Cold War Island

During the height of the Cold War in the 1950s the small island of Quemoy or Jinmen in the Taiwan Strait was the front line in the military standoff between Chiang Kai-shek's Republic of China and Mao Zedong's People's Republic. Local society and culture were dramatically transformed. Michael Szonyi uses oral history, official documents, and dissident writings to convey the history of the island during this period. In so doing, he sheds light on the social and cultural impact of the Cold War on those who lived through it, as well as on the relationship between China, Taiwan, and the United States at this critical moment. By analyzing the effects of Quemoy's distinctive geopolitical situation on the economy, gender and the family, and citizenship and religion, the book provides a new perspective on the social history of the Cold War, showing how geopolitics can affect individual lives and communities.

MICHAEL SZONYI is John L. Loeb Associate Professor of the Humanities in the Department of East Asian Languages and Civilizations at Harvard University. His previous book is *Practicing Kinship: Lineage and Descent in Late Imperial China* (2002).

Cold War Island:

Quemoy on the Front Line

Michael Szonyi
Harvard University

CAMBRIDGE
UNIVERSITY PRESS

CAMBRIDGE UNIVERSITY PRESS

Cambridge, New York, Melbourne, Madrid, Cape Town,
Singapore, São Paulo, Delhi

Cambridge University Press
The Edinburgh Building, Cambridge CB2 8RU, UK

Published in the United States of America by
Cambridge University Press, New York

www.cambridge.org
Information on this title: www.cambridge.org/9780521726405

First published 2008

Printed in the United Kingdom at the University Press, Cambridge

A catalogue record for this publication is available from the British Library

ISBN 978-0-521-89813-3   hardback
ISBN 978-0-521-72640-5   paperback

To Kathleen and Robert

Contents

Illustrations and tables

Tables

Preface

For half a century, Jinmen, or Quemoy, has frequently been represented through metaphor. It has been called the West Berlin of Asia and the Dien Bien Phu of China. It was the outpost from which the forces of freedom would launch their attack on communism, or the first domino whose fall would signal the failure of those forces. A second set of metaphors conveys the opposite impression of Jinmen's significance, suggesting that the conflicts over it have been mere theater. Dwight Eisenhower famously called tension over the island a "Gilbert and Sullivan war."[1] More recently, I heard a former US ambassador to Beijing liken the Taiwan Strait to "a Chinese opera – there are lots of drums and gongs but no one really gets hurt." I was initially inspired to write this book in part to explain why neither set of metaphors does a very good job of conveying the experiences of Jinmen residents. My greatest debt is to the many people of Jinmen, most of whom are not named here, for their willingness to welcome me into their homes and villages and share their oral history with me. I hope that those of them who read this book find my account of their lives fair and faithful, even if they do not agree with all of my analysis.

I am primarily a historian of Ming and Qing China, so readers may wonder at my choice of topic. In fact this book reprises, in a different time and a vastly different context, the themes of my earlier research on the relation of the state to everyday life. Specifically, my interest is in how people in Chinese societies have responded in quite unexpected ways to the larger forces that surround them but do not determine their lives. Failure, as James Scott has shown, has been the almost universal fate of state policies aimed at the transformation of society. Though Scott's interests are modern, his insight holds true in some ways even for the Ming dynasty. But even as policies fail to accomplish their intended outcomes, they may still generate unintended, unexpected, and yet hugely significant consequences. These local consequences can be as important to historical understanding as the central state policies that gave rise to them. This book also makes use of similar methodological approaches to my previous work, namely the combination of traditional textual studies with local fieldwork and oral history, and the use of local history as a means of asking larger questions. I learned these approaches as a student of Ming and Qing history while working with many other scholars, in particular those associated with the South China Research Center. Though this group borrows from anthropology its questions remain resolutely historical. One of the factors that made Jinmen interesting to me was curiosity about whether these methods might translate into other contexts. It is for readers to judge, but my own conclusion is that local history can be a powerful tool to explore the interaction of politics and everyday life in contemporary as well as earlier times.

These parallels do not explain how I first became interested in this specific context. I first visited Jinmen to attend an academic conference that ended on September 11, 2001. The subsequent turmoil forced me to extend my stay for several days. Visiting the island's villages, talking to local residents and learning of the work of local scholars is what sparked my interest in Jinmen's history. (To some degree the changed world that has emerged since then has also shaped my thinking on the key issues.) I thank Prof. C. K. Wang for the invitation that first brought me to Jinmen.

Robert Accinelli, Tim Brook, Beth Fischer, James Flath, Henrietta Harrison, Ian Johnson, Alan MacEachern, Francine McKenzie, David Ownby, and Robert Ross each read the entire manuscript, some of them more than once. Cynthia Enloe, Gregory Scott, Terry Sicular, and Wonwoon Yi commented on individual chapters. Many colleagues suggested sources, answered questions, or provided other help. They include Eileen Cheng-Yin Chow, Robert Johnson, Denis Kozlov, Li Cho-ying, Lin Hongyi, Lo Shih-chieh, Ed Miller, Rebecca Nedostup, Darryl Sterk, Nhung Tran, Lynne Viola, and David Wang (I apologize if I have left anyone out). Librarian James Cheng, Xiao-he Ma, and other staff at the Harvard–Yenching library were extremely helpful. In a matter of months, they made Harvard–Yenching what must be the greatest repository of Jinmen materials outside of the Republic of China. In Taiwan and on Jinmen, I received excellent research assistance from Chen Jiajia (Gia) and Zhang Jiying (Jackie). Bian Jinjing of the Jinmen county government facilitated my access to the Lieyu township archives; Huang Zijuan of the Jinmen National Park Headquarters provided much help. Huang Meiling was a very helpful host during my stays on the island. My other great debt is owed to two colleagues from Jinmen, Chi Chang-hui and Jiang Bowei. Both welcomed me into the small space of Jinmen studies where others might have guarded their territory. Jiang Bowei, with whom I have worked most closely, has truly been a model of scholarly generosity, a great colleague, and a great friend. I am also grateful to his research team at National Kinmen Institute of Technology, especially Weng Fenglan, for their help and gracious response to my many requests. I must also thank the other oral historians of Jinmen, especially Dong Qunlian, for their many excellent publications. Back at Harvard, students in my freshman seminar on the Cold War in Asia offered thoughtful critiques. Jeff Blossom prepared the maps. John Wong gave tireless and crucial help in the final stages of revising the manuscript. At Cambridge University Press, Marigold Acland, Sarah Green, and Rosina Di Marzo ably shepherded the book through the production process, and Jennifer Miles Davis was a great help in improving the text. Eileen Doherty prepared the Index and Nancy Hearst proofread the book. I am also grateful to two anonymous readers for the Press who helped me to see how Jinmen was part of a larger story.

Portions of the book have been presented at the University of British Columbia, the Central Party School in Beijing, Harvard University, National University of Singapore, and Xiamen University, and I thank the participants in each of these seminars. I am grateful to the following agencies for their support of my research: the Taiwan Studies Faculty Research Award Program for Canadians, sponsored by the Ministry of Education, Taiwan, Republic of China; the Social Sciences and Humanities Research Council of Canada, and the Clark fund at Harvard. Portions of chapters 11 and 12 have previously appeared as "The Virgin and the Chinese State: The Cult of Wang Yulan and the Politics of Local Identity on Jinmen (Quemoy)," *Journal of Ritual Studies* 19:2 (2005), and are reprinted by kind permission of the editors. Parts of chapter 10 are taken from a paper co-written with Chi Chang-hui for the 2007 Association for Asian Studies Annual Meeting.

That it is convention to close such remarks with thanks to one's family does not make the feelings less heartfelt. Kathleen and Robert, to whom this book is dedicated, have been patient with their father's frequent absences and overall distraction. When at the age of three Kathleen began staying up past midnight with her crayons "working," it was a good reminder that there are other things more important than books. I was glad to finally take them to Jinmen to see the place that has for so long been part of their lives; when we got there I found they opened many new doors for me. As for Francine McKenzie, I wish that I could find the words to express my gratitude for her support in so many ways.

CONVENTIONS

This book uses the *pinyin* system to romanize Chinese names and terms, with a few exceptions. In modern standard Chinese (Mandarin), the geographic subject of this book is romanized in *pinyin* as Jinmen. But most nonspecialists in the Western world know the island as Quemoy, a romanization of the island's name in the local dialect of Minnan. I hope readers will forgive my sleight-of-hand in using Quemoy in the title of the book, but Jinmen in the text. Also for reasons of familiarity, Sun Yat-sen is used for Sun Zhongshan; Chiang Kai-shek for Jiang Jieshi; Chiang Ching-kuo for Jiang Jingguo, and Kuomintang (KMT) for Guomindang. (Regrettably, this use of *pinyin* means that despite the success of Republic of China soldiers at defending the territory of Jinmen, this book actually contributes to the extension of mainland hegemony, at least linguistically, over the island.) The archipelago lying between Jinmen and Taiwan, also known as the Pescadores, is referred to here by its Chinese name Penghu. People's Republic of China (PRC) and China are used interchangeably to describe the political regime that has held power on the Chinese mainland since 1949; Republic of China (ROC) and Taiwan refer to the regime that has held power on Taiwan since that date. During martial law on Taiwan, the regime on the mainland was seen as illegitimate, and therefore it was never described as the People's Republic but rather by a variety of epithets such as "Communist bandits" or "bandits of Mao [Zedong] and Zhu [De]." Over time, these epithets became simply conventional ways of referring to the mainland regime. Therefore, in translating material, I have mostly substituted more neutral terms for the original ones, except where the source clearly uses the term with a strong negative sense. The various bombing campaigns against Jinmen are usually referred to in the Chinese sources using the month and day on which the bombing began (hence the 1958 campaign that began August 23 is known as the 8–23 Artillery War). I use the more familiar 1954–5 and 1958 Strait Crises.

For most of the period under discussion, the currency used on Jinmen was the Jinmen NTD (New Taiwan Dollar), equivalent in value to the standard NTD. Because many of the amounts cited in the text were provided in oral testimony, it would be misleading to convert them to constant dollars. To put these amounts in perspective, gross national product (GNP) per capita in Taiwan was NTD250 (US$50) in 1950; NTD5,200 ($130) in 1960; NTD11,680 ($292) in 1970; NTD57,000 ($1,400) in 1978, and NTD320,000 ($11,600) in 1996.[2]

Abbreviations

CCP	Chinese Communist Party
CCRM	Chinese Cultural Renaissance Movement
CO	commanding officer
DPP	Democratic Progressive Party (*Minjindang*)
JCRR	Joint Commission on Rural Reconstruction
JDHQ	Jinmen Defense Headquarters (*Jinmen fangwei silingbu*)
KMT	Nationalist Party (*Kuomintang*)
MAAG	Military Advisory and Assistance Group (US)
NTD	New Taiwan Dollar
PLA	People's Liberation Army
PRC	People's Republic of China
ROC	Republic of China
USO	United Service Organizations (US)
WZA	War Zone Administration (*Zhandi zhengwu*)
WZAC	War Zone Administration Committee

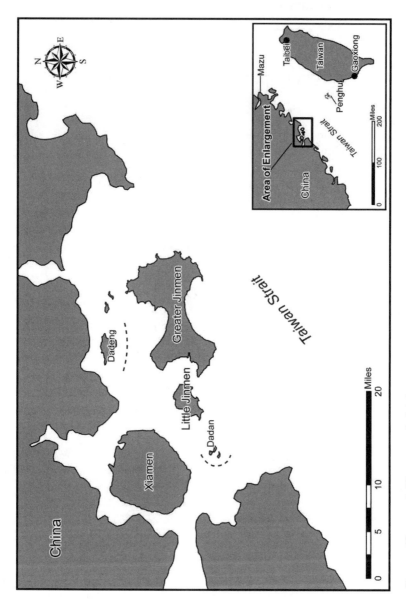

Jinmen (Quemoy), Xiamen and vicinity

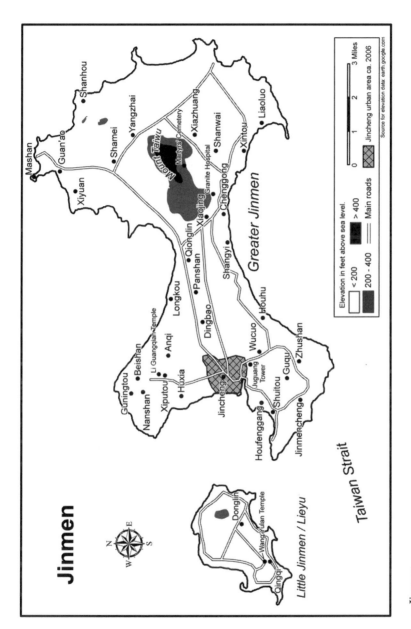

Jinmen

1 Introduction: ordinary life in an extraordinary place

Huang Pingsheng, a twenty-one year old farmer in 1958, remembers that he was watering vegetables in the family fields when he heard the first explosions – the boom of distant guns and then the louder sound of shell-bursts in the nearby hills. It was late summer, and the peanut harvest was ready to be brought in. There were other men working in the fields nearby, but most of the women were back in the village, preparing special foods for the Ghost Festival that would begin in a few days. In the late afternoon sun, Huang could see soldiers wending their way toward his home village of Xiyuan to bathe at the village well. At first Huang assumed the shelling was from an army training exercise, and he bent down to resume his work. But the noise did not die out as he expected. The explosions spread down the slope of the hills and onto the plains, toward Huang. This was no train-ing exercise, but the start of a great battle.

In the West, this battle became known as the Taiwan Strait Crisis of 1958. Huang and his fellow villagers call it the August 23rd or 8–23 Artillery War. Their home, the small island in the Taiwan Strait that was the epicenter of this conflict, is known in the local dialect as Quemoy. In this book, I refer to it instead using the island's name in standard Chinese, or Mandarin: Jinmen. For reasons that will become clear toward the end of this book, some forty years after these events Huang and dozens of other residents of Jinmen participated in a series of oral history inter-views, which is why his account is recorded. Perhaps his calm narration of events has something to do with his subsequent career as a policeman, but like many victims of war, Huang Pingsheng recounts his experiences in a matter-of-fact way, with little embellishment. He does not mention the shaking of the earth, the shells whistling through the air, the sky darkening with smoke.

Collecting his wits as the shelling grew more intense, Huang threw himself into a trench that ran alongside his fields. As he worked his way carefully homewards during lulls in the shelling Huang stumbled upon a concrete bunker full of troops. Though in other parts of Jinmen soldiers barred civilians from their bunkers, those inside this one allowed him to

1

take refuge. At dusk the bombing trailed off, and Huang left the safety of the bunker and continued back to his village. His house was deserted, so he became convinced that the rest of his family must be dead. But over the next few hours each of them straggled home safely from their own hiding places. In most homes, the first thing that needed to be done was to light incense to thank the gods and ancestors for their protection. This was a task that usually fell to elderly women – Huang does not say if it was his grandmother who did this in their house. As they did every night, mothers set water on the boil to cook sweet potato porridge for the evening meal, but many people were too tense to eat. Neighbors gathered on their doorsteps to exchange the day's gossip. Tonight of course the news was remarkable – who had been injured in the shelling; whose house hit; whose pigs killed. Xiyuan village escaped mostly unscathed from the bombardment on August 23, but the bombing would resume at first light the next morning. In the coming weeks some twenty of Huang's neighbors would be killed; nine of them buried alive when a shelter collapsed on them. The people of Xiyuan became used to life underground, in dank and dark shelters they hurriedly dug, packed with crying children, old folks chanting prayers to the gods, and wild rumors that the island would soon be overrun by hordes of Mao's soldiers.[1]

In most conventional histories the 1958 Taiwan Strait Crisis is told primarily as a story of diplomacy and high politics, of statesmen and their efforts to understand the tension in the context of global geopolitics.[2] What was the meaning of this attack by the People's Republic of China (PRC) on territory held by its enemy the Republic of China (ROC) on Taiwan? Why had China chosen this moment, and this tiny island, to heat up the Cold War? What would be the consequences? Chiang Kai-shek, the ROC president, turned to the US for support. President Eisenhower decided that Chiang's request fell under the Treaty of Mutual Defense between their two countries, and sent the Seventh Fleet into the Taiwan Strait. The Soviet foreign minister flew to Beijing to counsel Mao Zedong to stand down. Around the world political leaders and ordinary people wondered if this conflict might be the spark that would lead to a general war. But on October 6, after forty-four days of intense shelling, the guns of the People's Liberation Army (PLA) fell silent. All the parties involved claimed victory. One of the more dangerous episodes of the Cold War had come to an end, and once again Jinmen faded into obscurity.

In subsequent decades the diplomatic narratives of the crisis have given rise to a substantial analytic literature. Because the crisis of 1958 and a similar episode four years earlier had seemed to raise the possibility of war among the United States, China, and the Soviet Union, the story of Jinmen has come to figure with some prominence in the history of US foreign policy, Chinese foreign policy, Sino–Soviet and Sino-American relations, and in the theoretical literature on deterrence and brinkmanship.[3]

Though it will occasionally quote from this literature, this book does not contribute to these discussions. Rather, it looks at Jinmen from a very different perspective, asking how its inhabitants experienced these dramatic events and how they remember them today. It considers Jinmen as a human society embedded in a larger world. This book thus makes use of a historiographical tactic that has become common in recent decades. It deals with a topic, the Taiwan Strait conflict, that has previously been studied as a matter of high politics and international diplomacy, and examines it instead from the perspective of social history. But in common with the earlier literature, it argues that the study of Jinmen is of broader relevance, that it can tell us something about important historical questions. The transformation of Jinmen society was inseparable from the dominant international system of the time, the Cold War.[4] This book seeks to situate Jinmen within a broader framework of Cold War society and culture. It is an account of life lived in Cold War-time, of geopolitical confrontation at the levels of human experience and memory.

In this book I use Jinmen as a case study to explore four inter-related phenomena: militarization, geopoliticization, modernization, and memory. In its most common usage the term militarization refers to the process by which states enhance their capacity to make or defend against war or both.[5] For our purposes, it is more useful to adopt a broader understanding of the term, one that considers the impact of the military on society and the infiltration of military interests, values, and discourses into social life. Cynthia Enloe describes militarization in this sense as "the step-by-step process by which something becomes controlled by, dependent on, or derives its value from the military as an institution or militaristic criteria." Militarization in the broader sense is sometimes mis-represented as a means to accomplish militarization in the narrower sense, that is, as a way to create military power. But it is also a way to create and exercise political power more generally. On this broader definition, Enloe argues, virtually anything can become militarized.[6] Among the things that became militarized on Jinmen were rat tails, women's bodies, and basketballs. A new militarized economy arose to serve the needs of the garrison troops. A cult to the spirit of a drowned woman was militarized when it was patronized by army officers as a symbol of anti-Communism. The history of Jinmen shows us in microcosm some of the ways in which militarization can change a society.

Militarization on Jinmen was closely interconnected to geopoliticization. By geopoliticization I mean the ways in which life on Jinmen became connected to global politics. This process took several forms. Most obviously, Jinmen was affected by outside events tied to international politics, by decisions made in Beijing, Washington, Moscow, and elsewhere. The periodic bombings of the island were driven by issues that had little direct connection to Jinmen. Two years after the attack of 1958 PLA forces launched another barrage of some 170,000 shells on Jinmen, killing seven civilians, injuring forty, and destroying 200 homes. It was their way of "welcoming" US President Eisenhower on his visit to Taiwan. Another example of geopoliticization in this sense was the presence on Jinmen of US or US-sponsored entities, whose activities involved local people in the pursuit of American geopolitical interests. These included a Military Advisory and Assistance Group (MAAG) that advised the regular army; a CIA-proxy, Western Enterprises, that supported a guerrilla force in the early 1950s; and a US-funded development agency, the Joint Commission on Rural Reconstruction (JCRR).[7] Sometimes the geopolitical influence could work in the other direction. In the 1960 US presidential debates Richard Nixon charged that John F. Kennedy's questioning of the US commitment to the defense of Jinmen showed that he could not be trusted to stand up to Communism. To counter Nixon's charges, Kennedy's team put out a provocative statement of his willingness to intervene to roll-back revolution in Cuba. One can thus draw a connection between Jinmen and the abortive Bay of Pigs invasion of 1961.[8]

Geopoliticization also means the formal and explicit construction of Jinmen as a symbol in a larger international struggle. From the 1950s onwards, the island was invested, frequently and in a wide range of media, with great significance in regional and world affairs. It was a beacon of freedom for the enslaved masses of Asia, or the springboard for the coming war to free them. Jinmen was used as a metaphor for the determination of the Republic of China to resist the People's Republic; the commitment of the US-led Cold War alliance to resist Communism, and even the course of human progress. For flowery rhetoric none outdid a former Cuban ambassador to the ROC, who wrote in 1959, "The preservation of the principles which have shaped humanity is being decided at Jinmen. In Jinmen, the fight is for the rights of man, for freedom of the press, for the right to think for one's self and to believe in God."[9] A comprehensive account of the construction of Jinmen as a geopolitical symbol would have to take into account the various media used to communicate that symbolism and its reception in various times and places.[10] But I do not consider those issues in much detail here. For the construction of Jinmen as a geopolitical symbol was not, or not only, a matter of representation, like the writing of a text, but of social processes. My chief interest here is in understanding these processes and their consequences for the people of the island. Life on Jinmen was geopoliticized because what happened on Jinmen was thought to have geopolitical significance.

This in turn affected local life. Most importantly for this book, life on Jinmen was geopoliticized in the sense that geopolitics profoundly influenced many aspects of social relations, and became an important frame through which the people of Jinmen understood their own experiences. For the people of Jinmen, geopoliticization did not eliminate the quotidian routines that structured their lives – farming, marketing, paying taxes, raising children – but it affected them, becoming part of everyday life. The Cold War is remembered today less as an ideological confrontation than in terms of the minutiae of struggles of daily life – how people negotiated curfews, blackouts, and population registration rules; how illiterate farmers learned new agricultural techniques to produce goods that could be sold to soldiers; how families responded to the commodification of sexuality and danger of rape that seem universal wherever male soldiers are concentrated. Larger conflicts were major dynamos of social change, creating new patterns of interaction, new rhythms of life, and new attitudes to diverse issues.

The Cold War, and the Chinese civil war, were at one level struggles over mass utopias, that is, between competing visions of how society should be organized. But as Greg Grandin has written of the conflict in Latin America, "what gave that struggle its transcendental force was the politicization and internationalization of everyday life and familiar encounters."[11] One aim of this book is to show how international conflict became immanent in fields such as domestic life, religious practice, and economic exchange. It is an attempt to write a geopolitically informed social history, to show the importance of social history for understanding events that are otherwise allowed to generate their own meanings at a level of abstraction far above how they were experienced.

This study thus belongs to a growing body of work on how the local is embedded in the global. The interaction of global and local also shaped Jinmen's encounter with another great social force, the dramatic transformations that are usually labeled modernization. For the past century, the issue of how to modernize China, and what a modern China would look like, has been a central concern of Chinese political elites. Like the question of building the nation, with which it was closely connected, the question of modernization was not simply a matter of replicating a model from the West, but rather a diffuse pursuit of a complex target. In this work, I use the term modernization to describe not a specific set of conditions and values derived from Western experience but a complex of desired changes. This is not to say that modernity is an empty sign to which any meaning whatsoever can be attached; historical and contemporary factors impose limits on how modernity can be conceptualized. In China as in other non-Western societies the issue of how to reconcile modernity with Chinese tradition was a challenge that exercised many would-be modernizing reformers. The meaning of modernization is always negotiated and even contested, shaped both by global discourses and their local inflections.[12] Many of the changes desired by elites regardless of their political orientation were what might be called disciplinary schemes: education, to create modern citizens; hygiene, to create a population healthy in body as well as in mind; census-taking and registration, to allow the state to monitor that population. These took on particular and pressing importance under conditions of perceived military threat. The extraordinary situation on Jinmen made possible relatively unconstrained implementation of modernizing agendas, enabling and legitimizing distinctive forms of repression and discipline. The link between militarization and modernity, itself a form of mass utopia, produced distinctive modes of governmentality. Militarization and geopoliticization also influenced how modernization was defined, what goals were central and what peripheral. These processes came together in a phenomenon we can label militarized utopian modernism. This refers to the way appeals to external political circumstances legitimized authoritarian efforts to implement a distinctive project of social transformation shaped by a broader modernizing agenda. Militarized utopian modernism can be understood as a subset of James Scott's "authoritarian high modernism." Its distinguishing characteristic is the issue of perceived security threat and the resulting militarization of society.[13]

Memory is the fourth major theme of the book. The symbolic construction of Jinmen by the ROC state was aimed in multiple directions simultaneously, outwardly to ROC allies, especially the US, and also to the people of the ROC on Taiwan, as part of the project of mobilizing support and legitimizing authoritarian rule.[14] It was also directed inwards, toward the residents of Jinmen, as part of the project of creating them as an ideologized and mobilized anti-Communist polity. It is difficult to know now what people on Jinmen thought of the symbolic discourse about them in the 1950s and 1960s, whether they incorporated the image of themselves as heroic defenders of freedom into their own identities. But using oral history and materials from the democratization movement of the 1980s and 1990s, we can see how these previous policies shape memory and politics in the present day. Collective memory of the Cold War period is central to Jinmen residents' discussions of their own identity. In common with many other places around the world, collective memory has also become an important political resource for the people of Jinmen, shaping their relations with the state even after the end of the

Cold War. Though their own memories of the period focus mainly on everyday life, the people of Jinmen can and do remember their glorious contribution to the larger ideological and political confrontation, when it is in their interest to do so.

Jinmen in the world

One of the challenges of writing local history is to avoid the pitfall of singularity. There is much about Jinmen that is unique, but its history is also of broader significance. Comparing Jinmen to other late twentieth-century societies can shed light on several questions. First, there is the larger society of which Jinmen was a part, the Republic of China on Taiwan. Odd Arne Westad points out that post-Cold War triumphalism has obscured the fact that Taiwan and South Korea are the only sites of US Cold War intervention that achieved the desired outcome of stable growth and stable democracy.[15] The history of Jinmen shows some of the indirect consequences of that achievement, and thus can contribute to our understanding of the effects of the ROC's entanglement in the Cold War. The militarization of Jinmen meant that policies there were often an exaggerated version of policies implemented on Taiwan, and therefore it can tell us something about ROC politics. As we shall see, many Jinmen people speak about a division of labor between Jinmen and Taiwan, wherein Jinmen was responsible for military defense, enabling Taiwan to concentrate on and later enjoy the fruits of economic development. The study of Jinmen qualifies the well-known story of the rapid economic growth and eventual political pluralization of the Republic of China on Taiwan since 1949.

Second, Jinmen offers a useful case study with which to reflect on the similarities and differences between post-1949 China under Mao Zedong and Taiwan under Chiang Kai-shek.[16] What is most striking here is the frequency with which regimes shared and indeed borrowed disciplinary and repressive techniques from their own enemy, their own alter ego. Authorities in Jinmen often defined problems and formulated solutions in ways remarkably similar to how problems and solutions were constructed in the PRC. Some of the parallels are explicable in terms of their common origins. Both the Nationalist Party (KMT) and the Chinese Communist Party (CCP) were Leninist parties that emerged out of the political turmoil of early twentieth-century China. Other similarities make more sense in terms of the PRC and ROC's sixty-year (and counting) experience of cross-strait antagonism. Each of the two societies has sought to define itself in opposition to the other. In this process of mirror-imaging, to borrow John Borneman's description of East and West Berlin, the two states "fabricated themselves as moieties in a dual organization." On the other hand there was much mutual borrowing, some of it deliberate to ensure that the other side did not gain an advantage.[17] While policies on Jinmen were often crafted so as to draw attention to Jinmen's difference from the mainland, the process could also work the other way. We shall see over and over again in Jinmen's history examples of policies clearly intended to demonstrate Jinmen's distinctiveness from the mainland, but often in practice demonstrating the exact opposite. The parallelism thus speaks to our understanding of a modern Chinese political culture transcending explicit ideologies or the hubris of individual rulers.[18]

Jinmen also invites comparison with other highly militarized societies around the world. The dislocation and trauma caused by the abrupt fixing of highly politicized borders is similar whether the borders are between Jinmen and the mainland or between the two Berlins. The establishment and expansion of the garrison created economic disruptions, and opportunities, that resemble those in military base communities in many other places, from Subic Bay in the Philippines to Fort Bragg, North Carolina. The processes of mirror-imaging can also be detected around the world, but are particularly evident in the other divided states of the Cold War – Korea, Vietnam, and Germany.

The Cold War on Jinmen was experienced not as a discrete phenomenon but as one tied in manifold ways to the legacies of the Chinese civil war. This too was not unique to Jinmen. Everywhere the Cold War was experienced locally, tied to local and national conflicts and concerns. This was as true in the Third World where the Cold War was often wrapped up in anti-colonial struggles as it was in the First and Second, where the Cold War was one expression of broader debates about the meaning of modernity. In many places the Cold War, often as a cipher for existing conflicts, also lent a greater urgency to the pursuit of modernity and justified the militarization of this quest. The perception that modernization was essential to national security in the face of pressing danger, and the consequences of this perception for the articulation of modernization, was widespread in Asia and beyond.

In recent years two broad trends have emerged in the study of the global Cold War. One has been a reevaluation of the period in light of the partial opening of archives from the former Soviet bloc. But as Patrick Major and Rana Mitter point out, key elements of this "new Cold War history" are not really so new. The chief subject matter continues to be diplomatic and political history. Second, there has been a flowering of interest, a "cultural turn in Cold War history," in how culture and society shaped and were shaped by the Cold War. Much of this literature deals with the US and to a lesser degree the Soviet Union. It shows that even in the absence of war, geopolitical tension had many disruptive consequences.[19] Similarly, Cold War legacies continue to be important in many parts of the world. In some places, the challenge is to deal with the material consequences of the Cold War – environmental degradation, economic disruption, and social dislocation. In others, the Cold War also plays an important role in contemporary politics and memory. In Okinawa, for example, compensation for past suffering is an important element in local politics. In Vietnam, villagers and the state negotiate to produce a local politics of commemoration. The history of Jinmen is thus also part of the comparative social and cultural history of the Cold War period. Jinmen offers a local example of a much broader phenomenon, the geopoliticization of everyday life under the great ideological conflict of the latter twentieth century.

Perhaps Jinmen's experience may be relevant even beyond the temporal boundaries of the Cold War. The militarization of Jinmen from 1949 to 1992, when martial law was repealed, occurred under a condition of national emergency and martial law. The Italian political philosopher, Giorgio Agamben, points out that national emergency, for which his translators use the term "state of exception," is commonly misunderstood as a *de facto* response to a crisis. The central contradiction of the state of emergency or exception is that the necessity of this response is assumed to be an objective determination, but of course it is not. It is the result of a political decision. Since the state of exception does not simply mean the suspension of laws but the suspension of the legal and political order, the state of exception actually defines the limits of law. It is a juridical measure that cannot be explained juridically. It is not simply a form of dictatorship, but something different, wherein necessity becomes the ultimate source of law. Agamben also argues that though its very name suggests temporariness, the state of exception is in fact an emergent paradigm for political sovereignty in general. While the idea of a state of emergency has a long history in Western political thought, the twentieth century has seen it increasingly deployed as a mode of government. Agamben's main interest is in the state of exception as a problem of legal philosophy and ethics. But the issue of exception can also frame issues in social history. The crucial step is to move from seeing emergency as an inevitable response to objective conditions to treating emergency as a problem to be explained. For much of the period in question, until 1987, the entire Republic of China (ROC) was under a state of emergency, whose legal basis was the Martial Law and the Temporary Provisions Effective During the Period of Communist Rebellion. Jinmen's distinctive position meant that even Martial Law and the Temporary Provisions were considered inadequate to the situation. Distinctive systems had to be created to administer Jinmen and the other offshore islands. Jinmen thus became the state of exception within a state of exception. One way of looking at Jinmen is as an exemplary site for "testing and honing the functional mechanisms and apparatuses of the state of exception as a paradigm of government."[20] Its past is the history of a forty-year laboratory for fine-tuning the state of exception; its present a demonstration of the lingering consequences of that state.

Sources and outline of the book

This book is based primarily on oral history and archival documents. It uses about seventy oral history interviews that I conducted during repeated stays on the island between 2002 and 2007, and about 170 previously published interviews conducted by other researchers.[21] Working with oral history that has been collected by other scholars means confronting one of the fundamental axioms of oral history – that the interviewer's questioning techniques and methods of organizing material shape the results. For example, where one volume of interviews yields largely positive recollections of the period, another contains much more detail about government offenses and popular dissatisfaction. It is unlikely that one interviewer simply chanced upon interviewees who had suffered more than others; rather the distinctive responses reflect the interviewer's own interpretation of this period, expressed through the questions asked and the way the material is presented. Nevertheless, I have considerable confidence in the overall reliability of the oral history testimony gathered by other scholars. What I was told in my own interviews was consistent with what is written in the published material.[22] This of course is not to say that the facts are indisputable, but simply that there is general consistency across the two types of oral history evidence, my own and the published material. The question of whether this testimony accords with other historical documents is a rather different one. Indeed the different ways that local people interpret the past is itself an important theme of the book. Together, the oral histories help reveal the private experiences embedded in larger contexts and changes, and show how those involved remember these changes.[23]

The second main research source is village-level archives. These are files from six village offices that have been preserved since the lifting of martial law in 1992.[24] The archives cover the period from 1964 to 1992, with the bulk from the 1970s. Mostly the routine paperwork of village governance, they include such things as budgets for the construction of bomb shelters; forms used to apply for permission to buy a bicycle, travel

to Taiwan, build a house, or open a shop; and checklists for the maintenance of militia guns. They provide a record of the actual workings of the
regime of militarization, and complement the information provided in
oral history interviews.[25]

When martial law was lifted on the main island of Taiwan in 1987, a
dissident press sprang up, bringing to light previously suppressed information about the past four decades. Though Jinmen itself remained
under martial law, journalists from Jinmen sought to take advantage of
this new space that had been created on Taiwan. In 1990, they founded a
newsletter, *Jinmen Reports* (*Jinmen baodao*), to agitate for change from relative safety in Taiwan. Later, after martial law was also lifted on Jinmen,
the local daily newspaper, *Jinmen Daily* (*Jinmen ribao*), liberalized its
daily supplement (*fukan*) of readers' submissions. Residents of the island
and soldiers who had been stationed there began to submit essays, poems,
and stories about their personal experiences under martial law. For some
people, these writings became an important way of dealing with their past
experiences. Often highly opinionated, these present a third perspective
on life during the martial law period, shedding further light on issues that
arise in the oral history or the archives. As a genre of writing in newspapers of the ROC, the *fukan* blend fact and fiction; I therefore use these
essays mainly to explore personal memory and interpretation rather than
for the reconstruction of past events. Similarly, I use the dissident press
mainly to explore how certain questions became constructed as political
issues and what this can tell us about how history is perceived by politically engaged natives of Jinmen. Other sources include film, fiction, jokes,
diaries, and memoirs.

This book is divided into four parts. Part I covers the period from 1949
to 1960, explaining why Jinmen came to occupy its distinctive position in
cross-strait and global geopolitical relations, how a regime of militarization developed as a result of that distinctive position, and how this regime
began to reshape the daily lives of Jinmen residents. Part I also discusses
the three major episodes of military confrontation in this period, in 1949,
1954–5, and 1958. Part II continues the chronological coverage, discussing two major shifts in the militarization regime in the 1960s. The
main goal of the first two sections is to situate changing policies and their
consequences for local life in relation to the shifting geopolitical contexts,
in order to develop an explanation for the complex trajectory of geopoliticization and militarization of local society. Part III explores thematically
different aspects of social life over the whole period of martial law, with a
focus on how the people of the island experienced and negotiated with the
regime of militarization. Part IV discusses the process of demilitarization
and postmilitarization social life. The focus of interest in this part is how

the period of militarization is remembered, commemorated, and used to serve political purposes in the present.

Any historian of local society engages in a dialogue between the representative and the particular. For all its distinctiveness, Jinmen was hardly the only society of the late twentieth century that became highly militarized as a result of its implication in global geopolitical conflict. In the rest of this book we will consider how the study of Jinmen suggests new frameworks for interpreting the international history of the last half-century, and especially the Cold War, seeing it not simply as a political or military or ideological standoff, but in terms of cultural and social processes that could be broadly similar across different locales. There were many other places in the Communist and non-Communist world where, in the face of real or perceived threats, new techniques of militarization and mobilization were implemented in time of crisis. While Jinmen is only a small society, it throws these issues into the very sharpest of relief, allowing us to identify similarities with other societies and other times. With this in mind, let us return to Huang Pingsheng and his fellow villagers, and to their memories of times of war and chaos.

Part I

Geopoliticization ascendant

By the time of Huang Pingsheng's frightening experiences, the people of Jinmen already had considerable experience with the trauma of war. In the decade after 1949 Jinmen underwent three major episodes of direct military confrontation, the Battle of Guningtou at the start of the period in 1949 and the two Taiwan Strait crises of 1954–5 and 1958. The experiences of local people in these three episodes are discussed in three of the chapters of Part I. But regardless of their importance, these violent events do not tell the whole story of the island's history. There were other histories to which these battles were merely interludes. For the 1950s also saw the geopoliticization of the island and the beginnings of the system of militarization. I intersperse discussions of these alternative histories with the chapters on how each military confrontation was experienced.

2   The Battle of Guningtou

Late on the night of October 24, 1949, about 8,000 troops of the People's Liberation Army (PLA) Tenth Army embarked on hurriedly procured fishing boats from Dadeng island, a rocky outcrop north of Jinmen. A strong northeasterly wind was blowing, and the boats made good headway. But they were crewed by fishermen with no experience of keeping a large fleet in formation, and the convoy was soon spread out across the waters of the Taiwan Strait. The seas had risen and the troops, many of whom were on the ocean for the first time, became seasick, disoriented, and scared. The first boats to land, at about 1.40 a.m. on October 25, came ashore close to their intended landing site, near the village of Longkou on the narrow waist of Jinmen, where the plan was to cut defending forces in two. But the body of the fleet was straggling behind. It landed several miles to the west, on the broad western bulb of Jinmen's hourglass shape, near a place called Guningtou.

A Republic of China (ROC) army patrol on Jinmen spotted the first ships just before the initial landing and sounded the alarm (some local people say that the patrol had actually set off a land mine by mistake, leading to signal flares being fired in confusion and illuminating the attacking boats quite by accident). Troops were roused from the civilian homes where they were billeted and hurried to the beaches. By the time the unloading began, the beach had become a killing zone. Some PLA units lost a third of their soldiers before they had crossed the sands.

Within a few hours, the landing parties regrouped and put the defenders to flight. Realizing they had landed on the wrong site they tried to drive eastward. But it was too late. ROC troops in the eastern half of the island were already moving in to meet them. Beaten back into the northwestern parts of Jinmen, the PLA commander ordered his troops to dig in at Guningtou and its surrounding hamlets. There ensued over twenty-four hours of vicious urban-style fighting in lanes and courtyards. At one point, an ROC officer named Li Guangqian led his men in a furious and hopeless charge against a nest of PLA soldiers. Li was a thirty-two year old native of Hunan, a much-decorated officer during the anti-Japanese war. He was struck down almost instantly, probably by friendly fire.[1] We shall meet him again in chapter 11, for his was one of the many spirits that lingered on the battlefield, haunting the people of Jinmen.

Meanwhile, on the beach, the chaos of the disembarkation had caused fatal delay.[2] ROC troops brought barrels of oil and burned the PLA boats that had been stranded by the ebbing tide. PLA reinforcements reportedly watched helplessly on the shore opposite, firing into the air in frustration.[3] A thousand reinforcements finally arrived from the mainland early the next morning, broke through and joined the troops holed up in Guningtou. But it was much too late. The ROC army had its own reinforcements watching the battle from the nearby waters. As soon as the seas calmed enough to allow them to disembark, they marched along the western edge of the island and through the town of Jincheng toward the fighting.

Their commander was a man whose future would become closely intertwined with Jinmen, General Hu Lian. He was just over forty years old, and had been a soldier his whole life. He had fought against the warlords in the Northern Expedition, against the Communists in the 1930s, and against the Japanese. In September 1949 he was charged with regrouping units of the ROC army that had scattered and fled south in the face of the Communist onslaught. In the literature on the Battle of Guningtou, Hu Lian receives hagiographic treatment, given almost sole credit for the victory. But, in fact, by the time he arrived on the battlefield the outcome was all but decided. By late afternoon, the PLA soldiers had run out of ammunition, and the survivors tried to make their way back to the beach, hoping there might be boats to evacuate them. There were none. About a thousand made it to the beach, where they were surrounded. Half were killed during the course of the night; the survivors surrendered early on the morning of October 27. The Battle of Guningtou was over.

PLA forces suffered almost 4,000 killed and over 5,000 captured, against just over 1,000 ROC forces killed. When compared to the millions of troops mobilized on both sides during the preceding years of civil war, these are tiny numbers, and the Battle of Guningtou a mere skirmish.[4] But the battle did not seem insignificant at the time, nor would it in the ensuing decades. After months and years of defeat and retreat, Guningtou was immediately hailed as the first significant victory for Chiang Kai-shek's ROC forces. Chiang's son Chiang Ching-kuo wrote in his diary that the battle was "truly a case of defeat being turned into victory, a turning point in the battle to defeat the Communists and recover the country." Senior officers of the ROC National Army hailed it as a "spiritual victory."[5] The PLA also acknowledges that it was taught an important lesson at Guningtou. Its defeat revealed just how logistically difficult the planned attack on Taiwan would be. "Only if we conscientiously learn the lessons of the Jinmen campaign," wrote a senior Air Force officer recently, "will we be certain of victory in the future decisive battle of the Taiwan Strait." Guningtou continues to be cited as a salutary lesson in PLA writings on a possible invasion of Taiwan today.[6]

Jinmen before Guningtou

Jinmen is the name of an archipelago of islets on the coast of southern China. The two main islands, with a combined area of about sixty square miles, are Greater Jinmen and Little Jinmen, or Lieyu. Greater Jinmen is shaped like a dumbbell or hourglass, with two round bulbs connected by a more narrow waist. Little Jinmen looks like it would fit into the western bulb of Greater Jinmen, from which it is separated by just under a mile.[7] Three miles further to the west is the city of Xiamen and the mainland. People of Little Jinmen sometimes say "when the wind is right, we can hear their dogs and chickens." Taiwan lies just over 100 miles to the east.

Legends of human settlement in Jinmen go back many centuries, but the earliest reliable historical documents date from the Tang (seventh to tenth century), when the emperor first dispatched an official to the island. Several lineages that live on the islands today claim to be descended from his staff. Later deified as Lord Master of Benevolence (*Enzhu gong*), the spirit of this official is said to have come to the aid of the local people at several times in Jinmen's history, including the Battle of Guningtou. In the fourteenth century, an official of the Ming dynasty constructed a walled fort on the island. This man also gave Jinmen its name. Because of its strategic importance on key navigational routes, he called it Golden Gate (*Jin men*). In most ways, life on the island closely resembled that on the nearby mainland, with which Jinmen residents shared a common dialect and similar social, architectural, religious, and economic characteristics. One key difference was that whereas the plains on the mainland could sustain highly productive rice agriculture using water that drained from the inland mountains, Jinmen was far too dry to grow rice. But the peanut and the sweet potato, introduced into the region in the sixteenth or seventeenth century, proved well suited to the sandy soil of Jinmen, and probably led to the first dramatic increase in the local population, to around 50,000.[8]

But the seventeenth century was also a time of trauma for Jinmen. In mid-century, Manchu invaders occupied China and established the Qing dynasty. The Ming loyalist Zheng Chenggong (Koxinga) raised an army to try to dislodge the Qing, and based it in the Jinmen area. Later, when he withdrew to Taiwan, the Qing authorities ordered the whole of the south China coast forcibly evacuated to cut off his access to supplies and supporters. Residents of Jinmen fled to the mainland, and were not permitted to return for fifteen years.[9] When they did, the new town of Jincheng began to grow up around the small Qing garrison on the western shore. Pushed by poverty and pulled by new opportunities created by the expansion of European influence, Jinmen residents began to emigrate abroad in the nineteenth century, to Japan and Southeast Asia. It was mostly men who emigrated, leaving behind their wives and children. The island became part of a wide and dense network of circulation of people, goods, and ideas. At the time, the population peaked at about 80,000.[10]

In 1937, the Japanese army swept out of Manchuria and into China proper. Japanese troops landed on Jinmen in October, and held the island for the next eight years. Because remittances were cut off, the Japanese occupation caused great hardship for Overseas Chinese families on Jinmen, but otherwise it seems to have had little effect on local society. In the final years of the war, Jinmen men were made to work on a new airstrip for the Japanese army. This would be their first experience with forced labor, but not their last.

Jinmen and Guningtou

In the years after the Japanese surrender in 1945, China moved toward civil war between the Nationalist (KMT)-controlled Republic of China (ROC) under Chiang Kai-shek, and the Communists led by Mao Zedong. As elsewhere in China, the KMT imposed round after round of conscription on the island. At the same time as some local conscripts were leaving Jinmen, many more soldiers were arriving [Fig. 2.1]. Nationalist troops fleeing the Communist advance began to reinforce Jinmen in early 1948, first whole units, later rag-tag remnants of armies scattered by the fighting. Villagers recall their arrival as a pathetic sight. Sometimes five or six soldiers shared a single weapon. Many had lost their uniforms and wore shoes made of grass or helmets of woven bamboo. They were malnourished; lack of variety in diet had given them serious digestive problems. The "owners" of the public latrines of the island, who enjoyed the customary right to collect nightsoil for fertilizer, recall hearing the soldiers cursing and painful grunts, "like a pig being slaughtered" as they tried to relieve themselves.[11] The earliest arrivals set up their own camps, but as numbers grew, billets had to be found. Soldiers took over empty houses, barns, and public buildings – village schoolhouses, temples, and ancestral halls. By the fall of 1949, there were so many soldiers that they began to be housed together with local

Fig. 2.1 Jincheng in the 1950s (© Corbis)

families, sleeping in the main central hall and courtyard of the traditional style home [Fig. 2.2].

The soldiers made minor but growing exactions on civilians: chopsticks, bowls, tools, and furniture. There were frequent disputes. In what would become a significant pattern in subsequent politics in Jinmen, a new social grouping emerged to mediate between the troops and the villagers. Zhang Qicai was one of them. "Because I spoke some Mandarin, I could communicate with them."[12] Besides language, youth was the other key criteria distinguishing this group – the soldiers found it difficult to deal with the elders who traditionally took important decisions on behalf of the village. After 1949, these intermediaries would become the new elite of the militarized and modernizing society of Jinmen.

In the months leading up to Guningtou, the refugee troops and local civilians were put to work building up Jinmen's defenses. To provide the necessary supplies, empty or abandoned houses in the area were torn down, the beginnings of an imposition that would linger for decades in the hearts of Jinmen people. Officers commandeered men and donkeys to porter materials. "The soldiers tore down the houses, then the headman sent us to move the recovered materials." Most in demand were wooden doors, which could be used to cover a pit and turn it into a shelter. Oral

Fig. 2.2 Tank unit stationed in a village (by permission of Jinmen county cultural bureau)

history gives the impression that in 1949 soldiers confiscated virtually every door in Guningtou. At first villagers just nailed some boards together. But when the demands continued, they had no choice but to take down their doors and hand them over. Villagers were unhappy about this not just because of the loss of property, but because they needed them for the rough shelters they were building themselves in anticipation of an attack from the mainland. "We would just dig a pit in one of the rooms, cover it with a door, then pile oyster shells, sweet potatoes, and [granite slabs] in layers on top of the door."[13]

The expropriation of space that began when soldiers started using public buildings for sleeping quarters was now extended. The empty houses and public spaces that were torn down first were precisely where the troops had been housed, so more and more of them now had to move into private homes. And as the demand for building materials grew, even occupied private homes began to be identified for destruction. Villagers whose homes were destroyed were issued a certificate recording their contribution to the national cause and were told they would be compensated once the mainland was recovered from the Communists.

Officers were obviously aware of the potential problems of using civilian labor to dismantle civilian buildings, and assigned porters to work in villages other than their own. A man from Beishan hamlet of Guningtou recalls, "those of us who raised mules were assembled . . . to transport doors, stones and beams. The way it worked in those days was that mules from this village were used to move the materials from structures torn down in other villages. For example, I was sent to Nanshan and Anqi; and mule teams from another village were sent here." Still, even if some problems were averted, there were rumblings of discontent by those who were forced into labor. "We worked morning and night for a full month. The soldiers gave us a midday meal and fodder for our animals. But we had our parents and our children at home. They needed to eat too, but every time we asked to be allowed to leave, the officer refused."[14]

In late September 1949, the PLA's 10th Army Corps moved down the coast of Fujian Province. They rapidly captured several coastal islands with very little fighting, for most of the ROC troops fled at the first sign of the Communists. On October 15 the army launched its attack on Xiamen. It was over within two days. The speed of the takeover left many Jinmen residents stranded on the mainland. On the morning of October 17, a young Jinmen man named Wu Caisan was sent by his mother to Xiamen by ferry to buy cooking oil and medicine. By the afternoon, the ferries had stopped running, and it was more than forty years before he could return home.[15] Several thousand Nationalist defenders did manage to flee to Jinmen. The rest were captured or deserted. The stage was now set for the attack on Jinmen ten days later.

Rumors of an impending invasion began to circulate in the Guningtou area a few days prior to October 25. "With the naked eye we could see a lot of fishing boats assembling near the other shore," said one resident. Many families in northwestern Jinmen decided to flee to parts of the island that were more distant from the mainland. Familiar social networks were activated. When he first heard rumors of an attack on October 24, the father of Li Qingzheng took his family to Xiputou, "which was the natal home of my paternal grandmother." Afterwards, to get even farther away, he took them on to Houhu, where an aunt's sister lived. When the fighting broke out Li Jinchun's family fled in the night to one village, but villagers there were being impressed to porter ammunition back to the battlefield, so they continued on to the home of his elder sister. Wang Qinglin of Shangyi, six years old at the time, recalls being on the receiving end of the refugees. "I was a kid, so I didn't really understand the situation, but some relatives from Guningtou came and stayed with us for a few days to avoid the fighting."[16]

Not everyone fled Guningtou. In many families one person stayed behind to keep an eye on house and property. One father left his children in a ditch outside the village before going back to stand guard over the house. Often the elderly were left behind. Some explain that this was so the young and able-bodied would not be found and conscripted, others that an elderly parent refused to leave the ancestral home. Li Tiansong, who was only two years old in 1949, recalls, "My family worried that because I was so young, my mother would be unable to run very far while carrying me, so she and I were left behind to look after the house." They hid in the rough shelter that the family had dug underneath the home. When the PLA troops retreated back into Guningtou, ROC guns began to shell the area. One shell burst through the roof of their home and landed on the shelter, but did not detonate. "So when my grandfather registered me with the authorities, he called me Tiansong – 'sent by Heaven.'"[17]

The villagers' fears of being forced into labor were well founded. When the invasion began and ROC officers realized that they would not be able to hold the beach, they sent soldiers back to nearby villages to press villagers into service as porters. Wu Wujin was hiding in a shelter in his house when he was dragged out and ordered to help carry ammunition. He fetched his donkey and together with the other men of his village began to walk toward Guningtou. Before they got far, a shell dropped on the head of their party, killing the lead donkey. The other animals scattered. Wu and the men hid in a ditch by the side of the road. They stayed hidden all through the night and following morning (he does not provide dates, but it must have been October 26). Around noon, the fighting seemed to ease, and they decided it was best to return home. "But as soon as I stood up, a shell whizzed past, knocking out all my teeth." Villagers were also needed to carry the wounded. Unlike later on, when, as we shall see, civilian duties were strictly classified and allocated on gender and age lines, in the heat of battle the ROC troops simply seized whoever they could find. "In 1949, I was about twenty years old," remembers one woman. "At that time, it didn't matter if you were male or female, you had to carry the wounded."[18]

With no reliable information, families were reluctant to return home after the battle. But when the sounds of gunfire quieted, those who had been hiding in the open felt they had no choice. Some had not eaten for two days. But neither had some of the surviving troops, who were soon drawn by the cooking fires. "My mother started to cook noodles. While they were cooking, some soldiers walked in. They pushed us aside and just helped themselves. We had a rooster, a hen, three medium chickens and a piglet. They took all of them."[19]

Some of those who returned found their homes damaged, destroyed, occupied, or plundered:

You could only take refuge with your relatives for a while; you couldn't live there forever. So when the situation calmed down, the villagers all returned home. But many of their homes were mostly destroyed. All one could do was come to an agreement with the owners of one of the houses that remained. Many families lived together; in a single house there were often many families. There were no beds, no tables; [people just slept] on the ground. There was no hearth, so [people just] made one out of mud. It was like a beggar's life.[20]

"When we got back, our house had been emptied . . . The whole house was occupied by troops and our stores of sweet potato, peanuts and salt were gone." Li Qingquan's family had a hut in their fields; he went to try to protect it from being torn down when he learned that the soldiers were building bunkers nearby. When he got to the hut, the officer in charge told him, "You've come at a good time. We're short of labor; we need help moving these materials."[21]

Dead and wounded lay everywhere. Li Tiansong's mother, who carried him in her arms from the battlefield, later told him the corpses "looked like sweet potatoes drying in the field." Village headmen were ordered to conscript labor to bury the dead. From the mansion that the PLA had used for its field headquarters, more than eighty corpses were pulled. Some of the bodies were naked; probably these were KMT dead whose uniforms were taken by PLA soldiers to avoid capture. It was impossible to bury the dead with any propriety. Bodies were thrown in wells and manure pits, or in irrigation ditches and covered with earth. "We were all so young; we were terrified by the sight of the corpses, so we didn't do a very thorough job."[22] Within a few days, the rotting corpses began to stink and many of the villagers detailed to bury the dead fell sick.[23] Much of the land in the Guningtou area was subsequently abandoned, and some of it remains fallow today out of fear of disturbing the souls of the dead.

In the autumn of 1952, General Hu Lian, now serving both as the military commanding officer and the head of the civilian government, decided that the dead soldiers of Guningtou deserved a proper burial. In his memoirs, he explains that the international situation dictated the timing of his decision. During the American presidential election Eisenhower's foreign policy advisor, John Foster Dulles, had declared that the US would support the liberation of the peoples behind the Iron Curtain.[24] Since with American help Hu would soon be leaving Jinmen to re-conquer the mainland, he had his troops build a memorial cemetery. A site was selected on the lower slopes of Mount Taiwu, facing Xiamen, in February 1953. More than 4,000 corpses were found. The remains of ROC troops were exhumed and moved to the cemetery; those of PLA soldiers left where they were first buried.[25] But after three years, it would have been difficult, perhaps impossible, to distinguish the bones of friend and foe, which had been tumbled together in the days after the battle. There must be many PLA bones in the cemetery, and many National Army soldiers whose ghosts still haunt the battlefield of Guningtou, a topic to which we return in chapter 11. Already in 1952 the distinction between friend and enemy, crucial to the workings of government in Jinmen during the Cold War period, was blurred in a very material way.

In the days after the Battle of Guningtou radio broadcasts from the mainland warned civilians that a second attack was impending. This led to renewed efforts to build defensive fortifications. Most of Jinmen's fishing fleet was now broken up, ostensibly for the useful materials that could be salvaged. The real reason was probably to eliminate the possibility of flight or defection, forcing soldiers and the civilian residents to make their last stand on Jinmen. What people remember most is the toll in houses and buildings. The destruction was most serious in the Guningtou area itself, in part because so many of the inhabitants had fled. Before the battle, receipts had been issued for damaged property. Now empty homes were declared abandoned and torn down without even the promise of compensation. "We didn't know there was a rule about empty houses. When the soldiers started tearing things down, we were just worried about the chaos, so we packed up and left for town. After we left, *our* house was destroyed. About one hundred buildings in our village were torn down; only about one-third were spared."[26] Some of the most bitter memories are of the destruction of public or collective property, such as ancestral halls and temples. People rescued the images of the deities and moved them into their own homes. The new village school in Nanshan, financed by donations from villagers sojourning in the Philippines, was torn down. Even coffins, purchased in advance by their owners, were appropriated.

Guningtou is remembered as a great victory for the Republic of China, a turning point in the battle with the Communists.[27] The people of Jinmen today speak of it with pride. But their feelings were complex and ambivalent, for the battle and its aftermath were experienced as deeply traumatic. The consequences of having this heroic and geopolitical role thrust upon them would only become more profound with the passage of time.

3   Politics of the war zone, 1949–1960

The number of soldiers in Jinmen grew rapidly after the Battle of Guningtou, as more refugees from the mainland arrived and troops from Taiwan were sent to reinforce the great victory. "During the day, they just hung around the village. At night they went down to the beach to patrol. There were lots of deserters; when they caught one he'd be tied up, marched off and beaten. I saw this myself."[1] These changes on Jinmen were the localized expression of the larger geopolitical reconfiguration of 1949–50. Defeated on the mainland, the demoralized remnants of the ROC's Nationalist Party (KMT) regime retreated and regrouped on Taiwan. There, Chiang Kai-shek began to develop a plan for national survival, by reforming the party and securing the economic, political, and military foundations for the viability of the regime on Taiwan – and the eventual reconquest of the mainland. Within a few months the Korean War broke out. US President Harry Truman's subsequent decision to order the "neutralization" of the Taiwan Strait, preventing a PRC attack on Taiwan and an ROC attack on the mainland, meant that the unresolved aspects of the Chinese civil war were now internationalized, becoming part of the larger global Cold War.

On Jinmen, the larger issues translated into specific concerns – ensuring the defense of the island; making arrangements for the tens of thousands of troops, and dealing with the civilian population. The ROC government tried several approaches to the issue of governing Jinmen, before settling in 1956 on a structure called War Zone Administration (WZA, *Zhandi zhengwu*). In this chapter, I explore the history of administration on Jinmen, its origins, the rhetoric by which it was justified and legitimized, and the ways in which it operated and was experienced. Two specific policy issues, schemes for monitoring population and maintaining ideological unity, illustrate the interconnection between local politics on Jinmen and global geopolitics, and between militarization and modernization.

Ad hoc militarization

In the aftermath of Guningtou, Hu Lian and his superiors had to come up with immediate measures to maintain the security of the island. With Taiwan's defenses still undeveloped, Jinmen was of some military importance. Its position close to Xiamen, the nearest harbor from which the PLA might launch amphibious operations, meant that the Jinmen garrison could be used to delay or disrupt an invading force. But Jinmen was not just important for military reasons. Were Jinmen to fall, the great symbolic victory of Guningtou would be undone. The result was immediate security measures, a kind of *ad hoc* militarization. As the situation stabilized, longer term concerns were added: how to use the island for intelligence gathering and guerrilla action on the mainland, prepare for the coming counter-attack, and secure international, especially American, support for the ROC. To serve this international strategy, ROC authorities sought to construct an image of Jinmen as a bastion of freedom and a symbol of the commitment to the fight against global Communism. The first issue led to the restoration of civilian government, the second to the considerable expansion of the garrison. By 1956, the unexpected durability of the regime on the mainland meant that the planned counter-attack would have to be deferred indefinitely. The soldiers were on Jinmen to stay. The emphasis of policy now shifted to formalizing and systematizing the *ad hoc* measures that had been put in place over the past five years, resolving problems of coordination between the military and the civilian authorities, and demonstrating to the world the importance of Jinmen in the ROC's overall defenses. The result was the WZA system.

About a week after the Battle of Guningtou, civilian government on Jinmen was eliminated and authority over civilian affairs given to the commander of the Jinmen Defense Headquarters (JDHQ), a position held for most of the next decade by Hu Lian.[2] Unlike some later changes, this reform went beyond a mere change in terminology. New units were created within the garrison to administer civilian affairs, headed by appointees of the commander. Even as the civilian county government was dissolved, the provincial government of Fujian was being reconstituted on the island. By this time, the only parts of Fujian that remained under ROC control were the islands of Jinmen and Mazu. But it was deemed important to the ROC claim to be the sovereign government of all of China to maintain the fiction that the ROC still governed provinces other than Taiwan. The revival of the Fujian provincial government was part of this fiction. But this was a matter of appearances. The provincial government was an empty shell; the position of provincial chairman was simply the commander of the JDHQ *ex officio*.[3]

Three years later, in early 1953, county government was restored. No available evidence explains why this change was made. The reasons probably had to do with the ROC leadership's reaction to two geopolitical issues. The first was the stalemate of the Korean War. ROC planners may have concluded that with the PLA fully occupied in Korea and the US neutralization of the Strait holding, PRC adventurism was unlikely, and so it was possible to relax military control. The second issue was the growing recognition that the long-term survival of the ROC regime depended on continued US support. Jinmen could be useful in propaganda and public relations efforts to secure that support, as a symbol of the ROC's commitment to resist the Communist threat. Starting with the first US Congressional visitor only a few weeks after the Battle of Guningtou and the first correspondents from *Life* magazine in 1951, Jinmen increasingly became a favored stop on any anti-Communist's visit to Asia.[4] It was more difficult for Jinmen to serve this symbolic function convincingly while its people were under the direct rule of the army. The re-establishment of the civilian county government was thus a signal of ROC recognition that the real value of Jinmen was its image as a place of freedom, a part of Free China in contrast to Red China.

But the reorganization was largely nominal. The military remained in virtually complete control, and the commander retained his absolute powers. As one county official recalls of this time, "The commander was like the emperor. Whatever he said, that's what we did." Another remembers a meeting with Hu Lian's replacement as commander in 1954. "One time, the commander asked me 'do you have any hoodlums on Jinmen?' I answered, 'I can't say there are no hoodlums at all. Every place has got some badly behaved people.' Commander Liu asked, 'Why don't you just deal with them?' I said, 'But I'd need some legal basis to do so.' He said, 'Well then, just make up some new regulations and submit them to me. I'll approve them. Once I've approved them, you'll have your legal basis.' After our meeting, I did indeed draft some new regulations, and Commander Liu indeed authorized them."[5]

While the county government may have helped Jinmen's international image, its restoration created some unanticipated problems. One concern was coordination between the two authorities. The army depended on civilians for labor and various material requisitions. The new system interposed a new level of bureaucracy to procurement, creating inefficiencies and frequent conflicts over jurisdiction.[6] Another problem was that there was a substantial population on Jinmen whose status, civilian or military, was ambiguous. These were the thousands of soldiers of the Fujian Guerrilla Headquarters, created on Jinmen in 1951, and their dependents.[7] Their military activities were coordinated by a Central Intelligence

Agency (CIA)-front organization, but otherwise it was not clear under whose jurisdiction they fell. Politically, their existence "demonstrated" the continued existence of an anti-Communist resistance movement, so they could not simply be incorporated into the regular army.[8] But the county government had no effective authority over them. "At that time the guerrillas were very disorderly . . . They drank on the streets and there were often fights. You could say they had no military discipline to speak of."[9] Underlying all of these issues was a fundamental problem with the current arrangements, the ever-growing size of the garrison. Over the course of the 1950s, troop numbers would eventually reach a height of about 100,000, roughly double the civilian population (see Appendix).

There were thus practical and symbolic considerations behind the decision to revisit the question of how best to administer Jinmen. As policymakers discussed the question, they happened upon an existing framework that could be adapted to suit the island's needs. In the months following the withdrawal to Taiwan, Chiang Kai-shek had set up a research institute to plan for the restoration of ROC authority after the ultimate defeat of the Communists. The Bureau of War Zone Administration developed plans for undoing the damage that Communist ideas and institutions had done to Chinese society.[10] Ultimately the Bureau's work became the basis for a new political framework for Jinmen, one that would both demonstrate Chiang's commitment to keeping the islands under ROC control for the long term, and address the various problems with existing arrangements.

Theory and practice of War Zone Administration

The origins of the concept of War Zone Administration go back to the early days of the Chinese revolution, to Sun Yat-sen's doctrine that constitutional government for China had to be preceded by a period of political "tutelage" under military authority, to prepare the people for democracy. Chiang Kai-shek and his advisers elaborated on this notion in the years after 1949, most saliently as part of the justification for authoritarianism on Taiwan, but also as they thought about policies that would be needed once the mainland was recovered. Since the mainland was not enemy territory, one could not call such policies military occupation. But more than martial law would be needed to undo the terrible damage done by the Communists. WZA, temporary military control of national territory during and after the battle to defeat the Communists, was the formulation developed to solve this conundrum. Chiang decided that Jinmen (as well as the other offshore island group of Mazu) would become the testing ground for WZA. Of course, Jinmen had never been under Communist control, so a further manipulation was needed to make the scheme applicable – it would be known formally as the Experimental War Zone Administration. The whole of the Republic of China had been under martial law since 1946, so in a sense Taiwan itself was already under a state of emergency, or as Giorgio Agamben would put it, the state of exception. The WZA made Jinmen an exception within the state of exception.[11]

The WZA addressed the problems in coordination by clearly subordinating the civilian government to military command. The highest decision-making body on the island became the WZA Committee (WZAC), led by the head of the Political Warfare Department of the Jinmen Defense Headquarters and the most powerful man on the island after the JDHQ commander. A standing committee handled day-to-day decisions. The Committee's offices mirrored the civilian agencies of the county government, with a WZA cadre overseeing the work of every agency. An entire parallel structure to the civilian government was set up, separate but superior, staffed by officers of the military headquarters. This parallel structure resembled that in Taiwan, where the KMT penetrated both the state political system and most forms of social organization.[12] But there was one crucial difference. The parallel organization that penetrated all political and social entities, exerted overall control from within the entity, and determined appointments and promotions, was not, as in Taiwan, or for that matter in the PRC, the Leninist-style ruling party. On Jinmen it was the army [Fig. 3.1].

The main concession to public opinion under WZA was an appointed county consultative assembly but it met only irregularly and briefly and had no authority. We shall see below that village and township level elections were suspended indefinitely. Jinmen sent representatives to the two national assemblies in Taiwan, but until the 1980s, elections were uncontested. The WZA put forward sole nominees, who received the unanimous support of the 90 percent or more of eligible voters who cast their votes. The only legal party, of course, was the KMT, and it was subordinated to the WZA by the creation of a Special KMT Office that supervised the local party branch and had a veto over any elections to party branch positions. The Special Office was headed by the commander and the head of the Political Warfare Department – in other words, by the senior leadership of the WZA.[13]

Over time, an elaborate framework of rules and regulations was developed to clarify the division of responsibilities of the county government, the WZA, and the army. For example, the county government had a formal investigative and legal system, with branches of the relevant central government agencies such as the court, court of appeal, and so on. But a wide range of charges, anything that could remotely be tied to local security issues, including counterfeiting, murder, and sabotage, was automatically

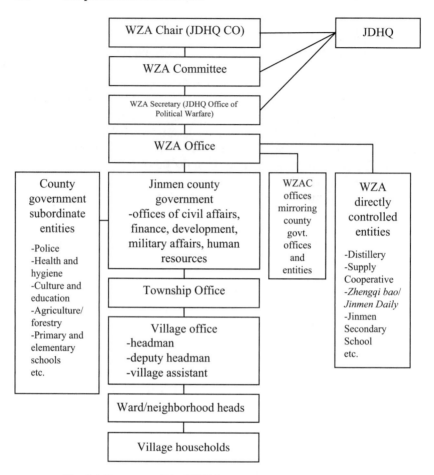

Fig. 3.1 Structure of the WZA bureaucracy

transferred to the army justice system. Thus in practice civilians were subject to military justice.[14] The ambiguity and indistinction between rule and application, rule and exception, and law and fact show Jinmen as a laboratory for fine-tuning politics in the state of emergency.

The WZA was explicitly articulated as a state of exception that justified the suspension of government regulations. But the state of exception is itself a form of government, so the limits of government authority were both suspended and not suspended. Cadres had to follow laws, but laws could be rewritten as necessary. The basic animating principle of the WZA was "unification of military and political; unity of army and civilians."[15] But there were fundamental contradictions internal to WZA. The civilian population was citizens of the ROC, and so the state had to acknowledge that it had certain obligations toward them, both present and future. These obligations were summed up by the slogan, "Administer, Instruct, Enrich, and Secure" (*guan, jiao, yang, wei*). Since the long-term obligation was to fulfill the national mission of defeating Communism and recovering the mainland, each of the elements in the slogan had to be interpreted in a dual-edged way. "Administer" meant guarding against Communist subversion as much as it did providing basic local services. "Instruct" meant instilling anti-Communist commitment as much as basic education. "Enrich" meant economic development, not only for the sake of civilian living standards but also to reduce their burden on the military. "Secure" meant not just policing, but mobilization of the population into the militia. The WZA system was a form of martial law, modeled on regimes of occupation and a model for a future occupation regime. The civilian population was thus both friend and enemy, self and other. These contradictions created distinctive modes of discipline, surveillance, and mobilization.

Village politics

During the initial reorganization of Jinmen government in late 1949, the island was divided into about 150 "administrative villages." The JDHQ chose a local man to serve as the headman of each village. They were selected on the basis of two criteria: the ability to speak Mandarin and literacy. "The most important thing was to be able to communicate, since at the time very few people spoke Mandarin."[16] As a result, most of the appointees were young men with little experience of village leadership, which made them more amenable to co-optation by the military administration. Youths who had befriended the troops in 1949 now found themselves political leaders. They had no say in the matter. As Wang Qingbiao, appointed in 1949 at the age of thirty, puts it, "It was obligatory. You'd have to work yourself half to death, but at the time the village headman was an assigned position. If you refused, that meant you were disobeying orders. Your thinking must have had problems; you were a Communist. So you didn't dare refuse."[17] Many in this first set of village headmen would play a crucial role in Jinmen politics for decades to come. They became the core of a new local political elite. Xue Chengzu was appointed headman of Zhushan. Born in 1924, he had been in the first class of the newly founded Jinmen Secondary School before it was shut down by the Japanese invasion. He was twenty-five when he became Zhushan headman, and held the position for the next eleven years. Several of his fellow classmates were also appointed headmen in 1949. Xue remains influential in village politics even to this day.

The youth of these headmen transformed traditional patterns of authority in the village. In Zhushan before 1949, village affairs had mainly been decided by an informal group of elder members of the Xue lineage and the wealthy patriarchs of Overseas Chinese families. These individuals were now largely shut out of the new formal administrative structure, though they continued to make their influence felt informally. Xue Chengzu reports, "For any village matters, I had to show them respect. If there were any disputes within families, or if the village was going to hold any collective activities, I asked their advice."[18]

The sense of intensified pressure that led to the establishment of the WZA reached down to the village. An early experiment with village-level elections in 1953 was abandoned, and for the next twenty years the WZA appointed village heads. New appointments also tended to be younger men with some education. Dong Zhenhan was appointed headman in early 1958. "I didn't want to do it, but the township said I had to, or I'd be offending the nation (*guojia*). I said, 'What do I know about the nation?' At the time I was twenty-seven years old."[19] The village headman was largely a nominal position. Real power in the village was in the hands of a cadre appointed from outside. From 1949 to 1956, this cadre was called the village political instructor (*zhidao yuan*); after 1956 the position was renamed deputy village headman (*fu cunzhang*). Political instructors were dispatched to every village in late 1949. Zheng Shihua, a native of Anhui and a soldier in Hu Lian's army, recalls:

In November 1949 I was sent to Panshan village to be the political instructor . . . The village headman was appointed. He didn't have to come to work everyday, and he didn't get a salary . . . He was the honorary head of the village. The political instructor was really responsible for all village affairs. Liaison with the outside, anything to do with the army was his responsibility . . . Orders from the higher-ups didn't usually go to the headman; they were sent directly to the political instructor.[20]

The dispatch of the new village cadres was an immediate burden on the villagers. They arrived with nothing, and so a first task was to round up supplies and requisition a house for their use. Xue Chengzu recalls having to go from house to house in Zhushan, trying to find furniture, including a door for a bed. The villagers' first impression of the political instructor was typically poor. One resident recalls, "When the instructors first came to the village they were extremely fierce. Their expectations of the people were totally military; they were extremely authoritarian, they treated the people as if they were soldiers." The instructors themselves saw it differently: "We were transferred out of the army, so we already knew what we needed to do. Training the civilian militia and training soldiers was basically the same."[21]

Xue Chengzu's first political instructor in Zhushan was a man named Wen Shizhong. Wen was a few years younger even than Xue. He had been conscripted into Hu Lian's army in 1948 while trying to get back to his hometown from school. Interviewed in 2001, he interpreted the political instructor system as a response to the KMT's defeats on the mainland. "At that time the government was mulling over the loss of the battle with the Communists on the mainland. [It concluded] that part of the reason had been the failure to mobilize the civilian population to support military logistics. So it began to organize the civilian population. The job was to get everyone enrolled in the organizational system." The political instructor played the key role:

The chief duties of the political instructor were to regulate the movement of civilians, militia training, and mobilization. The first thing was to monitor household registration. The focus was on eliminating traitors and preventing espionage, maintaining order, and making the household registration system tight and precise . . . As for mobilization, the main thing was leading work teams in constructing defense public works, including building roads and bridges, repairing roads, digging trenches, overseeing the construction of air raid shelters, constructing irrigation works, and so on.[22]

The range of duties did not shrink when the position was renamed deputy headman. "People at the time used to joke that 'Aside from delivering babies, every village matter, large or small, was [the deputy headman's] business.'"[23]

Defending against infiltration from the mainland was the most pressing task. As Wen Shizhong noted, the main instrument for this was the household registration system, which was the basis of an elaborate and strict surveillance regime over the civilian population. The system reinforced the close link that had long existed between the household and the state. In January 1950, an island-wide census was carried out, yielding household registers that associated each civilian with the house in which he or she lived. Village political instructors used the register and inspections to ensure that no mainland agents were hiding in civilian homes. "At that time household registration was very strict, and there were snap inspections . . . They'd divide up and inspect every family and every house. They'd inspect every room; they'd even look under the bed, to protect against any Communist spies hiding . . . The inspections were always in the middle of the night or early morning; at that time the villagers had all gone to sleep."[24]

Household inspections also gave the deputy the opportunity to search for prohibited items, such as radios, transmitters, and cameras, which civilians were forbidden to possess. There was also a long list of restricted items, comprising anything that could potentially serve as a flotation device: basketballs and volleyballs, bicycle and auto tires and inner tubes, and containers such as oil drums. These items were controlled to ensure that they did not fall into the hands of spies or would-be defectors. The deputy kept a list of these items attached to each household register, and checked off the list against what they found in their inspections to ensure that nothing was missing.[25] The household inspections also enabled political inspectors to search for military goods that had been pilfered by civilians or illegally sold by soldiers.

Civilians remember the inspections as a time when soldiers stole from them. Xue Liujin, a primary school student in Zhushan in the 1950s, recalls: "They'd seal off the whole village and roust everyone out of the house. We didn't even know what they were looking for. They'd just take whatever they wanted – anything that was valuable, anything they needed . . . There were no search warrants in those days."[26]

A pass system regulated movement. A resident who wished to spend the night away from his home required a pass from his own political instructor and had to register with the instructor at his destination. In practice this meant that a pass became necessary for many social activities. "If you went to visit your relatives, to attend a wedding or a sacrifice to the gods or ancestors, you had to apply for a pass. You had to walk there, and it took a long time, so you'd stay one or two nights. So you needed to get a pass. The pass system worked with the household register system. If there was an inspection, you had to be able to match the bodies to the register, and if not, you needed to have a pass."[27]

The regulatory system gained added force because households were linked together in a mutual responsibility system, with groups of five households required to police one another.[28] "If [a household inspection] found anything forbidden like military items, you'd be dragged off and detained. At that time, there was the five-household mutual responsibility system. So if by chance you were seized, you'd drag other people into it as well."[29] Because neighbors in the village tended to be kin, the mutual responsibility system could be an effective tool in ensuring compliance, since no one wanted to be responsible for getting their relatives locked up or fined.[30] On the other hand, the fact that members of a five-household mutual responsibility unit tended to be related could also work against the smooth operation of the system. One of Chi Chang-hui's informants recalls a time when his married sister returned to the natal home for a visit, and they neglected to register her. There was a snap inspection, but the sister evaded detection by sneaking out of the family home and into a neighbor's house. Then, when the inspection team had completed its work and moved on to the neighbor's house she snuck back into her own.[31]

Though there was no requirement that village heads and cadres be male, in practice no women were appointed or elected to these jobs until the 1990s. Since the political instructors and deputy heads were mostly demobilized soldiers, there was of course no possibility that these jobs could be filled by women. The one job women did take on was that of ward head. The ward head, responsible for a ward (*lin*) of five to twenty households, was appointed by the village officials to communicate orders to the villagers. That ward heads were often women was not due to deliberate effort but simply the fact that in many households women were the only literate members. Aside from areas of government that were dedicated to women's issues, the sub-administrative village level was the highest level of political authority that women ordinarily could attain.

Together the political instructor, household registration, five-household mutual responsibility, and ward systems created a new and intensive regime of surveillance that closely monitored the movements of the civilian population. But by targeting the household rather than the individual, and by relying on mutual responsibility, the regime was not a complete break from traditional patterns of village politics. Rather, it adapted existing approaches and understandings of state–society relations. This invites comparison both with modes of social control in traditional China *and* the interlocking system of party and state control on the mainland.

By giving political instructors responsibility for procurement of labor and supplies, the post-Battle of Guningtou system also began the formalization and systematization of civilian exactions. As Zhang Qicai recalls, it also created an identifiable target for villagers' resentments:

These village political instructors were heavy-handed; they didn't talk about feelings or face. When an order came down, they carried it out to the limit. Some village political instructors had problems of character or conduct . . . Many people in private called them "the undead". [The term political instructor (*zhidaoyuan*) is a near homophone in dialect for "one who can't be killed" (*sibuwan*).] Besides all of the other exactions, political officers were also responsible for village hygiene inspections, and many villagers found it too much . . . On top of all the training, exercises, assemblies, public works, who had time to do village hygiene? So it was no wonder that village hygiene was a mess. So wherever the instructor went he would curse, and wherever he cursed the duty team would follow [i.e. civilians would be forced to do labor]. His relations with the people became extremely tense, and he was much hated.[32]

The role of the village head in managing the interplay between coercion, persuasion, and the cultivation of self-discipline that constituted power in the village is captured well in the recollections of a deputy headman in the early 1970s. "For those who did not obey orders, the deputy headman had to assess the seriousness of the matter, and then give the appropriate level of punishment . . . If villagers didn't follow orders, the deputy village head could punish them by forcing them to do some village business or requiring them to do labor. If they didn't show up, the deputy head had lots of different ways to control them." For example, the deputy head could deny villagers permission to travel to Taiwan for work, study, or even medical treatment. In more extreme cases, he could put villagers in detention. "People didn't want to bring trouble onto themselves, so every person developed the habit of obeying the law."[33]

On the other hand, people were well aware that instructors played the key role in mediating state influences, and were critical of instructors who did not try to shelter the villagers. "When Ye Dehui was political instructor for the township, his demands for work were extremely strict, so some people were dissatisfied with him. Some people seized the opportunity when he was not at home to run into his bedroom and urinate on his bed." The household registration and pass system brought the cadres into close, even intimate relationships with the community in which they served. Hong Futian, who would go on to serve as the township head for Little Jinmen in the 1960s and 1970s, was in charge of registration at the township office in the 1950s. "Because of the population registration requirements, I got to know a lot of people . . . Once a husband and wife were arguing. The wife went back to her natal village. Her husband came to ask me for help. I went to her natal village and told them that the wife couldn't stay there because she didn't have permission." Hong reports that this happened more than once, and that couples continued for decades to thank him for his *ex officio* marriage counseling.[34]

The village headman had little real authority; the deputy headman had "powers of life and death" over the villagers. The relationship between the two was the crucial political relationship in village life during the martial law years. Longtime headmen like Xue Chengzu can rhyme off one after the other the names of the political instructors and deputy heads with whom they served. Headmen found themselves expected to mediate between instructors and other villagers. When a villager was detained, the dynamic between the two officials was crucial to obtaining release. Villagers could be held for up to several days virtually at the whim of the village deputy (longer detentions required approval from superiors, and paperwork). "The deputy headman had the authority to have you locked up on his signature, or even have you sent to the reform camp. Anyone who didn't participate in militia training, or didn't fulfill their hygiene work responsibilities, and didn't respond to warnings; anyone who didn't look after their weapon properly; even anyone who got drunk frequently – all the deputy head had to do was write a report and the magistrate would approve it, then the person who was disobedient could be locked up for up to two weeks." Villagers could be detained in the village office (in the early days this was generally an occupied house), in a pigsty or latrine, or in the nearest police station lockup. "Sometimes he just pointed at a spot on the ground, wherever, and said, 'Don't move. Stay here.' And you had to stay there; you couldn't move."[35] Typically when a villager was detained by the deputy, his family members would go to the headman, who would then intercede with the deputy to have the detainee released. So if the headman and the deputy did not get along, every villager suffered.

Deputies were rotated frequently, possibly in order to prevent them from forming ties with the villagers and neglecting their job of maintaining discipline. This became a particular concern as more of them realized that they were not going to return to the mainland, and became anxious to marry. Xue Chengzu was like many village headmen in serving as matchmaker for his instructors and deputies, starting with Wen Shizhong. As tales of matchmaking and marriages would suggest, the relationship between the political instructor and the villagers was not purely antagonistic. On the contrary, villagers sometimes saw their instructor's ties to the state used to their advantage. After about a year in Zhushan, Fu Wenmin was transferred to Liaoluo, a coastal village in the southeastern part of Jinmen (where the village head introduced him to his future wife). Fu interceded with the army – he had many contacts at JDHQ, having only just been demobilized – to allow the fishermen to go down to the beach after dark to lay shallow-water nets. The villagers all brought him fish in thanks. "In fact, the residents of Jinmen were all very innocent. I knew about the background of each of them. I was perfectly clear about whether or not there would be problems. Administering the fishermen was mainly a matter of ongoing inspections, to see how loyal and trustworthy they were."[36]

In the mainland villages opposite Jinmen, a more thorough effort was underway to destroy the structures of traditional rural life. Though the military officials who governed Jinmen did not set out on the same deliberate campaign of social change, the demands of military mobilization nonetheless had highly disruptive effects on village society. But just as on the mainland many of these older structures survived, mutating into new forms and taking on new political roles, martial law on Jinmen was hardly a solvent that simply dissolved existing patterns of authority and relationships.[37] The clearest example is in the persistence of patterns of mutual responsibility, which were deliberately reinforced by state policy. Efforts to construct a modern system of political control did not necessarily imply a focus on relations with autonomous individuals, but could rely instead on traditional units like the household, embedded in local social life. The distinctive characteristics of Jinmen profoundly shaped the emergence of new modes of governance. For example, the system of population surveillance and monitoring was intended to prevent infiltration and espionage by agents of the PRC. In practice though, this system came to serve much broader disciplinary functions. The specific articulation of surveillance, discipline, and violence that characterized Jinmen politics in the early years of martial law must thus be situated within the context of indigenous modes of governmentality, both pre-modern and modern, and above all, the international geopolitical situation.

Surveillance and repression

Though most residents of Jinmen today are quick to point out that by comparison with the regime on the mainland the WZA years were relatively benign, they are also determined to give voice to their memories of repression and fear. Everyone has an anecdote about a relative who was taken away and beaten on suspicion of Communist ties, a classmate who was detained and missed his only chance to take the university entrance examinations, a widow who searched for decades for news of her "disappeared" husband. Since democratization, local politicians responding to the requests of their constituents have begun to compile dossiers of archives on such cases, and these flesh out the oral history.[38]

The WZA rested, as we have seen, on a system of mutual responsibility. Its intelligence work rested on a system of mutual suspicion and fear. Both the WZA and the army had an intelligence service on the island. "The political air became very tense around the 1954–5 Crisis. The intelligence services used informers to get information about everything. People who wanted to get ahead became informants. They'd report everything. Even if half a dozen people just got together for a chat, they'd be investigated. What did you talk about? Who was in charge? Who was involved? What did you do?"[39] As in other places where state-sponsored white terror has been practiced, the result was a climate of fear and conservatism. "If there was someone who liked to stand out, liked to talk, liked to make a spectacle of himself, he'd be seen as having 'ideological problems,' which meant that his thought was too extreme. He'd be taken away, and he'd never return." People remember this as a time of arbitrary suspicion and detention, when the least offense could have disastrous consequences, and people could not even be sure what constituted an offense – a remark misinterpreted, a hummed tune that turned out to be a Communist song. Several people have stories about how some pre-1949 link to the mainland turned them into objects of suspicion. One tells the story of his father who had relatives in Xiamen. A letter from them, received before contact was cut off, was found in a rubbish pile by an informant. His father was held in a military jail for four months, at one point being forced to dig what he was told was his own grave.[40]

In July 1953, thirty-five year old Li Jiuli was seized by soldiers from his home in Guningtou. More than a year later his body was returned and his wife informed that he had been executed as a Communist agent. This was just over a week after the start of the 1954–5 Strait Crisis, and because of the shelling, he could not be given a proper funeral but was buried in a shallow grave outside the village. When she was interviewed by journalists in the late 1990s, Li's widow still did not know what her husband had done wrong. But she had long nursed speculation that he had been betrayed by a neighbor. This neighbor had sold a tire to a soldier who was caught building a raft to sail back to the mainland. The neighbor, to save himself, blamed Li Jiuli. Army documents recently released to the family confirm the story of the tire and provide details about the neighbor's accusations. He claimed Li was a Communist agent who had engaged in espionage and sabotage. There is no way to assess whether these accusations were true. In Jinmen in the early 1950s, they were a death warrant.[41]

Sometimes whole villages came under suspicion of contact with the Communists. Xiyuan, the village of Huang Pingsheng, the farmer with whom this book began, was one such village. The people of Xiyuan, which was close to mainland-held Dadeng island, had many relatives on the mainland. Apparently an informant reported that they were still in contact with their kin, and the whole village came under a cloud. An alternative explanation given by some informants is that a girl of Xiyuan was raped by a soldier shortly after 1949, and rather than dropping the matter as they were encouraged to do, village leaders pursued it and sought compensation. This earned them the enmity of the local garrison, whose officers labeled them a "spy village" (*feidie cun*).[42]

As on Taiwan, intellectuals as a group were suspected of having Communist tendencies (of course, intellectuals were also frequently targeted on the mainland, both for their supposed political inclinations and their bad class background). On Jinmen, the only intellectuals were the teachers. In the late 1940s, Wang Fangming had been recruited from his home on the mainland by a former classmate to teach at a Jinmen primary school. With the fall of Xiamen in October 1949, Wang became one of the many people, on both sides of the waters, who was cut off from their family. Wang seems nevertheless to have prospered in Jinmen. In the mid-1950s, he became principal of the Jincheng primary school. He married a local teacher in 1958. But one day in September 1968, Wang was taken away by officers from the Jinmen Investigation Office, the county-level intelligence service. Another of his classmates from the mainland, who had followed the KMT to Taiwan in 1949, had recently come under investigation for Communist sympathies. To save himself, he claimed that while they had been studying together during the war, Wang had joined a

Fig. 3.2 Children playing beneath anti-Communist graffiti (© Getty images)

student reading group that was actually a Communist front organization. Wang denied the charge, but the other members of the group were all still on the mainland, so there was no way he could corroborate his story. Under torture, Wang "confessed" to having joined a Communist organization on the mainland and he was sentenced to ten years. Thanks to a general amnesty, Wang became eligible for release in 1973. He continued to be closely monitored by police for the rest of the martial law period. In 1990, political liberalization on both sides of the Strait made it possible for Wang to return to his mainland home for a visit. He learned then that in 1968, the same year as he was arrested, his elderly father had been persecuted and killed in the Cultural Revolution because his son was a civil servant under the KMT regime.[43]

Conclusions

By 1956, the position of Jinmen in the ROC's overall strategy had moved through several phases. From a surprising victory to be defended at all costs, it had become a military base for the imminent counter-attack to recover the mainland. It continued to have a military function as the site for intelligence gathering and guerrilla harassment, but increasingly its real significance was political: as a symbol of the government's commitment to national recovery and anti-Communism. The Experimental War Zone Administration system was a political structure developed in service of these goals. A civilian government did exist, to demonstrate the contrast between the ROC and the political system on the mainland. But its powers were nominal; in all important respects it was subordinated to the military presence on the island. Military priorities and concerns dominated public and increasingly also private life, and contributed to the erasure of the distinction between the two. The WZA system sought to foster a docile population in service of geopolitical goals, developing and using new forms of discipline to monitor the population and its movements and to maintain ideological unity. During precisely the period that these policies were being developed on Jinmen, similar policies were being developed in the PRC. For example, the introduction of an internal pass system in the PRC occurred within months of the tightening of the WZA pass system on Jinmen. This suggests that what was happening on Jinmen cannot be explained solely with reference to the immediate concerns of the island's authorities, but also in terms of more widespread issues. With national development taking place under the shadow of a military threat that was local, but also tied to the larger Cold War conflict, modernization was defined in ways that prioritized the danger of infiltration, subversion, and sabotage. The need to monitor the population and train their bodies and their minds into docility was a central concern. For the island's residents the need to prepare for war thus profoundly shaped both the construction and the experience of modernity.

4　The 1954–5 Artillery War

In 1954, Zheng Qingli was fourteen years old. One afternoon he was playing basketball near his home in Jinmencheng, the village that had grown up on the ruins of the old Ming fort.

Suddenly I heard the sounds of shelling – "bong bong." At first, the shells landed mostly in the sea between Shuitou and Little Jinmen. We all scrambled up onto the old town wall to watch. We could see the shells firing from the Communist guns on the coast at Xiamen. As each shell was fired, [the gun] flashed – it was something to see. As each shell landed in the water, it sent up a spray of water – what a sight! Our navy boats were sailing back and forth trying not to be hit – it was like us kids playing hide and seek – it was cool . . . Then at about five or six o'clock, suddenly there was a loud sound "xiuuuu." A shell flew right over our heads and fell by the north gate of Jinmencheng. It landed on my aunt, killing her and the child she was carrying on the spot. The sudden huge noise scared all of us who had climbed on the wall to watch the excitement, and we scattered. This was my first experience of shellfire. At the time I was just a foolish kid. After I ran home there was nowhere to hide, so all I could do was hide under the bed, and pile some blankets on the bed, thinking this would protect me.[1]

Thus began the Taiwan Strait Crisis of 1954–5 or, as the people of Jinmen call it, the September 3rd Artillery War. Cross-strait tension had been building over the summer of 1954, though there seems to have been no awareness of this on Jinmen. At three in the afternoon on September 3, mainland guns opened fire with a ferocious barrage. Two US officers of the Military Assistance Advisory Group were among those killed on that first day. The heavy shelling continued. The chairman of the joint chiefs of staff, Admiral Arthur Radford, soon linked Jinmen to the nascent domino theory. "If we fail to resist this aggression, we commit the United States further to a negative policy which could result in a progressive loss of free world strength to local aggression until or unless all-out conflict is forced upon us." Radford urged President Eisenhower to consider the use of nuclear weapons against the PRC to stave off an imminent invasion.[2] The US ambassador in Taibei, Karl Rankin, was more sanguine and did not think an invasion was imminent, "My guess is that they are simply trying us out . . . If they can make it appear to all and sundry that the United

States is unable or unwilling to do anything about these offshore islands, the Reds will have won another round."[3]

The ROC had already been pressing the US to enter into a mutual defense arrangement to guarantee the security of Taiwan against PRC invasion. The crisis in the Taiwan Strait sparked the start of formal negotiations. The US secretary of state, John Foster Dulles, visited Taiwan to meet Chiang Kai-shek on September 9, and the ROC foreign minister traveled to Washington. On December 2 the treaty was signed. It committed the US to support the defense of Taiwan and Penghu only. In January 1955, the People's Liberation Army (PLA) destroyed the ROC garrison on Yijiangshan, an island off the coast of Zhejiang province north of Jinmen. Chiang then decided to abandon the other ROC-held islands off Zhejiang, known as the Dachen group, to avoid a humiliating defeat. Eisenhower then requested that Congress pass the so-called Formosa Resolution, which authorized him to use US forces to defend not only Taiwan and Penghu, but also any other territories that were necessary to ensure their defense. The Formosa Resolution was passed in late January. Jinmen now seemed to lie under the US security umbrella, even if the US was still unwilling to say so explicitly.

Chiang had hoped that in return for his relinquishing the Dachen islands Eisenhower would make a public declaration about Jinmen. So he was disappointed in the US, which had let its ally down just as it had in 1949. Reluctant to abandon any more territory to the Communists and still hopeful that he would one day lead an army to reconquer the mainland, Chiang quickly realized that he could make Jinmen "necessary" to the defense of Taiwan by committing a disproportionate number of his troops to the island. That is, if a successful attack on Jinmen would lead to huge losses to the ROC army and a potentially serious blow to morale on Taiwan, the US might be obliged to help Chiang defend Jinmen. Deployment of massive numbers of troops to Jinmen was Chiang's way to drag the US into the defense of the region (see Appendix).[4]

The intense shelling of Jinmen continued. In early March, US officials stepped up their efforts to stop the crisis by threatening to expand it. Dulles publicly announced that the US was preparing for the use of nuclear weapons to deter aggression against Jinmen.[5] At the time, it appeared that US deterrence worked. On May 1, the PLA scaled back its shelling of Jinmen, though it continued sporadic firing for the next several years. In 1957, an ROC report on the damages caused by the shelling since the beginning of the crisis said that a total of 59,923 shells had been fired on Jinmen, 61 civilians had been killed and 128 injured, and almost 2,000 homes destroyed.

Today, the prevailing scholarly interpretation is that by attacking Jinmen while the US was considering both a Mutual Defense Treaty and including Taiwan in multilateral defense plans for Southeast Asia, Mao was signaling that the PRC considered the US to be interfering in China's internal affairs, and warning that a defense pact with Taiwan would carry the significant risk of dragging the US into war. There had to be some response to this provocation, and Mao chose Jinmen to play this role. But the signaling did not fulfill its full objective, because while Chinese planners were correct that Jinmen was not important to overall US security strategy, they did not realize the importance of firmness and resolve in that strategy. The warning may even be said to have backfired, for it led the US to make a stronger commitment to Taiwan's security than Eisenhower had originally intended.[6]

Memories of battle

The calculations of statesmen and their generals tell us little about how conflict is experienced. The 1954–5 Strait Crisis may have been a battle of political posturing, but for the people of Jinmen it was still a battle. Collection of oral history on Jinmen began in the late 1990s, after the people of Jinmen had experienced forty years of militarization and military threat since the crisis. Their subsequent experience has shaped their memories of earlier events. The prevailing sentiment underlying many accounts of the 1954–5 Crisis is a self-deprecating awareness of their own naiveté. Though they had already lived through the Battle of Guningtou and the beginnings of militarization, on September 3 the people of Jinmen were still innocent. Many accounts follow Zheng Qingli in drawing attention to the way people put themselves at risk by watching the pyrotechnic display.

The naiveté and panic of the villagers in 1954, in contrast to their greater degree of experience and familiarity later on, have produced many jokes. There is the anecdote about a Zhushan man who went to Jincheng for a haircut. It was only half done when the bombing began, but he leaped from his chair and ran all the way home, with his hair half cut. There are countless versions of the story about the villagers who were drawing water when the bombing began. After they dropped their pail in panic, they had a hard time recovering it from the depths of the well.[7] Another way in which Jinmen people recount the transformation that they underwent during the 1954–5 Crisis is to tell of how they developed a new skill that became invaluable in the subsequent decades, the ability to determine the direction of a shell based on the sounds it made. "When the bombs were falling, we in the militia could tell from the sound where the bomb was coming from and where it was going to land. If you heard the sound pong-pong-pong, you knew that you were OK, that it was going somewhere else. If you heard a sound like fst-fst-fst, you knew the shell would land nearby, maybe within fifty feet."[8]

Besides the sense of panic, another memory that older residents share is of the immediate mobilization of the militia. The military had large stocks of ammunition at Shuitou, where the naval base was located. This part of the island was close and very exposed to the mainland guns, so it was decided to relocate the ammunition to the expanding central army base in western Jinmen, where Mount Taiwu obstructed the line of fire from the mainland. Dong Wunan was one of the militia who helped carry the ammunition across the island. "On the night of September 3, we had to carry one box of ammunition each – it weighed about 100 pounds. We set out from Gugang [his native village, about one mile from Shuitou] at nine o'clock, and carried the ammunition to Mount Taiwu. By the time we got there, the sun had already come up. That time there was one militia team that had five members killed."[9] While civilians in every time and place are made vulnerable by war, for the people of Jinmen militia obligations meant that when fighting broke out, they would be forced to move into the fray, not away from it.

Like the Battle of Guningtou that preceded it, experiences of the 1954–5 Artillery War varied considerably by one's location on the island. This was because the initial wave of bombing was targeted on the naval base at Shuitou, and many of the shells fell short. So the effects of the artillery barrage were at first felt most strongly on the western parts of Jinmen, in the vicinity of Shuitou, and on Little Jinmen, because it was closest to the mainland. Many people fled east. Chen Zonglun, also from Jinmencheng, decided to move a few miles east. "At first, I thought the shells wouldn't be able to reach Zhushan, so I took my family and stayed with my relative Xue Qingguo there. He already had a simple shelter. We stayed about a week. Then Zhushan started to be hit. We figured that if the whole island was within range of the guns, we might as well just go home. We dug our own shelter there. A few days later, we learned that Xue Qingguo had been killed when a shell landed on his shelter."[10]

On September 17 a direct hit on an ammunition dump at Guqu, near Shuitou, destroyed the entire village. One elderly villager wrote recently in the local newspaper of his memories of the disaster.

We had lost all sensation. The whole village was completely black with smoke. You couldn't see the fingers of your hand. When I crawled out from under the bed, I couldn't tell left from right, so I ran. When I was on the road to Dongsha, I looked back to the village. The sky was filled with smoke. Some people say that every house has a spirit in the rafters. When I ran out from the black village, I heard pitiful moans rising out of the burning flames. Later I asked an elder what the noise had been, and I learned that when houses are collapsing, the spirits of the rafters disperse. Even today when I think of that sound, my hair stands on end . . . [Returning the next morning, I saw that] not a single house was undamaged. Everything was in disarray. Throughout the village there were broken tiles and beams, and scattered shells both exploded and live. Several banyans – of the size that two or three people could encircle them with their arms – had been completely uprooted. The force must have been incredible. The whole village was dark, and there was the smell of powder. It was like hell on earth.[11]

Though Guqu was the most obvious localized devastation, 1954 marked the beginning of a general relocation in the social and economic as well as military center of gravity of Jinmen toward the better-protected eastern parts of the island. After Guqu, the most dramatic shift was the eclipse of Shuitou town. Before 1954, it had been the site of the naval base on Jinmen and Hu Lian's headquarters. Huang Xi'an used to help his mother sell snacks to the huge crowds of soldiers who came to watch opera performances. Now the numbers dwindled.[12] After 1954, when the naval base and headquarters were moved to eastern Jinmen, Shuitou went into a decline from which it never recovered.

When residents of Shuitou talk about the decline of their village after 1954, they blame the Artillery War for the end of the vibrant village night-life, with its opera performances and open-air teahouses. But there is more to the story than this. To make it harder for mainland gunners to target the island, in late 1954 a blackout was imposed on Jinmen. It remained in force for more than a quarter of a century. The civilian parts of the island had not yet been electrified in 1954, so residents lit their home with candles and oil lamps. Every structure now had to be equipped with blackout curtains to cover doorways and windows. The militia was given the task of inspecting homes regularly, and patrolling the community to look for any evidence of light seeping out. When running water was introduced to the towns and villages of Jinmen in the 1960s, a new level of monitoring became possible. Residents had to demonstrate that their homes were equipped with blackout curtains before they could be hooked up to the water supply.[13]

The 1954–5 Crisis also furthered the geographical isolation of Jinmen from the outside world. After 1949, the island's dense links with the nearby mainland had been completely cut. But shipping links continued to the other offshore islands that remained in ROC hands, and to Hong Kong. With Hu Lian's permission, the guerrillas used the Hong Kong trade to fund their activities – they purchased luxury goods such as perfume and stockings in Hong Kong and resold them at a profit on Jinmen, from where they could be transhipped to Taiwan. Shuitou was where the guerrillas unloaded their products, and Huang Xi'an remembers shopkeepers from

Jincheng coming with their donkeys to carry goods back to town.[14] The 1954 shelling made this trade too dangerous; the destruction of the Shuitou docks also meant that a new site would be needed to off-load cargo. To prevent the trade from interfering with regular military transport, the Jinmen Defense Headquarters (JDHQ) commander decided to ban the Hong Kong trade altogether.[15] With the abandonment of the northern offshore islands by the ROC, the coastal trade also disappeared. Jinmen, which had for decades been enmeshed in very complex networks of trade, money and people, was now cut off from all its contacts with the rest of the world except one, the sea and air route to Taiwan, and even that route was highly restricted.

Though the shelling subsided after a few months, the heightened level of militia mobilization did not. New tasks were assigned to help repel the invasion that was rumored to be imminent. One task that militia members remember well is the installation of anti-landing spikes all around the island. These were heavy iron bars, topped with sharpened spikes, that were set into concrete at an angle and sunk into the beaches. They were intended to keep the landing boats of an invading force offshore, forcing them to discharge their passengers in deeper water where they would be easy targets, and to pierce and ensnare the boats themselves, making it impossible for them to return to the mainland to carry reinforcements and resupply. Every militia unit was given a quota of spikes to install. The stakes could only be installed at low tide, and only at night, because during the day the militia soldiers made easy targets for the gunners on the mainland. "When they realized that we were doing it at night, they started targeting the beaches at night too."[16]

The 1954–5 artillery attacks are also remembered as a turning point in the construction of shelters, the other major new task for civilian labor. Digging and reinforcing shelters was not a new job. Many families had built rough shelters or dug caves after the Battle of Guningtou. The JDHQ had encouraged civilians to build shelters near their homes. "But people had a very perfunctory attitude, and the tools for digging were very primitive . . . so they couldn't dig very deep." "At that time the shelters were only dug very shallowly; as long as you could crouch down inside it that was good enough." Zheng Qingli's response to the shelling, to hide under his bed and pile blankets on top, was a common one. Now the military ordered that every village must construct deeper and more substantial shelters, adequate to house the entire population, within two months. These orders generated considerable resentment, but a few years later would play an important role in turning popular opinion around on the War Zone Administration. As Huang Pingsheng reports, "After the 1954 Crisis, the militia had to build shelters . . . At the time, I remember we used to curse the government. We civilians were already under so much pressure it almost killed us. Then to have this responsibility added on top; it was just too much." As head of the militia, Xu Rongxiang was responsible for enforcing the policy. "If I heard that a family was not building a shelter, I'd have them locked up. Lots of people hated me at the time for this, but later, they all thanked me."[17] For during the 1958 Crisis three years later, the shelters saved countless lives. Shelter construction was one more way in which the intensification of militarization on Jinmen affected the way civilians' lives were organized and lived. Though they did not know it at the time, the shelters would come to be a major part of their lives for the next quarter of a century.

The outcomes of the 1954–5 Crisis mattered greatly to the overall geopoliticization of the island, though not in ways that could have been predicted. Since the US–ROC agreements did not explicitly include Jinmen under the US security umbrella, but did authorize the US President to help defend territories essential to ROC defense, they paradoxically gave Chiang Kai-shek a strong incentive to dig in on the island. The greater the proportion of his forces on the island, the more persuasive his argument that they must be defended. Troop levels now rose from 60,000 in 1954 to a height of about 100,000. By 1957, as Dulles recognized, "the defense of the offshore islands was now so complete and so integral a part of the defense of Taiwan, that it was not to be compared with the fluid situation of three years ago . . . If there were an all-out attack on [Jinmen or Mazu], the United States should not sit to one side and permit the loss of these islands, because their loss would surely result in the loss of Taiwan and the Penghus."[18] By strongly investing in Jinmen, Chiang sought to link the fate of the island to the global Cold War by tying the United States to its defense. Militarization in the narrow sense of more soldiers also led to greater militarization in the broader sense. As the number of soldiers came to exceed the total civilian population, more and more elements of life on the island became shaped by and dependent on military concerns.

The 1954–5 Taiwan Strait Crisis is remembered today as the second of the great victories of Jinmen, won by the collective determination of the army and the civilian population. That the preponderance of evidence suggests that there was never going to be an invasion of Jinmen is not something that can easily fit into residents' framework of memory of the period. Civilian memories are most often of the shock and panic of the initial barrage, of their attempts to flee and find shelter, of the damage to life and property. Conditioned by later events, many of their memories focus on their naïve innocence when the shells began to fall on September 3. They remember clearly developments whose significance would only become evident much later in time, such as the transfer of the naval base and the subsequent decline of Shuitou, the spread of air-raid shelters, the nightly blackout, or the new tasks assigned to the militia. From the long-term perspective, however important the crisis was, both in international relations and in the personal recollections of the people of Jinmen, it marks less a significant juncture in the history of local militarization than an intensification of an ongoing process, the gradual subordination of civilian to military interests, and the articulation of civilian interests in terms of military values.

5 Militarization and the Jinmen Civilian Self-Defense Forces, 1949–1960

Everyone in Jinmen knows the joke about the old villager who was walking along the road in his militia uniform when he ran into a checkpoint. The military police at the checkpoint detained him because his uniform was unkempt and tattered, and demanded to know his unit. Confused and frightened, and in some versions of the joke misunderstanding the MPs' Mandarin, the man stammered out "I'm in Unit 805." Later, the MPs prepared a report on the poor discipline of this unit and submitted it to headquarters. To everyone's surprise, there was no Unit 805 stationed on Jinmen. It turned out the old man had got the better of them. He was a militia member, not a regular soldier. And 805 was not the name of his unit, but the cost of his uniform $80.50.[1] For Jinmen residents who lived through the War Zone Administration (WZA) period, the story speaks to powerful themes – their subjection to military discipline that they did not always understand, and their efforts to respond to that subjection.

The story of Unit 805 is also a compelling metaphor for the trajectory of militarization in a very specific sense, the incorporation of the people of Jinmen into an armed militia. As Aaron Friedberg has observed, "Of all the activities of the modern state, none is so immediate or dramatic in its impact on the lives of ordinary citizens as the extraction of manpower."[2]

In this chapter, I discuss the early history of the militia on Jinmen after 1949, showing the gradual formalization, systematization, and institutionalization of the *ad hoc* measures used in 1949. As I will show, this formalization was not simply a matter of rationalization of civilian labor for military purposes. The development of the militia reflected taxonomic impulses that constantly distinguished between militia and regular soldiers, even as the military functions of the two converged. Over time the militia came to be a vehicle for mobilization as well as extraction of labor and surveillance of the population. In other words, besides its military functions, it also came to have political functions, as part of the project of creating an anti-Communist polity on Jinmen. The clearest evidence of this was the commutation of militia duties. On the one hand, in the early

50

period, individual militia members were permitted to commute their labor obligations, either by hiring a replacement or paying money to the village officers to hire someone on their behalf. Later these options were phased out and it became increasingly difficult to avoid personally fulfilling one's assigned militia duties. On the other hand, in the interest of efficiency, many tasks that were formerly done by individual militia members were transferred to specialized laborers hired by the village. Other tasks, such as participation in military review, served primarily political functions, and therefore no one could be exempt. As militia service became increasingly also a political obligation, the functions of the household registration system were effectively reversed. As we saw in chapter 3, the system had originally been intended to guard against spies and infiltrators from the mainland, to ensure that no one was on Jinmen who should not be. By the late 1950s it became, in large part, a mechanism to ensure that no one evaded their militia responsibilities, and that no one who should be on Jinmen was not.

The story of the militia is continued in two later chapters. In the middle period of martial law, from the late 1960s to the 1980s, the militia's functions became increasingly militarized. No longer was the militia trained to provide logistical support to regulars; now their job was actually to fight in combat. Militia service constructed Jinmen residents as heroic defenders of their nation, and freedom itself. In the early period, the people of Jinmen were ambivalent about this construction, making use of whatever means they had in their power to limit its impact on their lives. Their initial resistance and sense of outrage at the demands made of them were largely submerged by the end of this period. But as we shall see in Part IV, it remained a part of collective memory, and re-emerged with important consequences as the militia system was dissolved in the 1990s.

In her study of militias under both the ROC and the PRC, Elizabeth Perry shows that, throughout the twentieth century, Chinese regimes sought to use popular militias for the purposes of both state-making and state-breaking, in the process articulating some of the central tensions in the construction of citizenship.[3] The militia of Jinmen reveals another dimension to the history of militias in modern China. Militia service is connected not only to the transformation of the militia members themselves into citizens. It can also serve an indirect role, as a political model of citizenship for the populace as a whole. The militia member becomes a symbol of the self-sacrifice expected of all citizens. When a government makes it seem that military service is a natural part of citizenship, it is expending political resources in order to keep hidden the separability of citizenship and militarization. On Jinmen, the ROC sought to localize this cost, expending it in one locale in order to convey the message to the whole populace.[4]

In October 1949, when the Battle of Guningtou broke out, army officers seized anyone they could find to provide services like portering of ammunition and evacuation of the wounded. This was entirely in keeping with their experiences on the mainland, and at the time would have been done with little or no reflection. When the Nationalist (KMT)'s National Army needed labor in Republican China, it took it. After the situation stabilized and it became clear that the army was likely to remain on Jinmen for some time and in significant numbers, arrangements began to be formalized. During the battle itself, as we saw, "it didn't matter if you were male or female, you had to carry the wounded." But soon the civilian population was divided by age and sex into several functional groupings, with teenagers and older men forming the "roadworks team"; the "women's team" providing aid at field hospitals, and adult males forming the "duty team" and required to perform a wide range of functions in peacetime and during combat. In 1950, this classification system was further refined, with teams divided into mule teams, transport teams, fire-brigades, and so on.

Many residents tried to evade militia service. This was not due to laziness. Rumors were circulating that the ROC forces would soon be evacuating the island, and taking with them all men of military age. Moreover, the frenzied defense preparations, and regular and frequent radio broadcasts from the mainland warning that Jinmen would soon be "washed in blood" when the PLA returned to revenge their defeat at Guningtou, convinced many residents that even if Chiang Kai-shek was not planning to abandon them, they might still be cannon fodder in an anticipated great battle. Chen Yongcai, about twelve years old in 1949, was hidden by his parents in a grove of trees to avoid being drafted to the duty team.[5]

This fear that providing labor service for the soldiers could have disastrous consequences turned the census of early 1950 into a farce. Men in their sixties and seventies today frequently told me in interviews, "I was born in [such-and-such] year, but my identity card says I was born in [a different] year." In other words, their parents delayed reporting their birth or otherwise falsified their reporting to the census-takers. With the age of duty-team service set at eighteen years, parents of sons who were nineteen or twenty claimed that they were twelve or fifteen. Du Tiansheng remembers that the political instructor in his village would pull down the pants of teenage boys and check if their testicles had descended. If they had he would simply add two years to the boy's age as recorded on the registration.[6]

The desire to avoid militia duty did not disappear when the situation calmed down, and people continued to look for ways to evade it. Oral history of Jinmen in the early 1950s suggests that militia duties occupied an extraordinary amount of time in the period, though there are great discrepancies among accounts. Older informants say that they trained for three to four months of every year.[7] This may be exaggeration on the part of people trying to magnify the extent of their sacrifice. (As we shall see, once compensation for militia service began to be discussed, they had strong material reasons to do so.) Fu Wenmin, Wen Shizhong's replacement as political instructor in Zhushan, remembers a bi-annual, month-long training in the early 1950s. Xu Rongxiang, who led the militia for part of this period, reports that there was regular training of four hours twice per week, and also an annual training period of thirteen weeks. But he also remembers that annual training only totaled 100 hours. So perhaps older residents are describing the duration of the training period accurately, but neglecting to mention that they did not train full-time during the period. The meaning of training was quite flexible in this period. Young men and old men belonged to the roadworks team, whose job was to repair roads damaged by shelling in combat. There were no paved roads on Jinmen; the packed earth roads were frequently washed out by rain or damaged by the passage of heavy military equipment. For the roadworks team, training was often simply an excuse to have them repair damaged roads.[8]

With the passage of time, requirements on the militia became more routinized. An elaborate regulatory framework developed.[9] A Militia Command (*zongdui*) headed by the county magistrate was created. In the same way as the county and sub-county government were controlled by interlocking "deputy" positions appointed by the WZA at every level, the deputy commander of the Militia Command was the deputy magistrate, who was simultaneously the head of the county military affairs office and a WZA Committee appointee. Underneath the Militia Command was a simplified version of the military hierarchy; each township had a militia battalion (*dadui*); each village formed a company (*zhongdui*); each village company was divided into platoons and each platoon into squads (*ban*) of ten to twelve men. The village company was commanded by the village deputy headman. Militia units were also formed in each of the entities under the WZA Committee, such as economic and cultural organizations and schools. Militia battalions were divided functionally, and also by age and gender, in a further refinement of the classification that had been becoming ever more elaborate since 1949. Teenage boys and girls of sixteen and seventeen and men between forty-five and fifty years of age formed the reserve platoon, responsible for surveillance, intelligence

Fig. 5.1 Militia training (from Ming Qiushui (ed.), *Jinmen*, by permission of Jinmen county cultural bureau)

gathering, and communications. Women aged between eighteen and thirty-five made up the women's brigade, which handled propaganda work, provided succor and nursing to the wounded, supported the weak and aged, and educated the youth in their duties to support the army. Men of eighteen to forty-five made up the main body of the militia, divided into defense, logistics, and medical brigades. In coastal villages, fishermen were organized into a boat brigade.[10]

Former militia members have little to say about militia training and exercises in the early years. It was monotonous and pointless. "We just did drill – attention, at ease, attention; how to march – things like that," is a typical response [see Figs. 5.1 and 5.2]. Xu Rongxiang, who headed the militia in the early 1950s, divided training up into three components: political education, military training, and military logistics training. "Political training included lectures on morale; basic knowledge of defense; basic soldier's knowledge; Communist brutality; Sun Yat-sen's last testament and the President's virtues. Military training included basic training, weapons training, target practice, and combat training. Military logistics training included stretcher training; counter-intelligence training, and battlefield medicine. [Training for] men stressed combat ability . . . For women, the emphasis was on developing their first-aid skills. During combat there were sure to be casualties. First-aid training

Fig. 5.2 Militia review, 1958 (by permission of Jinmen county cultural bureau)

taught women how to apply bandages and do emergency medicine."[11] As for exercises, "We didn't really do very much. We just followed [the troops] around. The important thing was for us to get used to the routine in case of combat."[12]

Thunder Exercises

The most memorable type of exercise was the lock-down and comprehensive search known as a Thunder Exercise. It was an open secret that Thunder Exercises were not military exercises as the term is usually understood, but temporary intensifications of repression and control, typically launched in order to locate a soldier who was thought to have deserted.[13] The frequency of desertion was highest in the early years of WZA, as soldiers from the mainland came to realize they were probably never going home. "Jinmen was famous for deserters. Every year there were a dozen or so. They thought you could swim over to the mainland because it was so close. In fact the currents made it impossible. The waves would push a man back. But if you didn't try and were brought back and captured, this was the road to death."[14] Many Thunder Exercises in the

1960s to 1980s ended when it was learned that the missing soldier had committed suicide, apparently a serious problem until more frequent leaves in Taiwan were allowed.[15]

Thunder Exercises could be very dangerous for civilians. Militia members who were found derelict in their inspection of the territory under their responsibility could be imprisoned and through the principle of mutual responsibility, neighbors and the officers of the village were also liable to be punished.[16] Deserting soldiers sometimes became desperate. In August 1953, a soldier deserted his post after having argued with his superior officer. He fled to the village of Wucuo, where he took refuge in a civilian house, and took a nineteen year old civilian woman hostage. Within minutes, hundreds of soldiers descended on the village and surrounded the house. The woman's grandmother ran up to the door of the house to beg for her life, and was shot. There were more shots fired and fire broke out inside the house. By the time the door was broken down, both the soldier and his civilian hostage were dead.[17]

Militia members also served guard duty. Sun Bingshu remembers serving for two hours at a time, twice a week, outside the township office. Militia patrols went through the village in groups of four to ensure that blackout measures were totally effective and no light was visible to draw the fire of PLA guns. There was no effort to rationalize such duties above the level of the village, so where one lived had a significant impact on one's militia obligations. As one senior officer recalls, "Militia from coastal villages were somewhat worse off. Sometimes they had to do night patrols, helping the army to guard against frogmen coming ashore." What made coastal patrols and guard duty particularly irritating was that they were intensified during holidays on the assumption that an attack was more likely when the regular army was relaxing. Patrols at such times were maximally socially disruptive.[18]

In the 1950s, the militia had fewer guns than members. "Each village might have ten or twenty guns . . . Squad leaders and higher cadres definitely had them. As for other militia members, it was only the rifle squads that had them. The stretcher teams and the transport teams weren't issued guns. Their equipment was a stretcher, carrying poles and rope. Even if they'd been issued a gun, they wouldn't have been able to carry it." This made sense at the time, for the militia's main function was to provide logistical support. For weapons training and exercises in those early days, neighborhood ward heads went into the countryside and cut branches and sticks to fashion wooden dummies.[19]

But eventually more guns were issued, though many were old rifles brought over from the mainland. In 1962, the WZA authority issued regulations for maintenance and inspection of militia weapons. Much of the surviving village archives consists of records of these inspections. When Hong Futian, the township head of Little Jinmen, called a weapons inspection he would gather the entire militia unit in the morning and not allow anyone to go home for lunch until their weapon was clean. In practice, even when weapons were maintained properly, the program contributed little to mobilization and self-discipline. Militia members did not always maintain their weapon themselves. Li Qingzheng, who was born in 1949, explains that he often maintained his father's rifle for him. And there were other problems of compliance. Xie Gulong, one of my oldest informants at eighty-seven years old in 2006, says that problems with weapons maintenance were the most common reason for which villagers were punished. It was thus further evidence for the seeming capriciousness of the system. "You might have to do a forced march, or run, or exercises. It really just depended on the mood of the officer." A former county official confirms that people were most often punished for failing to look after their weapons. "They'd never fired a gun, so they didn't know how to take care of it." Eventually a system of monetary rewards and fines was put in place to ensure guns were maintained.[20]

Militia labor

Besides its military functions, the militia also served as the organizational structure to coordinate civilian labor for a wide range of tasks [Fig. 5.3]. Wen Shizhong, the first political instructor for Zhushan, can still rhyme these off:

In the past the militia had many duties, including portering . . . construction work, relief and rescue work, grain storage, and logistical support. But the militia members received no salary or rations; they weren't provided with meals; they weren't provided with clothing . . . Many of the roads in the vicinity of their village were built by them; normally they also maintained and repaired the roads. Large construction projects were mostly done by the military; smaller ones were done by the militia. They maintained tunnels and shelters; they did forestation too – the military-restricted zones on higher ground were planted by the soldiers; militia members were responsible for those areas near the village. They also dug trenches, and looked after sanitation.[21]

Portering supplies was an important militia task in ordinary times as well as when Jinmen came under attack. To support the massive troop presence huge convoys of supply ships were sent regularly from Taiwan to resupply the island. The main items transported were food, coal, and weapons and ammunition. Almost 2,000 tons of rice was shipped each year.[22] Navy ships were unloaded initially at Shuitou and later at the new harbor at Liaoluo. The army unloaded its ships at Xintou, also on the

Fig. 5.3 Militia labor detail (© Getty images)

southeast coast near Liaoluo where, it was thought, they were safe from PRC guns (this assumption would be proven wrong in the 1958 Crisis, as we shall see). Portering was tiring, awkward work. Before the Liaoluo harbor was completed, cargo had to be offloaded to small fishing boats, then carried off the fishing boats and across the sandy beach. The rice sacks weighed 100 pounds; some villagers recall that recent graduates and wealthier townsfolk were unable even to lift them.[23] Each laborer was assigned a certain volume to carry per day, and was not allowed to quit until he had completed it. While on porter duty, militia members were billeted in local homes or temporary shelters built on the beach. They were issued only rice, so they quickly learned to bring along salted oysters and preserved vegetables to cook with the rice.[24]

As with other construction work, the main concern of the leadership was that the tasks were completed, not who completed them. Labor responsibility was assigned on the basis of the militia registers. In the early years it was common practice to find a substitute, typically a relative or neighbor. Since fishermen could not afford not to fish, they also frequently hired substitutes. Sometimes a militia member simply paid money to the village cadre, who in turn used it to hire replacements. One former militia member recalls that an official once pocketed the money and simply scratched the name of the militia member off the list. This meant that everyone else on the list moved up the rota. "So sometimes it happened that after you'd done your week, a week would pass and it would be your turn again. People got very angry at how unfair this was, and complained to the cadre. He just said, 'If you go or not is your business. The list of names [of men liable to provide labor] has already been sent.' "[25] Later, in at least some villages, this system was formalized, and a fee was levied on villagers to pay the cost of professional porters.

The total amount of labor was considerable. Dong Qunlian reports seeing documents that show that between late 1954 and the establishment of the War Zone Administration in mid-1956, more than 300,000 person days of militia labor were used to support military construction.[26] The total size of the militia at that time was around 10,000, so this suggests that militia members contributed about thirty days of manual labor per year in addition to their training and exercise duties.

Not all labor could be commuted. Some of the labor that was required or expected of militia members was clearly symbolic. In 1951, Hu Lian ordered the construction of a grand assembly hall outside of Jincheng town in honor of Chiang Kai-shek's return to the Presidency (Chiang had resigned *pro forma* in 1949 in contrition for the defeats on the mainland). The hall was built on very high ground so that it could be seen from the mainland, but this made it quite exposed to the wind. So it was to be enclosed by a stone wall. Hu decided that he and his officers and local students would help build the wall instead of doing morning drill. So moved were the local people by Hu's personal efforts, at least according to Hu's own memoirs, that they too joined in the labor and the wall was completed in only a month.[27] The labor of the militia could be symbolic in other ways. Recalls one former member, "When performing troupes came from Taiwan, or basketball teams came for friendly games, the atmosphere couldn't be too restrained. So to fill the seats, the superior officers ordered the militia to attend. If you didn't go, they'd take attendance at the event, and if your name wasn't checked, you'd immediately be sent to the police station and detained for three days."[28]

Political training was a large part of militia activities. In the months after the Battle of Guningtou, army headquarters organized a mandatory children's brigade to do intelligence collection and propaganda work. They were explicitly taking a page from the Communists, whose use of propaganda had been so much more effective. On holidays, political warfare officers distributed colored banners painted with slogans to the children, who paraded around shouting them. They were taught to write their own slogans. "Some old folks today have very nice calligraphy – it's because they learned it from the soldiers at that time." Children were also taught to perform anti-Communist skits, songs and dances, which they performed in the village and in the barracks. They were taught to recognize PLA weaponry and planes so they could do surveillance work if combat broke out. "You learned about patriotism and self-sacrifice, about sacrificing yourself for the nation. The kids thought this was glorious. They'd all been in school since they were eight years old, so they learned this." As in Taiwan itself, primary school students in the villages were mobilized to parade through their community early every morning before class, led by their teacher, shouting slogans – "Recover the Mainland; Oppose Communism and Fight the Soviets; Down with Mao Zedong."[29]

Besides the basic regulations covering the militia, in 1957 the Ministry of Defense also issued a related set of instructions covering rewards and punishments for the militia. The list of circumstances that justified rewards and punishments, and the rewards and punishments themselves, illustrate the expectations of the state on militia members. While the punishments imposed by village deputy headmen invariably seemed arbitrary and capricious to the villagers, the regulations provided the legal basis for them. Militia members and ordinary civilians were to be rewarded for "displaying the spirit of protecting one's homeland and defending territory to a high degree, and heroically assisting the National Army in combat during the anti-Communist anti-Soviet counter-attack to recover the nation." Civilians could demonstrate this either through active heroism, for example by interfering with saboteurs, seizing enemy property, or capturing enemy soldiers, or passively, by being killed, injured, or taken prisoner. Possible rewards included public commendation, construction of a public memorial, cash payments, and assistance with educational expenses. For those who failed to obey the orders of their commanders, or interfered with those following orders, or who failed to take action when enemy infiltrators were detected, there was a corresponding set of punishments, ranging from warnings, suspension, or dismissal for public servants, to cash fines, or forced labor for up to thirty days. Since over the period of martial law Jinmen militia members never in fact saw combat aside from the artillery bombardments, the most important justification for punishment, by far, was "evading legal obligations to perform militia duties, or not fulfilling them in a timely fashion."[30] Though few Jinmen residents seem to have been aware of the existence of the regulations, all who lived through this period knew of their implications.

Militia discipline was strict. One of the most commonly expressed complaints against militia officers, at all levels from the village deputy headman all the way up to the Jinmen commanding officer, is that they treated civilians just like soldiers, that they did not know the difference. One militia member recalls going to assembly with his uniform not complete, and being beaten on the spot before being sent to detention.

Discipline was framed in ideological terms – someone who was late for assembly was labeled a Communist spy, someone with ideological problems, before being locked up.[31]

Not surprisingly, for every story in the oral history of arbitrary punishment and discipline there is another anecdote of resistance. When ward heads were required to procure bricks from militia members so the soldiers could build bunkers and there were no bricks to be had, they would wait until the soldiers were occupied elsewhere, steal some of the bricks already on the work site, and then deliver the same bricks back to the soldiers later in the day. There are many stories of pilferage when the militia was moving supplies. The friend of a man who was caught pilfering cakes asked, "He had no choice – who told the army not to give us any rations?"[32] One case of pilferage occasioned the closest thing to collective resistance in any of the evidence I have come across. It seems a militia member working at the Xintou dock was so hungry he could not resist piercing a hole in a tin of pineapple he was unloading. When he was caught, the officer threatened not just to detain him but to send him to the army's reform camp. While a militiaman restrained the officer, over a hundred other militia released the offender and escorted him from the scene.[33]

The creation of the militia and the mobilization of the populace affected the people of Jinmen in profound ways that are explored throughout the course of this book. In popular memory, two of the consequences that come up particularly often are the constant sense of tension and the disruption of agricultural life. The tension is generally not articulated in terms of concern about an impending attack from the mainland or other military confrontation, but of pressure to fulfill militia obligations. As one resident of Jincheng town recalls of the years of bombing that began in 1958, "We were required to assemble at the bus station within thirty minutes of hearing enemy shells. If you weren't there for roll call, you'd be punished according to military justice. It was really strict. So to protect your own life, you didn't dare take off your uniform, and you left your gun hanging on the wall [where it was easy to reach]. As soon as you heard the alert, you had to put down whatever work you were doing and race off to assemble." A fisherman's wife recalls that it was no different in the villages. "Sometimes you'd be taking it easy and you'd be called to assemble. You had to go. Even if you were in the middle of eating, you had to put down your bowl and chopsticks and go. If you were called and didn't go, you'd be punished. The punishment was that your husband wasn't allowed to go out fishing. Once I was locked up; I was only released when I got sick."[34]

Militia labor was extremely disruptive to traditional agricultural patterns. Xu Pimou puts it very clearly. "I was a farmer. Most of the time

I sowed, spread fertilizer, weeded, and harvested. As soon as there was training or labor, there was no way to care for the crops. So it caused me big losses. It became a real question whether or not I had enough to eat. The consequences [of training] were so great it is hard to calculate them." The only way to deal with the situation was to work harder. "When the training began, the sorghum shoots had just sprouted. So I had to attend to them. I had no choice but to go water the fields in the early morning, and then go back at night after training was over."[35]

Conclusions

The first decade of the militia on Jinmen saw a number of changes, the most obvious being the gradual formalization of what had initially been an *ad hoc* system. The result was an extraordinarily highly militarized society, in which a significant proportion of labor was regularly if not entirely systematically extracted from the populace, male and female, adult and child. The militarization of the populace was represented as a purely military issue, but this was clearly a misrepresentation. The routinization and formalization of the militia were linked to and enabled by larger events. The Korean War had ensured the temporary survival of Taiwan. Jinmen remained key to Chiang's short-term plans to harass the mainland with small-scale military operations and to collect intelligence. As noted in the previous chapter, the US–ROC Mutual Defense Treaty and the Formosa Resolution encouraged Chiang to expand the size of the garrison on Jinmen so as to force the US to guarantee its defense. This conjuncture of geopolitical forces meant that the ROC army would remain in strength on Jinmen indefinitely and therefore encouraged the creation of formal structures to govern the relationship between the army and the civilian population. The militia was trained to provide logistical support for regular troops during wartime; it was also used to supply various types of other support during peacetime. The militia also acquired a political function, as the main vehicle through which the state sought to inculcate anti-Communism. Militarization was also political in the sense that it created new modes of discipline and control. As the concern of WZA leadership moved from simply getting tasks completed to using labor as a mechanism for political mobilization, the individual militia member's freedom to hire a replacement to perform a given task for him was increasingly constrained.

The creation of the War Zone Administration and the militarization of society meant that many of the tensions that are often associated with modernization were expressed distinctively in Jinmen. For example, the interaction between two modes of time, traditional agricultural time and industrial time, was experienced on Jinmen not as a conflict between farm work and factory work, but between farm work on the one hand and military training and forced labor on the other. The bureaucratization and rationalization of human relations that was implied by the WZA and militia systems were in practice only partial. The main sanction that was used to enforce the compliance of civilians, detention, was invariably mediated by personal relationships. Detention was ultimately at the behest of the political instructor or deputy headman, and depended not only on the violation of the rules but on the relations between the official and the offender and, indeed, on the mood of the official. Villagers were typically not detained for the maximum period that the rules allowed; rather, their families interceded with the village headman, who in turn interceded with the deputy headman or police cadre for earlier release. The timing of release, even more than the decision to put someone in detention, was thus the product of a series of personal relationships, some internal to the village, some between village representatives and state representatives. Though it was justified in a language of geopolitical security threats and rationalizing modernization, as it became intertwined with everyday experience militarization was still something to be negotiated.

6   The 1958 Artillery War

Ke Huizhu, who was fifteen years old in 1958, recalls:

At times, the shelling was so bad we didn't dare stick our heads out . . . When you heard the sound of shells filling the sky, you were so scared that you didn't even dare go out to pee . . . Even if you couldn't have three proper meals, you still had to eat something [so] during the night, when the shelling was lighter, the brave ones would crawl into the fields to dig up some sweet potatoes. But it wouldn't take long before the shelling started again; they'd only have time to fill half a sack of sweet potatoes before half-running, half-crawling back to the shelter. They'd be out of breath, unable to speak, with their legs all sore [Fig. 6.1].[1]

We return now to the scenes with which this book began, the extraordinary artillery attacks that began on August 23, 1958. Just as in 1954–5, the battle briefly but unforgettably foregrounded the close connection between Jinmen and global geopolitics. Politicians and the public in many countries speculated on the possibility that the sudden tension over Jinmen, an insignificant place they mostly knew little about and that seemed to matter little in world events, might somehow lead to serious conflict, even global nuclear war. In six weeks of intense shelling about half a million shells landed on the sixty square miles of Jinmen, almost 10,000 shells per square mile. The 1958 conflict, usually called the 8–23 or August 23rd Artillery War, is almost always the central episode in the oral history of the people of Jinmen, both a turning point about which many memories were formed and a reference point around which other memories are oriented. For some residents, like the baby born in an air-raid shelter and given the name Li Jindong, "Enters the shelter," the bombing is recalled many times every day. Many others, even those who escaped personal injury in the fighting, are permanently scarred by the conflict nonetheless. Township head Hong Futian's eldest son, for example, was evacuated to the main island. There he caught a fever that left him with severe brain damage.[2] Despite its centrality in world events and in popular memory, the 1958 war did not cause fundamental shifts in the experience of militarization on Jinmen. Rather, it intensified existing processes and ensured they would continue in the decades to come.

Fig. 6.1 Shelling over Quemoy, 1958

Where it did signal a major shift was in the underlying causes of further militarization. After 1958, militarization became increasingly detached from military threat.

In contrast to the general consensus on Chinese motivations in 1954, there is still disagreement about what led Mao Zedong to initiate the crisis of 1958. Some analysts focus on Chinese domestic issues, others on international causes. Some scholars argue that Mao wanted to eliminate what he perceived to be a real threat of attack from Taiwan, others that he used the attack as a "strategic probe" to test and if possible to complicate the US commitment to the ROC. Mao may have wished to signal disapproval of deepening US–ROC military cooperation, including the delivery of Matador missiles that could potentially be armed with nuclear warheads. Some argue that he also wished to demonstrate China's independence from a Soviet Union seen as increasingly revisionist, or that the attack was an expression of Mao's internationalism and Third World solidarity, that he wanted to send a message in response to perceived American aggression in the Middle East, where US forces had intervened earlier in the year in Iraq and Lebanon.[3] Recently, scholars such as Thomas Christensen, Chen Jian, and the PRC historian Xu Yan, have argued that the crisis needs to be understood in terms of the interplay of domestic *and* international factors. In 1958 Mao had launched an extraordinary social revolution, the Great Leap Forward. Intended to accelerate China's economic development by mobilizing the Chinese people so as to release their latent energy and talents, the Great Leap Forward imposed a huge physical and economic burden on the populace. Part of Mao's solution to the challenge of generating support for this program, Christensen argues, was "manipulating conflict [and] militarizing society."[4] On this argument, one of Mao's motivations in launching the attack on Jinmen was to create a sense of external tension and threat and thereby arouse popular enthusiasm for his domestic agenda. At the very least, regardless of his motivations in launching the attack, Mao clearly sought to use the Jinmen bombardment to support his domestic agenda. This explanation finds support in some recently released documents. For example, Mao told the Supreme State Conference on September 5, part way through the crisis, that "a tense situation can mobilize the forces, can mobilize the backward people, can mobilize the people in the center to rise up and struggle."[5] The Great Leap certainly did lead to a heightening of militarization within the PRC, expressed most clearly in the "Everyone a Soldier" campaign of late 1958.[6] As Christensen points out, the mobilization of popular enthusiasm was probably the one successful aspect of the otherwise disastrous Great Leap. But this mobilization came at considerable cost to the people of Jinmen.

Just as in 1954, tension in the Taiwan Strait built up over the summer of 1958. A railway line connecting Xiamen to the national railway system was nearing completion, making possible more rapid deployment of troops and matériel to the coast. In June, the People's Liberation Army (PLA) held large-scale exercises to the south of Jinmen. ROC forces on the island, at the time numbering almost 100,000, were put on high alert. Civilian travel was suspended. On August 20, Chiang Kai-shek flew to Jinmen on a morale-building mission. According to local lore, civilian officials knelt and begged Chiang for the good of the country to return immediately to the relative safety of Taibei. It was simply too dangerous for him to remain on Jinmen. Meanwhile, Mao was telling the Politburo that driving up international tension could be useful for the main task of supporting the Great Leap Forward. Such tension, he said, "can lead us to increase steel and grain [production] . . . If we have an enemy in front of us, tension is to our benefit."[7]

We know from the recent work of PRC scholars and the release of archives that Mao was making decisions about the Jinmen situation personally. Having changed his mind repeatedly, on August 18 he wrote to Defense Minister Peng Dehuai, instructing him to "prepare to shell

Fig. 6.2 "A new page in the history of warfare": damage caused by PLA shelling, 1958 (from Ming Qiushui (ed.), *Jinmen*, by permission of Jinmen county cultural bureau)

Jinmen, dealing directly with Chiang [Kai-shek] and indirectly with the Americans."[8] Mao ruminated for several more days before, on the afternoon of August 23, he gave the order to fire.

Only later did residents of Jinmen learn that the first sortie of shells, fired from a PLA artillery unit in Xiamen, had hit its target, the officers' mess of the Jinmen garrison located in a steep gorge of Mount Taiwu, killing three of Hu Lian's deputy commanding officers. But despite the accuracy of the shells, the timing was off. Hu Lian and Defense Minister Yu Dawei, visiting from Taibei, were still underground, so they escaped injury. There is a widespread rumor that moments after the first shelling, a colonel was overheard to say to himself, "Damn, just a few minutes too early." He was arrested and found to be a Communist infiltrator.[9] Many military details of the initial attack remain secret, but the number of military casualties in the first few hours probably lies somewhere between 200 and 600. Because the force of the attacks was on the Taiwu headquarters, civilian casualties on the first day were light – about twenty dead and twenty wounded. Over the course of the next six weeks, some 140 civilians were killed, and several hundred wounded. Thousands of homes were damaged or destroyed [Fig. 6.2].[10]

Memories of battle

Whereas Jinmen residents tell many stories of their own naiveté in 1954–5, their few humorous stories about 1958 tend to mock the soldiers, not themselves. In one village the troops had moved out of the homes in which they had been billeted for almost a decade and into newly built fortifications nearby in early May 1958 (this led some villagers to wonder if the army had had advance warning of the attack, and had decided to leave civilians in the dark). But they would sometimes come out of their hilltop barracks to bathe at the village well. On the afternoon of August 23, a group of soldiers were having their bath when the shelling began, and the villagers laughed to see them run back to their barracks, some half-naked, others still covered in soap suds. While civilians' own recollections do not minimize the horror of the events of those days, they also indicate a certain pride in their own *sang-froid*. Though not soldiers themselves, the people of Jinmen could now keep their heads under pressure even better than the less experienced soldiers. They were able to use the defenses they had constructed themselves for protection. "Hu Lian had told us, when you encounter shelling, get down. During his first term as commanding officer (CO), he had required that every plot of land should have an escape trench in case it became necessary. We also knew this from our militia training."[11]

Though the absolute number of civilian casualties may not have been high, the dead are central to people's memories of August 23. Those whose own relatives were injured tell their personal stories. Those whose immediate circle escaped injury tell the stories of women and children injured, though whether this is because of their own sense of outrage or the effective propagandizing of these injuries afterwards is hard to tell. Thus one hears often of the woman in Zhongbao village who was killed while running to the shelter. Everyone also knows of the old lady who was killed when she foolishly left the shelter to recover her jewelry.[12] Besides the dead and injured, the other focus of memory is life in the shelter. Eighty-two year old Li Jinchun still remembers many details of the early days of the August 23 war. "In the shelter, every family had their own spot. There was nothing you could do. The old ladies were the most terrified. They just sat there shaking all day. The old folks prayed to the gods and the ancestors, but it was no use. It didn't matter how many ancestors you had, the bombs kept coming from the east and from the west . . . Every family dug a pit outside, and carried their chamber pot out to dump it. It was really cramped; there was barely room to sit down. We laid some boards down on the ground to lie on. Everyone was terrified."[13]

Fig. 6.3 Cooking in a bombed out home (© Corbis)

Many memories of life during the shelling focus on food – growing, harvesting, and cooking [Fig. 6.3]. The experience of sneaking out during lulls in the shelling to gather sweet potatoes in Ke Huizhu's story was almost universal. She recalls one elderly neighbor who set up a stove in a ruined house next to the shelter. One day there was a huge barrage while she was cooking. When she brought the pot back into the shelter, to everyone's surprise it was empty. After it had cooled, they saw that two shrapnel fragments had landed in the soup and instantly boiled off the liquid. "Afterwards, everybody used to talk about how the boiled sweet potato soup was turned into boiled shrapnel soup." People today remember the bombing as a rare time of eating meat, usually eaten only on special occasions if at all. In 1958, the eating of meat was simply a practical response to the large numbers of animals killed.[14]

In the cramped and uncomfortable darkness of the shelters, cut off from all communication with the outside world, civilians were easily terrified. "When the shelling was at its fiercest, there were often rumors that the Communists were already landing, that there were landing craft at Xiamen that could cross at any time, that Jinmen couldn't be defended." There were rumors about spies and about the use of chemical weapons. There were rumors that enemy frogmen had struck coastal sentry posts, leaving not a single survivor and then slipping away like ghosts. And there were stories of direct hits on military bunkers that crushed the occupants so deep underground that militia teams could not even dig out the bodies. "One rumor followed another . . . there were so many rumors and not a single piece of information that could be confirmed. The pressure on our hearts grew greater and greater, and all day long people were just terrified."[15]

Just as they had been in 1949 and 1954–5, old networks were important in dealing with crisis. Families looked for shelter from their neighbors, and from wider kinship groups. In one household that did not yet have its own shelter, "my father was injured, and my mother had just given birth. So we had to rely on our neighbors to let us use their shelter." As the crisis wore on, ties between neighbors became strained. "My mother reminded me recently about how we were thrown out of the shelter because we hadn't helped to build it." As often happened in times of stress, affinal relations, or relations by marriage, were reactivated. A large family might turn to affinal relatives in different generations. For example, Huang Yongtuan, whose village was hit hard on the first night, went with his grandmother and his father back to his grandmother's natal village. His younger brother, three sisters, and mother meanwhile went to the mother's natal village of Chenkeng. And when they became too much of a burden on these relations, members of his family sometimes went to stay with his paternal aunt, his father's sister, for a few days. Thus three sets of affines all provided assistance to Huang's family.

Just as in 1954–5, Jinmen residents not only had to deal with protecting their own lives and property, they were also called up to provide militia services. In the early days of the crisis, when an invasion was thought imminent, soldiers were withdrawn from coastal fortifications to more secure bunkers on an inland second-line, presumably in accordance with predetermined defense plans. "We militia had to guard the coast. It was supposed to be to protect the people and defend the country. Really, they were sending us to the front line, while the regulars retreated . . . We had to stand watch in shifts through the night at the harbor. We were scared of the ghosts, and of frogmen sneaking in." Some villagers took advantage of the withdrawal of the troops to take shelter in their bunkers and pillboxes, which were far better fortified than the civilian shelters. But as it became clear that the Communists did not intend an invasion, the soldiers were returned to coastal installations. They ejected the civilians hiding in their bunkers, who returned to their villages to seek shelter there.[16]

Though the militia had served its assigned tasks in 1954–5, it was really with the 1958 Crisis that the legend of Jinmen's civilian soldiers began to develop, that they were constructed as a symbol of resistance, self-sacrifice, and patriotism that was widely deployed as propaganda. Chiang Ching-kuo, who was deputy-secretary of the National Defense Commission, visited Jinmen frequently during the last months of 1958. He is reported to have once said, "If only all citizens were as daring as the Jinmen militia, our nation would be capable of retaking the mainland quickly."[17]

Had there actually been an invasion of Jinmen, the militia might well have made their anticipated contribution, relieving the regulars from having to worry about logistics and support and freeing them up for combat. But we now know that Mao was never planning an invasion. Whatever the underlying causes of the attack, as a warning to the US, a salutary lesson to the Soviet Union, or domestic mobilization, by September Mao was confirmed in his decision that it would be counter-productive for Jinmen to fall to the PLA. The ROC presence on Jinmen was a reminder that both regimes agreed there was only "One China" that would one day be reunified. If Jinmen were to fall, it might be a first step toward the permanent separation of the two regimes, toward "Two Chinas." On September 22, Mao approved Zhou Enlai's recommendation to continue the policy of "shell but don't land" and "cut off [supplies] but don't deliver the death blow."[18]

Portering

PLA attacks on ROC shipping and the concentrated bombing of the island's harbors led the ROC leadership to conclude that whether or not the mainland was planning to invade the island, it was certainly trying to impose a blockade. Accepting that they could not ensure the safety of ships and aircraft, the ROC decided to suspend resupply. Matériel began to pile up on the docks at Penghu, the ordinary transshipment point. Within a week the pile of supplies had grown half a mile long and several yards high. Meanwhile, in Washington, President Eisenhower had concluded that the US could not appear weak in the face of Chinese action, and ordered an increase in military aid transfers to the ROC (including artillery capable of firing atomic weapons) and the reinforcement of the Seventh Fleet, already in nearby waters. Christensen calls the US fleet presence the "largest nuclear navy" ever assembled in history.[19] On September 3, John Foster Dulles proposed to Eisenhower that the Seventh Fleet provide support for ROC supply convoys. Eisenhower agreed and the next day Dulles made a public announcement at Newport,

Fig. 6.4 Militia porters (by permission of Jinmen county cultural bureau)

Rhode Island. Mao later claimed that this was a major victory for the PRC, which had lured the United States into a noose.[20]

In the first week of September, ROC resupply convoys set out from Penghu, accompanied by US ships. Fishing boats carried grain and coal, and navy ships artillery shells, ammunition, and other military supplies. The convoys were left unmolested in the international waters *en route* to Jinmen. As they neared Jinmen the US ships split off to stay out of waters claimed by the PRC. To avoid hitting US ships and escalating the crisis, the PLA held fire until the escort and the convoy separated. So the force of the shelling was concentrated on the waters around Jinmen and especially on the beach where civilian militia teams unloaded the ships, by hand, for hour after excruciating hour.

The most dangerous task for the militia was unloading the supply convoys [Fig. 6.4]. One village headman received word on September 26 that the militia team from his village was required for portering duty the following day. The next morning, jeeps arrived to take the militia to the beach at Liaoluo. In early afternoon, the village runner returned with a report that the team had come under heavy firing. The headman recalls:

At the time, the families of all the militia were waiting at home; they were already very nervous. As soon as they heard there was news, they all raced to the village office to ask after their relatives. Someone said, "Was anyone killed?" The village runner replied "Fatty." There were two guys nicknamed Fatty in the village then, one surnamed Xu, and the other surnamed Wang. As soon as the mother of Fatty Xu heard that Fatty had been killed, she started to wail. I tried to comfort her by saying, "we still don't know which Fatty it was. Calm down – it might not be your Fatty." After a while we learned that it was Fatty Wang. His full name was Wang Tiansheng. He had been hit in the stomach, and his guts had spilled out. When he was brought back he was still alive, but we didn't have any knowledge of medicine then [so we] did not give any emergency care. So he died.[21]

Two other porters from the village were also killed that day. According to War Zone Administration (WZA) statistics, a total of eleven militia members were killed while on duty during the 1958 shelling, and fourteen others seriously wounded. Almost all of these injuries occurred while militia members were unloading the supply convoys at the beach.[22]

Forty-four days after the start of the shelling, on October 6, 1958, Chinese Minister of Defense Peng Dehuai announced a unilateral seven-day cease-fire. We now know that his "Message to our Taiwan Compatriots" was drafted by Mao personally. Mao claimed this as a victory because it successfully entrapped the US. "Whenever necessary we can shell [Jinmen and Mazu]. Whenever we are in need of tension, we may tighten the noose, and whenever we want to relax the tension, we may loosen the noose. We will let them hang there, neither dead nor alive, using them as a means to deal with the Americans."[23] Further ratcheting up of tension might serve the goal of domestic mobilization but it would be counter-productive to other national interests if the US persuaded Chiang to withdraw from the islands. As a symbolic link between Taiwan and the mainland, abandonment of the island would be a setback to the goal of preventing permanent separation of the two regimes on either side of the Taiwan Strait. If Jinmen fell to the PLA, "Two Chinas" would be one step closer to reality. So the pressure on Jinmen had to be carefully calibrated, using the island to keep both the US and Taiwan in Mao's "noose." But Mao also seems to have been surprised by the strength of the US reaction, saying "The fighting over Jinmen and Mazu was just a few shells; I certainly never expected that the world would become so disturbed and turbulent."[24]

Evacuation

The government of the ROC had long since realized that, leaving all other concerns aside, there was great propaganda value in having a civilian population on Jinmen, heroically resisting Communist aggression. If the island were reduced to a military base, then the Communist attack was simply a military action. But as long as Jinmen was also a civilian community, the Communist attack could be portrayed in a much darker light. News stories from the island during the crisis played up both these sides: the horror of war on civilians, and the indifference of the defenders to the danger. On September 27, the *New York Times* ran the story "Quemoy Unbowed Despite Shelling." A few days later, the headline read "Children Live in Caves," and the story covered the threat of disease and exposure as winter approached. All 1,500 children on Little Jinmen were living underground, short of food, and with no medical supplies.[25] This dual rhetoric captures well the distinctive character of militarization on Jinmen, and the fluid boundary between civilian and military. On the one hand, society could be militarized in many ways that would serve military interests. On the other, the boundary had to be maintained for civilians to play their desired roles, both military and political. While the shelling continued unabated, it would have been impossible to evacuate the island safely. But the cease-fire raised a dilemma. Though Chiang refused to consider abandoning the islands, there must have been a discussion about whether the civilian population should be evacuated, both for their safety and to avoid creating the negative impression that the regime was needlessly exposing them to danger. This is the likeliest explanation for the staggered decision-making about evacuation. In the days after the cease-fire, the WZA announced that the students, teachers, and staff of Jinmen Secondary School would be evacuated to Taiwan. But a day or two later, the scope of the evacuation was expanded and all residents of the island were allowed to register for voluntary evacuation.

As residents today remember it, it was the wealthy who left in disproportionate numbers. "After the artillery attacks, we had no money. We were farmers – what would we do with our goats, our pigs, our chickens? We grew peanuts. With everyone leaving, there was no one to sell them to. So we had to stay."[26] Today, after two or more generations of Jinmen children have grown up in a world in which Jinmen is closely tied to Taiwan, in which Jinmen people fly to Taibei to do their shopping and Jinmen natives working in Taiwan fly home for the weekend, it is hard to recall a time when Taiwan was an utterly alien place full of imagined dangers that seemed even worse than the threat of falling bombs. But this is how many people remember their attitudes toward the evacuation. "Many people moved to Taiwan. We also wanted to go, but my father worried about how to make a living. He said, 'If we stay on Jinmen, even if things take a turn for the worse, we'll still have sweet potato to live on.'" "At the time, people's thinking was that if you didn't go, you had to be afraid of being killed in the shelling, while if you did go, you had to be afraid of starving to death."[27]

Some 6,500 people, about 15 percent of the total population, eventually joined the evacuation. Nine hundred students and teachers from the secondary school embarked on troop transits on October 9; the remaining civilians were taken on three ships on October 11 and 12. A large contingent of evacuees, about thirty families, was from Zhushan village. According to one of them the villagers believed that the ROC was likely to abandon Jinmen, so they decided it was better to leave ahead of time than wait until the last moment.[28] On arrival at the Taiwanese port of Gaoxiong, the refugees were given a resettlement allowance of NTD3,000, equivalent to several years' income for a typical Jinmen family. Because in the memory of those who stayed behind evacuation to Taiwan in 1958 was closely linked to class, the resettlement allowance issue is remembered with much bitterness today. It was the rich who left, people say, and government help only made them richer. But most evacuees had little success. Dong Wenju tracked down a relative living in a Taibei suburb who helped him find a job as a fruitseller. But having left the Jinmen militia, he now became liable for conscription, and served two years in the army. After demobilization, he became a construction worker. Other evacuees found work as manual laborers. Many remained only until their resettlement allowance ran out. "When they had spent their $3,000 with no result, they braved the danger and returned to their old home."[29] Population statistics give a sense of the scale of the return movement. At the end of 1959, the population of Jinmen fell to a low of 41,000. Two years later it had recovered to 47,500. About half the increase was due to returnees.[30]

The evacuation itself had diverse social impacts. The price of real estate in the towns collapsed, as shopkeepers decided to sell out and move their families to Taiwan. Many wealthy families on Jinmen today owe their prosperity to having purchased shops at this time. At the bottom of the market in 1958, a shophouse in Shanwai, including inventory, could be had for a few thousand NTD. Those who took advantage of the low prices could realize enormous returns – even aside from the profits that could be made from doing business with the soldiers, a topic we will discuss in chapter 9. "Those who were daring then got rich later."[31] To ensure the supply of fresh meat and prevent hoarding, the WZA ordered pigs slaughtered and sold at fixed prices. In another remarkable parallel with events on the mainland during the Great Leap Forward, when people learned that they would be forced to slaughter their pigs, they stopped feeding them, so all the slaughtered pigs were lean and underweight.[32]

On October 13, the PRC extended the cease-fire for another two weeks, though it was broken for one hour on October 20 to protest Dulles' visit to Taiwan. When the two weeks were over, Mao again issued a statement under Peng Dehuai's name. This "Announcement" restated that the Taiwan question was an internal matter in which the US had no business. It blamed the Americans for inciting the crisis by their meddling, and ended by hinting that the ROC leadership realized this full well.[33] After mid-October, with a few exceptions, the intensity of the shelling declined dramatically. In a decision that came to be a symbol of Jinmen, live shells were replaced by shells that exploded in mid-air, scattering propaganda leaflets, and shells were fired on alternate days only. Recently published material shows that this was also Mao's personal decision.[34] The public "Announcement" explained that the decision would allow the garrison on Jinmen to receive supplies and relax on alternate days, while constantly reminding both Taiwan and the US that Jinmen, and Taiwan, belonged to China.

So began one of the most bizarre aspects of life on Jinmen, the alternate day shelling. The phrase "shelling on odd-numbered days; no shelling on even days" (*danda shuangbuda*) came to symbolize both the ongoing low-level conflict and Jinmen itself. Between October 1958 and December 1979, every other day Communist batteries fired on Jinmen. The shelling usually typically consisted of several hundred shells, fired in the early evening. "You just went on living your life. It was just a question of who had good luck and who didn't . . . But at that time we were all good at listening to the shells. You only had to hear the sound of the shells and you knew if it was going to hit us here, or there. They hit a set area every day. When the first shell hit somewhere, you knew that all the shelling today would be around there. The next five or ten would all be concentrated there. It was just that every day the sequence moved on to another place."[35] Even the propaganda shells could still be dangerous. Sometimes the small explosives in the cap of the shell failed and the entire heavy shell fell to earth. The other big danger was the shrapnel shards after the casing exploded. "They could go down into the ground several yards; they could cut through walls."[36] So most Jinmen families were less sanguine about the shelling. Every odd-numbered day, the family would go to the nearest shelter in the early evening and remain there for several hours, until they were sure that the shelling was over for the night [Fig. 6.5].

Conclusions

The ROC government claims that over the course of the crisis the PLA fired more than half a million shells on the island. Civilian casualties were 138 dead and 324 injured. Over 7,000 structures, mostly homes, were

Fig. 6.5 Into the shelter (© Getty images)

damaged or destroyed.[37] Though the crisis as a matter of international geopolitics soon subsided, it continued to shape life on Jinmen for two more decades. Was the crisis a real turning point? It did not lead to major changes in the pattern of militarization of life on Jinmen, but rather an intensification of existing trends. This intensification was exemplified by the odd rhythms created by the need to take shelter underground every other day. It also took the form of greater mobilization of civilian labor to provide support to the military, and more generally the extension of military concerns and military goals into many new spheres of social life, from scheduling to domestic architecture. Whatever Mao's motivations in launching the attack, to the extent that he also sought to use it to exploit the sense of threat from an external enemy to mobilize the PRC's population, he unintentionally inspired a parallel response on the part of that enemy. That is, the ROC state on Jinmen in turn shaped its policies in ways that emphasized the threat from the enemy on the mainland. The result was heightened mobilization and militarization on Jinmen. Thus in this case PRC and ROC domestic politics moved virtually in lockstep, two gears linked by a third gear of Maoist foreign policy. On the other hand, 1958 did mark a turning point in the relationship between militarization and military threat. It became clear during the crisis that the PRC had no intention of conquering Jinmen, that to do so would be fundamentally counter-productive to Mao's wishes to prevent a *de facto* separation of the PRC and ROC regimes into "Two Chinas." The further militarization of Jinmen after 1958 was driven not chiefly by military concerns but by the larger political context. We will explore this shift in more detail in coming chapters.

Part II

Militarization and geopoliticization change course

By the early 1960s, the global Cold War was entering a new phase. The two superpowers moved toward uneasy *détente*, especially after the Cuban missile crisis of 1962 demonstrated the dangers of brinkmanship. The Sino–Soviet split complicated the previous bipolar order, though it took some time for the significance of the split to be recognized in the West. (Both the 1958 Strait Crisis and the Great Leap Forward were in part expressions of the PRC's challenge to Soviet leadership of the Communist bloc. Two Russian historians consider the 1958 Crisis an early harbinger of the global changes, "of paramount importance as a manifestation of the disintegration of the absolute bipolarity of the early Cold War."[1]) Construction of the Berlin Wall began in August 1961, producing some of the same traumatic dislocations as had the fall of Xiamen in 1949.

On Taiwan, successful land reform, infusions of financial and technical aid from the US, and an economic policy aimed at import substitution and industrial investment were leading to dramatic economic growth, with gross national product (GNP) rising an average of 9 percent per year from 1953 to 1982. Economic development supported better living standards and improvements to health care, education and other social services.[2] Industry became the leading economic sector, and the mainstay of industry shifted from textiles to electronics, machinery, and petrochemicals. Jinmen's experience was rather different: there was no industrialization to speak of, though many of the social developments were shared. GNP per capita on Jinmen, while increasing, began to lag significantly behind Taiwan. As Nationalist Party (KMT) rule over Taiwan stabilized, a system of universal male military service was implemented. Men on Jinmen were exempt from conscription because they fulfilled their service obligations through militia membership. This had two significant effects. First, as military service became a rite of passage for Taiwanese youth, the life course of Jinmen men began to diverge from that on the main island. Second, as the old soldiers from the mainland were gradually mustered out, the soldiers who came to Jinmen were increasingly temporary conscripts from Taiwan, whose experiences and expectations were very different.

Already by the late 1950s, Jinmen's military importance in the narrow sense had become much less significant. US neutralization of the Taiwan Strait meant that Jinmen would not be the springboard for a triumphant counter-attack on the mainland, even if ROC forces had the necessary military capacity (which they did not). Nor was ROC control over Jinmen critical to the defense of Taiwan, even if the PRC had been willing to risk US involvement by launching an attack (which it was not). With the strengthening of Taiwan's own defenses, the ability of the Jinmen garrison to warn of, delay, or disrupt an invasion force declined. Nor finally did the PRC leaders have any interest in taking over Jinmen alone, for this would only have been perceived as contributing to making the separation of Taiwan from China permanent (which neither they nor their KMT counterparts wanted). Moreover, politicians and generals in China, Taiwan, and the US were generally aware of these various factors, and therefore of Jinmen's overall insignificance in a purely military sense.[3] Jinmen's importance had become largely political. The huge troop presence on the island was a result of Chiang's efforts to force the US to commit to defending the island. Jinmen had thus become part of the larger political struggle between the PRC and the ROC and, because of the US alliance with the ROC, the global Cold War. Part II continues to trace the changing political significance of Jinmen in these conflicts and explore the consequences of the changes for local society.

The military danger to Jinmen peaked with the 1958 Crisis, and, with minor exceptions, the island would never again be the victim of massive and devastating artillery attacks from the mainland. But militarization, in the broader sense, continued over subsequent decades and in new directions. In the next two chapters, I outline two of these new directions. The first was a heightened attention to socio-economic development in the early 1960s; the second was a return to a focus on military preparedness in the late 1960s and 1970s. This phase in Jinmen's history further illustrates the complex trajectory of militarization, and how shifting geopolitics affected both militarization and approaches to modernization.

7   The 1960s: creating a Model County of the Three Principles of the People

Weng Mingzhi, a Jinmen native and former secretary-general of Fujian Province, recalls a campaign against sparrows in 1977, when he was ten years old.

At that time there were many birds on Jinmen, and they were eating the sorghum. So the township government bought some hunting rifles and lent them out to the villagers to kill sparrows. You'd borrow the gun, and use it to shoot sparrows. We kids used slingshots. You had to turn over a certain number of sparrow claws and sparrow eggs. You could steal eggs from the nests. At night we'd take flashlights and shine them into the nests. If a sparrow was in the nest, it would freeze. In the daytime the sparrows would fly away but at night they'd freeze and you could shoot them – pong, pong, pong – and down they'd fall. If kids didn't turn in sparrow claws, or rat tails, or flies – in those days we each had to turn in one matchbox of flies – then we'd get slapped on our palms. This was done all over Jinmen, so there were a lot of birds killed. Well, the following year, all over Jinmen there was a plague of carpenter ants. You'd see them all in a row crossing the road; you'd drive over them – bump, bump, bump – the air was full of them. My parents told us they were the spirits of soldiers killed at Guningtou.[1]

Campaigns to mobilize the population to eradicate pests such as sparrows were part of a host of economic and social development policies introduced on Jinmen in the early 1960s. This might suggest that the emphasis of politics had shifted to civilian concerns. But these policies were ultimately driven by and dependent on military issues and geopolitical priorities. They were militarization by another name, a form of militarized development. The juxtaposition of these two terms is crucial to capture the notion that even policies seemingly quite remote from the military sphere – agricultural extension, school construction, even rules against gambling – could still be tied to it. In this chapter and chapter 9, I discuss how two fundamental goals of state policy, modernization and economic development, were locally defined and pursued in terms of military and geopolitical interests and concerns. Of course, these two goals were mutually connected, even mutually constitutive of one another, but the policies devised to pursue them and the way residents responded to them differed in interesting ways, so I consider them separately. By modernization, to restate, I mean a constellation of social changes that were identified as desirable in the twentieth-century world, but whose precise definition remained contested. State policies and the popular responses to them reflect the intertwining of military concerns with the pursuit of modernity, and thus the elaboration of militarized modernity on Jinmen, a form of modernity with distinctive interests and obsessions. Despite the very different relative position of the two sides, there were remarkable similarities between some of these policies and those on the mainland. This suggests that geopolitical context alone is not enough to explain these policies. Elements of a shared political culture and the mirror-imaging process of self-fashioning also played a role.

Development planning

In April 1960, Chiang Kai-shek called for Jinmen and Mazu to become "Model Counties [for the implementation of] the Three Principles of the People." As Chiang later explained, "Jinmen is an island that is both on the farthest front line of the war, and also impoverished and underdeveloped."[2] The new campaign would remedy this situation by modernizing the island's economy and society. What did this mean in practice? The War Zone Administration (WZA) responded to Chiang's call with a series of multi-year plans for "modern political development in the war zone." The ultimate goal of these plans was to "use construction as the means to attain victory." This meant "training the masses, improving their livelihood, and reducing the burden [they impose] on the military." Though Jinmen's proximity to the enemy made any development difficult, the project was too important to neglect. If successful, it would serve to "attack the enemy, influence the world, and fortify the spirit of the people."[3] In concrete terms, this meant building infrastructure: roads, schools, reservoirs, power stations. Modernizing the material conditions of life for civilian residents was part of the project. So was molding them into modern citizens.

The campaign to construct Jinmen as a Model County for the Three Principles of the People, like the response to the 1958 artillery campaign that preceded it, has to be understood in relation to events on the mainland. By 1960 the failures of the Great Leap Forward were becoming evident, with production falling and shortfalls looming throughout the country.[4] Problems on the mainland were propaganda opportunities for the ROC. The Model County program, by shifting the focus of policy on Jinmen to social and economic development, was intended to demonstrate the superiority of ROC approaches to modernization and development over those of the PRC. As in 1958, mainland policies drove local politics, but this time the reaction worked in the opposite direction. In 1958, changes on the mainland resulted in policies that made Jinmen and mainland society become more similar; in 1960 the ROC response was to attempt to distinguish Jinmen from the mainland. According to the official statement of the plan, "our free and democratic political construction will strike a death blow to the bandit clique's People's Communes." Mao and leaders of other Communist states often indexed the transition to Communism to material prosperity and social welfare. The Model County program on Jinmen was intended to show the people of the mainland that the socialist road was leading them astray. On the other hand, Jinmen was becoming seen as a symbol that could be used to mobilize the citizenry of the ROC on Taiwan, "to move the people in the rear to collective struggle, in imitation of the people on the front line."[5] So the flipside of the high levels of economic and social development of Jinmen was the frugality, self-sacrifice, and discipline of its people. The Model County campaign was a form of political warfare, a program of development dictated by geopolitical issues and concerns.

The Model County campaign was also a movement of popular mobilization, of propaganda work, public covenants, inter-village competition, and organized discussions.[6] To understand the full significance of the campaign, it must be placed within the larger process of creating a modern citizenry that was seen as underlying any effort to create a modern society.[7] These measures can also be seen as part of the emergence of a modern biopolitics, the construction of a system of control that works not simply through punishment and repression, but through apparatuses that produce and regulate customs and practices, "techniques for achieving the subjugations of bodies and the control of populations" – in other words the regulation of life both from the exterior and the interior of its constituent bodies.[8] This biopolitics was shaped by discourses of modernization that had developed over the past decades of ROC control of the mainland as well as perceived geopolitical imperatives. Thus what constituted the modern citizen on Jinmen cannot be divorced from the context in which modernization was defined as a goal and pursued. But this was not unique to Jinmen. Everywhere the global Cold War tied modernization to military concerns.[9]

The ideological program of the Model County campaign echoed the New Life Movement first implemented on the mainland in the 1930s. As Arif Dirlik has shown, this was a conservative or reactionary effort intended to enhance the power of the state by promoting the self-molding of modern citizens, an attempt to mobilize the people into "voluntary functionaries of a bureaucratic machinery."[10] It was largely attenuated on Taiwan by the 1950s, but on Jinmen, the perceived pressing threat, the suspension of ordinary politics, and the small scale, meant that the campaign could not only be kept alive but even expanded. The New Life Movement on Jinmen was aimed at transforming individual morality and deepening popular mobilization. Competitions, mass meetings, and the identification of positive and negative models were its main mechanisms. While other policies mobilized civilian property and labor, the New Life Movement was a form of spiritual mobilization, that aimed to build confidence in the inevitability of ultimate victory, promote patriotism, and counter rumors and enemy propaganda. Every aspect was tied to Jinmen's distinctive geopolitical situation. Spreading military secrets, communication with the enemy, and evasion of labor duties were particular targets. Mutual aid was another important part of the movement, but what it meant in practice was that civilians should help the military and victims of enemy bombing. While Jinmen in the 1960s could not credibly be imagined as a place of luxurious and extravagant living, the movement also appealed for frugality, in clothing, eating, and especially ritual expenditure. There was also a set of behaviors that were specifically identified as "New Life" behaviors. Citizens were instructed to foster harmony and unity with their kinfolk; to respect their elders and help nurture their juniors.[11] Modern behavior was conceived as incorporating and revitalizing behaviors residing in traditional Chinese culture.

Hygiene had long been central to the definition of the modern citizen of the ROC.[12] The 1960s saw the elaboration of this concern with the promulgation of "Necessary Basic Knowledge for the Lives of Citizens," and "Standards of Etiquette for Citizens," providing instructions for modern hygiene down to the least detail. When eating, citizens should use clean utensils and sit upright and not too close to the table. They should wait for others to start eating, not be too loud, not spit out bones on the floor, and wait for the host to rise before leaving the table.[13] Chiang Kai-shek took a personal interest in hygiene promotion. He gave specific instructions on many of his visits to Jinmen, knowing full well that these instructions would be recorded by the accompanying officials and vigorously implemented. For example, during a visit in 1970, he issued instructions that kindergarten and primary school students should be taught to use paper handkerchiefs to blow their noses, and to place used handkerchiefs in garbage bins.[14] Perhaps this careful attention to hygiene can be linked to defense against Communist infiltration. Communism was a virus to be guarded against and annihilated, just as modern citizens would annihilate other pests. While instructions about how to behave at the table were only exhortations, other aspects of concerns about hygiene and contagion translated into more active social policies. The issue of rat control, while predating the formal call for the creation of a Model County, allows us to examine such policies and the discourses behind them in detail.

Rat tails and hygiene

Hu Lian's memoirs contain a detailed if perhaps apocryphal account of how he became aware of the rat problem on Jinmen in 1949. The staple ration for the troops at that time was steamed bread made from refined flour shipped from Taiwan. Troops from south China grumbled about this unfamiliar food. But they were thrilled to find that they could supplement their rations by catching snakes. A few months later, plague broke out on Jinmen, killing soldiers and civilians. A medical expert was sent over from Taiwan, and he identified the crucial causal link: "Previously, the snakes had hunted the rats, so it was hard for the rats to reproduce. Now our troops were eating the snakes, which was the same thing as helping the rats to make trouble."[15]

Plague was a perennial threat on Jinmen. The last great pandemic of the 1890s was said to have killed over 8,000 residents, almost a quarter of the total population. In 1946, some 300 people died, with almost 100 in the village of Qionglin alone. The following year, sixty deaths were reported.[16] After 1949, martial law and the extraordinary powers of the commanding officer made rapid and decisive responses possible. When plague struck one village, Hu Lian ordered it evacuated, sterilized, and sprayed with pesticide, and the residents inoculated. The outbreak was quickly quelled.[17]

In the first years of military administration of Jinmen, official discussion of plague conceived of it as a problem demanding technical solutions: inoculation, quarantine, and eradication of carriers. In 1950 alone, 120,000 inoculations were performed on Jinmen, presumably for every soldier and civilian on the island.[18] Plague was a military issue. Inspection teams invariably noted that by weakening Jinmen's military capacity, plague posed a serious danger to a place "of extreme strategic importance." Even more serious was the danger that plague on Jinmen might spread to Taiwan with disastrous results. When there was an outbreak in early May 1951, the island was put under quarantine, and air and sea links suspended to limit the risk of transmission to Taiwan.[19]

But the program to eradicate rats to prevent plague soon also became a matter of mass mobilization and of civilian–military relations. Hu Lian devised a policy requiring civilian households to meet a rat-killing quota that eventually was set at one rat per person per month. Compliance was ensured by requiring households to hand in the tails of the dead rats. In the second quarter of 1954, civilians turned in over 24,000 tails.[20] While the consequences of plague continued to be seen in military terms, the cause of transmission, the prevalence of rats, now came to be understood as a problem of the backwardness of the civilian populace. As an inspection team put it, "Jinmen's location is remote, and the people's minds are closed. They don't emphasize hygiene; one could say they don't even know what hygiene is. When there is sickness, they hire sorcerers and ask the gods to cure them. This illustrates their low level of knowledge."[21]

While Hu Lian's memoirs relate the growing rat population to the disappearance of its natural predators, and other sources explain it in terms of poor civilian hygiene, common sense suggests a third explanation. In the years after the Battle of Guningtou, the military presence on Jinmen meant that vast quantities of food had to be shipped regularly from Taiwan and stored on the island. Food reserves became an effectively inexhaustible food supply for rodents. The construction of large numbers of trenches, pillboxes, and underground bunkers created endless hiding places that poisoning campaigns were never able to penetrate thoroughly. Thus at least part of the reason why the military was troubled by rats on Jinmen was because its very presence made the island particularly hospitable to rats. Militarization on Jinmen sometimes created the very problems the militarized regime identified as needing to be solved.

By 1954, the problem of rats had been converted, in part, to a problem of mobilization. Ward heads were responsible for collecting tails from households. As one ward head recalls "I had to collect whatever the government ordered me to collect, such as rat tails." Compliance rates were an important criterion for the evaluation of village officials. Another village head remembers with pride his certificate for exemplary performance in the rat-catching campaign in April 1958.[22] Village headmen had various options to deal with those who did not submit the required number of tails. In 1964, villagers were warned that they would be punished with three days of forced labor if they did not meet their quota. Another deputy village head also recalls that those who did not submit their quota "found that things would be very inconvenient." Little Jinmen villagers who were behind in their quota were required to produce a tail at the village office before they could obtain the necessary permit to take the ferry to Jinmen.[23]

Residents were also mobilized for other hygiene-related campaigns, such as flea and sparrow eradication. The archives show that if nothing else the campaigns served their stated objective, as narrowly conceived. Many pests – rats, sparrows, and flies – were caught and killed by Jinmen villagers. As a focus of civilian mobilization, however, the results of the campaigns were rather more mixed. Villagers found ways to get around sanctions intended to encourage compliance. A Little Jinmen villager who was behind in his quota could always borrow a tail from a neighbor. There were also more devious strategies. Chen Huajin remembers cutting up rat tails into shorter lengths and claiming that each clipping was the tail of a different rat. In 1982, the hygiene office issued an outraged document that recently submitted rat tails were actually a kind of reed. Similar stratagems were also employed in the other campaigns. In 1977, the hygiene office notified cadres that if foreign objects were found among the dead flies submitted, the recorded weight would be reduced by 50 percent. Chen Huajin recalls using tea leaves and incense ashes to fill up the matchboxes of flies that he submitted.[24] It is perhaps too much to dignify these tales of tails with the term resistance. On the other hand it would also be wrong to dismiss them as nothing more than naive assertions of agency on the part of passive victims. Longtime Jinmen residents love to tell these tales of how they outwitted the foolish officials with their schemes. The humor of their folk-wisdom is a significant element in a form of counter-memory that runs throughout the recent history of Jinmen, not overtly challenging but still destabilizing the official rhetoric of selfless civilian devotion to the national cause, even in killing rats.

The simplest form of non-compliance was not to produce one's quota of rats. Statistics in the village office show that this was a perennial problem, and one that intensified over time, suggesting that efforts to generate new forms of self-discipline were utterly unsuccessful. Part of the explanation for this is that much of the deception in the campaigns was on the part of village cadres, who found it easier to try to meet the pest quotas personally than to educate, chastise, and possibly punish the residents under their charge. Li Zenghua, a former police officer and acting village head on Little Jinmen, recalls that there was once a shortfall in the volume of flies handed over. He and a colleague went to a garbage dump and spread out fish heads and insecticide. "Then we used a broom to sweep the flies in to eat the fish heads. It took till evening before we had enough, and the task was finished. As for submitting rat tails, if each household didn't submit the required number, we'd have to go to the market and buy [tails] for a high price. Each tail cost $3 or $5 – it varied. Otherwise we wouldn't reach our quota, and we cadres would receive demerits or punishments."[25]

As we shall see in chapter 9, civilians on Jinmen became highly entrepreneurial under the WZA. This entrepreneurship extended to the rat tails, and a market soon developed. The market was initially created because soldiers were also given a quota of tails. Soldiers were even more anxious than residents to fill their quota, for a shortfall meant they would be denied leave on Taiwan. Prices fluctuated in response to supply and demand, but in the 1970s a single tail could be had for roughly the price of a pack of cigarettes. Once the economies of Jinmen and Taiwan diverged because of more rapid development on Taiwan, soldiers tended to be wealthier than residents, and the price rose. Wu Guihai remembers that the market for tails led some people to specialize in catching rats. Those who did preferred to sell their tails to soldiers rather than village officials like Li Zenghua, because the soldiers would pay a higher price (the premium on purchases by soldiers was widespread in the petty economy of Jinmen, as we shall see in chapter 9). Eventually a kind of secondary market in rat tails emerged. Army cooks and procurement officers, shopping for vegetables for their canteen kitchens, would require vendors to include a certain quantity of rats' tails with their orders, otherwise they would threaten to switch to a different vendor. So vegetable vendors were also willing to pay higher prices for rat tails.[26]

Rather than internalizing the concern that poor hygiene led to disease and in turn to military dangers, Jinmen residents saw the fluctuating official emphasis on the campaigns as yet another example of the arbitrariness of WZA policies. "Whenever a new magistrate took office, there was a new style and new policies. Under the WZA system, the magistrate was always from the army, and each one had a very different style. Whatever the authorities wanted to accomplish, that's what they ordered. And you had to find a way to fulfill it. If they told you to catch birds, you had to catch birds; if they told you to catch flies, you had to catch flies; if they told you to kill rats, you had to kill rats. It was really pitiful, being a village cadre."[27] Residents, like soldiers, recognized that so long as the duration of the campaign was uncertain, it was not in their interest to be too energetic in the capture of rats. In 1991, the dissident newspaper *Jinmen Reports* contained a deliberately humorous report that soldiers killed only male rats. If they caught a female rat, the best thing to do was to cut off its tail and release it, so that it could have more offspring, and ensure that the supply of rats did not run out. There were many live rats, the story concluded, running about with no tail.[28]

To the extent that the pest problem was constructed as one of civilian backwardness and the need to modernize, it also contained the roots of its own failure. Mobilization campaigns seek to inculcate attitudes and behaviors, but the operation of campaigns is a question of monitoring and regulation. A meeting in 1978 to assess the current campaign observed that villagers may still have been killing rats, but they had become unwilling to cooperate with the operation of the campaign. "The people's standard of living has been rising. After catching a rat, they do not wish to cut off and collect the tail to submit it. This leads to problems in carrying out [rat catching campaign] work."[29] This did not necessarily mean that rural

residents were now seen as modern. Hygiene inspection teams continued
to find fault with practices that were marked as backward. Villagers
allowed their poultry to roam; they did not cover manure pits; they did
not sweep in front of their homes.[30] Failures of policy could be blamed on
the problems of the people, rather than the policies themselves.

By the late 1970s, the confusion of means and ends was complete. In
the hope of meeting targets, in the mid-1970s village offices had introduced a token reward of NTD1 for any rat tails that were submitted over
the quota.[31] But in August 1978, one village submitted no rat tails at all,
and other villages were short on their quota. A special meeting of the
county committee responsible for the anti-rat campaign was called. The
possible epidemiological and military consequences were not the issue.
Nor did the meeting consider that the shortfalls might reflect the success
of the campaign and the elimination of rats. Rather, the problem had
become precisely the campaign itself. The shortfalls meant that many
cadres had to be punished, and planning for the future had become
impossible. The chair proposed the usual range of technical solutions:
extending deadlines, adjusting funding, and more research into the
balance of incentives and sanctions. This research led to the conclusion
that if the market price for rat tails was higher than the campaign reward,
the solution was to raise the reward.[32] A problem that had been one of
popular mobilization was now simply a problem of economics.

The construction of the problem of rats shows the interplay between
military and modernizing agendas in Jinmen politics. In the eyes of planners, poor rural hygiene created the problem but strategic concerns gave
the problem its significance. Campaign-style mobilization served to
address both of these concerns, protecting Jinmen's combat capacity
while also modernizing its civilian residents. But with its focus on the
household as the unit of activism, and the persistence of informal and per-
sonalistic village relationships in ensuring compliance, the campaign was
also well rooted in historical modes of conducting politics. Individuals
and households negotiated with the campaign in various ways. Pest
quotas were sometimes resisted, sometimes undermined, sometimes
ignored. Two changes illustrate the development of mobilized modernity
on Jinmen. First, the campaign ultimately became the end in itself, as
issues of compliance and monitoring became paramount concerns while
the original goals of the campaign simply disappeared. Second, having
failed, or being perceived as having failed, at modernizing the villagers'
consciousness, the campaign became largely subject to market forces.
The problem of compliance could be met, it came to be believed, simply
by raising the financial incentives. Finally, the emphasis on civilian mobilization and the use of campaigns to deal with environmental problems

invite comparison to approaches to similar problems in the PRC, where the anti-four pests campaigns of the 1960s are often cited as evidence of the shortcomings of the regime. The history of Jinmen's anti-rat campaign also shows how approaches and methods developed during the WZA period lingered even after the restoration of civilian government. In 1995, the county government's hygiene office reported that the rat population was increasing. The county responded by ordering every public servant to submit two rat tails per month until the problem was solved.[33]

The biopolitics of a modern militarized citizenry

Besides the anti-pest and other hygiene campaigns, the WZA and the county government implemented a range of other programs aimed at turning the people of Jinmen into a modern, civilized, mobilized citizenry. Like the anti-rat campaigns, these programs were both universalized and localized; that is, they were constructed as tactics to attain what were seen as universally valid outcomes, but they were given special importance because of the specific local context on the front line of the battle with global Communism and the PRC. While the extreme degree of governmental control over Jinmen enabled an ambitious agenda of militarized utopian modernism, the content of that agenda was modulated by the assumptions of its authors and the active and passive resistance of those who were to be modernized.

One such policy, on names, remade the geography of Jinmen. There is a long tradition in Chinese thought of linking successful policy outcomes to giving the appropriate names to phenomena. On Jinmen, this rectification of names took several forms. The goal of creating a civilized Jinmen converged with efforts to promote nationalist ideology in the renaming of several villages. Villages with names that were seen as rustic and backward were given more politically inspiring names. Kekedun, "Oyster Mound," became Fuguodun, "National Recovery Mound." The written forms of some villages were replaced with homonyms or near homonyms that carried a political message: Chenkeng, "Chen Lowlands," became Chenggong, "Success." Liu Anqi, commanding officer (CO) of the Jinmen Defense Headquarters in the mid-1950s, explained that these changes were intended to confuse the enemy and build morale.[34] Efforts to rectify names also applied to individuals. In 1973, Hong Longyan (Dragon-eye Hong) was renamed Hong Minyi (Clever and Well-mannered Hong). Hong Daxiang (Elephant Hong) became Hong Dawei (Great and Martial Hong). Their original names were "not cultured" (*bu ya*), and therefore inappropriate. The range of names that were not cultured was broad. Anthropomorphic names, names that referred to agricultural products or implements, names that had vulgar connotations because they referred to sex or to bodily functions, or easily confused homonyms for any such names – all of these had to be changed.[35]

Policies on names were part of a system of regulation and discipline that was intended to create self-regulating militarized modern subjects of the people of Jinmen. Besides the arbitrary punishments of the state-sponsored White Terror and militia discipline, the system also included administrative detention and reform (*guanxun*) as well as the ROC criminal and penal laws. The detention and reform system defined the limits of acceptable behavior in terms of both acts and individuals, expanding the boundaries of punishable behavior far beyond the limits of criminal law. Such behavior included interference with or obstruction of government officials; rumor-mongering; slander of military officers or government officials; assembly of more than three men of different surnames with evil intent; bringing of spurious lawsuits; gambling; sneaking into theater or opera performances without paying; luring women into prostitution, pimping, or allowing prostitutes to stay in one's house; gathering to consume alcohol; and a variety of "inappropriate relations" with soldiers, for example conniving together to obtain and sell military supplies or using information about when units were being transferred to steal materials. The regulations identified as targets not only acts but also the "harmful elements" (*buliang fenzi*) who perpetrated them: hoodlums, vagrants, the unemployed, habitual violators of security, and, to cast the net as wide as possible, "those whose conduct cannot be improved without being put in detention." Many of these behaviors were criminal under the civilian legal code, and in theory the administrative detention system did not apply to violators of the law, who were to be tried and sentenced by the legal system. But in practice, the distinction was ambiguous and arbitrary. As one high official in the WZA put it, "under martial law, everyone on Jinmen was under the CO. He, or the deputy village head, would decide if you were a criminal, in which case you'd be locked up in the police station or put in detention." "Harmful elements" who committed crimes but were not charged or found not guilty at trial could still be put in detention at the behest of the local authorities.[36] Detention thus also served as a backup punitive system to ensure that those who cadres felt had violated rules on behavior did not escape punishment by virtue of legal procedures.

When a village official sentenced a civilian to administrative detention, the police transferred the person to a walled facility within the main army compound at Mount Taiwu, the Illuminating Virtue Training Team (*Mingde xunlian ban*). Simply put, the Training Team was the term for Jinmen's military prison *cum* reform camp. It was a facility run by the army, and most of its detainees were ordinary soldiers. The camp was one of the points where the distinction between soldier and civilian blurred, for the civilian authorities were able to detain civilians in the military prison for an unspecified term. (One issue on which the distinction remained relatively clear was finance; the county government paid a fee to the army for the upkeep of civilians in the Training Team.) In fact, former Jinmen officials suggest that the sorts of offenses that sent civilians to the Team, especially habitual gambling, petty crime, and profiteering, were precisely the sorts of offenses of which the soldiers sent to the Team were also guilty. While in the Training Team, civilians were reeducated and forced to labor. Reeducation meant ideological training; forced labor meant endless drill and manual labor on public works projects.[37]

The detention and reform system encapsulates many of the fundamental themes of the period. These include the combination of disciplinary and personal cultivation approaches to governmentality, the potential for resistance even in the most authoritarian settings, and the way the state of exception justifies both the suspension and the elaboration of ordinary politics for the sake of geopolitical expediency, in other words because of national emergency.

Crossing borders

Militarized modernity on Jinmen, especially the Three Principles of the People Model County campaign, was at least in part a response and a challenge to developments across the border on the mainland. I have so far said little about that border. Like other borders, it was not simply a line drawn on the shallow waters between Jinmen and Xiamen, but also a phenomenon invested with multiple meanings, a contextualized space, and a frame through which people – not only people on either side of the border but people in many more distant parts of the world – interpreted major issues. Boundary construction is always a problem-ridden enterprise, but perhaps never more so than in the divided states of the Cold War. Borders are never impermeable, but are always porous, physically, rhetorically, and conceptually, and this is especially true when the people on either side of the border are simultaneously citizens of a state that sits on one side or the other of an ideological divide *and* members of a nation, the Korean, German, or Chinese people, that transcends that divide.

To the extent that the Model County campaign was a form of political warfare or propaganda directed in part at the mainland, communication was essential to its effectiveness. Thus while the boundary between the PRC and the ROC was always conceptually ambiguous, on Jinmen the boundary between the two societies had to be made permeable in a very concrete way. Managing communication across the border was an important part of the project of militarization on Jinmen. There were three main mechanisms by which this communication was mediated: return of would-be defectors; local fishermen, and formal propaganda.

The first refugees or defectors from nearby mainland communities began to arrive on Jinmen in 1950, and the last were reported in the mid-1980s. Total statistics on "righteousness-loving compatriots" (*yibao*) who came to Jinmen are incomplete; one official source says there were more than 10,000 over the whole martial law period, while the Jinmen statistical annual lists 3,199 from 1954 to 1985. The category itself is problematic; it covers genuine defectors, mainland fishermen who were washed ashore, and mainland civilians and soldiers who were captured at sea. Regardless of their intentions, Jinmen authorities were always sensitive to the political uses to which they could be put. In the 1950s, defectors were celebrated for their courage in having made a bid for freedom, and called on to describe the brutality of the PRC regime. Reports of defectors make them out to be eloquent political spokesmen. Fourteen boatmen who fled to Jinmen in 1953 said on arrival, "When President Chiang was on the mainland, everyone lived in freedom and business was good. Since the Communist bandits have seized the mainland, the people suffer terribly. So we have decided to flee to the freedom of the motherland, and help President Chiang recover the mainland as soon as possible."[38]

By the 1960s "righteousness-loving compatriots" had also become vehicles for the transmission of propaganda back to the mainland. Most would-be defectors and refugees were eventually sent back. More than 90 percent of the 1,100 "righteousness-loving compatriots" reported between 1955 and 1964 were returned to the mainland.[39] In 1967 a "mainland compatriot reception center" was built to temporarily house would-be defectors. As one former officer told me of the reception center, "it was a military unit . . . It was called a reception center, but it was really a lockup. There was a team who interrogated and investigated them, and decided if they were legitimate. If they weren't, we put them in a small boat, rowed them to the mid-point [of the Strait] and told them to go back to the mainland. Before they left they were instructed that in the future, they should spread the message of President Chiang to their compatriots in the Communist areas . . . Using this method to propagandize to [mainland] fishermen has been very effective in winning the hearts of people on the mainland."[40]

The border was less permeable to other types of flows of people. Some of the most tragic stories of Jinmen under martial law involve families inadvertently separated because of the sudden impermeability of the border after 1949, a situation that changed little until the 1990s. Of course, such separations were both very common on Taiwan after the retreat of the ROC and also quite familiar to the people of Jinmen because of the long experience of sojourning Overseas Chinese. But the proximity of the border between Jinmen and the mainland made such separations especially poignant. In chapter 2, I mentioned the case of Wu Caisan, sent by his mother to buy peanut oil in Xiamen on October 17, 1949, and stranded there by the fall of the city for more than forty years. There were hundreds, perhaps thousands of similar cases.[41]

Another type of communication with the mainland was Jinmen fishermen, who worked in the liminal space that spanned the border. They became the objects of special regulatory concern, with even more elaborate systems of surveillance than ordinary residents. After several years when fishing on Jinmen was banned entirely, it was gradually re-introduced, with many restrictions, during the mid-1950s. Hong Rongbi, an old fisherman, recalls the difficulties of the early years:

We used to follow the tides. But after 1949, we had to obey the army schedules. The coast opened at 4 am, and closed at 5 pm. If you didn't come back on time, you'd be interrogated . . . Our boats had to be dragged ashore every night, and the oars and paddles locked up at the checkpoint . . . To gather shellfish or sand-worms [for bait] you had to get up before sunrise. If we went down too early to collect the shallow water nets, we had to dodge the searchlights from the check-point. It was really hard in those days.[42]

Ironically, the tight control over boats and propulsion tools like oars on the mainland was also used in ROC propaganda to convey the repressive-ness of the enemy regime. The fisherman defector interviewed by American journalists in 1961 told of how commune cadres locked away all oars every night. Stealing and hiding an oar while the rest of the commune was attending a mass meeting on "the war-mongering Americans" had been the first step in his escape to freedom.[43] The con-tradictory interpretation of the virtually identical policy, which was repre-sented as an indictment of Communist repression on the mainland while being a necessary security measure on Jinmen, points to the heart of the Jinmen authorities' policy on the border. In theory, it was to be made impermeable. In practice, it was necessary to permeate it for the political warfare work of Jinmen to be done. But the direction and content of per-meation was to be strictly managed.

Older fishermen still do not like to admit that they had any contact with mainlanders at sea. Hong Rongbi says, "Sometimes we saw Communist boats, but we didn't dare go near them. We were being watched. Anyway, I did inshore fishing, so I rarely saw them." But on another occasion he told me, "In the seventies we sometimes bought fish from mainland boats. But our fish was fresher, and could be sold for a higher price. Their fish didn't look fresh, and we didn't know what kind of preservatives they used – so we didn't do this for long."

While it is still a taboo subject among the fishermen themselves, the army and WZA saw fishermen both as means to spread propaganda to their mainland counterparts and also as possible targets for intelligence collection by the enemy. A handbook distributed in the early 1970s instructs them that if they encounter a mainland naval vessel, they are to "use the opportunity presented by conversation to communicate information about the prosperity of Jinmen and inquire about conditions on the mainland." If captured and interrogated about conditions on Jinmen, they should "indicate the prosperity, freedom, and security of the people. You may also discuss how the army loves and protects the people, and how things are better now than in the past." If they encountered mainland fishermen, their instructions were to "greet them with friendship, and explain our happy, secure, and free situation. Take the opportunity to learn about the enemy situation, and encourage them to surrender [i.e. to defect]."[44]

The third method of communication was direct transmission of propaganda. Here too the central issue was management and control of the flow of information. Both sides used identical techniques: loudspeaker and radio broadcasts, balloons and floats, and propaganda shells. Beginning in the early 1950s, radio stations and loudspeaker stations, reportedly with the largest loudspeakers in the world, were set up on Jinmen, to broadcast day and night.[45] Huge numbers of helium balloons and sea-floats laden with propaganda materials were released from Jinmen [Fig. 7.1]. Foreign visitors on a tour of Jinmen were often photographed releasing such balloons, doing their part in the anti-Communist struggle. Tens of thousands of floats were released every summer, when the prevailing currents were more likely to push them to the mainland. Besides propaganda materials, the floats contained food, clothing, cigarettes, soap, toys, watches, and radios, all items thought to be in short supply on the mainland (residents of the mainland opposite Jinmen have told me that these floats were well known to be booby-trapped, and the food inside them to be poisoned).[46] Propaganda leaflets told of the "prosperity and progress of Taiwan, Penghu, Jinmen and Mazu; activities of the Free World; living conditions of righteous compatriots [defectors] after their return [to the motherland]." Surviving examples include cartoons of Chinese Communism under attack from human rights, democracy, and freedom, accounts of economic development on Taiwan, and glossy photographs of female Taiwanese pop singers. Similar materials were enclosed in propaganda shells, hollow artillery shells that were designed to explode in mid-air, showering the materials onto the ground below.[47]

Fig. 7.1 Launching propaganda balloons (by permission of Jinmen county cultural bureau)

In the early years of militarization, when there were severe material shortages on Jinmen, the propaganda sea-floats often went astray. According to Hong Rongbi, "we used to pick up the floats and take out the towels, toothpaste, undershirts and cookies. Then we'd throw away the container and the propaganda leaflets." Here, too, there seems to be a lingering reluctance to be completely honest about past behaviors, as Hong was then able to show me one of the containers that was lying around his shed. "It was just like this, sealed with wax so water could not get in."[48] The containers can be found today in the homes of many older fishermen, often punctured and tied to a length of rope. The fishermen use them as floats for nets and traps, a very material example of the way Jinmen residents manipulated the geopolitically driven policies that surrounded them.

Jinmen was also on the receiving end of the PRC propaganda by artillery shell, balloon, or sea-float. Besides leaflets, in the early 1980s these items included video tapes, kites, balls, figurines, and seasonal fruits such as the famous Hami melons of western China.[49] Just as mainland cadres told civilians that propaganda items coming over from Jinmen might be booby-trapped, civilians on Jinmen were warned that the mainland materials were poisoned. The danger of propaganda items was that they might "poison the thinking of soldiers and civilians, and dull their anti-Communist and anti-Soviet commitment." There seemed no limits to the enemy's deviousness – in 1977 village officials were notified that four soldiers who had eaten from food tins that had come over with mainland propaganda had lost their minds.[50] Just as concern about hygiene was linked to the fear of Communist infection, concern about tinned food was a literal, even material expression of the fear of Communist poison.

The basic policy on leaflets was defined in a set of regulations issued in 1962: "Soldiers and civilians shall not read, recite, or conceal [propaganda materials]; they shall not look at the photographs or read a single character, but shall without delay submit [these materials] to the higher authorities to be dealt with."[51] Vast quantities of leaflets were turned in by Jinmen civilians. From 1975 to 1978, more than a million leaflets were gathered each year, roughly twenty-five items per civilian resident. While handing in propaganda materials was everyone's responsibility, it was clear that not everyone took it seriously. Staff at many government offices made only a token effort; the whole Civil Affairs Office of the county government was able to produce only a single leaflet in 1978, when almost 2 million were handed in across Jinmen. In contrast, the campaigns were highly effective in schools. In that same year, two primary schools accounted for more than half a million individual items. Teachers encouraged and gave small rewards to students who turned in the largest number of leaflets, as part of the overall ideological education of Jinmen youth. As we shall see in chapter 9, children were interested in collecting the leaflets and shells not just to earn the praise of their teachers, but also because they could sell the fragments to earn pocket money.[52]

The dangerous permeability and ambiguity of the border was symbolized on Jinmen in the specter of the frogman, the water-ghost (*shuigui*). The enemy frogman was not pure fantasy; there were certainly PRC efforts to infiltrate the island. But it would be all but impossible to write a history of their efforts. Rather, my interest here is what might be called the political work of the frogman image. That is, what was going on when people on Jinmen talked about frogmen? Frogmen were believed to be frequent visitors; the final examination for PLA frogman training was said to be to sneak over to Jinmen and bring back a souvenir. "If you brought back a head, you came first [in the class ranking]; if you brought back a can or something that you might just have found floating in the sea, you came last." Frogmen on military assignments took trophies – the ears of their victims. Enemy frogmen were sometimes invoked to explain the seemingly arbitrary movement of coastal watchpoints. "Once the frogmen came over and killed a whole squad in its bunker. The army kept it a secret, but we all knew about it. If a whole unit was destroyed by frogmen the army would seal up their bunker with concrete."[53] The image

Fig. 7.2 Frogmen heroes (from Ming Qiushui (ed.), *Jinmen*, by permission of Jinmen county cultural bureau)

of the frogman could mask other unpalatable realities about the ROC army. There was significant Communist infiltration of the army before 1949, and a few celebrated cases showed that espionage continued after 1949. When sabotage occurred on Jinmen, or signal flares went up in the night sky, it was more comforting to think of these as the acts of frogmen teams than to consider the alternative explanations. The danger of frogmen was also used as justification for accidents, like the shooting of a soldier who lost his way and wandered onto the beach at night. The frogman image was an ambiguous one, because the ROC had its own frogmen, who were represented in official material as the greatest of heroes [Fig. 7.2]. Just as PLA frogmen-in-training were required to sneak ashore on Jinmen in order to graduate, ROC frogmen had as their final examination to sneak into Xiamen. The parallelism between the two sides is reflected in a popular story about a class of frogmen-in-training from

Jinmen, on their way to complete their final assignment. Making their way along the sea floor, they ran into a graduating class of PLA frogmen, on their way to Jinmen to accomplish the same task of souvenir-hunting. The two groups immediately realized the situation, backed away from one another, and continued their assignment.[54] Ultimately the political work of the enemy frogman was to serve as a symbol of danger and the need to maintain vigilance because of the permeable border. It was not that there was danger because there were frogmen, but that there were frogmen because there was danger.[55]

Conclusions

In the early 1960s government planners developed a comprehensive plan for economic and social development on Jinmen. This plan was driven largely by geopolitical and military concerns, specifically the desire to demonstrate the superiority of the ROC's political and economic system over that of the mainland, where the Great Leap Forward was bringing unprecedented catastrophe. Therefore, this new focus on development should not be interpreted as a break from militarization, but rather a shift in its direction. I have labeled it militarized development, to convey the idea that even civilian economic development can be tied to military concerns and priorities. Militarized development also represents a shift in the way changes on the mainland affected Jinmen society. I argued in the previous chapter that the intensification of militarization in the late 1950s had links to Mao's foreign policy adventurism that, in turn, as other scholars have pointed out, was linked to domestic agendas in the PRC. This adventurist foreign policy had a ripple effect, shaping state policies and, in turn, social experience on Jinmen. Unlike the militarization sparked by the 1958 Strait Crisis, in which PRC domestic policy and social life on Jinmen were linked by the gear of foreign policy, militarized development was a direct response to PRC domestic policy, specifically the failures of the Great Leap Forward. When the two phases are considered together, militarization on Jinmen looks like the domestic political equivalent of an arms race or security dilemma. That is, every time domestic mobilization was ratcheted up on one side, it was increased on the second side in response. On the other hand, domestic mobilization could also increase when one side perceived weakness in the other.

The fundamental goal of social policy on Jinmen was to create a mobilized anti-Communist polity. Even this goal was in part driven by appearances, by the desire to demonstrate that the ROC regime was capable of demanding and obtaining the same high levels of mobilization as the PRC. In the course of this mobilization, there developed on Jinmen many phenomena that we associate with modernity – new forms of surveillance, control, and self-discipline, and new modes of classification and recording of information about people. This has some implications for our understanding of modernity in general. Much of the literature continues to treat modernity as a body of knowledge that exists in the abstract and that first appeared in the West. On this interpretation, modernization elsewhere in the world is the process of adopting this body of knowledge. Economic or domestic political factors, industrial capitalism or liberal democracy, are typically seen as the key drivers or indicators of this larger process. But for Jinmen, and for much of the rest of Asia, modernization, whatever it might mean, was undertaken during war or mobilization for war, and was driven by perceived security threats. Modernization was therefore inextricably tied to militarization. On Jinmen, it was the local inflection of the global Cold War and the unfinished business of the Chinese civil war that defined the course of militarized modernization. Besides a new biopolitics of citizenry that invites comparison with many other modernizing societies, the particular fixations on hygiene and ideological education are remarkable for their similarity to policies on the mainland. These similarities cannot be explained in terms of the specific and opposing ideologies to which the two regimes claimed allegiance; rather, they must lie in the common experience of leaders and thinkers of both regimes in the practices and discourses of modernization of early twentieth-century China and the Cold War mirror-imaging process. Second, to the extent that militarized development was a propaganda tool, it depended for success on communication with the intended targets of that propaganda. Regulation and manipulation of the theoretically impermeable border between Jinmen and the PRC and its citizens on the mainland was therefore also a crucial element in development modernization on Jinmen.

The people of Jinmen were made modern and made citizens under conditions wherein power lay above law. The state of emergency itself was central in the making of the people. This of course was precisely one of the criticisms that was made against the Communist enemy of the ROC a few miles across the Taiwan Strait.

8   The 1970s: combat villages and underground Jinmen

In 1980 Chiang Ching-kuo, who had succeeded to the ROC presidency soon after the death of his father in 1975, composed a commemorative essay to celebrate the construction of a new hotel on Jinmen. Located outside the town of Shanwai near the Jinmen Defense Headquarters (JDHQ), the Hall of Welcoming Guests (*yingbin guan*) was a luxury guesthouse, capable of accommodating about ninety visitors. What made it distinctive was that it was located in caves carved out of the granite sides of Mount Taiwu. Chiang's essay explains the purpose of the project: "We shall not passively accept insult but aggressively convert insult into strength. Jinmen is already established as a model for the people of the world . . . Compatriots at home and abroad, and anti-Communists around the world, all wish to see this imposing maritime anti-Communist Great Wall in person . . . So it became necessary to build this guesthouse."[1]

The Hall of Welcoming Guests was but one of a number of massive construction projects in the late 1960s and 1970s. Huge tunnels large enough to house entire naval flotillas were excavated. The central complex under Mount Taiwu was expanded. JDHQ also built the world's first hospital carved entirely out of granite, reportedly able to withstand a direct atomic hit [Fig. 8.1]. Jinmen's villagers were made to build more and larger shelters, and in some villages to excavate tunnel complexes beneath their homes. These changes, together with reforms that gave active combat responsibilities to the militia members, were known as the "combat village" (*zhandou cun*) system.

How was the overall military situation changing in this period? After 1958, there was never again a serious threat that the island would be invaded (we have already seen that in fact invasion was unlikely even in 1958, though Jinmen people were unaware of this at the time). Though the mid-1960s had seen renewed mobilization of PRC society with the outbreak of the Cultural Revolution, within a few years rapprochement with the US was underway. Mao Zedong died in 1976. After a period of uncertainty, Deng Xiaoping succeeded to the position of supreme leader and launched China on its current course of economic reform and

Fig. 8.1 The Granite Hospital. The hospital was finally closed in 2006
(photo by author)

opening up to the world. Whatever Deng's plans for Taiwan, it is reason-
able to assume that he did not intend to drop an atomic bomb just outside
Xiamen harbor. It was thus precisely as the direct military threat was
receding that the JDHQ and War Zone Administration (WZA) were
expending vast sums of money and energy to expand and fortify the
island's defenses. These efforts led to a further intensification of the militarization of local society. This chapter discusses these new policies and
their effects, and then tries to resolve the paradox.

Theory and practice of combat villages

The turning point in this new intensification of militarization of the
civilian populace can be traced very precisely to 1968, when Chiang

Ching-kuo announced a major shift in Jinmen policy, effectively abandoning the focus on social and economic development that had been launched by his father eight years earlier with the Three Principles Model County campaign. On March 12, the younger Chiang, then minister of defense, ordered that "In the construction of Jinmen from this point forward, the emphasis should be on military preparedness. It would be best if less money was spent on projects not connected to military needs. In this way even more funds can be spent on the battlefield, in order to fortify defense works."[2]

The man charged with implementing Chiang's orders in the civilian realm was an officer named Xiao Zhengzhi, a lieutenant of the Nationalist Party (KMT)'s grand master of political warfare, General Wang Sheng. In April 1968, Xiao became head of the Political Warfare Department of the JDHQ, and therefore secretary-general *ex officio* of the WZA Committee. He soon began to lay the plans for a wholesale reorganization of the militia. The changes were unveiled on August 12. The timing may have been linked to the approaching tenth anniversary of the 1958 Crisis, for rumors had spread that the People's Liberation Army (PLA) had vowed to avenge their earlier defeat within ten years, and the situation on the island became extremely tense.[3] The heightened danger was also explicitly linked to the larger regional Cold War conflict. The Tet offensive by the Vietnamese Communists in January 1968, and developments in the demilitarized zone between the two Koreas, were seen as part of a larger plan of Communist aggression, necessitating stronger preparations for war in response.[4]

The animating principle of Xiao's program was "every individual a combat fighter; every village a base for combat." The militia, whose function had previously been chiefly logistical, was now to become a combat force, blurring the functional distinction between the militia and the regular army.[5] More of the population was now drawn into military duties. While the principles of recruitment for the formal militia remained unchanged under the combat village system, many previously exempt groups were now incorporated into auxiliary units. Married women were formed into a supplementary team to take over the logistical functions formerly performed by the militia, to do psychological warfare, and to look after the wounded. Boys and girls aged twelve to fifteen made up the "Young Lions team" to patrol the village and control traffic. Children under eleven and seniors over fifty-six were trained in evacuation to help whoever was left into underground shelters. In some ways, this was a throwback to the arbitrary labor exactions of the early 1950s, when anyone was liable to be conscripted into service. The difference was that civilian responsibilities were now clearly specified and formalized.

The combat village system gave a military role to virtually the entire civilian population. Released from their former logistical responsibilities, the main body of the militia could now be given a new task, direct engagement of the PLA. In the event of an invasion, the "mobile team" of men aged between sixteen and thirty-five was to respond in four phases: "attack the enemy outside the village . . . prevent the enemy from entering the village . . . destroy the enemy in the village . . . pursue the enemy as he flees." If paratroopers were dropped in the vicinity, the "defensive team" of older men and unmarried women was to kill, capture, or delay them until regulars arrived.[6]

Whereas militia training in practice had previously meant either drill and exercise or civil construction under the guise of training, now it became necessary to train militia in a wide variety of combat functions – how to respond appropriately to different scenarios, how to ambush and trap the enemy, how to secure a perimeter, how to guard prisoners. A most graphic example was a militia course taught on Little Jinmen in 1971 about how to set and remove traps. Militia members were taught to suspend artillery shells from trees, and set up tripwires to trigger the shells' fall. Everyday objects like agricultural implements could be mounted on springs and concealed within the home so as to maim careless enemies [Fig. 8.2].[7]

To be able to fight in combat the militia needed to be adequately armed. "Every person who is capable of carrying a weapon shall be issued one. Annual and irregular training will be used to provide the necessary training and exercise. Everyone must be able to shoot, to target accurately and to fire accurately."[8] Though weapons maintenance and training had long been part of militia training, as we saw in chapter 5, the army had been unwilling or unable to provide enough guns. Now every militia member received a modern rifle, "even better than what the regular army had."[9]

The other major change was a new approach to defense construction. Whereas previously the militia had built defense works that would be manned by the army, now the village itself was to become a fortification. Every village, and even the land around the village, was to be rebuilt. "The topography in the area around the village should be changed to make it impossible for the enemy to conceal himself." The geography of Jinmen had long been remade by the needs of the army. Now the physical environment of even the village itself was becoming militarized, subordinated to the concerns of military planners. Inside the bounds of the villages, a central stronghold and one or more fortified shelters were to be built. The layout of all of the structures of the village, not just defense works but also civilian homes, now required coordination. Civilian homes were to be

Fig. 8.2 How to build a trap (from a militia training manual) (photo by author)

equipped with camouflaged firing holes for use in combat. Plans were drawn up to mine or otherwise render unusable buildings that might be useful to an invading force.[10] The people of Jinmen had long since become accustomed to their land being appropriated for army uses, and their homes damaged in shelling contests. Now the state's power to demand use of and even changes to private and collective village property was formalized. It is an irony rarely lost on Jinmen people today that though the propaganda sent from Jinmen to the mainland trumpeted the sanctity of private property, their own rights in this regard were somewhat qualified.

In the first years of combat village construction, militia members dug more than ten miles of tunnels under Jinmen's villages and built hundreds of highly fortified bunkers from which machine gun attacks could be launched at the enemy.[11] In 1976, Xiao Zhengzhi, now deputy commander of the General Political Warfare Department, returned to Jinmen on a tour of inspection and ordered a further expansion of the system. He called for the creation of "Underground Jinmen," linking the existing blockhouses by a tunnel network, enabling the militia to defend against attack by withdrawing underground and counter-attacking by surprise. Qionglin was chosen as the first implementation site. Its strategic position on the narrow waist of Jinmen certainly made it a logical choice. But local residents have a different explanation for its selection. Jiang Bowei, who studied the village in the early 1990s, was told that in the early 1950s, a soldier had been found murdered near the village. To punish the village as a whole, it was labeled a "spy village" (*feidie cun*) and subject to even stricter surveillance than Jinmen as a whole. Relations between the villagers and the nearby military bases remained tense, and villagers believe that the army selected Qionglin as the first combat village to finally exact revenge on the villagers.[12]

Cai Fulin, who became deputy village head of Qionglin just as the construction was getting underway, recalls: "There were many exits to the tunnel system, located all over the village. Some led to bunkers, some were in people's kitchens, some were in public places. The command post was located under the village offices. The post was built first, then a building was constructed on top of it, then the village offices were moved into the building." Most upsetting to the villagers was that a tunnel was dug under the ancestral hall, and an exit hole built into the hall itself. The Qionglin model combat village, completed in March 1978, was the largest militia works to date in Jinmen. Over the next five years, it was duplicated in seventeen other combat villages.[13] "Production aboveground; life below-ground" became another guiding slogan for Jinmen society.

Village police supervised the construction of traps and escape routes between houses. By the 1970s many residents of Jinmen were wealthy enough to construct new houses. Homebuilders were required to construct a shelter in the basement [Fig. 8.3]. The village policeman's approval of the shelter was needed before the house could be connected to the water supply or electrical system. The policeman also had to ensure that new constructions did not interfere with the overall defense capabilities of the combat village. For example, if a new structure would obstruct the firing line of a village bunker, the policeman could either withhold building permission or require that the owner pay for the construction of a new bunker.

Rules on travel to Taiwan became more elaborate. Jinmen residents, especially young people, had been moving to Taiwan in large numbers ever since the mass evacuation of 1958 (see Appendix). Contrary to what many people on Jinmen now believe, there were few legal restrictions on moving permanently to Taiwan in the 1960s. A would-be migrant had to

Fig. 8.3 Household shelter in a home built in the 1970s (photo by author)

arrange to have his household registration transferred to the new residence on Taiwan, and demonstrate that he was neither leaving behind any debts on Jinmen nor abandoning elderly relatives who required support. A resident traveling temporarily to Taiwan had to apply for an exit permit from the WZA authorities. Now, the rules were tightened to prevent militia soldiers from evading their militia duties. From 1975, except in cases of serious illness, exit permits were not issued for two months preceding scheduled militia training or when the militia was doing defense work construction or other logistics support. The exit permit system worked alongside but now completely reversed the original functions of the household registration system. The household registration regime had been created chiefly to counter PRC agents infiltrating Jinmen, that is, it worked to keep people out of the island. Now, its main function was to regulate the travel of residents to Taiwan and ensure they did not evade their militia responsibilities. In other words, the system now worked chiefly to keep people in.[14] As many people on Jinmen say, the elaborate regulatory procedures meant that "it was harder for us to go to Taiwan than for a person from Taiwan to go abroad."[15]

The origins of the combat village model

The combat village quickly became the dominant model in the local planning discourse. While other elements of local development were not officially abandoned, they were adjusted and subordinated to the combat village plan. Thus in 1976, when planning began for the next phase of the Three Principles Model County campaign, the plan began by noting, "In this phase of construction of Jinmen, the basic principle is coordination with military defense work. Construction work is to be expanded in combat villages; this construction will allow combat requirements to be attained."[16]

Before his transfer to Jinmen, Xiao Zhengzhi's previous posting had been with the ROC's Military Assistance and Advisory Group (MAAG) in South Vietnam, to which the ROC had been providing aid in the form of political warfare advisers, medical teams, and agricultural advice since October 1964.[17] Apparently, while in Vietnam, Xiao had become interested in a South Vietnamese anti-Communist program called *Ap Doi Moi* or *Ap Tan Sinh*, "New Life Hamlets." This was a rural pacification program that in the mid-1960s had replaced the discredited Strategic Hamlet program. In 1968, the ROC Ministry of Defense produced a long and widely distributed report on *Ap Doi Moi*, suggesting the program be adapted for use on Jinmen.[18] The documentary evidence thus gives the impression that Xiao learned about a particular approach to fighting Communist infiltration while serving in Vietnam, and then applied the same model on Jinmen, where it was renamed the combat village model.

The problem with this explanation is that it is complete nonsense. The *Ap Doi Moi* program involved army regulars with US support sweeping an area of Communist fighters to allow government workers to move in and train the hamlet's militia, improve its administration, set up welfare activities, and provide farm credit.[19] This was nothing like the combat village system. In fact, the *Ap Doi Moi* comparison was simply a cover-story for the real influence on Xiao's thinking during his time in Vietnam, the guerrilla activities of the Viet Cong. The combat village system sought to emulate the capacity of the Viet Cong to guard strength underground even when the enemy entered the village. This was an open secret among officials on Jinmen. As Cai Fulin recalled, "The initial thinking came from tunnel warfare in Vietnam. [The idea] was to protect military forces underground in time of combat, and then have them burst out to the surface and fire."[20] The tunnel complex of Qionglin, open to the public today, closely resembles the famous Viet Cong tunnel complex of Cu Chi, outside Ho Chi Minh city (one reason for the resemblance is that tunnels in both complexes have been widened and their walls smoothed out to make them safe for tourists) [Fig. 8.4]. The militia training was similarly

Fig. 8.4 Qionglin tunnel complex (photo by author)

aimed at teaching the guerrilla warfare and popular mobilization techniques that the Viet Cong were using so effectively in Vietnam.[21] Of
course it was quite unacceptable politically to admit that there was anything to be learned from a Communist enemy. So a fiction, that the real

inspiration came from the Republic of Vietnam government and its US ally, was manufactured. The attempt to transpose an approach to militarization that seemed to be effective to a different context shows that ultimately militarization was about techniques of creating and using power more than supporting ideological positions. But as a former deputy headman sardonically recalled, the system turned out not to be terribly practical for the needs of Jinmen. "The idea for combat villages came from Vietnam. But the two places are totally different. The topography and the geography are really different. The only thing that we could do was to dig tunnels. So [Xiao] mobilized the police to supervise the militia to dig lots of tunnels."[22]

The geopolitics of the combat village

Viet Cong tactics were part of a military insurgency aimed at overthrowing a national political authority and driving out its superpower ally. On Jinmen, the authorities faced neither an insurgency nor a counter-insurgency, and the hope was to solidify not eliminate the relationship with the superpower ally. That militarization on Jinmen reached its apogee in the 1970s and 1980s can be interpreted as strong evidence in support of Giorgio Agamben's arguments on the obfuscation at the heart of the state of emergency, the way the state of emergency mis-represents itself as a matter of security when it is also a matter of politics. For this high point of militarization, in which every civilian became a potential combatant, and every community a potential combat zone, was reached at a time when the actual military threat to Jinmen had receded considerably. Sino–American rapprochement and the seating of the PRC at the United Nations were serious diplomatic setbacks for the ROC. But Beijing, meanwhile, was shifting to a more conciliatory approach to the ROC. The rise of Deng Xiaoping and the start of reform led to both a general withdrawal of the PRC state from society and a stronger commitment to a peaceful external environment. Both these factors, a less militarized and mobilized society, and a state that was generally interested in avoiding conflict to focus on economic development, greatly diminished the likelihood of military action against Jinmen. Jinmen was already relatively unimportant to the security of Taiwan. Now even the security threat to Jinmen itself was declining. Even as the combat village system remade the topography of Jinmen, it became increasingly unlikely that the system would ever be put to the test.

If the military threat was so obviously diminishing, what explains the further intensification of militarization? The answer is that this phase of militarization was driven primarily by political and not military concerns.

These political concerns were both international and domestic. The Cultural Revolution and rumors of an attack to mark the tenth anniversary of 1958 may well have played a role in the initial decision to set up the combat village system. But as the system evolved over the next decade its chief impulse became the twofold goal of exaggerating the threat posed by the PRC in order to bolster wavering international support and domestic legitimacy. This involved representing the cross-strait conflict in terms of a stark bipolar Cold War world that by the early 1970s no longer existed. The combat village system was part of the project of building Jinmen into a symbol that harkened back to that world and therefore inspired the unity of purpose of the earlier Cold War. The political work of the combat village system and of Jinmen in general in this period was both to convey the impression of constant cross-strait tension and threat, and to support an already largely outdated geopolitical perspective that tied Jinmen to a global Cold War, rather than simply the unfinished business arising from the Chinese civil war.[23]

The international element of this propaganda strategy proved largely ineffective. Taiwan's diplomatic and international standing continued its inexorable slide. The US and most of the ROC's other allies began to switch diplomatic recognition to Beijing. The ROC was increasingly excluded from or constrained in international fora. But this did not lead to the abandonment of Jinmen as a propaganda symbol, merely to its redirection. Though this was a gradual process, if one had to specify a turning point it would be the breaking of diplomatic relations between the US and the ROC and the establishment of relations between the US and the PRC on January 1, 1979. This effectively meant the final abandonment of US support for the ROC claim to be the legitimate government of all of China. That this did not lead to the end of ROC propaganda about Jinmen had much to do with the domestic situation. The KMT regime was also facing pressing challenges at home. To simplify a very complex story, economic development had created a significant middle class, many of them of Taiwanese rather than mainland origin. Some members of this group became increasingly assertive in demands for political liberalization. Gradually, much of the KMT leadership came around to the idea of political reform. But this did not mean giving in to all the demands of the nascent opposition. Reform had to be fast enough to prevent social turmoil, but gradual enough to maintain stability and ensure that the KMT retained overall political dominance. In this context, the extraordinary levels of militarization on Jinmen in the 1970s make sense as propaganda for internal consumption, intended to stress the persistent external military threat in order to justify continued authoritarianism and lack of political reform, and once that battle too had been lost, to justify the slow pace of the reform. On Jinmen itself, WZA instructions on propaganda work for 1977 call for the threat to be stressed at all times. Propaganda work should "expose the Communists' United Front plotting toward our base area, to encourage all the compatriots of the nation to be alert against infiltrators, to be united in the face of divisiveness, to not accept the provocation of evil men, to be unmoved by evil talk, and to support the government's resolute anti-Communism to the utmost."[24] To ensure that the message reached its intended audience, the ROC Ministry of Education asked the Ministry of Defense to revive the suspended "summer combat camp," so as to give teenagers from Taiwan the chance to experience militarized life on Jinmen and thereby support the inculcation of patriotism.[25] Jinmen's militarized state demonstrated that there were real threats that could not be neglected. Unlike in the previous phase of intense militarization, Jinmen now grew more militarized as mainland society grew less. But the key independent variable influencing the degree of militarization was no longer in the mainland; now it was in Taiwan.

As Jinmen grew more important as a propaganda symbol, demonstrating the persistent danger of the PRC and the ROC's vigilance in standing up to the threat, the militia served increasingly as a showcase for foreign and domestic observers. After the Qionglin tunnels were completed in 1977, the village frequently played host to visitors, much to the inconvenience of residents. Cai Fulin, deputy headman at the time, recalls,

For Chinese and foreign visitors to Jinmen, the Qionglin tunnels became a highlight that had to be seen, and viewing the village's militia in training was also something not to be missed . . . While the visitors were visiting the tunnel structure, I would use the village loudspeaker system to broadcast: "Emergency situation! Emergency situation! All militia members must stop what they are doing, put on their helmets and uniforms and report to the village office." Within a few minutes the militia members would rush to the office to collect their weapons and ammunition and assemble. At this time, the visitors would be coming up from their tour of the tunnels, and would watch the militia exercises. I would issue orders: "First Company to this pillbox; Second Company enter the tunnels; Third Company into your homes," and so on . . . Immediately the militia would take their positions. Then I would use the loudspeakers to broadcast the enemy situation: "The enemy is here . . . enemy guns are there . . ." There were lots of different demonstrations – defending the village, putting out fires, psychological warfare and so on.

The task of constantly having to perform for visitors became a real burden for the villagers, and created new tension between them and the deputy headman. Cai Fulin soon found it unbearable and requested a transfer:

The militia members did not get any compensation; at best they only had to do [exercises] in a rotation, but the frequency of VIPs was very high, about once or twice a month on average. And [ordinary] visitors came endlessly. It was a big burden on the villagers, and so they became very resentful . . . I was stuck in the middle.[26]

Life during wartime is always disruptive and exhausting, and always creates tension within communities. But Cai Fulin's problems stemmed not from the tense military situation, but from the distinctive role that his home played in the larger conflict between the PRC and the ROC, and in the international and domestic issues facing the ROC government.

Ideological education and mass campaigns

The new course of militarization on Jinmen from the mid-1960s also took the form of a series of mass campaigns. These ideological campaigns had a threefold purpose. First, they were intended to maintain discipline on Jinmen itself. Second, they were intended to highlight the contrast between the ROC and the PRC, as an example to influence international public opinion. Third, they were intended to highlight ideological unity on Jinmen as an example to promote discipline in Taiwan society. The most important of these campaigns were the "Glory of Ju" (*Ju guang*) and Chinese Cultural Renaissance movements.

The expression "Glory of Ju" is today invoked in the names for many different things in the ROC, from geographic terms like village names and names of streets to brand names for a variety of products. But all of these references ultimately can be traced back to a single defining moment, which can in turn be traced back to a tale from ancient history. In 1951, according to Hu Lian, the local elite of Jinmen asked Chiang Kai-shek for a piece of his calligraphy to commemorate one of his visits to the island (since the request was relayed through Hu Lian, one wonders about the spontaneity of this request). To Hu's surprise, the indefatigable Chiang responded early in 1952, with a four-character phrase, *wuwang zai Ju*, or "Never Forget our Time in Ju." This was a reference to an episode in ancient history when a sovereign who had lost most of his territory to an enemy found refuge in the Ju region and eventually turned the tables and reconquered his kingdom.[27] Hu had an enlarged copy of Chiang's calligraphy carved on a stone outcropping on a slope of Mount Wutai, and later ordered the construction of a second monument, the Glory of Ju Tower [Fig. 8.5]. Built in the "national style" of architecture developed in Nanjing in the 1920s, the tower is oriented on an east–west axis, so that its main entrance faces west, looking toward the mainland. It soon became one of the best-known symbols of Jinmen.[28]

In 1964, young conscript soldiers in Jinmen apparently spontaneously decided to revive the flagging spirit of "Never Forget our Time in Ju."

Fig. 8.5 The Glory of Ju (Juguang) Tower (photo by author)

Their efforts were picked up by the Ministry of Defense, then endorsed by Chiang himself, who launched a national mass movement by the same name.[29] The Chinese Youth Anti-Communist National Salvation League took a leading role. "Our efforts have brought about ten years of peace and prosperity. But as the period of peace lengthens, some people inevitably gradually forget that we are at war and society in the cities has come to resemble a dancing party."[30] The Never Forget our Time in Ju movement soon petered out in society at large, but it remained important in the military, where "Glory of Ju" was the name given to weekly compulsory political education. Beginning in 1976, all militia units on Jinmen, as well as staff at schools and government offices, were required to participate in Glory of Ju training. "The goal is to heighten the patriotism of the citizenry and strengthen their anti-Communist consciousness."[31] The practical arrangements suggest that the possibilities of mass mobilization on Jinmen were already reaching their limits. Government offices and schools set aside four hours per week, just as in army units, to gather for lectures and discussion. But militia members were required only to study political texts and supplementary materials independently. With the added burden of labor to construct the combat village tunnel networks, presumably it was too much to also require a half-day of the militia's time each week for political education. "Glory of Ju" day, for a long time held on Thursdays, is used today as a metaphor for a quiet time when no people are about and no business is done. "Glory of Ju" teaching materials provide a clear index of WZA perceptions of the major political education challenges of the day. Through the 1970s, the main issues were to explain the deteriorating international position of the ROC and encourage continued vigilance against conciliatory PRC policies. Thus each improvement in the PRC–US relationship generated a body of texts that interpreted the change as further evidence of Communist ambition and aggression.

In 1968, as the Cultural Revolution raged in China, Chiang Kai-shek promulgated a cultural campaign known as the Chinese Cultural Renaissance Movement (*Zhongguo wenhua fuxing yundong*) (CCRM). A self-conscious appeal to Chinese tradition had characterized cultural discourse in the Republic of China during its first decades on Taiwan. Cultural politics became intertwined with nationalism as the KMT government sought to "invoke, resuscitate and reinvent tradition for the purpose of legitimizing its own vision of modern society."[32] Chiang and his cultural officials claimed that the KMT was the defender and guardian of traditional Chinese culture, and, in turn, of the Chinese nation. Their definition of culture was highly conservative, in reaction to the radical vision of the Chinese Communist Party (CCP) on the mainland. The CCRM elaborated on and formalized the selective appropriation of putative traditions for political ends "seizing the attention and sympathy of the international community, using culture in the forefront, to reshape the world situation."[33] In July 1968, at the very time that the combat village plan was being unveiled, a CCRM office was established on Jinmen to promote village education, citizenship training, and the reconstruction of important historical monuments. The forms of citizenship training harkened back to the New Life Movement and subsequent efforts to promote forms of citizenship that combined modern scientific hygiene with traditional ethical norms. One can still see in many Jinmen homes wall posters outlining "What every citizen must know." The text combines the need to maintain a hygienic household with the need to respect the elderly and live frugally. A similar mixture characterizes the educational efforts – besides standard Chinese, English, and mathematics, the CCRM office also sought to promote knowledge of the great sages of Chinese philosophy, and began a lecture series on the Four Books of the Confucian canon. The movement envisaged a new symbolic role for Jinmen. "Everyone already knows the strength of Jinmen's defenses . . . It is like the sharp tip of a sword piercing the vital organs of the Communists on the mainland . . . Everybody also knows that on Jinmen the government is peaceful and the people harmonious, the military and civilians are united, society is well-ordered, and the people prosperous and happy. It is like a brilliant light in the darkness, inspiring the boundless admiration and envy of the suffering compatriots on the mainland. But it may be that people are not yet entirely familiar with the work of cultural renaissance on Jinmen. The spirit of humaneness and righteousness, the prosperity of society, and the evidence of well-mannered behavior are everywhere to be seen." All three of the virtues of Jinmen are, in this essay, aimed at the mainland. By the 1970s, they were equally aimed in the opposite direction, back to Taiwan.[34]

In its efforts to maintain militarized discipline, ideological education on Jinmen from the late 1960s through the 1970s reflects typical problems of late authoritarianism, and paralleled efforts on Taiwan. What is most interesting about their expression on Jinmen is the explicit intertwining of geopolitical concerns, domestic issues, and the attempt to use Jinmen as a model for the larger ROC society. Already in the mid-1960s we find warnings against the illicit import of pornography, which is "bad for combat spirit."[35] In 1978, the county orders an inspection of male cadres and militia members. Owing to "wartime conditions" those with long hair must have it cut.[36] There were prohibitions against men having long hair on Taiwan and other places in the region as well at this time; on Jinmen the connection between long hair and national security is explicit. In 1980 in Jinmen older high-school students are ordered to do militia training for several days during the summer holiday, in order to "train them for combat, fortify their anti-Communist confidence, and strengthen the militia in support of its mission to protect one's family and defend the homeland." In service of this goal, male students must not be allowed to grow their hair long.[37] The regime of militarization had always stressed the need for vigilance against both external and internal enemies. In the early phases of militarization, internal enemies had meant Communist infiltrators. Now enemies abroad are encouraged by enemies at home. Teaching materials for Glory of Ju day political education in 1977 urge vigilance against the Communists' ally, the Taiwanese independence movement. Both are the sworn enemies of the Chinese people.[38] What all of these campaigns suggest is that the basic transition of the combat villages also occurred in the domain of political education. Where a decade earlier Jinmen had been constructed as a model of difference in the face of society on the mainland, it was now increasingly being constructed as a model of difference from society on Taiwan.

But this was a rearguard action. By the late 1970s, there is a rising sense of desperation, if only in the open acknowledgment of problems, about the civilian–military relationship on the island. "Everyone knows," writes one local official, "that the army and the civilian populace are one family. But lately some foolish local youths have been causing problems. We must stop this, and promote a patriotic spirit of respect for the army."[39] As we shall see in Part IV, this cause would soon be lost.

Conclusions

The combat capability of the Jinmen militia went up dramatically after 1968. This was not because the likelihood of military conflict over Jinmen had increased; indeed it decreased considerably over the next decade. Rather, it reflected a change in the political role of the militia. In the 1950s the militia had been used to mobilize the people of Jinmen itself. Now it was being used to mobilize others, as a national and international symbol of ROC anti-Communism.

Even as the direct military threat to Jinmen began to recede, the late 1960s saw a fundamental reorientation in the nature of local militarization. The main function of the militia shifted from providing logistical support for the regular army to engaging in combat with the enemy. Jinmen's villages were no longer civilian population centers to be protected and defended by the army, but military installations in their own right. New militarized ideological campaigns sought to construct and disseminate the heroic militarized version of Jinmen's popular martial anti-Communist spirit and mobilization to the rest of the ROC and to the international community. Other campaigns also sought to valorize selective elements of what was seen as Chinese tradition, to draw attention to differences between the PRC and the ROC. What draws all of these changing policies together and explains why they were implemented even as the actual threat was declining is a basic shift in the causes of militarization. By the mid-1960s, the course of militarization was being determined not by military issues but by political ones, specifically the increasingly shaky international position of the ROC on Taiwan, and the crisis of legitimacy facing the KMT government within the ROC. The combat village system and the Glory of Ju and other campaigns sought to respond to these challenges by heightening the sense of Communist threat and constructing Jinmen and its people as heroic resisters of that threat. The combat village system was largely shaped by another Cold War conflict, that in Vietnam, but the inspiration from Vietnam was not the ROC's ally, the Republic of Vietnam, but their joint enemy, the Communist National Liberation Front. This episode of borrowing techniques from an ideological foe shows that militarization could be as much about effective techniques of power as it was about ideologically inspired commitment. Regardless of its origins, militarization in this phase continued to disrupt the lives of Jinmen's residents. The developments of this phase demonstrate further that militarization is a complex phenomenon intended to serve multiple goals and with complex and not always anticipated consequences.

The heightened mobilization of the combat village system draws attention to some of the central paradoxes of Cold War militarization. The rhetoric of militarization, especially during the combat village phase, required that the people of Jinmen be constructed as voluntaristic heroes capable of independent action. But an extraordinary apparatus of surveillance and discipline was necessary to sustain this construction. The ideological campaigns against the enemy constantly stressed the subjection of its populace to the political whims of their leaders. As slogans broadcast by the Jinmen militia to the mainland put it, "The Chinese Communist Party treats you as human targets, to be fought for back and forth. But when the fighting is done, it is not the CCP leaders who will be dead, but you."[40] But this criticism could equally be made of the KMT's use of the people of Jinmen. The ironies of the situation, not lost on local society, were rarely addressed explicitly. When they were, they were justified in terms of the state of emergency, the extraordinary situation that justified the suspension of the normal order. That the demands made on those living in the emergency seemed to grow, even as the seriousness of the emergency diminished, points to the fundamental misrepresentation at the heart of the state of emergency in Cold War Jinmen but also in other contexts in Asia and beyond. Emergency measures are portrayed as purely objective responses to circumstances, when in fact they are political decisions that can be analyzed like any political decision.

Part III

Life in Cold War-time

Histories of the Cold War typically interpret the three decades from the 1960s to the 1980s in terms of a threefold periodization: an easing of Cold War tension, *détente*, and a renewal of tension beginning around 1979 with the Soviet invasion of Afghanistan. This periodization may be valid at a high level of generality, but only at the cost of privileging the diplomatic arena and the interaction of the superpowers. The further one moves from Washington and Moscow and toward local communities in the US, the USSR, and elsewhere, and the more broadly one considers the social and cultural effects of the Cold War, the more problematic this periodization becomes. Part III consists of three chapters that explore different aspects of social life in this period, with a focus on how the people of the island experienced and negotiated with the WZA regime. The first of these chapters, on the economy, deals mainly with the material dimension of militarization; the other two chapters, on religion and gender, focus on discursive aspects. The purpose of these chapters is not simply to show the people of Jinmen resisting the repressive and disciplinary systems that were put in place over them or to highlight their agency within those systems, but primarily to show how the "capillaries of militarization" worked their way into a wide range of social institutions seemingly little connected to the battlefield.[1] Together the three chapters show how the project and experience of militarization were inflected by the specific expression of geopolitics on Jinmen. Each of them invites comparison with other societies affected by geopoliticization, as part of a larger comparative cultural and social history of the Cold War.

9 Combat economy

Wu Chaoxi, or Maestro Wu as he is known in his shop's promotional materials, is Jinmen's best known entrepreneur. Wu was originally an itinerant blacksmith. In 1944, when US planes shelled Japanese positions on Jinmen, Wu realized that the shell fragments from the bombing were made of much higher quality steel than anything found on the island, and he began to collect them to use in his smithy. The two crises of 1954–5 and 1958 provided him with an effectively endless supply of top quality raw materials. A decade later the family business was booming. His son remembers: "We'd buy shells from the people. Kids would collect the shells, and trade them for candy. You could use them in village shops to buy eggs or whatever, and then the shopkeeper would resell them."[1] Among the many products that a rural blacksmith had to be able to make and repair were knives, especially the heavy rectangular-bladed cleavers (*caidao*) that are the essential tool for Chinese-style cooking. Cooks in the army canteens all needed cleavers, and Wu's were the best. His cleavers gradually became an indispensable memento of a tour of duty on Jinmen, not just for cooks but for every soldier.[2] With tens of thousands of troops cycling through Jinmen each year in the 1960s, the market was substantial. Some critics say that today the family buys ordinary steel from wholesalers just like any other hardware factory. But their shop floor remains piled high with rusty shell cylinders, and Wu's son can fashion a shard of one of them into a shiny cleaver in minutes [Fig. 9.1]. He dismisses the accusations. "Enough shells fell on Jinmen to keep us in business for a hundred years, a thousand years. Why would we cheat people?"[3]

Like thousands of other Jinmen families, Maestro Wu's story is one of adaptation to the distinctive economic context that was created by geopoliticization and militarization. Some of the changes to the economy of Jinmen look very familiar to us – young men and women pulled from the land by the lure of opportunity of industrial jobs in distant cities. Other changes seem more distinctive – local industries that arose, by government plan or through the workings of the market, to serve the soldiers, or the

Fig. 9.1 Maestro Wu's workshop. His son is cutting out a shell fragment
to begin the knife-making process (photo by author)

repeasantization of residents as demand for agricultural products soared.
But here, too, there are resemblances to communities elsewhere that were
located in or near large military bases. There are two main dimensions to
the overall story. The first is the state's interventions in the economy.
These can be understood as the local inflection of a global discourse of
state-mediated development that would come to be known as the developmental state.[4] On Jinmen, geopolitical conditions and concerns limited
the choices that were available to state planners and made certain outcomes especially desirable. This was part of the larger mirror-imaging
process whereby policies on Jinmen were often devised so as to highlight
the contrast with the mainland. While these state policies certainly had
some impact, an equally important element in the overall economic transformation came from the decisions and behaviors of local people. The militarization of society created new sets of incentives for them. They
responded to these incentives in ways that were quite unpredicted by state
planners, setting up small businesses on an extraordinary scale.

Despite the ROC demonization of the PRC command economy, state-
owned enterprise was an important part of Taiwan's economic development. But petty entrepreneurship also played a key role in the dramatic

economic transformation of the main island. In this sense, some of the basic patterns of economic development on Taiwan were shared on Jinmen. But like state economic planning, entrepreneurship is also highly specific to context. The geopolitical context on Jinmen was sufficiently different that the form of entrepreneurship that arose there diverged significantly, as did the economic outcomes. Entrepreneurialism challenged the state's capacity to control local society, and created many tensions between villagers and the local government and between villagers and the military. This highly context-specific pattern of economic development on Jinmen has left a major legacy there today, a distinctive form of dependency that resembles that found around military bases around the world, and that continues to challenge both state economic planners and local families.

The traditional economy

The general impression one gets of the traditional economy of Jinmen before 1949 is of generalized poverty, with isolated peasants barely surviving in the face of limited resources, predatory local elites, and the ever-present threat of natural disaster. A common folk saying is used to convey the poverty: "By the time a girl has grown up and married she will not have tasted two pecks of rice."[5] But another piece of folk wisdom, similarly intended to convey a sense of poverty and isolation, actually reveals that the situation was rather more complex. People often say that Jinmen produced only enough food for four months of consumption; for the rest of the year, the island had to rely on imports from the mainland. Famine was rare, so what this really conveys is that Jinmen was sufficiently tied into larger commercial networks that people were able to sell what they produced – peanuts, sweet potato, salt, and fish – and purchase adequate food for their own consumption.

Jinmen was also integrated into the larger world through its labor networks. Increasingly from the mid-nineteenth century onward significant numbers of Jinmen men had gone abroad to seek their fortune, and there were communities of Jinmen natives throughout Southeast Asia. Few migrants fulfilled their dreams of fabulous wealth, but their remittances were nonetheless important to the prosperity of their villages, and the overall economy of Jinmen. A 1940 survey found that almost one-third of Jinmen's 8,000 households had a family member living abroad. Besides Overseas Chinese villages, the other prosperous settlement on Jinmen was the main town of Jincheng. To a young Central Intelligence Agency (CIA) agent posted to Jinmen in 1952, the town's appearance remained "completely medieval, with wooden structures along the narrow streets.

They slightly overhung the roads like some village in Shakespeare's England."[6] The exception would have been a single fine street of brick shops, "Model Street" (*mofanjie*), built in 1924 by the chamber of commerce, whose leaders were mostly returned Overseas Chinese, in the hope of catalyzing the modernization of the local economy. After the Japanese surrender in 1945, old commercial networks were revitalized, and living standards rose. But 1949 would change everything.

The militarized developmental state

The months after the Battle of Guningtou saw massive disruption of the local economy, as discussed in chapter 2. Besides the devastation of the battlefield, covering much of the northwestern arm of the island, the new geopolitical situation eliminated many familiar ways of making a living. I have mentioned already how the island's fishing fleet was largely destroyed, ostensibly to obtain materials but probably also to prevent soldiers defecting back to the mainland. Among the materials seized by the army were many items essential to the village economies such as the flat stones used to cultivate oysters and the retaining walls of salt pans. Cut off from their main suppliers and markets in Xiamen, most of the island's merchants found it impossible to continue their traditional lines of business by late 1949. The other destabilizing factor was demographic. By the end of 1949, the total population of Jinmen including soldiers had leaped to over 100,000. There were serious material shortages. Shortages led in turn to inflation, fueled in part by the booty that some Republican soldiers brought over with them from the mainland. Theft, pilferage, and intimidation caused serious tension between soldiers and civilians. Farmers had to guard their fields to prevent soldiers from stealing the unripe crops. "They stole all our crops; it was like we were working for nothing."[7]

The Jinmen Defense Headquarters (JDHQ) under General Hu Lian worked quickly to stabilize the economic situation. Currency and price controls were imposed, and a supply cooperative established to coordinate shipments from Taiwan.[8] As the overall situation became more stable, thoughts turned to long-term planning. The most elaborate intervention in the economy was land reform, begun in late 1953, interrupted in 1954 by the first Taiwan Strait Crisis, and completed in 1955. The small scale of Jinmen permitted relatively simple approaches to pursue the goal of "land to the tiller" (*gengzhe you qi di*). Most tenants were simply given title to the land they worked and the original owner compensated according to a standardized land price. This was rather different from Taiwan, where landowners were paid with long-term government bonds. "So the peasants were able to obtain land without recourse to violence and therefore remained calm, and landlords were able to receive immediate compensation rather than payments over a long period of time, and so were also pleased."[9] A loan from the US-funded Joint Commission on Rural Reconstruction (JCRR) provided the funds to compensate landowners.[10] The statistics show why the process was painless. The vast majority of family holdings were small; only 11 percent of land was rented, and in all of Jinmen there were only thirteen households that could be considered large landlords with holdings of over forty *mu* (2.7 hectares). Before land reform, 89 percent of land was worked by owner-cultivators; after land reform the figure rose to 92 percent.[11] In other words, the consequences of the process were utterly trivial. The military leadership must have been aware of this. Some even argued that given the military situation, land reform was a needless distraction.[12] But the decision to go ahead with land reform was ultimately a political one, and its main purpose was to highlight the failure of land reform across the Strait. "Land reform on Jinmen is a policy aimed at implementing the principle of people's livelihood, to attain the goal of land to the tiller. Its methods are peaceful, scientific, and non violent . . . This policy implemented on the front line of Jinmen is in sharp contrast to the bloody 'land reform' on the opposite shore, behind the Iron Curtain."[13] In other words, land reform on Jinmen was a propaganda measure, intended to draw attention to the violence of land reform on the mainland and thereby generate international sympathy for the ROC's cause of national recovery. Land reform was intended primarily not to serve the cause of economic development, but as "the most effective weapon in the political and economic combat with the Communists."[14]

Oral history confirms the insignificance of land reform in the lives of ordinary people. Almost no one has anything to say about the subject. When pressed on the issue, informants dismissively point out that land on Jinmen was so poor as to be almost worthless. One certainly could not survive simply by obtaining the deed to a plot of land. But there is another more important explanation for the lack of attention in popular memory. Even as land reform was being implemented, significant quantities of land were being seized by the army. There are no reliable statistics on the total amount, but when a system was created in the early 1990s to compensate residents for seizures of land, over 8,000 separate claims were filed.[15] A former magistrate estimates that even after much land was returned to civilians in the last decade, at least one-third of the total area of the island remains in the hands of the army.[16] Thus two unspoken truths, one historical and one related to the post-1949 situation, undermined the overall significance of land reform. First, the ecology of Jinmen meant that few people would or could make a living purely off the land, so even the most thorough of reforms would not lead to a dramatic relief from poverty. Second, and far more important, the overwhelming factor shaping the distribution of land was precisely the military's arbitrary seizure of much of the residents' property. Land reform did nothing to address this issue. While the oral history has little to say about land reform, many people do recall with great energy the destruction of homes and especially the seizure of wooden doors. It may be that resentment about loss of doors has come to be an acceptable metaphor for the larger issue of arbitrary seizures in general, a taboo subject for most of the last half century.

Comparing Jinmen with the mainland and Taiwan draws attention to the importance of context and political will in shaping the impact of land reform. On the mainland, land reform had enormous political impact. It fulfilled one of the fundamental promises made by the Chinese Communist Party (CCP) and, through its violence, put hundreds of millions of peasants through a baptism by fire that committed them to the new order. And it had a major leveling impact on society, destroying the landlords as a social class. Its long-term economic consequences on the mainland are hard to measure because land reform was so quickly followed by collectivization. On Taiwan, land reform is credited with a massive increase in agricultural productivity, releasing labor and surplus investment funds that would fuel the impressive economic growth of the 1960s. Its political effects, while not as dramatic as on the mainland, were still significant. The power base of the traditional rural elite was shaken, creating a vacuum that was filled by groups that could be co-opted into the Nationalist Party (KMT).[17] On Jinmen, land reform had none of these effects. It neither boosted economic productivity nor caused a social transformation. But it was nonetheless accounted a great success. Land reform illustrates another of the unanticipated consequences of the geopoliticization of the island, the subsuming or subordination of otherwise dominant discourses of economic development and modernization to perceived geopolitical needs, sometimes militarized in the narrow sense, sometimes militarized in the broader sense of being political or propaganda gestures driven by the larger military conflict.

Industrialization, state-owned enterprise and agricultural extension

Land reform on Jinmen was primarily a political issue, aimed at drawing attention to the contrast in governance between the ROC and the PRC, rather than improving the lot of the local people. But economic well-being itself soon became a political issue. When people today talk about the early 1950s their recollections focus heavily on poverty and shortfalls. Villagers often begged food from the soldiers. A former soldier remembers that "whenever we ate, the kids from the village would stand around waiting with bowls and pots. As soon as we finished, they would collect the leftover rice and dishes and take them home."[18] Students in primary school were fed with donations from US aid agencies. "There was cereal and powdered milk. The cereal was full of bugs; you boiled it up and then strained out the bugs that floated to the surface. The powdered milk had hardened into bricks. You had to bang it against the wall. We got steamed bread at school, but we'd hide it in our pockets to take home to our parents who had no food at all." The burlap sacks of relief food were recycled into clothing. "You'd have 'Gift of the United States people' written on your chest."[19] It therefore became politically important to "turn the poor soil of Jinmen into a prosperous oasis, creating a wealthy society and a firm fortress of freedom."[20] Of course, the small scale of Jinmen meant that the illusion of prosperity could be created simply by increasing the amount of aid from Taiwan. But this would have increased the costs of administering the island, costs borne by the Ministry of Defense, and would also be less effective politically as a demonstration of the ROC's superiority.

Early efforts to promote industrialization, both public and private, foundered under problems caused by the military situation: political instability in general and supply insecurity specifically.[21] Lack of industrial development is the second main cause for the demographic decline of the island after the evacuation of 1958. Beginning in the late 1960s, more and more young people left the island to look for work elsewhere. Their traditional emigration destinations closed off by more restrictive immigration policies by the newly independent states of Southeast Asia, Taiwan became the most important destination. From the 1960s to the late 1980s, almost 20,000 Jinmen residents moved to Taiwan, where they joined the exodus of working-age people from the main island's rural south.[22] Some followed family members who had been evacuated in 1958; most were young people who went seeking jobs or to obtain higher education. They settled chiefly in the industrial suburbs around Taibei, in towns such as Yonghe, Zhonghe and Sanchong, where they found work in the export-processing industries that contributed to Taiwan's economic revolution. (Another reason people moved to Taiwan was to join the army. For children of poorer Jinmen families, joining the military was often the only way to obtain an education. Chen Shuizai, county magistrate in the 1990s, recalls, "I was in the first class at Jinmen secondary school after it returned to Jinmen [after the 1958 evacuation]. My family had no money to send me to university, so I decided to go to military college, in exchange for serving ten years in the army."[23])

Efforts at local industrial development were not a complete failure. The main success story involved Hu Lian's introduction of sorghum (*gaoliang*) in 1950. Sorghum became a symbol of the search for an economic foundation for Jinmen under conditions of militarization. According to Hu Lian's own account, he promoted the cultivation of sorghum as a source of fuel, as a windbreak to prevent soil erosion, and as a food supply. It soon became clear that the local people could be made to grow the sorghum, but they would not eat it. Like the soldiers from south China who would not eat steamed bread, the villagers found sorghum unfamiliar and unappetizing. They preferred their traditional diet of sweet potato.[24] Like so many of the issues Hu faced, this created a political issue, a problem of appearances. Sweet potato, boiled into gruel or cut into strips and dried, was the familiar diet for most residents. But this was a consequence of the overall poverty of the island. The sweet potato was disdained in Chinese culinary culture, seen as a food for the poor, a crop that respectable people would feed to their animals, not to their families. Before 1949, the well-off on the island would have eaten rice, imported from the mainland through Xiamen. After the initial crisis of 1949 had passed, the expanded garrison on Jinmen was supplied mostly with rice from Taiwan. This meant that the soldiers ate rice while civilians ate sweet potato. The different cultural value placed on the two staples undermined the notion, expressed on wall slogans and much outwardly directed propaganda, that "soldiers and civilians are one family."

Hu Lian then hit upon an alternative use for sorghum that would solve the problem. Sorghum can also be used to distill alcohol. Alcohol was one of the chief forms of recreation for the troops, especially in the early years before the army and the villagers responded to the demand for entertainment. More than 100,000 bottles of spirits were shipped per month for the troops. It occurred to Hu Lian to try to produce these spirits locally. The first Jinmen sorghum liquor went on the local market by late 1950, at prices significantly cheaper than liquor from Taiwan. It soon came to dominate the market. Now the full genius of Hu's plan became apparent. His officers used the revenue from the operation of the liquor factory to purchase rice on Taiwan. The rice was then shipped to Jinmen, where it was exchanged with farmers for an equal weight of sorghum. One of the main events of the agricultural calendar became the annual visit by factory representatives to every village. They drove trucks loaded with rice, and exchanged the sacks of rice for sacks of sorghum.

The market price of sorghum on Taiwan was typically between one-third and one-half the price of rice. Jinmen's farmers immediately saw the advantages of growing sorghum. The exchange by weight worked greatly in their favor, and amounted to an indirect subsidy from the Ministry of Defense to the farmers of Jinmen. But this was beside the point. The rice exchange program meant that the citizens of Jinmen could now be seen eating the same high quality food as the soldiers without adding to the logistical burden on the military. Within a few years, many Jinmen farmers had cultivated much of their land with sorghum. (They typically reserved a portion of their land for sweet potato, and another portion for high-value crops like vegetables. I explain why vegetables were so valuable below.)

The liquor program eventually became even more successful than Hu had hoped. By the mid-1950s, Jinmen sorghum liquor had become extremely popular in Taiwan. In the early years, the factory was under the control of the War Zone Administration Committee (WZAC), and its operating profits accounted for most of the administration's reported income. After 1970, operating profits went directly into county coffers, and typically amounted to around half of locally generated revenues. (But for both entities this was only an unknown fraction of the total budget, for most transfers from the Ministry of Defense and the central government do not appear in the statistics.[25])

The sorghum program was only part of the larger program of economic development on Jinmen. Economic development was an end in its own right, but it was also linked to other political and military concerns, such as the need to demonstrate the superiority of policies on Jinmen compared to those on the mainland and the need to reduce the burden of supplying Jinmen from Taiwan. Economic development itself became militarized. The ways in which economic development was conceptualized illustrate well the interplay between the island's geopolitical situation and more general discourses of development. On the one hand, the unstable political situation made investment and even supplies of materials uncertain, so there was little chance that industry would play a central role. Jinmen's economy would have to remain largely agricultural. On the other hand, the state would play a central role in mediating development, an assumption that ran through much of the writing and thinking on Taiwan's development, and throughout much of the world, during the 1950s to 1970s.

The problem of economic development is another illustration of the ways in which modernization and militarization could create the very problems they sought to address. One of the central problems of the economy on Jinmen, the symbol of its backwardness and impoverishment, was the heavy reliance of the population on a single staple, the sweet potato, and the consequent lack of diversification in the economy. But the cause of this situation did not lie in the backwardness of the economy. Rather, it was the political circumstances that had cut the island off from the commercial and labor networks in which it had previously been embedded.

The huge investment in infrastructure in the early 1950s was frequently represented as part of the program of state-mediated economic development. For example, a dense network of roads was constructed, and there were major improvements to irrigation, especially the capacity to store water. But the chief concerns behind these efforts were basically military; contributions to economic development were incidental to this larger purpose. Where state efforts were most targeted to the civilian economy was in the area of agricultural policy. The JCRR played the crucial role in this area. An initial inspection by the JCRR identified three main issues – plague and disease prevention, forestation to prevent erosion, and agricultural extension to increase productivity. Disease prevention efforts have been touched upon in chapter 7. Forestation work was at least partly a military concern that was represented as a development issue, for Hu was also worried about providing cover for troop movements and military installations. Forestation was also tied to the issue of popular mobilization, as militia members as well as soldiers were charged with planting and caring for seedlings. "In the 1950s, every tree had a little plaque with the name of the person responsible for planting it and looking after it," recalls one former magistrate.[26] The third focus of JCRR work was agriculture. "Agricultural technology and knowledge are backward. Agriculture, forestry, fishery, and husbandry should make use of modern agricultural methods in accord with local agricultural customs." But political concerns were always close to the fore. "Jinmen is close to the mainland, and combat may break out at any time."[27] With JCRR support an agricultural experimental station introduced hundreds of new crop strains. The JCRR also supported the Farmers Association that was created in 1953. Initially, the association seems to have been yet another example of the tendency to create organizations that mirrored organizations being founded on the mainland, the point being to show that the Jinmen version was less repressive and more effective than its mainland counterpart. But by the late 1950s, JCRR aid was transforming the association into a major force for improving agricultural production. Using JCRR funds, the association provided large quantities of fertilizer, pesticides, seed, and feed to local farmers. It also provided farm loans, a key factor in allowing local farmers to expand their production. Besides local farmers, JCRR work also involved extension work with the garrison. In 1955, the Ministry of Defense asked the JCRR to submit a proposal for "victory gardens." The idea was to provide soldiers with equipment and expertise so that they could farm the lands around their bases in their spare time, reducing the level of imports needed, easing pressure on the local market, and improving soldiers' standards of living.

Given that the objectives of the agricultural development program were both economic and political, to assess those programs we need to consider the results in both realms. In agriculture, the major development in the martial law period was the massive increase in sorghum production. But this had little to do with agricultural extension work *per se*; it was a response to the effectively infinite demand for sorghum of the liquor factory. Other staple crops such as barley, wheat, soybeans, and peanuts showed smaller increases. The exception was sweet potato. Average annual production rose from between 5,000 and 10,000 tons to over 35,000 tons. This was apparently largely a result of the introduction of higher-yield strains of potato from Taiwan by the JCRR.[28]

The political record was less mixed. The JCRR itself published numerous pamphlets celebrating the accomplishments of Jinmen. "Jinmen today is a structure built up through the collective efforts of the soldiers and civilians of the whole nation and is a most concrete and excellent example of international cooperation. The island of Jinmen leaves a deep impression on the minds of the freedom-loving people of the whole world. It will also enable every person of the free world to share the honor of having done his part and feel proud of himself."[29] A 1956 *New York Times* article relates "a story of adversities, natural and man-made, of courageous endurance, and of dawning improvement in the lot of the people." After the early successes of the JCRR at improving self-sufficiency, its plans became more ambitious. "Why not convert this unlikely heap of sand and stone, under the Red Guns, into an object lesson in progress to the Red-held mainland?"[30] As evidence of the success of agricultural extension, propaganda materials included photographs of young farmers holding giant sweet potatoes and enormous melons. These photos resemble those in publications of the US 4-H agricultural extension program, but are also eerily similar to the photographic evidence of the triumphs of the Great Leap Forward on the mainland. For in the curious mirror-imaging of Cold War cross-strait antagonism, neither side could afford to shy away from any battle, no matter how fantastic. The appropriate response to claims that the enemy could produce giant vegetables was not to dismiss such claims, but to assert that one's own system could yield vegetables of an even more staggering size [Figs. 9.2, 9.3].

Fig. 9.2 A bumper crop of sorghum (from Ming Qiushui (ed.), *Jinmen*, by permission of Jinmen county cultural bureau)

The logic of this propaganda reveals a number of internal paradoxes or contradictions. First, the people of Jinmen were free agents, but they also had to be the beneficiaries of the army and, in this case, the US. Praising the peaceful appearance of Jinmen, two American observers note, "Somehow it is all a deception, for the mainland behind the peaceful vale [sic] is ugly and dangerous, as the people of Jinmen well know, and on Jinmen itself there are soldiers, more soldiers than civilians. They run the island. They are responsible for its improvements, its roads, its trees, its wells and system of irrigation, its schools . . . its safety. With the technical aid and assistance of the US JCRR, they have made Quemoy island a cross between a fertile garden and a tremendous military position."[31] Second, the capacity for endurance was represented as an essential part of the distinctive character of the people of Jinmen, a symbol of their heroism. How could they suffer from material privation while at the same time enjoy such great economic development? The resolution of this paradox in representation lies in understanding that the capacity to

Fig. 9.3 Giant vegetables (from Ming Qiushui (ed.), *Jinmen*, by permission of Jinmen county cultural bureau)

endure privation and rising prosperity were simultaneously a stick with which to beat the Communists and a demonstration of the legitimacy of the regime.[32]

Despite its accomplishments, real and rhetorical, agricultural development on Jinmen faced some simple facts. No amount of agricultural extension could deal with the basic ecological constraints coupled with the island's isolation. The potential of state-mediated development was limited. Sorghum spirits and other state-owned enterprises provided some employment for local workers, and contributed funds to local government. But it was impossible for Jinmen to industrialize, or to develop flourishing export-oriented commercial agriculture. The real key to economic growth on the island depended on dramatically shifting the economic opportunities, incentives, and constraints faced by local families. Militarization did just that, but completely inadvertently and unexpectedly. Just as on Taiwan, it was the market-driven choices of individuals and households that were primarily responsible for economic transformation. But as we shall see in the next section, the market on Jinmen was unique. It was not integration into global capitalism but geopoliticization that determined this market.

G. I. Joe business

In the mid-1970s, there were almost 4,000 registered businesses in Jinmen. The population at the time was around 60,000, and the number of households around 10,000.[33] Thus about 40 percent of households were operating a business. This must be among the highest rates of entrepreneurship in any society in history. In fact, the rate of business ownership was even higher than this, as many families ran small-scale operations and did not bother to register them. Almost half of the registered businesses were licensed as "special category shops" – cold drink shops and teahouses, snack shops, barber shops, and pool halls – enterprises whose business was conducted largely or entirely with garrison soldiers. In the local parlance, this type of trade was called *A'bingge* business, *A'bingge* being the common slang term for a soldier. At the risk of imposing a very different sensibility, I translate the term as G. I. Joe business. The peculiar demographic situation on Jinmen, where soldiers outnumbered civilians, turned the civilian population of the island into petty traders on an extraordinary scale. Despite various state-mediated development schemes, it was G. I. Joe business that became the mainstay of the local economy, with diverse consequences for local life.

Though Jinmen people do not include it within the category of G. I. Joe business, the most widespread form of economic engagement with the garrison was the produce trade. There are no reliable statistics for this type of commercial agriculture, but many, perhaps most, rural families were involved, further testimony to the extraordinary entrepreneurialism driven by the military presence. The trade began even before the fall of the mainland, during the troop build-up of 1949. Many informants relate how they were inspired to sell produce to the troops because of the huge price increase as demand exploded. As one man recalls, "At that time there were so many soldiers. People were amazed at how much they ate, how much they consumed. Take vegetable sellers for example. Any extra vegetables were quickly sold out . . . If you sold vegetables for a day you could make three or even five ounces of silver."[34] Market gardening was particularly attractive to many families because it required no capital and promised quick returns. "There were already lots of soldiers then, so I planned to go into business. I talked it over with Mother and she disagreed, because we had no capital, so I gave it up. At that time, the troops needed to eat vegetables, but there were very few people on Jinmen who grew vegetables. When the cooks bought vegetables, a whole silver dollar could buy only three *jin* [about five pounds] of cabbage, so I started growing cabbage." Farmers concentrated on fast-growing vegetables, and they were eventually able to grow produce from seed to market in only a few weeks. The JCRR-supported agricultural experimental station helped these efforts by importing and disseminating information on new vegetable strains. Hong Hongcheng, who quit school as a teenager in the early 1950s, recalls that at that time raising vegetables was considered a highly rewarding career. "At that time, a civil servant earned a salary of NTD350 per month. You could make NTD400–NTD500 a day [growing vegetables]. My uncle graduated from middle school and got a job in the county government. My grandmother wouldn't let him take it. She said, 'If you go, your salary won't be enough to raise your brothers and sisters.' " By the time Hong had married and received a share of the household estate when it was divided in 1961, the family's holdings were put entirely to vegetables.[35]

A daily produce market soon developed in Jincheng. Farmers from all over the island would converge there every morning. Wang Yingchuan remembers:

In the years around 1970, I grew a lot of vegetables. I sold most of them to the troops. Every morning I'd get out of bed really early, usually at 3 or 4 in the morning . . . If you got there early you could get a good spot, and you could have a look around or have a snooze. Before the market opened, the vegetable whole-salers would come take a look; they'd buy your whole load, then sell it to the troops. You could sell yourself, but that would take more time, and you might not sell everything. In the early days business was good . . . I could sell all [my produce] to a single company. Usually the deal was for the whole load. If they bought Chinese cabbage one day, then everybody ate Chinese cabbage; if they bought leafy cabbage the next day, then everyone ate leafy cabbage.[36]

For the army, there was no getting around the need to ship ammunition, grain, fuel, and processed goods to supply the garrison on Jinmen. But the independent decisions of Jinmen farmers to grow and sell vegetables did relieve the army of one concern. Another foodstuff that needed to be supplied was fresh meat. There was little tradition of raising pigs on Jinmen; in 1952 there were fewer than 800 animals on the island.[37] (This was no doubt a significant decrease from 1949 because much local livestock was stolen by soldiers in the chaotic period after the Battle of Guningtou.) By the early 1950s, the JDHQ was shipping about 2,000 pigs per month to Jinmen to meet local needs. Once again, local farmers responded to the new incentives created by the troop presence, and reduced the burden on the state by going into the pig-rearing business. Hu Lian comments that by the time he returned to Jinmen in 1958 for his second tour of duty as commanding officer (CO), "there were more pigs than people."[38] This was a slight exaggeration. In the mid-1950s Jinmen farmers raised around 20,000 pigs.[39] "In those days, if you raised eight pigs you were pretty well off. We had twelve, and four of them were killed in the [1958] bombing."[40]

In a pattern of economic activity that is common to highly militarized societies, the most successful raisers of pigs and the largest number of pigs were in villages located near military bases. Mash made from sorghum or sweet potato was the main feed for pigs, but pigs grew faster when they were also fed slops, the spoilage, leftovers, and waste from human food consumption. The richest slops were those discarded by the army canteens. On such rich feed, piglets could be raised to a size of 200 pounds and be ready for slaughter in six to eight months.[41] There is a joke told about a farmer who fed the pigs on nightsoil that he collected from the soldiers' toilets. Once when units were being rotated, he grew concerned that he might not have enough food for his pigs. So he foolishly began asking questions about the size of the unit being transferred into the nearby base. Of course, this raised suspicions that he was a Communist agent, and he was locked up.[42]

In the name of improving rural hygiene, under the Model County campaign farmers were ordered to remove pigs from their homes or makeshift sties adjacent to their homes and raise them in purpose-built pigsties. The sties themselves became part of the larger system of hygiene work and inspection. As ward head Yang Yonghe recalls, the hygiene demands were completely unrealistic, further evidence of the arbitrariness of the WZA system. "There was a hygiene inspection every week. It was so strict that there couldn't even be flies in the pigsty. If any flies were found you'd be told you were damaging hygiene, and for sure you'd be punished."[43] Regardless of the degree to which one considers hygiene socially constructed, the rules on pigsties show once again how the militarizing regime produced some of the very problems that it sought to address. Jinmen villagers did not raise their pigs in their homes because they were uncivilized and backward. They raised pigs in their homes because they were afraid, with much justification, that their pigs would be stolen. It was improvements in military discipline and in ensuring adequate provisions for the troops that made them accept the order to build dedicated sties, not improvements to their level of civilization.

Two entrepreneurs

The other side to G. I. Joe business was the retail and service trade. The vast majority of these businesses were located in the island's villages. In the early 1950s, they provided goods and services to the soldiers stationed in their own homes; as the troops moved out to newly built bases, village shops became their chief recreation sites. The shops typically charged about twice what comparable goods and services cost in town, but they had the unbeatable advantage that the soldiers could visit them in their spare time without taking a bus into town.

Zhai Fen was born in 1953. Though compulsory elementary education was introduced when she was fourteen years old, "I only went to school for a few days, and then I didn't have time." Her mother had died when she was eight, so Zhai had to look after her two younger siblings. By the time she was a teenager, she was also an important breadwinner, doing laundry for the nearby soldiers. At age twenty-two, she was married to a nearby villager. "My father liked him, so he chose him. He was introduced by a matchmaker, and I had to marry him. I didn't want to marry him. I wanted to be a nun." When she married, she moved to her husband's home village where there were more soldiers. "There were more barracks there; there were soldiers all around." So the volume of her business expanded, from some twenty uniforms a day to 200 to 300. Soon she had enough savings, over NTD5,000, to open an ice cream shop. The shop played music for the customers; she taught herself to read from the liner notes of the records. Later she reinvested profits from the ice cream shop into a variety store, and then a snack shop. After about a decade, her husband moved to Taiwan to work as a construction laborer. Zhai soon followed. She closed up her businesses on Jinmen and set up a roadside food stall selling local Jinmen-style snacks in Taiwan. With the family savings, they bought a house in Taibei, where her four children now live. But she never cared for life in the city, so she abandoned the food stall, returned to Jinmen and resumed her laundry business. Today she runs a souvenir stall outside one of Jinmen's main museums (among her wares is contraband smuggled from the mainland – an issue to be discussed in the final chapters). "Now I go back and forth all the time; if I'm not here I just close up the stall . . . Where do I like best? Wherever I am, that's the best."[44]

The story of the Sancenglou, "Three Story Building," of Little Jinmen illustrates how the G. I. Joe business shifted in the later years of martial law. Its proprietor is Xiao Shengyi, born in 1949. His parents, like so many other residents, had begun doing laundry and selling drinks and cigarettes soon after 1949. He attended only primary school, and went into the business in the early 1960s. In the 1970s and 1980s, Xiao's wife ran the shop, while he ran an unlicensed taxi business using their goods truck. This business grew out of his habit of giving rides back to base to soldiers who had come in to shop in the store. When soldiers went on leave, Xiao's day started very early. "I'd drive them from their unit to the battalion headquarters [to get the necessary stamps on their pass], then to regiment HQ, then to division HQ, and then to the docks. Then I'd come back and start cooking." Their memories of this period are of unrelenting toil. "We didn't even close for the [Chinese] New Year's holiday. In fact, we were even busier than usual. The army units all had competitions and we provided the food and wine for the meals. Our only vacation was on Glory of Ju day [the weekly political education session when troops were confined to barracks]." Business was busiest when new conscripts arrived. "Their officers would bring them here to show them where the store was. There would be seventy or eighty of them at a time. They just had to line up; how could I keep track of them all?" When units were rotated around the island, "this was really good for us too, because the newly arrived units had to buy everything. The departing unit would leave nothing behind; they'd even smash the light bulbs."[45]

In 1987, using the profits from the business, Xiao and his wife built a three-story building. The first floor housed the variety store, the second a restaurant, and the third was the family's living quarters. The construction cost around NTD2 million, paid in cash, for no bank would issue mortgages for property on Jinmen. It was the highest structure in the village. When an officer came to inspect the house, to make sure there was the requisite bomb shelter and firing holes, "he said to us, 'You're so rich. Why don't you just move to Taiwan?' This was very funny. If we moved to Taiwan, who would sell things to the troops?" At the height of the business, Xiao reports, monthly income was about NTD300,000. They hired three young women from the village to help, at a salary of NTD20,000. "In the old days there were lots of ways to make money. If you wanted an old lady to come in and tidy up for you, you had to pay her NTD10,000 a month, and she still wouldn't want to do it."[46]

The most common businesses according to records from 1959 were barber shops, bath houses, tea shops, snack shops, laundries, pool halls, book rental shops, and variety stores selling daily necessities.[47] Laundries were probably the most numerous of all. These informal businesses were unregistered, so there is no way of knowing how many families in total did laundry for the soldiers. In the village of Guan'ao, which had a population of about 1,000, anthropologist Zhang Mingchun found eighteen families who took in laundry for the troops. Of all the G. I. Joe businesses, laundry work was the easiest to enter. It required almost no capital; one had only to spread the word that one was willing. "I didn't really have a shop. I just worked very hard. I put up a sign with a few characters, and the soldiers dropped off their clothes. I washed about twenty or thirty sets a day."[48] Laundries were expected to do minor repairs as well, so sewing machines became part of the normal dowry for village women. "My wife washed the clothes; my daughter mended. I can't remember how many sets she did per day; I just remember that she washed all morning and ironed all afternoon."[49]

Besides laundries, the other ubiquitous business was the variety store. Like laundries, it is impossible to determine just how many variety stores there were, because many were unregistered. But Zhang Mingchun found thirteen in Guan'ao, accounting for over a third of all G. I. Joe businesses. This too is surely an understatement, for some variety shops were nothing more than a table set up in the front of a courtyard. Products included dried goods such as rice, tinned food, and cooking oil, and items for daily use such as soap, cigarettes, toilet paper, stationery, and, later, telephone cards. Village variety stores were unusual among G. I. Joe businesses in that while they existed to meet the demand from the soldiers, they were also patronized by local residents. The typical division of labor in a household with a variety store was that the husband was responsible for purchasing goods from wholesalers in Jincheng town and carrying them back to the village on foot, using a carrying pole, while the wife handled shop operations. Many variety stores also had snack shops attached. They were mostly informal and had no set menus. The women of the household simply cooked fried rice, noodles, or dumplings. Business was best on days when the canteens were closed and soldiers were expected to eat field rations. Snack shops could also provide more elaborate meals – the custom among soldiers was to hold a series of dinners for friends during their time on Jinmen: a feast when a soldier had one year of service remaining, when he had 100 days remaining (this was called "breaking one hundred"), and on one's last night on Jinmen.

With the passage of time, more businesses were set up to provide entertainment. Until the arrival of karaoke and, later, video games in the 1980s and 1990s, billiards was the most popular form of recreation on Jinmen, and many villagers set up small-scale pool halls with one or two tables in their homes. Because of the cost of the table and equipment, about NTD3,500 in the 1960s, pool halls required rather more capital to open, and it was often successful storekeepers who diversified into the pool business. Unlike laundries and variety stores, pool halls more commonly hired outside labor. The soldiers liked to be served by young women, and so many pool halls hired a teenage attendant.[50]

The vast majority of businesses were family businesses, located in the family home and staffed with family labor. Women typically provided most of the labor, which they balanced with childcare and domestic chores. Men who were employed outside the home worked after hours, and farmers in the slack periods. Children also helped after school, and the need to work in family businesses is often the reason given for why someone dropped out of school at a young age. G. I. Joe business was also family business because of its sources of capital. Capital usually came from agricultural income or savings, or loans from family members. At the height of the militarized period, G. I. Joe business income typically accounted for most household income, though most households continued to earn other sources of income as well. Because of the need for surveillance and discipline, the various campaigns for civic construction, and the promotion of education for propaganda reasons, the public sector on Jinmen rapidly grew very large relative to the economy as a whole. By 1954, there were already over 400 public sector employees; the number rose to over 1,000 by the late 1960s, and remained at that level for the next two decades. With the total number of households fluctuating between 6,000 and 10,000 in the 1960s to the 1980s, the implication is that about 10 to 15 percent of Jinmen households had one member receiving a government salary.[51] Zhang Mingchun found that it was precisely these families that were most likely to open a shop.[52]

G. I. Joe petty commerce militarized the labor of all family members in the sense that it was organized to produce goods and services for soldiers. The labor system in G. I. Joe businesses resembles that in other, less militarized Asian societies, in that low-cost female and child labor was utilized by family business such that there was no clear line between work and home and no overall ethos of production. G. I. Joe business had a complex effect on gender arrangements and expectations in Jinmen families. My impression is that it was businesses in the middle range that had the most destabilizing impact. In families where the wife simply took in some laundry, or sold a small quantity of sundry items from a stand in the home, business participation and the greater female contribution to household income typically did not lead to a breakdown in traditional patriarchal arrangements. Nor were traditional arrangements dramatically undermined in large-scale operations like Maestro Wu's, in which the male members of the family labored full-time, and women worked for the business on top of their domestic tasks, often out of sight of the customers. The situation in such enterprises resembles the family workshops of Taiwan, where new economic practices often reinforced rather than weakened existing family patterns.[53] Where G. I. Joe business does seem to have had a big impact is on families like Zhai Fen's. Her business was the main source of household income. Though she was married through a matchmaker on her father's instructions, her economic role gave her unexpected authority in the household. "I decided most things in our family. He [my husband] did not have a lot of responsibilities; he was just like an employee." Her husband concurs, and indicates moreover that her decision-making authority extended beyond business activities to broader family decisions. "Because she earned money, she could make decisions . . . for example about buying property. From choosing the location, to making the final decision, it was she who made all the decisions. I just went along once she had made up her mind; I respected her decision."[54]

While the businesses look very simple, in fact their proprietors were constantly searching for innovation and diversification. In order to grow beyond a very low threshold, most families had to combine multiple types of businesses. Typically, G. I. Joe business began with laundry, and then expanded into other areas such as snacks, entertainment, a variety store, hair-cutting, and so on. Some families were simultaneously involved in five or six different lines of business. "We sold drinks, washed clothes, sold ices, ran pool tables. Our house was like a department store; whatever the soldiers needed, we supplied."[55] Some of the more successful retail businesses later expanded into the wholesale business, using capital and connections acquired in the 1950s to supply the increased number of businesses in the 1960s and after. Because barriers to entry were low, there was fierce competition, so families felt compelled to move constantly into new product lines and even new lines of business to maintain an advantage. One of the newest products introduced in snack shops in recent years has been fried instant noodles – a package of noodles is fried with eggs, vegetables, and meat. As the proprietor of one snack shop wrote, "If you don't know what fried instant noodles are, and if you've never tasted them, then you're really behind the times on Jinmen."[56]

Because the G. I. Joe business economy was mostly unregulated, there are no reliable statistics on the overall size of the trade. The dissident journal *Jinmen Reports* estimated that in the late 1980s, military consumption pumped NTD200 million into the Jinmen economy each month. When a division of 10,000 troops was withdrawn, expenditures dropped by NTD50 million per month.[57] This dependence on the troop presence made for one of the great paradoxes of Jinmen society during the period of militarization and one of the many ways in which local life was geopoliticized. Geopolitical tension was good for business. More tension meant more troops, and more troops benefited the local economy. The more the situation calmed, the worse off the residents of the island became. This paradox reached a climax in the early 1990s, when demilitarization threatened the entire economy of Jinmen, and forced the central and local governments and the civilians of the island to look for new ways to make a living.

Problems of G. I. Joe business

The combat village program and the laying of mines reshaped the geography of the island. So did G. I. Joe business. The town of Shanwai was

Fig. 9.4 Shanwai in the 1950s (by permission of Jinmen county cultural bureau)

largely a product of the trade with the soldiers. It was first planned in 1951 to resettle families displaced by the Battle of Guningtou. But G. I. Joe business drew more and more residents to Shanwai [Figs. 9.4, 9.5]. In the early years of martial law five other villages also underwent dramatic growth.[58] The reason is straightforward; all were located near divisional headquarters. As a resident reports, "Dingbao used to be considered a prosperous village. When there were a lot of troops stationed on Jinmen, Dingbao was the headquarters for the Jinxi division. At the time, the village had a cinema; there were a lot of army consumers. Lots of people from other towns raced to Dingbao to open shops. It was like there was a sea of people."[59]

Civilian populations congregate around military bases in many places in the world, because bases offer defensive protection, or because they create economic opportunities, or both. But military bases make dangerous neighbors. In combat, they draw the fire of the enemy. Even in peacetime, they house weapons and heavy equipment that make for frequent accidents. And soldiers themselves are often dangerous to civilians. The relocation and reorientation of Jinmen's populace around the military

Fig. 9.5 Shanwai today (photo by Jiang Bowei)

bases for the sake of commerce is one important indication of the way
daily life became militarized. Once the troops had moved out of people's
homes and into their own barracks, G. I. Joe business was the chief
medium in which soldiers and civilians interacted. A soldier stationed on
Jinmen in the 1980s told how he was struck by the mutual reliance of the
soldiers and civilians. "For the enlisted men, the shops were a kind of
refuge" from their officers.[60] There are many stories of warm relations
between soldiers and shops they patronized; older residents recall being
invited to feasts at the barracks on national holidays, and exchanging gifts
of seasonal foods. Relations were often highly informal; regular customers
would do their own cooking in the shops, or simply watch videos or television when these became widespread. Soldiers and shopkeepers were also
natural allies against their common enemy, the military police (MPs).
"After curfew, the MPs would come and look for any soldiers. They'd
hide inside [our shop] and watch television . . . We'd be the sentries, if we
saw MPs outside the village, we'd tell the soldiers – hurry up, come inside.
One time, someone poured a bucket of water down from a window onto
the MPs. Sometimes we would drive the truck right up to the door and
sneak the soldiers in. If we ever got caught, we'd just say, 'We're in business; if the soldiers come in, that's their mistake.' "[61]

But G. I. Joe business also created a range of problems and tension
between civilians and the soldiers themselves. A common source of

tension was store credit. Soldiers were often in debt to the local shopkeepers, repaying their debt every month when they received their pay or when their family in Taiwan sent them money. Every shop had a secret set of books in which the names of customers and their debts were recorded. Xiao Shengyi estimates that he typically held debts of NTD2 million at any one time, a few thousand dollars for each of the thousand or so nearby soldiers. The books were secret because it was forbidden to extend credit to soldiers. Police officers frequently reminded village officials and shopkeepers that credit was prohibited, "in order to maintain the reputation of the army and prevent conflicts between civilians and soldiers." Periodically, shopkeepers were asked to sign a voluntary pledge that they would not offer credit.[62] It was an open secret that every shop had to give credit or risk losing business. But because life on Jinmen would become unbearable if a soldier could not enjoy the comforts of the nearby shops, default was rare. Xiao Shengyi recalls only three major episodes; in each case the soldiers had accumulated huge debts of over NTD100,000. Nonetheless, credit and the recovery of debt was a constant source of friction for anyone involved in G. I. Joe business.

Another source of concern to local officials was the diversion of military goods into the civilian economy. Chen Bingren identified the illicit sale of military matériel as one of the two chief disciplinary problems during his tenure. Generally, the offenses were small in scale, at least at first. Old and discarded uniforms were sold into society at large, making it impossible to distinguish clearly between soldiers and civilians. Or a peddler who sold vegetables to army canteens began to buy overstock or past date goods such as tinned meats from the canteens and then resell them. Everyone treated the prohibition on resale of military goods as a bit of a joke. But then the peddler moved into the illegal trade in oil, and this was more serious. Civilians, who needed fuel for agricultural machinery and fishing boats, were warned of serious punishments for illegal purchase of military fuel in 1963, but the problem was perennial; a decade later residents were again being exhorted at village assemblies not to purchase fuel for military use.[63]

The larger concern was the potential danger to military discipline and respect for military authority. A police report on the problem of civilian shopkeepers conniving with soldiers to undermine curfew and the MPs who enforced it calls for better education of civilians, "so they will not harm military discipline and public order." Precisely because the shops were refuges from the army, they could easily become the site of forbidden activities, such as gambling. The "voluntary" pledge by which shopkeepers certified that they would not offer credit also included clauses that gambling would not be allowed. One of the ghost stories told about

Jinmen illustrates how the issue of gambling intertwined several concerns about military discipline and civil–military relations. The story is set in a mahjong den located on the second floor of a variety store. As one of the characters says, "mahjong dens are found everywhere on Jinmen." The protagonists are three soldiers who spend the night playing with a stranger. When they have cleaned him out and he leaves, their winnings turn suddenly into the paper money that is burned for the spirits of the dead. They inquire with the shopkeeper, but he did not see the stranger enter or leave. But when they tell him the stranger's name, the shopkeeper recognizes him as an old customer who had racked up enormous gambling debts, both to soldiers and local ruffians. Overwhelmed, he had committed suicide shortly before his service on Jinmen was over.[64]

Besides gambling, G. I. Joe businesses were also sites of drunkenness and this led frequently to fighting. Zhai Fen explains that she once had to break up a fight at her snack shop. "Once a group of soldiers was eating. One of them was leaving Jinmen, and they had gathered to send him off. I don't know why, but they started to fight. We pulled them apart and tried to calm things down. If there had been an investigation they would have been punished. Also, they would have been confined to barracks, which would have been bad for business. So we calmed them down."[65] If civilians were involved, fighting was an offense serious enough to have one sent to reform camp. This seems to have become more of a problem in the later years of martial law, and was especially troubling because it highlighted the undercurrent of tension between soldiers and civilians that threatened the image of unity and common purpose that was so central to Jinmen's political functions.

The heavy reliance of the civilian populace on G. I. Joe business created an additional resource to control that populace. Because this control was exerted directly by the military, it does not show up in the civic government archive. But details of it emerge in the oral history and the dissident press. The broadsheet *Jinmen Reports* ran several stories in the early 1990s that illustrate this control. For example, in May 1991, a fight broke out between five drunk soldiers and two civilians. The following day, villagers were informed that the village would be off-limits to soldiers for one month. MPs were stationed at all entrances to the village to keep the soldiers out. A similar incident occurred two years later when a dispute at the Little Jinmen pier led MPs to ban soldiers from local shops.

The capacity to regulate G. I. Joe business was not only used to ensure self-policing by residents; it could also be employed to smooth over tension between soldiers and civilians. The import of motorized vehicles into Jinmen was strictly controlled for military reasons, for too many civilian cars might interfere with the movement of military vehicles. In the

1980s, successive COs authorized the import of about eighty cars to serve as taxis. The archives contain details of the lottery that was used to allocate licenses. By 1984, there were officially 200 taxis on Jinmen. But *Jinmen Reports* states that there were in fact 201 cabs operating. The story of the extra cab was that a village woman had been gathering empty bottles outside a barracks when she was raped and killed by soldiers. As part of the settlement of the matter, her husband was issued a taxi license.[66]

The reliance on G. I. Joe business made locals very vulnerable to changes in the provision of services to the troops and even more to the overall number of troops. The first issue arose in 1979, when in response to complaints about the high cost of goods on Jinmen relative to Taiwan, the army decided to expand the network of army stores where soldiers could purchase goods for personal use at subsidized prices. This aroused great concern among villagers, who appealed to officials not to harm their livelihood in this way.[67] But far more serious was the withdrawal of troops from specific bases, and eventually from the island as a whole. Xiao Shengyi recalls the drawdown in troops from Little Jinmen as the beginning of an irreversible decline in his family's business. "In 1997, an entire battalion was withdrawn. This was the first place on Little Jinmen from which the troops were pulled out. There wasn't much warning; the order was issued and a month later the troops were gone. So we started drawing down our stocks." They have never been replenished.[68] Today the settlements that sprang up around army bases that have been abandoned are ghost towns.

Conclusions

With the exception of labor migration to Taiwan, militarized modernity did not mean the incorporation of Jinmen into systems of global capitalism. Rather, Jinmen after 1949 was largely isolated from the rest of the world. But Jinmen was not cut off from the global circulation of ideas. The economic policy of the Jinmen authorities after 1949 was the local inflection of a global discourse of development. Throughout the region, in both Communist and non- or anti-Communist states, states undertook to reform land ownership and guide industrial development. But on Jinmen these policies were not primarily aimed at economic results, except in the sense that reducing dependency on imports from Taiwan served military interests. Nor were the goals political in the narrow sense of being aimed to bolster internal support for the regime and prevent infiltration by revolutionary groups. Rather, these were policies aimed at demonstrating the superiority of the sovereign government of Jinmen over its sworn enemy and alternative. The WZA was the development state as geopolitical propaganda. On the whole, these policies were not very effective. In many ways the Taiwanese economic miracle simply bypassed Jinmen. Because much of the local economy was informal, it is difficult to make meaningful comparisons, but income levels on Jinmen lagged well behind Taiwan. The basic reasons for this are obvious. For geopolitical reasons there was almost no industrial investment on the island. While there had been massive infrastructural investment on the island, it was driven largely by military concerns. The gradual divestiture of state economic assets and the consequent increase in entrepreneurship that were crucial in the development of Taiwan and more recently of the PRC did not occur on Jinmen. The few large-scale businesses on the island remain state-owned. Many young people have left the land; most have moved to Taiwan. Even with this demographic outflow, many residents continued to be farmers. A specific household division of labor, in which one member was a public servant, teacher, or soldier while the others continued to farm, became very common. Large numbers of children abandoned their education to help with farm work or the family G. I. Joe business, further complicating the notion that Jinmen was simply pursuing an alternative path to modernity. Though state-mediated development had not modernized Jinmen's economy to anything like the same degree as Taiwan, people's livelihood nonetheless saw dramatic improvement. But this improvement should not be ascribed to state policy so much as to individual and household entrepreneurship. Petty capitalism was irrepressible. It was the decisions of thousands of civilian families in response to a newly created set of incentives that boosted civilian incomes.[69] Their actions structured a massive transfer from the Ministry of Defense to the civilian economy, via procurement budgets and soldiers' salaries [Fig. 9.6].

Framed in this way, the story of Jinmen also seems to anticipate the effects of globalization on the region. Mark Berger argues that the globalization project can really be understood as the eclipse of discourses of development that focus on the role of the state by neo-liberal approaches that make the profit-maximizing and consumption-oriented individual the universal subject of development. Berger adds that this does not imply, as some predicted, the end of the nation-state, but rather a shift in its role.[70] Geopoliticization and militarization made this process distinctive on Jinmen.

There were political consequences to the distinctive economic situation on Jinmen. In the 1970s and 1980s, overall income levels were rising, but the nascent middle-class was entirely dependent on the military presence. There was a relatively large number of bureaucrats in the civilian and military organs, but many of them either maintained homes on or planned to

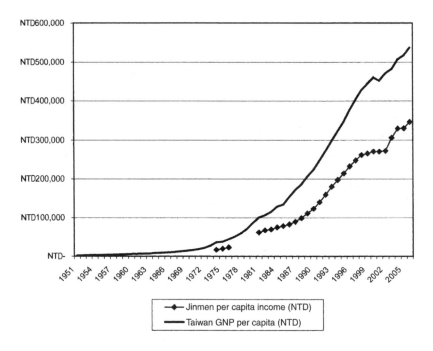

Fig. 9.6 Per capita income for selected years, Taiwan vs. Jinmen[71]

move to Taiwan. So the middle-class did not play the same role in pushing for political reform, democratization, and demilitarization as it did in other places, including Taiwan. Finally, the high levels of dependence on military spending, itself a function of geopoliticization, left the island extremely vulnerable to changes in the geopolitical context, changes that would profoundly reshape island society in the 1990s. In this regard Jinmen's experience looks very much like that of other military base economies around the world, including in the superpowers.[72] The interconnection between national security threats, real or imagined, and economic development creates similar uncertainties and challenges in different places, though the precise outcomes may differ. On Jinmen as elsewhere, the geopolitical struggle between nation-states was largely responsible for the context in which residents operated, but it was the decisions of these residents that largely determined their economic fates.

10   Women's lives: military brothels, parades, and emblems of mobilized modernity

In Lü Jiang's 1984 short story "Two Dads" ("*Liangge baba*"), a teacher in a southern Taiwanese village struggles to understand the complex family arrangements of one of his pupils. The child, he learns, was abandoned as an infant and adopted by a household consisting of two old soldiers from the mainland and their common wife. Though she is habitually drunk almost to the point of incoherence, the wife explains that she had been sold into prostitution by her parents at the age of thirteen. Many years later she found herself working in an army-run brothel on an offshore island that must be Jinmen, where she met the two clients who became her husbands. Together they now sought to build a new if unconventional life on Taiwan.[1] Lü does not get into details, but perhaps the woman might have worked in the brothel at Shamei, one of several abandoned brothels that can still be found on Jinmen. Today it is easy to scale its concrete walls. One enters a compound formed by two long buildings on either side. Each building is divided into a dozen identical rooms, with a number above each door. Rubble is strewn throughout the tiny rooms, many of which retain their original furniture – a double bed, a water basin, and a wardrobe. In one room are the scattered contents of files and account books. Together these two sources, one textual and one material, introduce us to a Jinmen institution, the military brothel, known colloquially as 831. Its history traces out the connections between militarization, sex, and gender in the martial law period.

Militarization on Jinmen was a gendered phenomenon, experienced differently by women and men. Women, like men, had to be mobilized to serve the nation. But mobilization took different forms for women and men. These differences were shaped by ideologies and underlying cultural logics about the different identities and behaviors that were appropriate to men and to women, and militarization in turn contributed to changing ideas of what was appropriate to each gender. Official documents and propaganda typically describe women in terms of two archetypes or symbols: the soldier and the wife-mother. Oral history, with both women and men, identifies two other categories: the prostitute and the

G. I. Joe entrepreneur. These are more than mere ideological constructions; they correspond closely to the actual ways in which women's relationships with society at large and specifically with the military were
articulated.[2] It was not only the soldiers but all four categories of women
who were militarized (G. I. Joe entrepreneurs have already been discussed
in the preceding chapter and are not dealt with further here). But, as
Enloe points out, women who serve the military differently tend not to see
themselves as bound together by shared womanhood or by shared militarization.[3] Membership in each category demanded a particular expression of the ideal of the self-sacrificing woman serving the nation. In this
chapter, I explore the various roles assigned to women in order to draw
attention to three themes. First, militarization rested on the gendering of
society toward certain forms of femininity and masculinity. Second,
Jinmen as elsewhere saw the construction of a patriarchal conception of
women as the embodiment of tradition and cultural authenticity within
modernity. But militarization complicated this conception.[4] Third, the
gendering of militarized modernity was not simply imposed by the state,
but also involved the agency of the women involved, for whom this gendering could play a crucial role in the formation of their own subjectivity.
While questions of the different expectations of men and women in the
war zone run through this work, it is still useful to isolate the issue of
gender and gender roles, because isolating sex and gender as a specific
and significant domain for regulation and reform is precisely what army
and civilian authorities did. We can then see more clearly how the consequences of these state efforts intertwined with other issues.

The year 1949 was a turning point for gender relations as for so many
other aspects of local life. But to make a tidy juxtaposition between a traditional gender system before martial law and modernity thereafter would
be a gross oversimplification. While people often say that life on the island
was very traditional before 1949, Jinmen was hardly stuck in eternal and
unchanging ways. Newspapers from the 1930s are full of accounts of
efforts to create modern women on Jinmen. Nevertheless when the soldiers arrived, it was to a society in which marriages were arranged and
women were expected to mostly avoid contact with men outside their
family. The billeting of soldiers in civilian homes was thus an immediate
challenge to local standards of propriety, fracturing familiar dualisms
between public and private, inner and outer.[5] The greater concern, one
shared by people living in militarized societies everywhere, was the threat
of sexual violence. Rape was the silent consequence of the intersection of
the homosocial world of the army with the civilian populace.

In the tense atmosphere of the early 1950s sexual violence by soldiers
against civilians seems to have been common. "There were many women

raped in Shanhou, Shanwai, and in Jincheng. Everybody talked about it. Soldiers who committed rape were punished very severely, but it happened anyway. The girls who were raped always left for Taiwan. They couldn't stay here because everyone knew what had happened." Informants recall horrifying stories like that of a woman shot on her wedding night by a soldier she had rejected, or the wife of an Overseas Chinese killed along with her two children when she refused a soldier's advances, or the man killed trying to prevent the rape of his daughter-in-law by a soldier.[6] One of the reasons for the positive impression of Hu Lian in local memory is that he is credited with imposing discipline on the soldiers and therefore freeing civilians of the scourge of rape, along with many other problems. In the eyes of many Jinmen informants, Hu's main method to deal with the problem of rape was to create a vehicle for official military prostitution.

Women as prostitutes

The story of the military brothel system allows us to trace a history of the regulation of sexual relations between soldiers and women. As far as I have been able to ascertain, no women civilians from Jinmen were directly involved as sex workers (some local men were involved in the administration of commercial sex, as we shall see). Two factors nonetheless argue for its inclusion in this book. First and most important, the military brothel system was an important part of the overall regime of militarization and management of army–civilian relations. Second, the system had significant consequences for the women of Jinmen even if they were not directly involved in it. I have chosen not to try to interview former sex workers. Even without their testimony, the memoirs and oral history of local men and women, together with other documents from a variety of sources, make it possible to reconstruct the history of military prostitution on Jinmen. The main shortcoming of this approach is that by excluding the voices of the most central and most vulnerable participants it carries the risk of minimizing or obscuring the more brutal and dehumanizing elements of the system.

Chen Changqing, who today runs a bookshop in Shanwai town, became a clerk in the political affairs office of the Jinmen Defense Headquarters (JDHQ) in 1965, at the age of nineteen. There he was responsible for the various social welfare provisions for the garrison, including army stores, movie theaters, and on-base barbers and laundries. His most important job was to administer the military brothel system, formally known as "soldiers' paradise" (*junzhong leyuan*) or "special assignation teahouse" (*teyue chashi*), but always referred to as "831." Most people say that 831 was the

Fig. 10.1 Military brothel in the 1950s. The couplet to either side reads: "serving the three armed forces/lifting morale" (by permission of Jinmen county cultural bureau)

number of the brothels' dedicated telephone exchange, but Chen says this is wrong (and he can recall the telephone numbers of the old brothels to support this). He says the name comes from the Chinese telegraphic code for a vulgar character for vagina, 83111. In the military, he says, 831 became the slang term for a woman.[7]

The founding of the brothels is routinely credited with a dramatic reduction in rape. "The special assignation teahouses made for a big improvement in public order on Jinmen." "When the army first came to Jinmen, there was no discipline. There were many cases of fighting, of theft, and of rape . . . In 1951 the first soldiers' paradise was set up in Jincheng . . . Only then did the number of rapes go down significantly, and public safety was secured."[8] New brothels were established as troop levels rose, and by the time Chen took up his position, there was a total of ten, with between ten and forty sex workers each [Fig. 10.1]. The head of the 831 system in the early years was an old pimp and brothel owner from Shanghai. Most of his staff was demobilized soldiers, but some locals worked as guards, book-keepers, and caretakers. They were employees of the War Zone Administration (WZA), whose Fifth Bureau was responsible for administering the 831. Unlike some other twentieth-century societies, where careful efforts were typically made to create the impression that the military and by extension the state was not directly involved in the sale of sex, the brothels were unambiguously part of the army. This makes it relatively easy to situate the 831 in the larger project of militarization, to uncover its links to strategies, administrative frameworks, and profits. The JDHQ budget for 1954 contains a line item for military brothels, covering the costs of constructing new brothels, recruiting new sex workers, and monitoring their hygiene and political consciousness. In practice though, according to Chen, the 831 were effectively run as a private business by the old pimp. "As long as he kept good relations with the commanding officer and the procurement officer of the key units, and submitted the profits each month, he basically ran the show."[9]

Many people on Jinmen believe that 831 sex workers were prostitutes who had been convicted of selling sex outside of the licensed prostitution system on Taiwan. A 1960 magazine article includes an interview with a young woman who reports that she was arrested for street-walking on Taiwan and given the choice of jail or service in a Jinmen 831. But there is more evidence that sex workers came voluntarily, and much information about the recruitment process.[10] Of course, histories of prostitution in other times and places teach us that it is very rarely if ever an occupation that is truly chosen freely, and typically the outcome of some combination of violence, poverty, and lack of options. Chen Ailing, a local woman whose father ran a snack bar in one of the brothels, recalls that most of the sex workers she knew shared similar tragic pasts – some had been sold into prostitution as teenagers; for others, poverty, illiteracy, and lack of alternatives explained their entry into commercial sex work. They had come to the offshore islands for different reasons. Some were too old to attract custom on Taiwan; others hoped that the austerity of Jinmen would make it easier to save money and leave the business sooner. Despite the brutality of the system many appreciated the anonymity of Jinmen. "No one knew them here; that's why they came." After school, Chen would help them write letters back to their families. "They would just want to say – everything is fine; I hope the family is well; I have a good job; I'm sending you some money."[11]

Besides the tragic pasts of the prostitutes, the system shared much in common with militarized prostitution in other parts of Asia, and the system's operation would have been familiar to US servicemen in Korea or elsewhere.[12] When a new prostitute arrived on Jinmen, her photograph was hung with the room number to which she was assigned on a board beside the ticket booth. A customer purchased a ticket for a specific number, and then waited his turn. Soldiers placed their helmet outside the numbered room to keep their place in line; one could tell a popular sex worker by the long row of helmets outside her door. In larger 831, pool tables or a snack shop were set up in the courtyard to entertain waiting soldiers. In the 1950s and 1960s the brothels were always busy; on days when whole units were given leave, the courtyard was "busier than a movie theater." Brothels were open seven days a week, with three shifts from 8 am to 11.30 am, 1 pm to 5 pm, and 6 pm until curfew at 9 pm. The only time off was on Thursdays, when the soldiers were busy with political education. In the 831, Thursday morning was devoted to sanitation and the afternoon to compulsory medical inspection by military doctors, before business as usual resumed for the evening shift.[13]

Without interviewing sex workers it is impossible to get a clear sense of the rate at which they serviced customers. The author Li Ao, whose writing is often deliberately sensationalist, writes that the typical figure was thirty to forty per day, that a woman who serviced more than fifty received a reward from the brothel, and that one brothel let off firecrackers when a new record was set. Sang Pinzai, a former child soldier who worked in a Mazu brothel in the late 1950s, gives a figure of sixty customers per day. Li Ao also reports that workers were punished, sometimes beaten, if they fell below a certain quota. Chen Changqing contradicts this, reporting that even a figure of ten to twenty customers a day is an exaggeration and that women who did not service sufficient customers were eventually simply sent back to Taiwan. Regulations from the mid-1980s, when the brothels had been fully privatized, set ten patrons per day as the minimum standard. Women who failed to produce 300 tickets per month for three months were subject to dismissal.[14]

In the 1950s, prices for sex were NTD10 for enlisted men and NTD15 for officers, at a time when monthly salaries for soldiers ranged from NTD7 to NTD12, and from NTD18 up for officers. Chen recalls some old soldiers boasting that they spent their entire salaries on visiting the 831. The next date for which there is reliable information is 1986, when a JDHQ report gives the figures of NTD250 for officers, NTD200 for non-coms, and NTD150 for enlisted men. While monthly salaries had by this time risen to several thousand dollars for an enlisted man, this did not necessarily mean that the cost of purchasing sex had fallen. One ticket now purchased a "session" of only seven minutes, so patrons typically purchased multiple tickets. Throughout the period as a general rule prostitutes kept 60 percent of their earnings, and 40 percent went to the 831.[15] This meant that there was a strong incentive for prostitutes to get around the ticketing system, and it was an open secret that they saw customers outside of normal hours for a discounted rate.

At its height, there were about 250 sex workers in the 831 system on Jinmen. Without reliable figures for the number of customers, it is not possible to determine the funds the system generated. But even a rough calculation, assuming the low figure of ten clients per day and that all clients were enlisted men, yields a figure of NTD750,000 gross per month. "The brothel managers could make great fortunes. Everyone knew that the biggest money was on Jinmen, because it was a captive market. Even girls who were past their prime on Taiwan could still make money." According to Chen, the profits remitted to the JDHQ funded most of the other welfare activities for garrison soldiers – including laundry, bathing, library, hair-cuts, theatrical entertainments, and prizes for the various competitions.[16]

The most flourishing time for the 831 system was the late 1950s, when troop numbers were at their highest and many of the soldiers were old mainlanders, who had little hope of marriage and family life before the Nationalist Party (KMT)'s already long-delayed defeat of the Communists and return to the mainland. In what seems to have been an ironic gesture toward this problem, there is reported to have been a special "wedding style" category of service in 831. For a higher price, the soldier was served a meal with the prostitute and allowed to stay overnight in her room.[17] Brothel rules forbade prostitutes from forming relationships with their customers but it did occasionally happen that a prostitute and a soldier developed a relationship and even married. Many of these couples moved to Taiwan but eventually returned to Jinmen. "The old people all know about it, but no one says anything."[18] It was more common for old soldiers to be frustrated in their advances. There is one well-known case of a prostitute who borrowed a large sum of money from an officer after promising to marry him, but then rejected him, whereupon he murdered her.[19] During the 1958 Crisis, like virtually all other aspects of life on Jinmen, the brothels shut down. But they reopened as soon as the PRC declared the cease-fire, giving rise to the joke that while the Communists "shoot on odd-numbered days; rest on even," the 831 "shoot on even-numbered days; rest on odd." But the system soon began a long decline. By the early 1960s, more and more of the garrison soldiers were conscripts from Taiwan. They were younger than the mainlanders; they served limited terms in the army, and many had girlfriends back on Taiwan. Most expected to return to Taiwan and marry. So while the 831 remained the only legitimate outlet for heterosexual desire during one's time in the army, it was not, as it was for the soldiers from the mainland, the only outlet they could expect for the rest of their lives. No longer were there soldiers who boasted that they spent their entire income on prostitutes.[20] As trade began to slow, recruitment dropped and the prostitutes grew older.

Relations between sex workers and local people seem to have varied over time and according to the age cohort of civilians. Perhaps because they have personal memories of the time before 831, older civilians typically report cordial relations. "They were just doing their job, why criticize them?" "We earned money from them so how could we be rude to them?"[21] But discrimination seems to have risen over time. Younger informants comment: "We civilians had a bad impression of the prostitutes; they stank of perfume, and they wore clothes that were too revealing. But they were big spenders, so nobody dared to be rude to their face. Except in the market, there was very little contact between the prostitutes and civilians." "We discriminated against them; if you sat down next to one of them, people would talk."[22] Even today, when locals talk about tourists from Taiwan, they sometimes say of a woman who is seen as inappropriately dressed, too aggressive, or too highly sexualized, "She looks just like an 831 girl."

For ordinary male residents of Jinmen, 831 were places of great mystery. It was strictly forbidden for civilians to use 831 services. Locals who worked in the 831 were constantly pressured to bring in their friends.[23] But this was a very serious offense; if discovered both the would-be patron and his contact were liable to be sent to reform camp. Village officials were frequently instructed to ensure that a rigid separation be maintained between the civilian population and commercial sex workers. A 1965 memo from the commanding officer (CO) instructs the military police (MPs) who guarded the brothels to be vigilant about non-military personnel sneaking into the brothels. The police were to keep a careful watch on local "bad elements" to ensure that they did not lure the sex workers out of the brothels to do business with civilians. This separation was a perennial concern. Over a decade later, the county magistrate repeated the order that civilians and service workers were not permitted to "engage in inappropriate sexual conduct." The rest of the order suggests a further analogy between prostitutes and soldiers. Just as G. I. Joe shops were forbidden from extending credit to soldiers, civilians were also ordered not to lend money to or gamble with prostitutes.[24]

The sex industry was classified, categorized, and structured to ensure that certain kinds of men only had sex with certain kinds of women. Distinctions, between officers and enlisted men, between soldiers and civilians, between those who earned a salary from the state and those who did not, had to be maintained. Military sex was disciplined sex. Regulations posted outside the brothels required patrons to be sober and to be dressed in an orderly way. Military sex was also "scientific" sex, with various measures to ensure health and hygiene. Some of these measures, such as the requirement that patrons drink water before sex and urinate afterwards, may not necessarily have accomplished their narrow objectives, the prevention of sexually transmitted diseases. But they reflect an impulse toward the regulation and management of sex for the larger public interest. In a military brothel on Taiwan, Li Ao found a set of rules including a section on "Enjoyment." Among the regulations to ensure sexual pleasure are the following:

> Inspect the service worker's health inspection certificate.
> Penetrate the vagina slowly to avoid injury.
> While taking your pleasure, do not forget your own knowledge and responsibilities.[25]

Sexual pleasure as a matter of knowledge, regulation, and self-discipline – could there be a more clear expression of Foucault's biopolitics, "the entry of life into history"?[26]

While any structured arrangement for sexual relations is by nature political, the military brothel system on Jinmen was politicized in a more narrow sense. The dominant objectives of militarization – vigilance against the foe and ultimate national recovery – were imbricated in the sexual encounter between soldiers and prostitutes, with each having their own role to play. Slogans posted on brothel walls reminded the soldier that the pursuit of pleasure should not interfere with his real goals. "Exercise restraint; Conserve time and energy; Enjoy yourself but remember your duty," were slogans that warned against allowing physical pleasure to weaken or distract the soldier. In one brothel, Li Ao reported seeing a poetic slogan intended to remind soldiers of their unfinished duty to recover the mainland:

> Be compassionate toward these powdered women by the bedside.
> Remember the fine ladies of the homeland.
> Seize the heights of ecstasy.
> But guard against lifelong regrets.[27]

For the sex workers themselves, commercial sex was represented as their distinctive sacrifice for the national purpose. As the couplet outside one 831 read "The hero risks his life on the frontier; the heroine contributes her body to serve the nation."[28] This construction of sex in military brothels as civic contribution was reinforced by the practice of singling out a small number of sex workers with exemplary performance and respect for regulations to receive an award on Women's Day, just as other outstanding civilian women were singled out for their own performance as wives or mothers.[29]

Military brothels are a product of the assumption that armies need prostitution to confirm militarized forms of masculinity.[30] Soldiers have sexual needs that must be met in order to keep them in fighting trim, and prostitutes should meet those needs in order to protect civilian women. As Chen Changqing puts it, "The 831 is an important part of Jinmen's history, because it provided a big help to Jinmen. After 1949, if the men hadn't been able to release their sexual energy, it would have led to violence. There would have been all sorts of cases of soldiers killing others or themselves. If it weren't for the 831, there would have been much more violence."[31] There was a brief period when pool halls were forbidden from hiring female attendants. This renewed concerns about the danger of rape. Said one official, "We improved the 831 by getting some more beautiful girls from Taiwan." Thus sexual desire in the military was a purely technical issue, requiring creative management to resolve. This comment also reminds us that the political authorities on Jinmen were also gendered. As Enloe's work shows, political elites are not just elites, they are typically male elites. Historians are more apt to see gender differences among people without much power. It is equally important to consider how those who make the decisions do so based on their own ideas about gender.[32]

The official rhetoric on military prostitution is perhaps where the WZA regime was at its most frank about the predatory nature of the military and the vulnerability of civilians. The 831 protected civilians who were in need of protection. This protection had to be provided, both for the sake of the civilians themselves and because sexual predation would harm civilian morale and cause tensions with the military. Military brothels are thus part of the larger vision of military–society relations. One of the basic techniques of militarization is the imposition of strict classificatory boundaries, for example between women who provide sexual services to soldiers and those who do not, and between those who are permitted to make use of prostitutes and those who are not. Problems are presumed to arise when these boundaries are ambiguous or indefinite. But efforts to seal off 831 from the society in which they were located were doomed to failure; local civilians were needed to provide services within the 831, and the 831 were an eternal source of fascination for local people. Civilian views of 831 sex workers, a mix of curiosity and disdain, generally did not connect them to their own militia service. But there is actually a strong parallel. Both involved the self-sacrifice of women in specific ways for the national cause. In other words, both were part of the gendering of militarization.

Military wives

Enloe calls the efforts that states employ to keep different groups of militarized women feeling separate from one another "maneuvers." WZA maneuvers were mostly successful. Local people sharply distinguish between 831 workers and local women. But marriage on Jinmen in the martial law period was also inseparably linked to 831, for together they comprised the two major legitimate modes of sexual relations between soldiers and civilians. Especially in the early years, there were considerable similarities. Both involved the commodification of sexual services. Marriage, on Jinmen as elsewhere, was not simply an institutionalized form of intimacy, but also a site where different types of exchanges took place, and these exchanges were profoundly affected by militarization. Propaganda material on Jinmen often referred to the destruction of the family by Mao Zedong and his supporters. If given the chance, they would surely do the same on Jinmen. But the real challenges to the traditional family on Jinmen came less from the mainland than from within, from the interaction of local society with the conditions of martial law.

Soldiers from the mainland began to marry local girls immediately after 1949. The phenomenon was never isolated as a distinct category in compiling statistics so the exact numbers are unknown. But according to Chen Zonglun, who dwelt at some length on the issue in his oral history testimony, and whom I will cite repeatedly below, the numbers were significant. "In 1949, after the ROC army was based on Jinmen, troops and civilians all lived under a single roof. So it was hard to avoid feelings from becoming aroused. Many women were married to soldiers; in total over one thousand. My own estimate would be that it was about one in five of the female population, a substantial number." In a clear example of the geopoliticization of life on Jinmen, the number of marriages rose as the international situation stabilized. Many older soldiers were already married on the mainland. Married or not, few soldiers were interested in marriage when Jinmen was simply a temporary stopping point in a long campaign. "Are you kidding?" said one old soldier, when asked about whether he considered marriage when he first arrived on Jinmen. "How could I marry? We were going to recover the mainland – how could you worry about getting a wife, about looking after a wife and raising kids?"[33] But as it became clear that they would not be returning to the mainland, more and more mainland soldiers sought to find local wives.[34] Thus the shifting geopolitical context in which militarization was embedded shaped changing patterns of marriage for women on Jinmen.

Informants, both former soldiers and their local wives, are typically reluctant to discuss their feelings about marriage. But we can learn something about the motivations for and consequences of soldier–civilian marriages by looking at what sorts of soldiers found wives on Jinmen. Many soldiers tried to form relationships with local women. The laundress Zhai Fen recalls, "when I washed clothes, they would put love notes in the pockets. They never said anything, they just put notes in the pockets, inviting me out to see a movie or whatever. When I washed the clothes, I would find the notes." But like most women in the G. I. Joe business she pretended not to see the notes and never responded to these advances.[35] Higher ranking officers and cadres had the most success forming relationships with and marrying young local women. When a village girl married a high officer in the 1960s, "the family's fortunes changed 180 degrees."[36] Most of the couples in this category were later transferred to other posts on Taiwan, and there are few of them living on Jinmen today. A second category was lower ranking officers and older enlisted men, like Zhang Zhichu. This group also includes soldiers who became village political instructors or deputy headmen. They often married older women, widows, and the abandoned wives of Overseas Chinese, to whom they were typically introduced by village headmen who hoped thereby to tie their loyalties more closely to the village (see chapter 3). Many of these men already had wives on the mainland, and this led to complications decades later, when retired servicemen were first allowed to return to the mainland. The third category, and one that informants most like to discuss, was canteen workers and cooks. They needed no matchmakers. In the 1950s they were attractive marriage partners because they could provide food, even if only canteen leftovers, when it was in short supply. Chen Huajin tells a joke about a captain and a cook who were pursuing the same local woman; the woman chose the cook. Why? "We [civilians] ate sweet potato, and they ate rice. In the morning, they had steamed bread to eat." Many informants say that in the 1950s, even officers had a hard time finding wives, but not canteen cooks. Young women had a common saying to reject the advances of unwelcome suitors: "I won't marry a cook or a squad leader; why would I marry a poor imp like you?"[37]

The marriages of local women to garrison soldiers had transformative effects on Jinmen society. But the motivations behind these marriages would be very familiar to scholars of the pre-modern Chinese family. To be considered legitimate, the marriage had to be sanctioned by if not arranged through the bride's parents or her in-laws in the case of a widow. These marriages, whether it was a widow finding support for herself and her children, or a younger woman marrying a canteen cook, fit neatly into older logics of using offspring, male and female, for purposes of family strategy, present and future. "If you married [your daughter] to a soldier, you would have enough to eat. It was like you sacrificed one daughter so her brothers and sisters could eat."[38]

Though romance with a local woman remained for soldiers a stereotype associated with service on Jinmen, the number of marriages with soldiers trailed off from a high point in the 1950s.[39] As the economic situation on Jinmen improved, local families no longer saw the marriage of their daughters as a sensible survival strategy.[40] But the main reason for the change was that the garrison was increasingly made up of conscripts from Taiwan who did not see the women of Jinmen as their only possible marriage partners. There was also growing recognition on the part of the authorities that relationships between soldiers and local women were harming morale and causing problems for the overall relationship between the army and local society. This was an extension of the same logic behind the creation of the 831 system. Just as brothels were needed to regulate sexual conduct and prevent rape, consensual sexual relations were also a source of tension and demanded a response. The solution seems to have been a deliberate campaign of disinformation. A rumor began to circulate that any Taiwanese soldier who married a local woman would be required to remain on Jinmen for ten years before he could return home. "It wasn't true; it was just meant to discourage soldiers from getting married here."[41]

Even though the number of marriages decreased, the tension created by the possibility of local women forming relationships with soldiers never disappeared completely. As late as 1978, we can find in the archives the case of a Jinmen man and his wife who quarreled over his refusal to grant her permission to travel to Little Jinmen. After the wife's disappearance the husband began to speculate that she was having an affair with an army lieutenant who had recently transferred to Little Jinmen. The episode entered the archival record when the cuckolded husband, apparently lashing out in frustration, speculated to the authorities that she might have left Jinmen without the proper exit permit.[42]

The large number of local women who married soldiers was a challenge to the masculinity of Jinmen men, who lived in a culture in which marriage was the fundamental marker of masculinity and a crucial marker of the passage to social adulthood. As Chen Zonglun puts it, the new situation altered the longtime pattern caused by male labor emigration, of women outnumbering men. "By the late fifties and early sixties, the population imbalance had reversed. In the marriage market, the situation was more males over females. Since the population was so unbalanced, there were many men who didn't find partners, and had to live a solitary life." The demographic imbalance created by marriages to soldiers caused an immediate reaction in the marriage market. The age at which women married began to drop, as local families sought to arrange marriages for their sons with girls who had not yet entered the marriage market. A booklet published by the Asian People's Anti-Communist League, a KMT front organization, in 1959 reports that on Mazu, the shortage of women had become a pressing concern: "Most fishermen constantly face the threat of a life long celibacy due to the scarcity of the fair sex. Almost every teenage girl is betrothed to someone. There simply is not enough time for the young girls to attain full womanhood."[43] In many

Table 10.1 Marital status of adult population[44]

Year	Total population over 15 *sui*	Never married		Currently married	
		Male	Female	Male	Female
1956	27,089	4,182	2,056	7,922	8,889
1961	25,192	3,758	1,242	7,874	8,487
1966	27,109	3,728	1,688	8,651	9,353
1971	31,481	4,495	3,138	9,860	10,410
1976	32,871	6,298	3,557	9,592	9,782
1981	30,255	5,705	3,076	9,132	9,377
1986	31,100	5,769	3,322	9,436	9,579
1991	29,760	4,925	2,855	9,709	9,396

middle-aged couples on Jinmen today, there is an age disparity of a decade or more. Many middle-aged women married in their early teens. This is reflected in the statistics as shown in Table 10.1. The higher number of unmarried males than females likely results from local women marrying soldiers and the reduction in the age of marriage for women; the two factors cannot be disaggregated given the available statistics. Similarly, the higher number of married females than males likely results mostly from marriages with Overseas Chinese before 1949, and marriages with soldiers thereafter, but the relative weight cannot be determined. While modernization is often associated with a rise in the marrying age for women, militarized modernity on Jinmen had precisely the opposite effect, reinforcing and even intensifying the pattern of early marriage. The propagandists made this too part of the self-sacrifice expected of women in the war zone, the loss of childhood to the pressure to marry even before attaining "full womanhood."

The second effect on the marriage market was a localized one. Marriages to soldiers undid some of the disruption caused by the disappearance of the mainland from marriage arrangements. Before 1949, many women from Guningtou were married into villages on the mainland. Chen Zonglun comments: "I've heard that the largest number of girls to marry soldiers was in Guningtou, because it had the largest number of girls of marriage age. This was because of some special circumstances. Jinmen has many small surnames and weak lineages. They didn't dare take Guningtou girls as their wives, because they worried that if their wife's family was so large and powerful, if there was trouble within the family, the wife's natal family would come to their support . . . So there were a lot of girls from Guningtou who were already past marrying age and still hadn't found a husband. Luckily the troops arrived, and they were able to find a home."[45]

The third effect on the marriage market was to raise the relative value of women. This found concrete expression in the appearance and then dramatic inflation of brideprice, which seems not to have existed on Jinmen before 1949, but became universal thereafter.[46] The local term for brideprice is "*san ba*" (three eights): NTD8,000; 800 (some say 8,000) *jin* (roughly one pound) of pork; and either 8 ounces of gold or 800 ounces of silver. In fact, there was no fixed brideprice; "three eights" is simply a euphemism for high brideprice.

The burdens and social stresses of inflated brideprice came to the attention of the WZA, which ordered an investigation into "three eights" and other traditional customs that needed to be reformed or eliminated. These were seen in terms of the backwardness of traditional village life, and as problems for the modernizing state to address. The intimate links between power and knowledge have become a subject of social investigation in many settings, including colonial contexts. One of the ways in which authoritarian politics in postcolonial societies has been naturalized is through the drawing of a clear line between colonial knowledge production and national knowledge production, with the power–knowledge relationship presumed to be more violent in the former and the knowledge produced more tied to the project of domination and control. But this distinction overstates the case. When ROC cadres conducted their interviews, wrote their reports, and formulated their recommendations about marriage practices on Jinmen, they were participating in a civilizing mission that looks very similar to colonial missions elsewhere. They constructed problems in ways that opened up possibilities of monitoring, regulation, and punishment. Though the reports did sometimes identify the role of the military in causing the problem, the larger issue was the need to transform the consciousness of villagers. This was to be accomplished through a combination of discipline and punishment: legal prohibitions; dispatch of cadres to the villages to instruct and educate the villagers, and forced labor for any who did not heed the instruction and continued to demand or pay brideprice.[47] The representation of the "three eights" system is yet another example of how modernity creates its own targets of intervention, and how the modern state defines modernity in opposition to an alternative that it may have itself created. For high brideprice on Jinmen was not in fact a lingering backward practice for the modernizing state to act upon, but a product of the very presence of that state.

Besides banning "three eights," the county government set up other policies designed to eliminate other marriage practices that were seen as traditional and wasteful. Hu Lian saw marriage as an important point of intervention into the private lives of local people, or rather, an opportune moment to remind them of the nexus of public and private, of personal and political. As a gesture to marrying couples, he allowed his jeep to be used for the ritualized journey of the bride to her new home. This meant that any Jinmen bride could now be "carried in a sedan chair," something that traditionally only the wealthy could afford. Every month he registered new marriages and sent a message of congratulations and "instructions on the ways to construct the nation and to build a family."[48]

In 1953, the county government went a step further by promoting a group wedding ceremony [Fig. 10.2]. The Jinmen group wedding was not the first time collective weddings were held in the ROC. Susan Glosser has shown how the ROC state held group weddings, in order to promote frugality, from the mid-1930s to the late 1940s.[49] The revival of the practice in Jinmen, like the continuation of the New Life Movement (see chapter 7), suggests that one consequence of the state of emergency can be the recycling of previously abandoned social engineering policies. The heightened state control justified by emergency can give such policies a greater chance of success than in their original incarnation. The first group wedding on Jinmen was such a success that it became an annual event, held every New Year's Day. By the mid-1970s, the invented ritual had become highly elaborated. There were detailed instructions on the appropriate clothing: grooms wore black suits and shoes with a white kerchief; brides wore "white formal wear" and white high heel shoes. In other words, this was an idealized recreation of a Western-style and therefore modern marriage ceremony. The staging of the wedding was a ritual representation of the political hierarchies of Jinmen, with the commanding officer of the JDHQ serving as each couple's witness, and lesser roles for the secretary of the WZAC and the county magistrate. Just as in the earlier weddings discussed by Glosser, this eliminated any role for parents and other kin, so the consequence was that the state "tacitly assumed" the role of the family.[50] The collective wedding was represented as a voluntary demonstration of frugality and modern-mindedness. But couples were pressured to participate. One document that appears year after year in the archives is a form on which village cadres listed the names of couples known to be engaged, so that township officials could persuade them to participate in the next group wedding.[51] The group wedding did not always accomplish its object of frugality, for some couples followed the wedding with a traditional feast, thus transforming the group wedding into a further elaboration of traditional practices and completely

Fig. 10.2 Collective wedding in the 1970s (from Ming Qiushui (ed.), *Jinmen*, by permission of Jinmen county cultural bureau)

defeating its purpose.[52] In response, the county started to require participants to agree not to hold any other ceremony and, if they wished to hold a feast for friends and families, to conform to limits on the number of guests, dishes per table, and total expense.[53] (To get around this restriction, married couples often arranged for several tables of guests to be concealed in private homes nearby the restaurant or public hall where the feast was held.[54]) The largest collective wedding was held in 1971, when sixty-six couples participated. But by 1978 the ritual was discontinued, ostensibly because "social mores had gradually become more open, and marrying couples knew [the importance of] frugality and limiting excessive expenditure."[55]

The phenomenon of disproportionate numbers of civilian women marrying soldiers is a common one in militarized societies. Though the two are rarely considered together, it is typically also an issue closely tied to the question of military brothels, since access to women as wives and as prostitutes are both forms by which visions of militarized masculinity are confirmed. The intimate scale of Jinmen allows us to see, anecdotally if not statistically, the demographic consequences when women marry soldiers, creating a shortage of marriage partners for local men. Two consequences of this are entirely predictable, a decline in the age of marriage for women and an increase in the value of women on the marriage market. In the case of Jinmen, this increase of value was quite explicit, and can even be quantified in terms of the exchanges that constitute marriage. A rise in the age of marriage for women, and a decline in the level of economic exchange associated with marriage, are often seen as social changes that typically accompany modernization. The appearance of the opposite processes on Jinmen shows not only that there are many ways in which modernization can unfold, but that militarized modernization can lead to very distinctive outcomes. The interest that the WZA and its bureaucracy took in civilian marriage is part of the larger project of governmentality, of regulating and educating for the purposes of strengthening compliance. What makes the Jinmen case so interesting is how explicitly the personal and the political dimensions of the modernizing and militarizing agenda were linked. Collective weddings would eliminate bad customs, customs that were perceived as lingering elements of tradition rather than what they really were, products of the very process of militarized modernization.

Women as wives and mothers

Once married, women entered the category of wives and mothers, and became central instruments in state efforts to transform the family. In Jinmen as in other modernizing regimes, the family was both an object and tool of governmentality. Policies sought to rationalize, standardize, and institutionalize the family in order to shape the individual.[56] Women were assigned a special role in this project. Consider the slogans that were posted around villages for the Women's Day festival of 1976. The first is a general appeal: "Mobilize and arise, women of the whole country; dedicate yourselves to anti-Communism and patriotism." Other slogans identify specific tasks for women in this struggle:

> To regulate the household is to serve the nation; to serve the nation one must first regulate the household.
>
> Promote moral virtues: filiality and family-mindedness; obedience to one's seniors; respect for one's elders, and nurturing of one's juniors.
>
> Respond to the government's calls; thoroughly implement frugality and stockpiling.
>
> Exert oneself for the rejuvenation of society; implement the Required Knowledge for Daily Life of Citizens.[57]

These slogans suggest a number of conclusions about the fundamental objectives of female political participation. First, married women's citizenship responsibilities were primarily in the domestic sphere. Their contribution to national goals lay in managing their own homes. As in many other societies, women were expected to play a dual role, leading the way for modernizing reforms to personal conduct while also serving as guardians of national tradition, or at least the selective appropriation of certain cultural elements and practices that sanctioned authoritarianism and could be represented as being elements of national tradition. One important virtue to be shared with one's family, and one that tied wives to sex workers, was the virtue of frugality, which took on added meaning on the front line. There were two things going on behind these gendered appeals to traditional virtues. First, these policies contrasted with the destruction of Chinese tradition and the amoral society on the mainland. Second, by associating the maintenance of these virtues with women, Jinmen authorities drew attention to the contrast between the supposed erasure of gender difference on the mainland and the survival and support of naturalized difference on its alter ego.

As in other Cold War contexts, household consumption was gendered as a feminine issue, placing women "at the center of the regime's efforts to negotiate its relations with the people over the crucial territory of living standards."[58] Regulation of the household also meant maintaining household hygiene. There were detailed instructions on what this meant in practice: rules on storage; household cleaning; maintenance of the surrounding area, and keeping of livestock.[59] Keeping a tidy home was militarized, because this was a responsibility assigned to militia members. So failure to keep the area tidy meant one was subject to military discipline, even arbitrary detention at the whim of the deputy headman. For reasons that are discussed in the next section, women left the militia when they married. Thus in most married couples the husband but not the wife was a formal member of the militia. But hygiene remained primarily the responsibility of the woman of the house. In the US in the 1960s, taking the lead in civil defense preparations came to be seen as an important part of being a good wife.[60] On Jinmen, because civil defense was highly structured through the militia system, being a good wife meant, in part, ensuring that a husband's civic defense responsibilities were fulfilled. When Xu Shupei, who had left the militia on marriage, was asked about militia duties, she answered, "Aside from sweeping up and hygiene, I wasn't responsible for any other labor. As for exercises and training, I did not participate much."[61] By remembering her husband's hygiene obligations as her own militia duties, Xu internalized the notion that a wife fulfilled her civic responsibilities by ensuring that the hygiene work assigned to her husband was completed. The regime of family regulation had come to shape her individual subjectivity.

For the most part, female political activity remained localized within the household and the domestic sphere. There was however one sanctioned form of female activism that brought women out of the home and into the barracks and that shows clearly the gendered division of labor in the militia. This was *laojun*, or "greeting the troops." *Laojun* is the term used in the ROC to describe civilians who offer morale, welfare, and recreation services to servicemen. It is to the ROC army what United Services Organizations (USO) work is to the armed forces of the US. As in other countries, "greeting the troops" was seen as a task best fulfilled by women, who could partially replicate the domesticity from which military service had removed the soldiers. The basic trend in the history of *laojun* on Jinmen is the increasing involvement of the local civilian population. In the early 1950s, *laojun* chiefly involved professional entertainers and distinguished visitors from Taiwan. By the 1970s, ordinary civilians, especially civilian women, were frequently and regularly visiting army barracks to entertain and support the troops. Even those civilians who did not personally "greet the troops" were involved in the practice through compulsory donations of money and goods to be given to the troops. The many washerwomen on Jinmen who participated in the G. I. Joe economy were already militarized, but laundry became further militarized when civilian women were expected to launder soldiers' clothes as civic duty. Cigarettes and hand towels became militarized when villagers were forced to purchase them and hand them over to village deputy headmen to give to the troops.

When Chen Zonglun was appointed village head in 1957, "there was already a female militia organization in the village, and they already did *laojun* activities. But this meant basically sending female militia into the bases at New Year and other holidays to help the troops with laundry and mending." In many cases of course this was exactly what these women did in their everyday lives. The only difference was that when they did laundry as part of *laojun* activities, they did not get paid for it. "But there was not yet any singing or performance. After I became village head, we started to choose some female militia members who were gifted at music, and organized a 'Little Chili Peppers' entertainment troupe . . . They would assemble every day at the village office to give singing lessons to the women and give performances." The introduction of this activity caused tension with local people, who found such behavior by women to be totally inappropriate. "In the early days, people were quite conservative, they didn't like the idea of their daughters giving performances. They couldn't accept it, but there was nothing they could do. This was a government regulation; who would dare oppose it? If you didn't obey you'd be punished."[62] Thus *laojun* inevitably had consequences for the remaking of traditional gender expectations. It created new possibilities for female activity, without necessarily eliminating female difference.

While in practice "greeting the troops" was coordinated by village leaders and school teachers, in theory it was the responsibility of two women's organizations, the Women's Association and the Chinese Women's Anti-Communist Anti-Soviet Alliance. The histories of these organizations show that, in common with other revolutionary societies, the legitimacy of female political activism on Jinmen always depended on the primacy of the national cause; efforts aimed at changing the lives of women were subordinated to efforts to mobilize women for tasks that served the national political agenda. The Women's Association had been established by the local KMT party branch in 1946, with funding from the county government. Its activities were suspended in 1958 during the shelling, and revived the following year. These activities included *laojun*, organization of annual celebrations on Women's Day, promotion of female education, and training of women in handicrafts. The Anti-Communist Anti-Soviet Alliance was the mass organization for female relatives of serving soldiers in the JDHQ. Founded at the behest of Madame Chiang Kai-shek, its activities also consisted mainly of providing support to the troops. These two organizations seem to have been the full extent of the organized women's movement on Jinmen. Military emergency, like anti-colonial and nationalist revolutionary movements, or for that matter anti-Communist movements, imposed strict limits on the range of acceptable political behavior.[63] Groups were expected to organize to serve a fixed hierarchy of goals, with national security firmly at the top. Any efforts to alter the hierarchy or needlessly undermine existing social arrangements implied a commitment to parochial interests that was illegitimate, irrelevant, and potentially subversive.

Women as soldiers

Besides prostitute and wife-mother, the woman as soldier was the third category into which women on Jinmen were pigeonholed. In official representations, this was the category that received the most attention. The many glossy photographic publications about Jinmen that were published in the martial law period invariably include a photograph of female militia soldiers drilling or on parade. In one of these, published in 1971, a team of fighters is running toward the camera, rifles held aloft, wearing white bobby-socks and khaki skirts, while their male officer rides alongside the team in his motorcycle in a standard military uniform [Fig. 10.3].[64] The juxtaposition of these images of femininity and militarization tells us that there was something more complicated going on than simply women being soldiers.

In virtually every modern society where the issue has arisen, the question of women as soldiers has been politically charged. Enloe's research shows that military leaders typically oppose female military participation

Fig. 10.3 Female militia team (from Ming Qiushui (ed.), *Jinmen*, by permission of Jinmen county cultural bureau)

and, even if persuaded of its temporary need, seek to limit its duration and maintain clear distinctions between soldiering of different sexes. For many feminists, in contrast, military service by women is seen as a crucial rite of citizenship and of equality.[65] But in most cases female military participation does not mean that gender differences in citizenship disappear.

Prasenjit Duara and others have shown how in colonial and postcolonial societies patriarchy was not so much broken down as reconfigured into a modern form. He discusses two broad forms this reconfiguration may take. In one form, first identified in South Asia in the work of Partha Chatterjee, women are represented as embodying the authentic core of the nation, and the domestic sphere they inhabit as the one refuge from colonial domination. In the second, which Duara explores in twentieth-century Manchuria, modern patriarchy allowed women to move outside the domestic sphere, "but sought to wrap the woman-in-public with the flag of civilizational authenticity represented by the historical rhetoric of self-sacrifice and virtue."[66] Jinmen, and other highly militarized twentieth-century Asian societies, represent a third model, in which women are called upon to be active outside the household in the all but unprecedented role of soldiers.[67] In some cases the justification for the militarization of women is revolutionary transformation; in others it is an emergency that threatens national survival and calls for new levels of sacrifice. But either way, female mobilization is implemented in ways that do not necessarily eliminate gender difference.

In this section, I explore the question of women in the militia from several perspectives. The first two issues, the rules of female participation and the functions performed by female militia members, shed light on how the gendering of military service fit into the larger regime of militarization. The third, a discussion of how individual women negotiated their service responsibilities, explores how this regime was experienced by the women subject to it. The decision that women should participate in militia service was an integral part of the construction of the modern woman on Jinmen. But the nature of that participation was shaped both by the unquestioned assumptions of military and civilian leaders and by the ways in which women themselves negotiated with the militia system. The outcome was a recasting of gender relations, but by no means the elimination of gender difference. For example, the exclusion of married women from the militia, itself a product of certain assumptions about gender roles, had significant implications for transforming the people of Jinmen into citizens of the Republic of China. In time, the fact of female participation became the most widely publicized and celebrated aspect of militia service on Jinmen. Indeed, Jinmen's female militia soldiers became a widespread symbol of the island itself. But this celebration was not intended to demonstrate that women on Jinmen had attained equality with men. Rather, it was a reminder of total militarization, a marker of the state of emergency.

In the early months of martial law, adult women like men provided labor in support of the army. While this was generally understood as simply an automatic response to the emergency situation, it was also rationalized in terms of the political need for popular mobilization, the failure of which was blamed in part for the collapse on the mainland. But as civilian support became systematized and regularized with the formal creation of the militia, women were assigned functions to which they were considered biologically or socially most suited. Special women's units were created in each village militia to perform these functions. As with male units, female unit functions were divided into peacetime and combat roles. In the 1950s and 1960s, some of the functions assigned to women's teams were propaganda and psychological warfare during peacetime, and first aid and care for the wounded and guarding of prisoners during combat. The thinking behind these combat roles was obviously that women should be kept away from the front line and actual fighting, which is why stretcher duty was assigned to male units. Predictably, functions performed by women were distinguished from and considered less important than those done by males, to the point that some female informants did not consider their service obligations to be part of militia duties. One woman, when asked if she participated in the militia, replied, "No, I participated in the women's brigade."[68]

Changing rules on female participation before 1968 shed light on the intersections between militarization, modernizing classification regimes, and traditional cultural practices and expectations. Female militia service required that several distinct understandings of the appropriate public role of women be reconciled. Concerns about militarized modernity demanded that all citizens be mobilized to serve the cause of national defense. When the militia system was regularized in the 1950s, adult women were required to participate until they became pregnant with their first child. This was because the traditional social expectation was that childrearing was a female task. During pregnancy female militia members would be unable to train, and after childbirth they would be occupied with childcare responsibilities. As one woman put it, "When women married and got pregnant, they would go with their big stomachs to the militia officer. When he certified they were pregnant, they could withdraw from the militia. So the joke was 'if you want to get out of militia service, you have to let the officer rub your belly.' "[69]

For a married woman, serving in the militia thus became a very public expression of failure to fulfill the traditional obligation of a wife, to bear children. "If you were married but hadn't become pregnant, you had to keep going. After I was married, it took me nine years before I got pregnant. I watched the others who married and got pregnant leave [the militia]. Every year there were new faces; they would get pregnant and leave, and still I was stuck on the women's team. I was extremely embarrassed; my time stretched to more than ten years."[70] These comments encapsulate ambivalences about militia service that were distinctive to women. Women, like men, complained about the burdens and inconveniences of militia service. But women also had to deal with the contradiction that while continued service might be an honorable fulfillment of one's duties as a citizen, it was simultaneously a statement of one's failures as a woman within the patriarchal family.

Sometime in the 1960s or 1970s the criterion for exemption from militia service was changed from pregnancy to marriage. Though there is no documentary evidence for this change, I suspect it was a matter of administrative simplification. The bureaucratic system set up to monitor the population, including the household registration system and the militia eligibility system, could not easily accommodate population mobility due to marriage. The problem was that marriage in Jinmen was surname exogamous and virilocal. These are technical terms for a simple, social reality – women married men of different surnames, and moved to their husband's village. So when a marriage took place, the bride had to be withdrawn from her father's household registration *and* from her militia post, and transferred to her husband's household registration *and* the militia unit in his village. The register recording the rifle or other weapon assigned to her in her natal village had to be revised, and someone else given responsibility for maintaining the gun. The new village had to find her a weapon. None of this was impossible, but it made a lot of work for village cadres. And, because it was assumed that a newly married woman would soon become pregnant and leave the militia permanently, it was a waste of resources. It was probably complaints from village cadres that led to the change in policy – a form of administrative simplification driven by the limits on the technical capacities of grass-roots administrators.[71]

The inertia of traditional ideals of female behavior and the imperative for universal mobilization continued to interact in shaping the rules and practices for female militia participation. After 1968, the introduction of the combat village system drew more women into combat roles, though married women remained exempt from annual training requirements. Now all women between the ages of sixteen and forty-five were formally enrolled in the militia. Together with the older men, they formed "defensive teams" whose role in combat was to interfere with landings by paratroopers and defend the village itself, while the "mobile team" of unmarried women and younger men went out to engage the enemy. But the expectation that women would be occupied with childcare responsibilities that would distract them from their duty made it desirable to limit their roles. Thus the regulations were that any woman with two or more children under the age of five would not be issued weapons in combat.[72]

In the early years, most village women would have been illiterate, and this was a problem for military training. To be effective militia members, women had to learn to read. So political instructors organized a women's literacy class, and "forced all the women to participate."[73] The texts for some of these literacy classes survive, and these show how the classes were vehicles not only for literacy, but also for mobilization and inculcating militarized values. One of the early lessons, entitled "The time for self-defense is now," compares the militia to animals' natural defenses. Like the animals, "humans too must use their own capacities to struggle for the right to exist . . . Friends! We must not be like beasts, dumbly watching the Communists hurt us. Can we forget the blood of our relatives? Blood must be repaid with blood."[74] The results of such lessons were predictable. "The women were very stubborn; we just killed time. We didn't learn a thing."[75] One unanticipated consequence of the decision to use the militia system as the primary agent of modernization meant that those who did not participate in the system were effectively excluded from the process of creation of modern citizens. Specifically, women who already had children or were of child-bearing age in 1949 did not belong to the one organization charged with literacy and Mandarin instruction, effectively condemning them to a life of partial citizenship. Traditional notions of gender roles became reinforced through administrative decisions that ultimately undercut the ostensible goal of universal mobilization and modernization.

The problem of female militia illiteracy should have mostly disappeared by the 1970s. As part of the program of constructing Jinmen as a Model County for the Three Principles of the People, the county government had invested heavily in schools, and Jinmen was in fact the first place in the ROC to introduce nine-year compulsory public education. Even so, female participation rates continued to be low, and there is some question about the effectiveness of education. A female essayist who entered the militia in the early 1970s when she turned eighteen reported that during her first session of annual training, she and the other women were given lectures and then tested on the material. "But we hadn't had much schooling, and we rarely wrote. So we couldn't even write our own names. Eventually the instructor just told us to look up our names on our household registration booklets [and copy them]. We were all right as long as the test was true-false."[76]

The link between women's reproductive biology, culturally constructed notions of appropriate conduct, and militia service gave women some space in which to negotiate their militia obligations. Male cadres accepted the logic that menstruation interfered with one's capacity to perform military duties, so women who could provide a doctor's note confirming they were having their period could gain exemption from training and exercises. Staff at local clinics were reportedly willing to connive at deceiving militia officers.[77] Many older people recall how shocking it was, both for young women and especially their parents, when they were informed that they would be required to serve in the militia. "Some girls were afraid of being in the militia. So they got engaged quickly, and there were lots of early marriages. Then as soon as they were married they wanted to get pregnant."[78] Thus efforts to evade militia service may have been another contributing factor to the reduction in the age of marriage in the years after 1949. It was not childbirth *per se* that exempted a woman from militia service but childrearing, which was assumed to be a woman's task.

"If you didn't want to be in the militia, you had to have a kid. If you didn't have a kid, you could adopt one. This happened quite often in Zhushan. You'd adopt the child when it was only a few months old, before it had been registered in the household registration."[79] Such adoptions were often arranged with close relatives. They were really just an adaptation of the traditional practice of adoption within lineages to ensure continuity of the male line, and more broadly, of flexible approaches to family and kinship to serve individual and household strategies. "This sort of thing was common at that time, and it wasn't illegal."[80]

Female soldiers of Jinmen

Today, many people, men and women, have nothing but complaints about their militia service. Such complaints, coupled with accounts of the various ways in which militia service was evaded, leave the impression that its reception by the people of Jinmen was entirely negative. One gets a very different impression from materials produced at the time. These celebrate the female militia soldiers of Jinmen as embodying new and modern ideals of femininity. A serial published by the WZA, *Jinmen Today*, devoted a special issue to the militia in 1974. We are introduced to nineteen year old Li Mengqi, the senior officer in the Nanmen neighborhood unit of the Jincheng militia. "Not only is she beautiful, but she adopts a serious attitude to her work. She is filial to her parents, and looks after her siblings thoroughly . . . She is truly an exceptional representative of modern women." Like Li, Weng Shuhui combines highly traditional virtues – she mends clothes in her spare time to help her parents support her siblings – with those of a mobilized citizenry. She stands out because her commitment to the national cause goes beyond what is required of her. "She says that if her country needs her, even if she has already married, she would willingly come forward and devote herself completely to the cause of protecting her homeland, entering into the ranks of the combatants."[81]

It is easy of course to dismiss such sentiments as pure propaganda. But at least one group of female militia soldiers continues to take great pride in its service, though this pride mingles with resentment at the harsh system and, as we shall see in a later chapter, demands for proper compensation. These are women who were chosen to travel to Taiwan to participate in the annual military review on the October 10 National Day holiday. A Jinmen militia team numbering 400 soldiers, half men and half women, participated in the military review annually between 1975 and 1987. The main criterion for selection to the team was physical – men had to be over 170 cm tall and women 158 cm. Township militia units identified unit members who met the criteria, and they were then ordered to a training camp where they were tested for their drilling abilities. The selected team began full-time training in late August. Most people remember the beginning of this training in relation to August 23 – training began soon after the anniversary of the 1958 bombing. In early October, the team would go to Taiwan for a final week of training with colleagues from the Mazu militia, with whom they would march together on National Day, October 10.

There was initially much enthusiasm for participating in the review. People were honored to be selected, and enjoyed the trip to Taiwan and the attention. But over time, the novelty wore off, and by the early 1980s there was much less interest. This was often explained, by male officers, as a problem of reconciling the demands of training with women's own femininity. "From the perspective of the Jinmen civilians, the National Day parade was a real burden . . . The training lasted three to four weeks, and it couldn't be put off, regardless of the weather. Women value beauty, so they were especially unwilling to participate."[82] Xu Minghong recalls, "All that training under the hot sun was very hard. It was especially unsuitable for women. Women like white skin, and training under the hot sun they would get dark, so no one wanted to participate. But it was semi-compulsory at that time. If a family had two or three daughters, they had to send one. One had to participate."[83] As enthusiasm began to wane, concerns grew about the possibility that women might try to evade their responsibilities. In the 1950s and 1960s, the WZA had dealt with the related problem of men trying to leave the island before annual exercises by tightening up the exit–entry control system. Now these same measures were applied to the pool of National Day review team members. Since by this time only unmarried women over the age of eighteen were in the militia, they became the target group. Unmarried women were added to the categories who were not permitted to receive exit permits to go to Taiwan in the summer months, and registered residents who were temporarily in Taiwan were required to return to Jinmen in time for the selection for the team.

While grumbling and evasion grew, some participants saw militia service as signifying both female equality and commitment to the national cause. Lin Jindou said, "Though we didn't have to do as much as the men, we still had to get a lot of training, and some of us even participated in the annual exercises. The level of difficulty we had to endure was no less than that for men. At the time, the circumstances of the nation were quite exceptional. The Communist armies might come over and invade. So learning some combat skills to protect yourself, and some nursing skills to look after others [was a good thing] – if there was ever a crisis, you'd be able to help yourself and your family. Even if it had been even more difficult, I'd still have embraced the challenge, and exerted myself to the utmost to do my duty."[84]

Like sorghum liquor and the "Never Forget our Time in Ju" inscription, the female militia demonstration team became a powerful symbol of Jinmen on Taiwan. (In a somewhat similar way, highly militarized women were also a potent political symbol on the mainland.) As the director of the team in 1981 says, the team's participation was very important for Jinmen. "Otherwise, most people would have a hard time even finding Jinmen on the map. But today everyone has a high level of awareness of this tiny speck of land – that's because our militia always performed so well, and lots of media came here to do interviews. During the military review ceremony, many other countries came to participate, so it also drew the attention of the international media."[85]

Women who served on the demonstration team in the early 1980s often say that the highlight of their participation was when they acted as extras in a 1982 film about the militia, *Women Warriors of Jinmen*.[86] No one would call this film an artistic masterpiece, but it is useful to us nonetheless because it draws out some of the complex symbolism and stereotypes of female soldiers on Jinmen. Like other Taiwanese films of the era, the film consists of several character-driven subplots. The main story concerns Bitao, the daughter of a fisherman and girlfriend of a frogman. When her father is murdered by People's Liberation Army (PLA) soldiers while at sea, she swears vengeance. Her commanding officer, Jianying, hated by most of the soldiers for her strictness, offers condolences, and explains that she too has suffered at the hands of the Communists. Her family was wiped out in the 1958 bombing. In a flashback, we see Jianying as a small baby, her hair cropped short, surrounded by explosions and flames. Though there is no railway on Jinmen, for some reason she seems to be sitting next to a railway tie. This is a reference to the iconic photograph of an abandoned child in Shanghai during the 1937 attack by the Japanese, and therefore equates the PLA with the Japanese, and the heroic people of Jinmen with those who resisted the Japanese on the mainland.[87] Jianying's tragic past explains why she is so strict with her charges, to ensure that they never relax their vigilance. Her own long-suffering boyfriend writes to her from Taiwan, threatening to break off their relationship if she does not agree to join him and leave the militia. But Jianying refuses. After her own father's death, Bitao asks her soldier boyfriend to teach her hand-to-hand combat. Encountering an enemy frogman on the beach at night, Bitao sacrifices her future happiness and her life by blowing herself and the frogman up with a grenade.

Two other subplots focus on the potentially transgressive consequences of women being soldiers. Suyue ignores the wishes of her family and all propriety to pursue her relationship with a soldier from Taiwan. Xiaoyu also has a Taiwanese boyfriend, but when his father visits Jinmen to meet her, she behaves like a vulgar boor, showing him no respect and eating like a man. Neither of the two take their soldiering very seriously, seeing it as an opportunity to meet boys and to curse Jianying. During a training exercise, the two girls become trapped, but Jianying comes to their rescue. She is gravely injured, and her leg is amputated. Suyue and Xiaoyu now realize the error of their ways, and vow to devote themselves to their militia duties and their sacred duty to protect their homeland. Ultimately the transgressiveness of female soldiers is contained by their self-sacrifice to the national cause. The film ends with the boyfriends of Jianying and Xiaoyu commiserating about the long wait before their girlfriends complete their militia duties and can marry. Of course, as we have seen, the reality was the opposite. Jinmen women typically did not delay marriage in order to continue serving in the militia, but advanced their marriage so as to avoid or shorten their length of service. But by drawing attention to the profound consequences of militarization for gender relations, the film highlights themes that were significant indeed.

Conclusions

I have sought to elucidate in this chapter some of the myriad ways in which emergency on Jinmen was gendered, how it was experienced differently by men and women, and how it simultaneously reinforced and transformed gender expectations and roles. The three categories of prostitute, wife-mother, and soldier defined women's potential positions in militarized society. (The G. I. Joe businesswoman was a fourth category, but since it has already been discussed in a previous chapter and did not officially exist, it is not necessary to raise it again here.) At first glance, nothing might seem more different than the images of proud female soldiers parading before state leaders, and prostitutes living and working in brutal conditions in military brothels. But while there were huge differences between these categories, there were also common links. Each of these categories performed roles that were essential to the smooth functioning of the militarized regime. Regardless of their assigned functional role, women were expected to sacrifice themselves for the sake of the national cause; indeed, whether it was as 831 prostitute or militia soldier, self-sacrifice became a defining element of womanhood. Second, while women were seen as guardians of national tradition, their social position was seen as an important indicator of modernity, of the casting off of backward habits of the past in favor of scientific and rational approaches. Duara writes that nationalist patriarchy constructed the self-sacrificing woman as a symbol of the national essence.[88] This was partially true on Jinmen, where a putative Chinese cultural tradition was selectively appropriated and assigned to women and the domestic sphere to protect. But women could only partially remain enclosed in domesticity. The state of emergency and the threat to national survival also required that women be mobilized for military purposes – to maintain the sexual vigor of the troops in the case of prostitutes, to provide support and domestic services as wives-mothers, and to participate in combat as female soldiers. In most societies, women are usually brought into military roles reluctantly and to meet temporary requirements. Dividing time into war and peace allows for the "convenient notion that any mobilization of women soldiers is short term and basically anomalous."[89] On Jinmen, the state of emergency blurred the distinction between war and peace. Women were charged both with protecting the national tradition, illustrating militarized modernity, and, by virtue of their role as soldiers, serving as markers not only of modernity but also of the state of emergency.

The functional role of Jinmen's female militia shifted in tandem with the island's role in international geopolitics. As Jinmen moved from having significant military functions to serving primarily as a political symbol of Communist threat and anti-Communist vigilance, both for the Taiwanese polity and the rest of the world, the significance of Jinmen's women soldiers shifted from providing support to the troops to demonstrating that women too had their role to play in the global geopolitical struggle. It is no coincidence that it was precisely as the geopolitical struggle changed again in the mid-1980s that Jinmen's female militia ceased to perform that role in the highly visible venue of the National Day parade.

As in so many other ways, Jinmen's intermediate position between Taiwan and the mainland can shed light on processes on either side of the Strait. The management of prostitution on Jinmen is one area where the two societies diverged. On the mainland after 1949 the elimination of prostitution was a symbol of China's emergence as a modern healthy nation.[90] On Jinmen, the specific context of militarization required a different position, one that is more common in military bases around the world. While in many societies prostitution is seen as a threat to the social order, around military bases prostitution is often considered potentially beneficial to the social and economic order. The focus is not the elimination of prostitution but its containment and regulation. On the other hand, the celebration of egalitarianism of women and men in the Jinmen militia was somewhat similar to the Maoist response to sexual difference.

Just like on the mainland, egalitarianism was expressed in terms of specialization of roles, often rationalized as responses to straightforwardly biological differences. In Maoist China, women's participation in labor would in theory eliminate inequality between the sexes but in practice tended simply to add to the burden of expectations. On Jinmen, the politics of women's status was always subordinated to national security, so there was never such an explicit commitment to female liberation. But the outcomes were much the same nonetheless. On Taiwan in the 1950s and 1960s, attempts to fix women in their household were supposed to restore the integrity of Chinese culture, but ended up providing an important source of unpaid labor for small-scale family entrepreneurialism. A similar situation obtained on Jinmen, but because of the military situation, that entrepreneurialism was directed not toward household workshops but G. I. Joe business. Just as there are similarities in how expectations of women changed, there are also similarities in the way some things did not change. In both the PRC and Jinmen, inherited assumptions about sexual difference persisted. On the mainland, these differences were often cloaked in the aura of science. On Jinmen, the fact of emergency obviated the need for this legitimization. In both societies, it was assumed that the state should specify and regulate the contexts in which sex was legitimate. On the mainland, there was only one such context – marriage. The distinctive characteristics of Jinmen, namely the need to support assumptions about martial masculinity, justified the inclusion of another context – the brothel. This meant that female sexuality was not defined exclusively in relation to husbands and reproduction. But the assumption that marriage and procreation are inevitable for ordinary women was shared. This is why Jinmen women were mustered out of the militia at marriage.

In many societies women have become signifiers in discourses related to the construction and transformation of national categories. On Jinmen, and in the PRC, women, especially militarized women, were signifiers of a different kind, of political difference and self-sacrificing citizenhood. During the period of militarization, social relations on Jinmen were recast in light of military threat. This threat was the rationale for changes to gender relations but it also limited the depth of the changes. Thus militarization did not simply expand rights and opportunities, it could also constrain them. Militarization and female mobilization for combat did not mean the end of patriarchy so much as a reconfiguration of it.

11   Ghosts and gods of the Cold War

One consequence of the intertwining of the global and the local on Jinmen has been in the supernatural realm. The fierce fighting in 1949, the ongoing bombardment campaign, and the death of ROC soldiers far from their homes and families on the mainland have turned Jinmen into a land of countless ghosts. Encounters with these ghosts are part of the lore associated with military service on Jinmen, and Jinmen ghost stories are a distinctive sub-genre of the category of popular supernatural fiction in contemporary Taiwan. There are tales of the ghosts of dead soldiers who linger on Jinmen and haunt civilians, and of ghosts of Jinmen villagers, their repose disturbed by military construction, who haunt the soldiers.[1] There are also more material traces of these ghosts. Temples to them are found everywhere on the island. These temples are not merely evidence of the persistence of tradition in the face of modernization, for they also reflect state efforts to use the power of memory and religion to shape society. They are both a site of interaction between state regulatory regimes and social life and another example of the geopoliticization of everyday life for the people of Jinmen. Popular religion on Jinmen is yet another area where state agents and civilians have engaged in contests of meaning and interpretation over issues created by geopolitical context.

Temples to Patriotic Generals

In the fields around Guningtou, one often happens upon simple structures, a few yards square, with walls of bare concrete and corrugated tin roofs. In front of each structure is a shaded platform with an incense burner. The interior typically contains a single altar with a statue of a deity and a table on which offerings can be placed. On the side wall there may be banners donated by thankful petitioners whose wishes have been granted by the intervention of the god. The outward appearance of the shrine is similar to that of the countless shrines to local deities found throughout southeast China and Taiwan, commemorating the spirits of hungry ghosts, anonymous humans who died under mysterious circumstances or far from home. In many of the Jinmen shrines, the image of the deity is not of a celestial bureaucrat in the robes of a traditional Chinese official as is the case in temples elsewhere. Rather, the god is represented as a contemporary man, wearing military fatigues, an ROC army cap, and sometimes holding a sub-machine gun or other weapon. On Jinmen, these gods are known as Patriotic Generals (*aiguo jiangjun*), and they are believed to be the souls of soldiers who have died on the island. The high concentration of temples around Guningtou is the consequence of the battle fought there in 1949.

The outstanding scholar of popular religion on Jinmen is Chi Chang-hui, who has located more than forty such shrines on Jinmen.[2] In general, these shrines appeared as a result of mediumistic revelation. For centuries, male and female mediums have been a way for Jinmen residents to communicate with the spirits of the dead and with gods. In the 1950s local mediums began to report that they had been possessed by the spirits of dead soldiers. These spirits asked the local people to build a shrine and to provide them with offerings, threatening that they would cause mischief if their wish was not granted. Sometimes the spirits were anonymous or unknown to the villagers; sometimes they identified themselves precisely and specifically, invoking memories that the villagers shared. Thus in Huxia, the spirit of a soldier who had killed himself in a village well possessed a local medium and asked for a shrine. Another temple has been built on the site of a bunker that was hit in 1958, instantly killing the squad within.[3] Often the process of building a temple begins when a body is found. Around 1976, two bodies washed up on the beach near Houfenggang. They were wearing only shorts, so the villagers knew they were frogmen. They were given a rough burial. Some time later, a woman whose fields were nearby the burial site fell ill, and asked a village medium for help. The spirits of the two dead men then appeared to her in a dream, asking for a proper burial and to receive offerings. The woman then built a small shrine. "She didn't know if they were ROC frogmen or Communist frogmen, so she just called them Patriotic Generals."[4]

The largest shrine to a Patriotic General is a magnificent temple on the road to Guningtou. The deity worshiped here is Li Guangqian, one of the heroes of Guningtou, who late on the first day of the battle was killed leading his men on a brave charge against a nest of PLA soldiers.[5] Some years later, troubled by strange noises in the night, nearby villagers asked their female medium to seek the cause. She was possessed by Li, who called on the villagers to erect a shrine and provide offerings. After inquiring with the Jinmen Defense Headquarters (JDHQ) authorities, and learning with amazement that all of the personal details provided by the medium actually corresponded to the dead hero Li Guangqian, the villagers complied with his request. Then in the 1970s, the spirit asked for the temple to be enlarged. This time the villagers turned to the army, requesting financial assistance. The commanding officer (CO) ordered the magistrate to contribute a large sum that made possible the construction of a huge temple, with an impressive entrance gate, a spirit way of stone animals, and a meeting room and museum behind the main shrine. By the late 1970s, the site had become both a shrine where local people made offerings and requested protection and also a place for political education and commemoration of heroes of the ROC army. When the county government celebrated the thirtieth anniversary of the Guningtou battle, it ordered a large-scale communal offering. The planning document for the celebration instructs, "At least two thousand civilians (male/female/young/old), students, as well as commanders from every area and heads of enterprises and the old and distinguished shall attend, to supply [adequate worshipers] for the shooting of a film [of the event]."[6] State efforts to harness and channel the power of Li Guangqian are but a small part of the project to control and monitor popular religious practices on Jinmen. A closer look at religious policy further illustrates how militarization and modernity have been linked on the island.

Control and surveillance of popular religion

Long before 1949, the Republic of China had been committed to the reform of Chinese popular religion as part of the larger goal of modernization. The Republican period, as Prasenjit Duara and Rebecca Nedostup have shown, saw periodic and largely unsuccessful campaigns to demarcate a boundary between religion and superstition and to weaken the power of institutional religion.[7] After 1949, on Taiwan as well as on Jinmen, official policies to regulate popular religion concentrated on eliminating practices seen as backward and wasteful, and ensuring that religious organizations did not threaten government control. Some observances were banned outright. For example, many villages had temples to plague deities known as Kingly Lords (*wangye*). To protect the village from disease, these temples held periodic rituals in which the gods were invited aboard a magnificent papier-mâché boat that was then floated off into the sea. Restrictions on group activities on the seashore made these rituals illegal. Before 1949, there had been a number of temples on Jinmen whose annual festival included multi-village processions in which the main deity was carried from village to village, providing an opportunity for feasting and social networking for people from different villages. Some of these festivals were prohibited; in other cases the ritual was limited to a single day, which made it impossible to process the deity to multiple villages. The festival of Middle Origin (*zhongyuan*) was another periodic festival that was restricted after 1949, though not overtly. The highlight of the festival was the *pudu* (universal salvation) ritual, a rite for the delivery of the souls of the dead. Traditionally, neighboring villages held the festival on different days, allowing villagers to attend more than one festival and deepen social connections. For security reasons, the military limited the celebration of the festival to one day, thereby making it impossible for people to attend celebrations other than in their own village. This policy was also intended to reduce expenditure on the festival, the thinking being that there would be less competitive expenditure. Frugality in expenditure became identified as a crucial contribution in the struggle with the Communists.

Efforts to regulate and restrict popular religious expression met with resistance. Villagers found pretexts to hold ritual operas. They sponsored opera performances for the enjoyment of the soldiers rather than the gods; this was a patriotic gesture rather than an expression of backwardness and wastefulness.[8] As people grew wealthier there were also cases of outright resistance. In 1977, a villager hired an opera troupe to perform at his ancestral hall without permission, knowing both that he would be fined and that most of the fine would go to the township's social welfare fund.[9]

The cult of Wang Yulan

The cult of Wang Yulan, among the most important cults on Little Jinmen, provides a useful case study to explore struggles over interpretation of popular religion. The cult originated in the propitiation of the ghost of a female corpse that floated up to the island in the summer of 1954. The corpse was buried, and villagers made offerings to her spirit at the site where the body was discovered. A strange glow and the sound of weeping emanated from the grave. Some informants report that the engines of army jeeps always died as they drove past the grave. Within a few months, the spirit possessed a local medium, and, as a commemorative inscription records, told her sorry tale:

My surname is Wang, and my given name Yulan. I am from Xiamen, aged seventeen, from a poor family. On the afternoon of July 9, while I was gathering clams at the seashore, brigands from the Zhu–Mao soldiers [i.e. Zhu De and Mao Zedong; in other words, soldiers of the People's Liberation Army] surrounded me, [intending to] shame me. I swore to die before submitting. [I] Yulan tried every measure to resist. But the bandits' bestial conduct was impossible to predict. Angry and ashamed [of themselves], they became enraged, and even more heartless and brutal, stripping me naked and throwing me into the sea.[10]

The initial process of a corpse washing up on the beach of Little Jinmen is consistent with a broad pattern in traditional Chinese popular religion whereby the spirit of a person who dies an untimely death or a mysterious corpse is perceived as a potentially malevolent force to be feared, a hungry ghost, and is sacrificed to in order to forestall unfortunate consequences. Even in its earliest phases the mythology attached to this particular corpse reflects some of the distinctive features of the situation in Jinmen. Some villagers say that Wang's body was first discovered by soldiers, whose officers then ordered a meeting of community leaders and demanded to know if any local girl had gone missing. The leaders insisted she was not from their village. But the corpse gave a sign that she was among her relatives, which convinced the villagers that they had some connection (*yuanfen*) with her, and decided to bury her. The early 1950s was when military hegemony over the people of Jinmen was being consolidated, and this story of the village leaders being dragged before the officer suggests the real source of their fear and danger. While the power of the military may have seemed unlimited, the story of the dying engines is a wry comment that however difficult the soldiers made life for the villagers, they, like everyone else, were still subject to the power of the gods. Another story that circulates widely tells that before soldiers got involved, the body was actually discovered by two locals, one of whom, known as Ah Hong, ran a photography studio and owned a camera. He is said to have taken photographs of the naked corpse, which miraculously had not deteriorated, and sold the pornographic photographs to local troops. The spirit of the dead girl was furious, and Ah Hong soon fell ill and died. The tale of Ah Hong touches on the sexualized aspect of the corpse, a theme to which I will return below, her potential for malevolence, and ambivalence about the changing economy of Jinmen, whose residents increasingly relied on commercial exchange with the military.

According to Hong Duoyu, an eighty-one year old blind man who now looks after the temple, after the spirit of Wang Yulan possessed the medium the villagers wished to build a temple in her honor but they were too poor. So Wang appeared to the top-ranking officer on Little Jinmen, 81st division commander Tian Shuzhang, in a dream and asked for his assistance, whereupon Tian had his troops build a small temple in the village of Qingqi. (When interviewed in 2002, Hong Duoyu reported that the deity had never again manifested herself through a medium, a claim reflecting a highly divisive issue in contemporary local politics, discussed in chapter 12.) Tian composed an inscription for the temple, which he named the Temple of the Chaste Maiden (*lienü miao*) [Figs. 11.1, 11.2]. After explaining the circumstances of Wang's death, the appearance of her corpse, and the temple's construction, it concludes:

Fig. 11.1 Exterior of temple of Wang Yulan (photo by author)

It is truly painful. Between Jinmen and Xiamen, fierce sea creatures come and go. How was she able to float to this place, and tell her story of injustice? While alive she was able to resist; when dead she threw herself toward freedom. The brutal and immoral regime of the red bandits moves both Heaven and man to indignation. How divine and remarkable [is Wang's spirit]! Today the whole world's anger against communism is at its high tide, and the revolutionary resistance to brutality rises like the wind. Autocracy must be defeated, and brutal governance must be destroyed. The facts are so. In order to comfort her virtuous spirit which has died prematurely, I have lovingly composed this record, in order to commemorate her purity and chastity.[11]

Tian's endorsement of Wang Yulan for her "purity and chastity," and for her ultimate self-sacrifice in support of these values, fits into a long tradition of official support for traditional female virtues. Systematic regulations regarding the awarding of honors for widow fidelity and women who preserved sexual purity even to the point of suicide had been in place in China since the fourteenth century.[12] But the officer's patronage of the temple was not simply an extension of this tradition of state support for feminine virtues, which had formally come to an end with the Revolution of 1911. Rather, it was part of the self-conscious appeal to Chinese tradition that characterized cultural discourse in the Republic of China during its first decades on Taiwan. Allen Chun has shown how cultural politics became intertwined with nationalism in this period, as the Nationalist Party (KMT) government sought to "invoke,

Fig. 11.2 Image of Wang Yulan in her temple. Note the gifts of skin cream at the lower front of the image (photo by author)

resuscitate and reinvent tradition for the purpose of legitimizing its own vision of modern society."[13] Chiang Kai-shek and his cultural officials claimed that the KMT was the defender and guardian of traditional Chinese culture, and in turn of the Chinese nation. Their definition of culture was highly conservative, in reaction to the radical vision of the Chinese Communist Party (CCP) on the mainland. Thus Wang Yulan's self-regulation of her sexuality, which in traditional Chinese morality could legitimately be expressed only after her parents' consent to her marriage, and only with her husband, was implicitly contrasted to the licentious and unfilial sexual freedoms believed to be spreading on the mainland. Even the choice of a hungry ghost/god as nationalist symbol is telling of the conservatism of KMT cultural discourse. While the early Republican state had imposed strict controls on popular religion as part of its campaign of control and modernization, after 1949 the repression of popular religion eased, at least rhetorically, for the Republic of China's new self-image as the protector of traditional Chinese culture and values rested on its contrast with the alien and atheist Communist movement. Chiang himself had signaled this shift in 1953, with the publication of two supplementary chapters to Sun Yat-sen's *Three Principles of the People* which became the main early statement of nationalist cultural policy on Taiwan. "In plotting to disrupt the Chinese society and exterminate the Chinese nation," Chiang wrote, "the Chinese Communists begin by persecuting religion and restricting our freedom of religious belief . . . Only when we realize why the Communists must get rid of religion root and branch before they can succeed in conquering the whole world and enslaving all humanity shall we be in a position to estimate with complete understanding the full significance of religion both to the individual and to society at large." Religious ideas were now seen as essential to human development and social stability. "A man without faith has no purpose in life and a society without religion has no spiritual stabilizing force."[14]

Tian's interpretation of Wang Yulan, an expression of this official cultural discourse, thus diverged from the popular model of deification of a hungry ghost while reflecting the distinctive geopolitics of Jinmen. Tian represented her as a symbol of the virtues of traditional Chinese culture, of heroic resistance to Chinese Communism, and thus as a metaphor for the Republic of China which he served. With Taiwan as a base for the eventual recapture and liberation of the mainland from the forces of Communism, all citizens of the Republic of China were to devote themselves wholeheartedly to this task, and thus needed to be inculcated with a spirit of self-sacrifice and service to the true ideals of the Chinese revolution. Tian portrayed Wang Yulan as a nationalist hero and patriotic martyr, a useful propaganda symbol in service of this goal.

Even as the ROC was building an image as the defender of tradition, the meanings of that tradition were being redefined. For example, the Japanese influence on Taiwanese culture, and notions of Taiwanese distinctiveness, were systematically purged from official cultural discourse. As Chun puts it, "Insofar as tradition was invented or reconstituted, by nature it also had to be a kind of mystification which coincided with the hegemonic process of state formation." This mystification was not entirely persuasive to the people of Little Jinmen. As a former village official, now a Daoist priest, said of the initial construction of the temple, "She was rescued for political reasons . . . At that time, on the mainland they were destroying temples, so she showed Taiwan was different."[15]

Soldiers, villagers, and Daoists

From the mid-1950s onward, the ritual practices of the cult developed along two intertwined paths. The first involved the military. Military planning has had a direct effect on the history of the cult. For example informants say that the corpse of Wang Yulan was originally buried at a place called Tongshan. At some point, the decision was made to lay a minefield at Tongshan. To forestall opposition, soldiers disinterred the corpse of Wang Yulan and transferred it to a new concrete grave, which they constructed, beside the temple.

But the relationship between the military and the cult was much more complex than this. The officers and soldiers of the garrison on Jinmen also participated personally in a distinct set of cult rituals. ROC officers often participate in the ritual life of the community in which they are stationed, worshiping at the chief temples of the locality. For the military, this worship is understood as having a dual character: it is both religiously instrumental, in the sense that the officer requests protection for the troops under his command, and socially instrumental, in that it is intended to solidify the links between the troops and the community (similarly, a ranking officer often donates commemorative plaques to ancestral halls of local lineages).

It is unclear when military officers began to worship regularly at the temple of Wang Yulan; presumably this began not long after Tian Shuzhang ordered the construction of her temple. This worship continues to the present day, though with the downgrading of the military presence on Little Jinmen in the late 1990s from division to brigade, it is now the local brigade commander who performs the ritual. The current commander, a career officer, participates as an honored guest in the annual temple festival of the deity. He also visits the temple to worship on the first and fifteenth of every lunar month, with the assistance of a young conscript. The soldier arrives first, to lay out the offerings of fruit on plates that he brings with him, and to ready the incense sticks and paper money to be burned. The officer is delivered to the temple in his black car. He offers incense at each of the incense burners of the temple and adjoining tomb. To save him time, his assistant then burns paper money in a furnace beside the tomb, while the officer himself bows before the temple and returns to his waiting car. In interpreting the ritual, the commander identifies several different dimensions to his participation. He worships at the temple because it is customary. "It was originally the garrison command that developed this tradition . . . When I first came here, the officer I replaced brought me here and explained this to me. I carried it on, and will pass it on to my replacement." He also sees an instrumental dimension. Since the soldiers under his command venerate the deity, it behooves him as commander to pay her respect. "I originally didn't have this belief, but now that I have been stationed here, I come here so that my soldiers will feel better." For the same reason, he also attends services at a local Christian church occasionally. Worshiping at the temple is good for his relations with the community, which is why he also visits the local temple to *Baosheng dadi* ('Great Emperor who Protects Life'), the other important temple on Little Jinmen. Finally, the officer sees a civic dimension to his participation. Here, he touches directly on Wang Yulan's transformation from ghost to god. "Any thing which is beautiful and admirable may become a deity. This is not only because they can help us, but also because they can educate us. We admire the morality [they demonstrated] while alive, and respect them."[16] Here the officer is referring to the virtues of Wang Yulan as first articulated fifty years ago by his predecessor, Tian Shuzhang. Wang's embodiment of the traditional female virtue of preserving chastity even to the point of death makes her an admirable symbol of traditional Chinese values.[17] This in turn makes her a symbol of resistance to the political force that, in the official cultural discourse of the ROC, seeks to destroy those values, the Chinese Communist Party. Military veneration of Wang Yulan is thus part of a campaign of popular mobilization in the nationalist project of the ROC state for most of the past half-century, a project which sought to link the identity of all its citizens, but especially those on front line islands like Jinmen, with the defense of their Republic.

The military officer's interpretation of his ritual practice is rather different from that of the local people, even if the basic ritual structure is identical. Village women come to the temple on the first and fifteenth of each month, and many come every day as well. A smaller number of men worship. At each of the five stations of the temple (outside burner, two side shrines, center shrine, grave), worshipers clasp their hands together and speak directly to the deity. Typically, the worshiper addresses the deity, then names all the members of her family, asking for general protection and sometimes specific boons for each individual. The requests will be familiar to anyone who has observed ritual performance in a temple in Taiwan or southern Fujian: prosperity for those in business; safe return for those away from home; examination success for adolescent children; sons for married children. Lastly, the worshiper identifies herself to the deity, saying, "I am believer so-and-so, of such-and-such place." The worshiper may cast divination blocks and use them to obtain a divination slip. Hong Duoyu can interpret the obscure content of the slip. The burning of paper money is a step that cannot be neglected, for it is essential to the reciprocal exchange that the worshiper seeks to enter into with the deity. Thus despite military efforts to transform Wang Yulan into a nationalist symbol of resistance, to the local people she remains a supernatural being of great power, who has a personal connection to their community and whose aid can be enlisted in support of their personal struggles.

People in Little Jinmen believe that it was precisely this power that led to the flourishing of her cult, in particular when she came to the assistance of a wealthy and prominent man named Lin Depu. Like many residents of Little Jinmen, Lin, who was born in 1910, had traveled abroad to Brunei to seek his fortune, just as his father had before him. He became a successful businessman, and in 1958 was appointed *kapitan*, leader of the local Chinese community, by the Sultan. In 1976, he returned to his home village with his family, and visited the temple to worship. According to the local folklore, at the time his business was suffering, but soon after his visit to the temple, it began to prosper again. In thanks, he donated money to rebuild and enlarge the temple. According to an inscription carved when the reconstruction was completed, "Unfortunately, when [the temple] was originally built, the construction was humble and rough, and the size of the hall was small. Visitors [who wished to burn] incense sometimes had a sense of being crowded." After Lin's intervention, "the temple's appearance was imposing and the hall impressive, and everything was brand new."[18] Thus for the people of Jinmen, the cult's growth depends primarily not on Wang's utility as a political symbol but on her efficacy.

Much of the popular folklore of the cult also diverges from or challenges official explanations that worshiping Wang is a civic ritual of honoring a moral exemplar. Many stories portray her rather as an efficacious supernatural patron of the military as well as ordinary folk. But geopolitics is still never very far from these stories. One village woman explains that the soldiers had first built the temple to Wang Yulan during the Strait Crisis of 1954–5, when an officer, presumably Tian Shuzhang himself, was rescued by the deity. "He was caught outside during an artillery bombardment, and happened to be near her tomb. He embraced the tomb and was protected. So he decided to build the temple." According to Hong Duoyu, "If it had not been for her, Jinmen and Little Jinmen would both have been destroyed during the two [Strait] Crises [of 1954–5 and 1958]. At that time, the bombs fell like bees. But they fell into the hills, away from the people."[19]

Ideas about gender and the sexuality of Wang Yulan, expressed both in folklore and in ritual, are ambiguous, blurring the firm line between military and popular interpretations of the deity. Much of the popular folklore about Wang Yulan is highly sexualized. Most informants believe that she must have been either raped or nearly raped at the hands of the soldiers. Otherwise, there would be no reason for her body to have been naked. As an inscription at the temple puts it, "She encountered criminal rogues, who observed her beauty and harbored evil designs. They became brutal, and she threw herself into the sea and sacrificed herself."[20] Her sexuality is also highlighted in the story of the pornographic pictures. On the other hand, the military interpretation of Wang desexualizes her, presenting her not as a victim of lust, but as a heroic emblem of chastity. Some informants also try to minimize the sexual themes of her story. For example, Hong Duoyu, the blind temple-keeper, tells visitors to the temple a sanitized version of her story:

Wang Yulan traveled to Xiamen, where her father was working. At that time, people used wood as fuel. So she went down to the sea to collect driftwood. She had to pass a checkpoint. The Communist soldier saw her going down to the seashore. But he went off duty, and forgot to tell his replacement about her. When she passed the checkpoint on her way back, the watchman demanded to see her identification. She was only seventeen years old, and didn't have any identification. She tried to explain, but the soldiers accused her of being a spy for the KMT. They insulted her. She said, "You are treating me like an animal, not a human being." Then she threw herself into the sea.[21]

Steven Sangren has argued that understandings of female deities are informed by ideas of purity and pollution and the association between female pollution and women's social roles in Chinese gender conceptions. Female deities, therefore, must overcome the stigma of pollution associated with menstruation, sexual intercourse, and childbirth.[22] Stories that link Wang Yulan to a tradition of righteous martyrdom by adolescent women in defense of chastity enable this purification.

As with many local deities in Chinese popular religions, the cult of Wang Yulan has been incorporated into the Daoist liturgical tradition, and in this sense too she has been desexualized, for the more like a god she becomes, the less she demonstrates the sexualized aspect of a human being. Every year that local finances permit, a collective sacrifice (*gongji*) is held on the fourteenth day of the fifth lunar month, the day Wang's corpse was discovered. Like many temple festivals in Chinese popular religion, this ritual is celebrated with two simultaneous liturgies. A local Daoist priest is hired to perform a simplified version of a *jiao*, or offering rite. Since the structure of the *jiao* ritual has been well documented already,[23] the only point that need be noted here is that during the ritual, the temple is reconstructed as a representation of the cosmos, and places of honor are yielded to the elemental powers of Daoism. Wang Yulan herself is not the focus of the ritual, but its performance in her temple indicates that the local Daoist understands her as one of the myriad spirits of the supernatural realms. Future revelation may specify her place in it. Hong Duoyu goes a step farther in incorporating Wang Yulan into the Daoist pantheon. He explains that she is the maternal grandchild of the Jade Emperor and sister to the Queen Mother of the West. The popular term for Wang Yulan, Immortal Lady (*Xiangu*), also reflects popular understandings of her as belonging to the larger pantheon of deities.

The second part of the ritual, which goes on simultaneously, belongs to the community, which is interested in paying homage to its protectress. A member of the temple management committee provided an outline of the community liturgy. It consists of twelve steps, involving offerings of incense, wine, fruits, and sacrificial meat; the reading of a sacrificial text, and sequences of prostration, with musical performance to open and close the sequence. While the Daoist liturgy is identical to liturgies for rituals to other popular religious deities, the community liturgy reflects the ambiguities of Wang Yulan's status in two ways. First, in a Chinese temple festival the liturgy of the religious specialists, be they Buddhist or Daoist, typically takes precedence, and the elders who perform the sacrifice follow the instructions of the presiding monk or priest. But at a crucial juncture in the festival of Wang Yulan, it is the community liturgy that takes precedence. This is reflected in the second step of the liturgy: "presiding elder takes his position." The "presiding elder" is a role that is played by the ranking military officer and civilian official on Little Jinmen. They cannot stand around waiting to be told what to do by a Daoist priest. For their convenience, the community offering rite begins when these two officials arrive. As the Daoist priest puts it, "when they arrive, I have to stop."[24] Another distinctive feature of the ritual is the sacrificial text (*zhu wen*) itself, which is prepared by the Daoist, but which incorporates much of the nationalist discourse promoted initially by the military. A recent version reads:

Sacrificial text
On the 14th day of the 5th month of the 78th year of the Republic of China [1989] vice-commander of the Jin[men] defense command, General X, leads the representatives from all the various groups of Lieyu [Little Jinmen] and others
To carefully conduct the ritual of sacrifice of animals, fruits, wine and incense before Immortal Lady, the Chaste Maiden Wang, saying:
Model of feminine virtue; four virtues all replete/ She confronted death and did not yield
She opposed brutality and sacrificed her own body/ Eternally pure as jade
Her will to protect her chastity is firm/ She refused to be shamed
Treating her own life lightly she sacrificed herself in adversity/ A martyr for the nation
Near and far all praise her/ The spirits are pleased and the land is at peace

A temple is erected to commemorate her/ All people venerate her
The incense fires flourish/ Repeatedly she has shown her efficacy
Protecting and aiding the military and the people
The tragic brutality of the Communist bandits/ Creates disaster for the nation and kills off the people
Gods and men are together indignant/ Ultimately, they will surely be destroyed
We are blessed to have arrived at the festival of the deity/ Our veneration and sacrifice are in earnest
We beg that you accept the offering.

These ambiguities in the rituals of the annual temple festival demonstrate on the one hand the limits of religious interpretation imposed from above, and on the other hand the potential of this superscription of interpretation to affect popular practice. The military presence plays a role in the ritual performance of the local people, and their faith in the deity no doubt plays a role in continued military patronage. But while successive military officers beginning with Tian Shuzhang have sought to define Wang as a patriotic martyr, the embodiment of traditional Chinese virtues that will ultimately lead to the victory of the Republic of China over the Communists, few worshipers of the cult are willing to accept completely this interpretation. Though they are evidently willing to see her sacrifice as part of the explanation for her distinctiveness, for them she should be venerated because of her power to affect their lives. These two interpretations, mutually reinforcing in some ways and contradictory in others, intertwine in the private and collective rituals of the cult. The early history of the cult can thus be interpreted in part as an expression of the struggle over Jinmen identity, between a state which represents Jinmen as a pure symbol of anti-Communist struggle and the people of Jinmen, whose values include the shared memory of the miracles of their gods and their own faithful transmission of history and ritual, who see themselves as a product of their past and thus insist on a more multi-faceted conception of their own identity, and for whom the subordination of local society to military interests generates deep ambivalence.

Geopolitics and interpretive styles: Wang Yulan as floating signifier[25]

In the 1950s dozens of Patriotic Generals possessed local mediums and appeared in the dreams of ordinary people. In the same period, in southern Europe, there was a rash of religious apparitions and visions. William Christian argues that religious visions are rather common. What is unusual is for such visions to generate widespread attention. When they do, this is an indication of a time and place of "social need or alertness to messages from heaven." Both the European visions and the appearance of the Patriotic Generals can only be understood by locating them in the larger context. According to Christian, the European visions and apparitions were "emotional counterweights to the deep divisions of the postwar period," in other words, they were responses to the Cold War. Christian focusses on the potential of these visions to unify communities and nations.[26] Our micro-analysis of the cult of Wang Yulan makes it possible to move beyond this generalization and explore the different ways in which she has been understood.

In *Unities and Diversities in Chinese Religion*, Robert Weller suggests that different interpretations of a single ritual act can be mapped across a spectrum of styles of interpretation.[27] For the worship of Wang Yulan, we can identify several different axes of interpretation within a larger spectrum. The first is the axis from ghost to god. When Wang's body is first discovered, it is understood as the physical traces of an outsider with no ties to the community. Her spirit is a potential source of danger, and therefore to appease that spirit the villagers bury the corpse and make offerings to her. Today her worshipers see her as a powerful being who has the potential to provide assistance and protection. In other words, she is a god. In slightly different ways, this is also the interpretation of the military authorities and Daoist priests who officiate at her rituals. This axis is therefore basically aligned along the temporal dimension, with the understanding of Wang as ghost giving way to the understanding of her as god with the passage of time. A second axis is that from concrete efficacy to abstract symbol. In the eyes of her local worshipers, she is a god because of her efficacy, or *ling*. But she is also a symbol of sexual purity, and a symbol of resistance to the Communists. While the shift from one end of this axis to the other has also taken place over time, the rise of interpretations of her as symbol has not erased interpretations that focus on her power. This axis is better thought of as aligned along the social dimension, with the symbolic interpretation prevailing among outsiders such as the military and civil authorities. But there is considerable overlap, as for example with Hong Duoyu, who simultaneously holds both views. A related axis, familiar from Robert Hymes' study of bureaucratic and nonbureaucratic forms of interaction with Chinese deities in late imperial times, is the axis from personal to impersonal relations.[28] Village women have an intimate and personal relationship with Wang Yulan, evident when they name themselves and ask for specific boons for their family members. But for the Daoist priest and the military commander, Wang Yulan is an impersonal spiritual force, worthy of respect but generally kept at a distance. Thus this axis is also aligned along a social dimension, but it may be that those who treat the deity as an impersonal symbol do so quite deliberately. The commander, for example, as representative of the modernizing ROC state for his subordinates, may hold this interpretation in part to discourage his soldiers, and perhaps even himself, from other interpretations that he sees as backward and superstitious.

Finally, we can identify a fourth axis, one that ties Wang Yulan, Li Guangqian, and the other ghosts of Jinmen to the wider world. This axis is from the dead as subject to the dead as agent, from a state perspective that sees the dead as objects of political control to a popular perspective of the dead as conscious historical actors and agents. In Vietnam, Heonik Kwon and Shaun Malarney have explored how a traditional religious institution, the commemoration of the dead, has become a "technology of national integration."[29] State patronage of Wang Yulan, like their examples from Vietnam, is part of a ritual politics of nationalism. This ritual politics intersects with an older politics of interaction between living and dead.

One way of understanding the history of the cult is to see it as the consequence of the *aporia* or undecidable alteration between the ends of these various axes. It is precisely the ambiguity between ghost and god that sets in motion the chain of events that follows the discovery of her corpse. It is the parallel ambiguity between concrete efficacy and abstract symbol, and between personal and impersonal interactions, that creates a common interest among villagers and the local military in promoting the cult, leading to the construction and reconstruction of the temple. Ambiguity in interpretation allows a single deity to be understood simultaneously as a protective spirit originating in the worship of a hungry ghost and a nationalist hero on the front line of global geopolitical conflict. In its early phases, the history of the cult of Wang Yulan is precisely the story of the interpenetration of these two modes of interpretation, one stemming from popular culture, the other promoted by militaristic official culture. This flexibility of interpretation has implications for understanding contemporary popular religion. While the argument of a straightforward link between modernization and secularization has been widely discredited, the persistence of popular religion is still often seen in terms of survival in the face of the challenges and threats of modernity. The history of the cult of Wang Yulan, and its patronage by local agents of a state with an explicit modernizing agenda, suggest by contrast that in certain contexts the modernizing state can actually contribute to the persistence and elaboration of popular religious elements. Clearly state efforts to transform local cultural practices into political resources do not rob these practices of their meaning in the eyes of adherents. On Jinmen, the negotiations over the interpretation of Wang Yulan, as well as other deities that have emerged out of the geopoliticization of everyday life, show yet another side to the militarization of society and culture on the island. We shall see in the next chapter that these negotiations have only become more complex with the passage of time.

Part IV

Demilitarization and postmilitarization

Even as the militarization system with all its diverse consequences for social life reached full maturity in the 1980s, forces were already in motion that would lead to its dismantling. Demilitarization would have consequences just as significant, and as unexpected, as militarization. And attention to the process of demilitarization, as to that of militarization, shows how local society on Jinmen continued to be closely intertwined with national, regional, and global geopolitics, how decisions made in distant places for unrelated reasons continued to affect the day-to-day life of the island's residents in unanticipated ways. The outcomes of demilitarization, like those of militarization, resulted from the interaction of broader geopolitical forces with local agents and local circumstances.

Like militarization, we can distinguish two meanings to the term demilitarization. The narrower of the two refers to the ROC state's reduction in its capacity to make or defend against war on Jinmen. Concretely, this meant the withdrawal of troops from the island. The broader sense is the disentangling of other dimensions of social life from military interests and discourses. It is this broader sense in which we are mostly interested here, though again the two meanings cannot be completely disentangled.

Internationally, the first inklings of the changes that would later lead to demilitarization of Jinmen can be traced back to the PRC's new role in the international system in the early 1970s, in particular Sino–American rapprochement and the seating of the PRC delegation at the United Nations. These marked the start of the long process of Taiwan's isolation in international diplomacy. Sino–American rapprochement meant the gradual delinking of Jinmen from the global Cold War. But after decades of US intervention, the cross-strait relationship and the remaining unfinished business of the Chinese civil war, including the status of Jinmen, could not be tidily resolved. In a sense, after the 1970s Jinmen was still on the frontiers of a cold war. But it was a different cold war.

The PRC's new focus on economic development, summarized by the slogan "reform and opening up," led to a warming of cross-strait relations in the period. Though China would not yield on asserting its right to use military force against Taiwan, over the course of the 1970s its leaders adopted a generally conciliatory policy that sought peaceful reunification. But the decreased likelihood of a PRC attack on Taiwan cannot directly explain demilitarization on Jinmen, for as I have shown in previous chapters, Jinmen's military significance had been trivial since the 1960s if not earlier. That a high level of militarization had been sustained since then was due largely to political rather than military factors. By the early 1980s Nationalist Party (KMT) efforts to shore up international support by drawing attention to the Communist threat from the mainland had failed. As argued in chapter 8, the key political objective of militarization of Jinmen now shifted to focusing popular attention in Taiwan on the mainland threat in order to justify and legitimize continued KMT authoritarianism. The critical changes that enabled demilitarization were therefore not primarily in the cross-strait relationship itself but rather in domestic political changes in the Republic of China on Taiwan.[1]

12 Demilitarization and postmilitarization

In December 1978, Jinmen went on high alert. Militia commanders were warned that "[Communist] bandits and illegal elements may take advantage of the situation to infiltrate and engage in sabotage." Security was tightened on the coast. Civilian morale became a major preoccupation. The Jinmen Defense Headquarters (JDHQ) issued a pamphlet calling on the people to maintain unity in the face of adversity, and warning of a sinister new ruse by the PRC.[1] What sparked this anxiety was a major development in international affairs, the normalization of Sino–US relations. On January 1, 1979, the US officially recognized the PRC and broke off diplomatic relations with the ROC on Taiwan. This was a deep blow to the KMT regime. On the very same day, the PRC issued a "Message to Compatriots on Taiwan," calling for the establishment of direct links of trade, transportation, and postal services and talks between the two governments (the statement uses the term "Taiwan authorities" for the ROC), as a prelude to peaceful reunification. As a gesture of sincerity, the announcement concluded with the news that after more than twenty years, the alternate day bombing of Jinmen and Mazu would be ended. In a separate statement, the PRC minister of defense revealed that he had issued the cease-fire order. "Taiwan is a part of our country, and the compatriots of Taiwan are our brothers. For the convenience of compatriots from Taiwan, Penghu, Jinmen, and Mazu, whether soldiers or civilians, to come to the mainland to visit relatives and friends or for other reasons, and for the sake of shipping and productive activities in the Taiwan Strait, I have already issued the order to the front line units of Fujian to cease the shelling of Jinmen beginning today."[2] As I have discussed previously, for most of this period the shelling had consisted mostly of propaganda rather than explosive shells, and had not targeted civilians. So the local people had become largely inured to the danger. "We weren't much affected [by the end of the bombing]. We had already got used to hiding every odd-numbered day in the shelters. The biggest difference was that there used to be movies only on even days. Now we could go see movies every day."[3] But the end of the bombing did mark the end of a phase of Jinmen's history and the militarized rhythm of daily life. No longer did the people of Jinmen live alternate nights in shelters.

In the short term these changes did not lead to significant demilitarization of Jinmen. It took almost a decade for large numbers of troops to be withdrawn, further demonstrating that the actual military threat had long been decoupled from the militarization of the island. While warmer relations across the strait were certainly part of the reason for the reductions, the more important factor was political change on Taiwan. In the late 1970s and early 1980s the domestic political developments mentioned in chapter 8 deepened. As it became evident that there would be no reconquest of the mainland, the KMT faced a growing crisis of legitimacy, and its justifications for the state of emergency were called increasingly into question. President Chiang Ching-kuo and other ROC leaders had also become convinced of the need for political reform. By the 1980s, economic prosperity had created a large middle-class that was beginning to demand more political rights. An opposition movement made up of native Taiwanese who desired Taiwanese independence was growing, and its leaders formed a political party, the Democratic Progressive Party (DPP) in 1986. There was also growing international pressure for democratization. In 1987 Chiang repealed martial law on Taiwan. After his death the following year, his successor, Lee Teng-hui, signaled his intention to continue reforms.

Simultaneous with these changes came a relaxation of the restrictions on contact with the mainland, a policy shift that was partially, but only partially, a response to overtures from the PRC. In 1981, the PRC's National People's Congress proposed a plan for reunification whereby Taiwan would become a Special Administrative Region, retaining considerable autonomy. The following year, this proposal was elaborated by Deng Xiaoping, who coined the phrase "One Country, Two Systems." While the ROC government maintained its ban on direct official contact, private economic ties began to grow as Deng Xiaoping's domestic reform policies took root and Taiwanese businessmen began investing on the mainland. In 1987, demonstrations by ex-servicemen anxious to visit their ancestral homes before they died forced the ROC to lift the ban on travel to the mainland. Taiwanese began to visit the mainland in large numbers, and cross-strait trade and investment exploded.

The Jinmen Democracy Movement

Political change was slower to come to Jinmen than to Taiwan. The divergence in political structure was already apparent by the early 1980s, when a visiting Chiang Ching-kuo jokingly told some local officials that visiting assemblymen from Taiwan had been very impressed with the clean environment, frugality, prosperity, and low crime rate on Jinmen. When they asked how this had been accomplished, they were told it was because Jinmen had no county and municipal assembly.[4]

Immediately after the 1987 lifting of martial law on Taiwan, the government issued a statement that for security reasons martial law would remain in force on Jinmen and Mazu. But the lifting of martial law on Taiwan created new space for political dissent, and demonstrations and parades became a familiar sight on the streets of Taibei. As we have already seen, politically active Jinmen natives took advantage of this space in ways that would have been suppressed on Jinmen itself. Within a few weeks of the lifting of martial law on Taiwan, a charismatic young journalist from Jinmen named Weng Mingzhi (whom we have met already as an intrepid killer of swallows) led the newly formed "Jinmen–Mazu Unity and Self-help Committee" in a demonstration to demand the lifting of martial law on the offshore islands as well. A few months later, the group issued an eighteen-point manifesto that articulated a host of simmering resentments, with complaints about militia service obligations, restrictions on media, military interference in various aspects of private life, and even the treatment of employees at the distillery and other state-owned enterprises. The authorities on Jinmen soon responded with a rebuttal, challenging the Committee's claim to represent the Jinmen populace and praising the accomplishments of the War Zone Administration (WZA) system. In the most familiar legitimizing tactic of the state of emergency, the response ended with an ominous warning that lifting martial law, or even questioning the current arrangements, could potentially have disastrous consequences:

Jinmen and Mazu are only separated from the coast of Fujian by a single stretch of water. They are entirely exposed in the range of the Communist bandits' artillery. It is 100 percent a war zone. Should one lightly discuss lifting martial law? For the residents of Jinmen and Mazu, the maintenance of martial law, the implementation of WZA, and the organization of the civilian militia etc. are entirely consistent with the safety, interests, and good fortune of the people, and moreover also with the prosperity of Taiwan and Penghu.[5]

While martial law remained in place, in 1989 the first multi-party elections were held for Jinmen's seats in the ROC's equivalent to a parliament, the Legislative Assembly. Weng Mingzhi was chosen as the Democratic Progressive Party (DPP) candidate, but the WZA placed him and other Jinmen dissidents on a blacklist. They were refused entry permits and could not return to the island to campaign. In an ironic reference to the anti-PRC propaganda of the past, Weng distributed his campaign literature by attaching it to balloons that he released at the Chiang

Kai-shek Memorial Hall in Taibei, hoping they would float across the Taiwan Strait to Jinmen. The KMT party machine went into operation, and its candidate won easily. Weng and other activists continued to organize demonstrations, many of them characterized by an ironic sensibility. In 1989, for example, they held an exhibition of "Prohibited Items" outside the Legislative Assembly, laying out basketballs, tape recorders, inner tubes, and other items whose import and use were still highly restricted. The following year, a group of young Jinmen intellectuals in Taiwan, with the quiet support of several older journalists on the island itself, founded a newspaper, *Jinmen Reports*, to agitate for political change. It circulated among the community of Jinmen expatriates on Taiwan, but could not legally be brought to Jinmen itself.

In an effort to shore up popular support, the county government decided to address several complaints raised during the 1989 campaign. For example, civilian telephone calls to Taiwan, which only a year earlier had been ruled out as an unacceptable risk to military secrecy, were now permitted, a great convenience to the many Jinmen families with members working or studying on Taiwan. Such reforms were small but significant, for they were a first indication of WZA responsiveness to public opinion. Other incremental changes followed. The much-hated entry–exit permit system was eliminated in 1990, making it possible for Jinmen residents to travel freely to and from Taiwan. There was little discussion on this issue. With large numbers of Taiwanese traveling to the mainland via Hong Kong, and smaller numbers of mainlanders coming to Taiwan, the original purposes of the system, to prevent infiltration from and defection to the mainland, were utterly antiquated. The functions that had later become attached to the system, ensuring that Jinmen residents fulfilled their militia duties and thereby reinforced the island's image as a stalwart defender against the ever-present military threat, were also increasingly made irrelevant by the transformations in Taiwan–mainland relations and in Taiwan itself. In retrospect, the end of the permit system can now be seen as marking the real beginnings of demilitarization. For the first time, an important dimension of social life that had been controlled by military concerns was delinked from those concerns. But a major breakthrough eluded the activists.

In April 1991, President Lee lifted the "Temporary provisions effective during the period of Communist rebellion," measures that had been in place since 1949, and that gave extraordinary powers to the President, effectively suspending the constitution. The next day, the minister of defense again announced that martial law would remain in place on Jinmen and Mazu. "So long as the Chinese Communists do not renounce the use of force, the temporary martial law on Jinmen and Mazu will not be lifted."[6] For the people of Jinmen, this was a repeat of 1987, with a major liberalization on Taiwan promptly followed by an announcement that the status quo would remain on Jinmen. It seemed that Jinmen was still to remain hostage to larger geopolitical struggles.

The reaction from the opposition movement, now seasoned by several years of experience, was immediate. A newly created umbrella organization declared a sit-in at the Legislative Assembly. Their demands included an immediate end to martial law and the implementation of full constitutional government; protection of basic rights; the dissolution of the WZA; and direct elections to the position of county magistrate. There were also more concrete and immediate demands – an end to media restrictions; the lifting of travel restrictions for non-residents; and the legalization of tourism. Dissidents compared Jinmen to other Cold War border sites such as Panmunjom, arguing that tourism could help the local economy. If state policies had isolated Jinmen from its traditional networks, such comparisons and the contacts that followed them marked the beginning of efforts to imagine new ones. Over the ensuing ten days, the demonstrators used an expanded repertoire of activism to draw attention to Jinmen, rightly concerned that the changes on Taiwan would overshadow the stagnant situation on Jinmen. A group of female militia members burned their uniforms; the demonstrators paraded a papier-mâché model of the Tang dynasty official who was credited with the founding of Jinmen, the Lord Master of Benevolence, calling for his help in their political struggle.[7]

Even as official and non-official contact between Taiwan and the mainland grew, the KMT, though committed in principle to unification, had consistently rejected Deng Xiaoping's calls for reunification. This rejection was expressed in a concrete way on Jinmen. Deng's formulation, "Let One Country/Two Systems Reunify China" had been posted on an enormous billboard on the coast at Xiamen, large enough to be read on Jinmen. Residents of Xiamen could read the opposing sign from the Jinmen side: "Let the Three Principles of the People Unify China." Jinmen activists now began to use the same slogan to taunt the ROC government. Was not the maintenance of martial law on Jinmen, with all its attendant consequences, a case of "One country, two systems"?[8]

As in 1987, the demonstrations of 1991 were followed closely by several concrete but minor changes. The demonstrators were thus able to point to these as indicating that their tactics had been successful. In fact, their perception overstates the case. According to Chen Shuizai, the county magistrate at the time, the Ministry of Defense had already by May 1991 come to the decision that the WZA should be dissolved and martial law lifted, well before the demonstrations began. Chen, a former army colonel, was parachuted into the magistracy on May 3 after the unexpected resignation of his predecessor. At the time, Chen was serving in the office of the Chief of Staff in the Ministry of Defense. "There were lots of issues" for the magistrate's office, he says, "how to develop the county, and how to deal with the effects of the withdrawal of troops. The job needed someone with experience dealing with Jinmen, and a military background."[9] His predecessor, the first native of Jinmen to serve as county magistrate since before 1949, resigned only a few months into his term, reportedly because he could not deal with the pressure of the post. Chen would then go on to oversee much of the demilitarization of the 1990s.

The end of emergency

The breakthrough that the dissidents were hoping for came a year later with the sudden announcement that martial law on the island would be lifted, effective November 7, 1992. The WZA and the militia were summarily dissolved. Two of the institutions that had structured life on Jinmen for decades simply disappeared.

In retrospect the end of the militia was less sudden than it appeared at the time, for militia obligations had actually been decreasing for a decade in response to grumbling from within the militia, criticism from dissidents on Taiwan, and the declining political and symbolic importance of the militia. The length of annual training had been gradually reduced. Allowances were introduced to compensate militia members for time spent in compulsory training. But the final dissolution of the militia was nonetheless a momentous step.

If they were no longer to serve in the militia, it stood to reason that young men on Jinmen would become eligible for conscription into the regular army; there was much debate about when this liability would take effect. There were other immediate concerns, such as how to dispose of the militia's antiquated weapons. As one former militia official put it, "The militia had about the strength of a [regular army] division, so [dissolution] raised the same sorts of problems as those that a military unit being dissolved would face."[10]

Administratively at least the dissolution of the WZA proved straightforward. There was already a county government in place; it was simply given real authority over various areas where its authority had previously been nominal. The county magistrate's relationship with the JDHQ commander and his chief of staff remained the most important political relationship; now they simply worked directly with one another rather than in their capacity as members of the WZA Committee. But like the end of the militia, the dissolution of the WZA created many new problems. For example, hundreds of thousands of mines needed to be located and removed.[11] Other issues, while less significant, were still complex. Jinmen's roads, built to facilitate coordinated military transport and confuse invaders, had to be widened and straightened. The changes were of such magnitude that an immediate restoration of constitutional governance was deemed impossible – the term restoration itself is a misnomer, for Jinmen had never been under constitutional government since the movement of the ROC to Taiwan. Instead the Ministry of Defense drew up a plan to ease the transition, in other words to bring the state of emergency to an end. The Regulations for the Safeguarding and Guidance of Jinmen and Mazu (*Jin–Ma anfu tiaoli*) were issued in the summer of 1992, just before the lifting of martial law.[12] There was much discussion in the Jinmen dissident movement about whether the regulations were in fact simply the re-introduction of a new form of control, a "semi-lifting of martial law."[13]

Chen Shuizai's background and connections in the military became very important, because with the dissolution of the WZA the institutionalized links between the military and the county government disappeared precisely at a time when the relationship was undergoing major changes. The most obvious of these changes was the demilitarization of Jinmen in the narrow sense, as the majority of troops were withdrawn from the island. The ROC government had begun discussing troop reductions in the mid-1980s, ostensibly in light of improving cross-strait relations. In fact, political reform on Taiwan was also important in their thinking, because as the KMT sought a new basis for legitimacy by expanding political participation and democratization, the legitimizing role played by the Communist threat declined. In 1983, one of five army divisions was relocated to Taiwan. Four divisions were stationed on Jinmen throughout the 1980s. But the divisions were being hollowed out, something that was evident both to the conscripts serving in them and the shopkeepers and other service workers who relied on their trade. "When I served on Jinmen, the numbers of troops was way down. But they did this by reducing the number of soldiers in each unit, not by cutting whole units. So my company had about thirty soldiers in it, when it really should have had over one hundred. This made sentry and patrol duty really onerous, because we were supposed to keep doing the job that the unit had done when it was much larger. Many sentry posts just had to be abandoned."[14] By the time this soldier, a conscript officer, was posted to Jinmen in 1993, the number of troops had been reduced in this way by about half, to a total of 31,000. In 1997, the ROC military implemented a general downsizing. The four divisions on Jinmen were now downgraded to brigades. The total number of troops was now 16,000. By the early twenty-first century, the number shrank even further, to under 11,000 (see Appendix).[15]

In many places in the world where local economies have become heavily reliant on the presence of the military, economic hardship and collapse are the immediate and frequently unanticipated consequences of demilitarization. Among Chen Shuizai's first big challenges was to shepherd the island through the economic turmoil caused by the troop withdrawals. Most pressing of all was the need to secure the finances of his own county government, which could no longer be assured of large subventions, through the WZA, from the Ministry of Defense. Lobbying in Taibei for central government funds became a novel but increasingly important part of the job of county magistrate. "We had to try to develop a social welfare system – we wanted it to be as good as in Western countries. But we needed money. So my attitude was that we had to be self-reliant." Looking for a more permanent solution, the county government borrowed funds to expand the distillery. Its multi-billion NTD annual income has become the mainstay of county government finance, and has allowed it to set up an impressive welfare program, with residents of Jinmen receiving free medical care, free education (universal in the ROC, but on Jinmen students also receive free meals at school), free public transport, and a small monthly pension for seniors. While Jinmen residents had for decades sought to transfer their registration to Taiwan in order to avoid militia duty, some Taiwanese residents now began to transfer their registration to Jinmen in order to receive benefits, and the island's long-term population decline stopped.

Though it is perhaps in the nature of modern governments to perceive a problem of inadequate finances, the boon from the liquor plant meant that the issue of county finances turned out to be relatively straightforward. There remained the larger issue of the island's economy as a whole. The thousands of households that relied on G. I. Joe business had already seen their income drop precipitously over the course of the 1980s. When martial law was lifted, the gross domestic product (GDP) per capita of Jinmen was about US$4,000, or only about two-thirds that of Taiwan as a whole.[16] Everyone knew that this statistic was inaccurate, since much of the economy was underground. Many owners of G. I. Joe businesses kept two sets of books, one for their own use and another to show to tax authorities.[17] But the island's economy and the standard of living of its inhabitants were manifestly behind those of Taiwan. The Taiwan economic miracle seemed to have largely bypassed Jinmen. Further decline was likely as troop reductions continued. The backwardness of Jinmen was particularly striking because it continued to be compared to the city of Xiamen, only a few miles away. By the 1990s Xiamen, one of the first Special Economic Zones created under Deng Xiaoping's reforms, was a burgeoning economic center, with rapidly rising foreign investment, construction, population, and standard of living. "People looked at the bright lights and tall buildings of Xiamen and asked, 'Why is our Jinmen still dark and quiet at night?' "[18]

Even with the improvement in cross-strait relations, the same problems of geographic isolation and geopolitical insecurity that had stood in the way of economic development in the 1950s and 1960s persisted. With Taiwanese investment shifting onto the mainland at a furious pace in the early 1990s, planners there were finding it difficult enough to retain investment on Taiwan itself, let alone direct it to Jinmen. The solution that was hit upon was to try to develop tourism as the basis of the local economy. Jinmen was like other places of heightened geopolitical significance that the end of the Cold War left with few resources for economic development. Tourism seemed to offer the best solution. Tourism had actually been growing surreptitiously since the late 1980s, under cover of official visits. The infrastructure that had been set up to bring local and foreign visitors to Jinmen to experience life on the front line and to be reminded of the Communist threat was reoriented by entrepreneurial officials to generate funds. Family members of conscripts serving on Jinmen were permitted to visit. As in other contexts where militarization depended on universal military service, allowing parents to visit their sons in the army was seen as a useful way to build support for, or at least forestall opposition to, continued militarization. Even before tourism was legalized there were an estimated 15,000 annual visitors from Taiwan to Jinmen through these two modes.[19] The ban on tourism was lifted in 1993. Response on Jinmen was mixed, since proprietors of G. I. Joe businesses recognized immediately that they would not necessarily benefit if their customers changed from soldiers stationed for months on end into tourists visiting for a few days.[20]

The local government and the ROC legislature now raised the possibility of establishing a national park on Jinmen. Having experienced the often negative consequences of unregulated tourism development in a number of places on Taiwan, the authorities were anxious that Jinmen would not suffer the same fate.[21] The environment of Jinmen required protection from tourists, and the tourists required protection from the environment. There were a number of environmentally fragile areas on the island from which the military had withdrawn, and there were serious safety concerns involving land-mines, buried ordinance, and abandoned bases. Also, with urban and village development having been tightly constrained for so long, Jinmen had become a museum of traditional architecture as well as of the Western–traditional hybrid architectural style created by returned Overseas Chinese. Historical preservation was a pressing concern now that restrictions had been lifted and many old houses abandoned. The original brief by the ROC's National Park Administration called for the transfer of much of Jinmen – 35 percent of Greater Jinmen and 70 percent of Little Jinmen – to the control of the new park. When word leaked out, there was immediate public opposition. People worried that the park would stifle economic development, exactly the opposite of what the lifting of martial law was supposed to accomplish. There were public meetings held with residents in 1994 and the planning bodies eventually reduced the projected scope. By late 1995, the planning and consultation was complete, and the national park was formally established.[22]

The tourism business by that point was already booming. In 1994 there were over 350,000 tourist visitors. The following year, the number jumped to almost half a million.[23] Many of these visitors were former soldiers or conscripts who had served on Jinmen, and so nostalgia was an important element to tourism. A museum at Guningtou features a documentary film about the battle; the film is presented as the reminiscences of an old soldier revisiting the battlefield with his grandson. Scholars have remarked on the structural similarities between tourism and pilgrimage, both of which involve transformation through spatial transition.[24] For most Taiwanese visitors, tourism to Jinmen is a journey to a place of heightened historical rather than spiritual significance; the islands have been sacralized by military conflict. Jinmen also provides an opportunity to gaze on the mainland, that is, for an ordered visual encounter with difference. (Today many Taiwanese visitors to Jinmen have already traveled to the mainland, often to Xiamen, where they have had the opportunity to gaze back upon Jinmen.) While tourism is often demonized for its commodification of the authentic, on Jinmen it is not the pristine or primitive that has been commodified, but the militarized and mobilized. If authenticity means faithfulness to an inherited set of practices reproduced in a specific locale for specific purposes unconnected to the market process, authenticity in Jinmen is distinguished by its link not to the pre-market past but to the geopolitical past.[25]

Perhaps because of the obvious limits of an industry dependent on nostalgia, plans to further develop tourism grew more elaborate, even outlandish. In 1994, county authorities commissioned a study on the possibility of establishing an international casino as a way to increase local revenues and further promote tourism and the economy. A tourist infrastructure was quickly emerging to meet the demand. By 1994, there were dozens of illegal hotels operating in the villages. In the absence of regulation, too many firms sprang up to chase too little business, and the resulting competition drove profits down for all. The transport business was a good example. Within a year of the opening of tourism, ten bus companies were created to move tourists around the island. Daily capacity soon reached almost 4,000 passengers, but with only 1,000 arrivals per day, and most tours lasting two or at most three days, there was considerable over-capacity and prices fell.[26] The upshot was that tourism, while benefiting the overall economy of Jinmen, did not benefit all its residents equally. "Who benefits from all this tourism?" asks Hong Duoyu, the blind temple-keeper at the Wang Yulan temple. "The hotel owners, the restaurant owners, and the bus companies. Ordinary people just suffer from higher prices."[27]

The rise of tourism presented new opportunities for some. With artillery shell cleavers already a famous product of the island, Maestro Wu's family business prospered. They opened new retail outlets especially for tourists. Domestic and later international journalists visited the shop and interviewed Wu Dawei. "The media made the knives a symbol of Jinmen." Several competitors joined the market, which grew to over NTD30 million (US$1 million) per year. But the Wu family still claims about half the total market.[28] It is this huge expansion that has prompted suspicion that the cleavers are no longer manufactured out of old shells but out of ordinary scrap steel. Other tourist-oriented industries, like peanut candy and sorghum liquor, have also prospered. As part of the larger policy of exchanging rice for sorghum, Jinmen farmers have always been given a few bottles of liquor several times per year at the seasonal festivals. As the number of tourists grew, local people began reselling their allotment to tourist shops in town. Locals also looked for ways to maximize their earnings from this practice. The obvious answer was to become a licensed liquor retailer, enabling one to purchase more liquor at the wholesale Jinmen price, then resell it to tourist shops. By the middle of 1994, there were over 7,000 licensed liquor retailers on Jinmen. To put this in perspective, about one in every three households was running a liquor shop. The vast majority of these shops was simply *pro forma* – they bought and sold liquor without ever necessarily taking physical possession of a single bottle. As they had been doing for decades, the civilians of Jinmen found loopholes in the system of militarization and demilitarization, and exploited these to their benefit as best they could.

But most families involved in G. I. Joe business have not prospered since the end of martial law. "Since the troops have been withdrawn, there's no longer a sea of people. The shopkeepers' business isn't as good as it used to be. Without the consumers from the military, there's nobody from outside to buy things. Lots of shops have already closed down." As Xiao Shengyi, the Little Jinmen shopkeeper puts it, "Since the withdrawal of the troops, the economy has deteriorated. The tourists leave Little Jinmen every night, and only a few shops make any money – selling

Fig. 12.1 Shuttered G. I. Joe shops in Xiaojing (photo by author)

kitchen knives, candy, and liquor. In the old days, there were lots of ways
to make money . . . Now everyone is competing for a small number of
jobs."[29] In every village of the island, one can see abandoned G. I. Joe
shops. Xiao's comment draws attention to another consequence of demilitarization and tourism, the reversal of the geographic shifts that occurred
in the 1950s. At that time, the economic center of the island shifted away
from Jincheng toward the central military complexes around Mount
Taiwu. Shanwai, especially, developed because it was near the major con-
centrations of troops and because it was protected by the mountain from
mainland shells. Other towns like Donglin on Little Jinmen flourished
because of their location near divisional headquarters. Today, the less
central parts of Shanwai and Donglin have become like ghost towns, and
Jincheng has resumed its traditional position as the most vibrant community on the island [Fig. 12.1].

831 in the new Jinmen

With these developments remaking so many aspects of Jinmen society,
one would not expect the commercial sex business to remain unchanged.
In the late 1980s, the military brothels, or 831, were privatized. The ROC
army was getting out of the sex business. We have no direct evidence of
the reasons for the changes, but it appears that the basic issue was shifts in

Fig. 12.2 Former military brothel converted to karaoke parlor. In 2007, police closed the business because it was being used for prostitution (photo by author)

public opinion in Taiwan and a new sensitivity to that opinion on the part of the army and the Ministry of Defense. The only concrete evidence available is the legal documentation pertaining to the contracting out of the 831 to private entities. In late 1986, a contract granted management of six brothels to a Jinmen company in exchange for a monthly fee [Fig. 12.2]. The company guaranteed that it would staff the brothels with between fifty and seventy sex workers, "beautiful in appearance (under thirty years of age), healthy and of high quality." The rules of recruitment, management, compensation, access, hygiene, and health were simply transferred over from the existing regulations. The Political Warfare Office of the Ministry of Defense retained overall supervision of the brothel system. Despite privatization, there were several factors that necessitated continued surveillance by the army. No matter who was running the brothels, ensuring that commercial sex did not threaten sol-diers' fighting trim was still important. So protection against sexually transmitted diseases remained a concern. The brothels also needed to be monitored to ensure that intimacy did not lead to breaches of security. As a place apart from civilian society, it was up to the army to ensure that workers in the brothels did not have prohibited or restricted items such as radios, cameras, flotation devices, and pornography. In yet another expression of the link between external and internal vigilance, sex workers themselves had to be free of suspicion of sympathy for or ties to "Communists, Taiwanese independence [supporters], or saboteurs."[30]

The stress on maintaining a firm line between soldiers, prostitutes, and civilians was also inherited from the earlier system. Categories of eligibility were clearly specified: serving soldiers and officers, and retired soldiers without family, a group consisting mainly of the old mainland soldiers who had never married but had settled down on Jinmen, were the main categories of customers. Civil servants from off-island remained an ambiguous group. They were not soldiers, but those who were unmarried and were not permanent Jinmen residents were also allowed to use the brothels at set times, presumably because unmarried men, regardless of their profession, were seen as potential dangers to civilian women. All other civilians were forbidden to use the brothels. A clear line between civilian women and prostitutes persisted. The management contract for the brothels specified that it was forbidden for "upright women" to enter the brothels and "engage in inappropriate conduct." At the same time, even after privatization, 831 prostitutes were still understood as women mobilized for the national cause in their own distinctive way. For this reason, the tradition continued of selecting exemplary employees as "model women." The army paid for prizes for the model sex workers on Women's Day each year.[31]

Given that the number of brothels and prostitutes remained virtually the same, and assuming that rates of use remained constant, the military brothel remained a profitable business in the late 1980s even though the number of troops had begun to decline. So it was no surprise that after an initial two-year contract, the management company was eager to sign a two-year extension in 1989. But domestic events in Taiwan intervened. The comfort women of the Second World War was becoming a topic of much public interest in Taiwan, following the public campaigns of former comfort women in Japan's other pre-war colony of Korea. Opposition legislators in Taiwan seized on the continued existence of the 831 at a time when the tragedy of the comfort women was coming to light to criticize the government's military policies. In late 1990, the management contracts were revoked, and the military brothels on Jinmen shut down after some forty years of operation.

Precisely because the 831 system had been kept so separate from civilian life, there seems to have been no support whatsoever for the move on Jinmen. On the contrary, there was actually considerable opposition. Those who benefited economically from the sex trade complained that they were hurt by its closure. Most of the staff of the brothels were retired soldiers. Thrown out of work and with no marketable skills, a group of them petitioned the county government to reopen the brothels. They were not thinking only of themselves, they insisted, but also of the larger civilian society. "For years," they wrote, "Jinmen has been orderly; society has been peaceful and sex-related crimes very rare. This must be credited to the existence of the brothels. It is a common saying that if there were no public toilets, people would urinate everywhere. The closure of the brothels will likely damage Jinmen society, and people are very worried about this." In other words, the military view that brothels were essential for the protection of local women against rape by soldiers had now become accepted by local civilians. Within the next year, the rape of a civilian woman by a soldier was reported to police. There had allegedly been several cases of rape already, including a horrific case involving a child, but these had been hushed-up. The civilian voices now calling for the reopening of the brothels grew. The county's Consultative Assembly called for the establishment of a purely civilian prostitution system, with no formal connection to the military, but necessary to respond to the pressures caused by militarization. "At present," ran their proposal, "it is difficult to balance the needs of soldiers and civilians on the offshore islands. We are concerned that conflicts may arise between soldiers and civilians, and rape and other crimes proliferate, causing a crisis." The proposal was rejected, but it was clear that civilians and civilian authorities accepted the underlying thinking. Referring to the rape case, magistrate Chen Shuizai called the presence of male soldiers on Jinmen "a bomb that could explode at any time."[32]

This final chapter of the history of military prostitution reveals one way in which the distortions of society and culture produced by militarization persist even after demilitarization. The understanding of militarized masculinity that had been produced by the military in the 1950s and 1960s had come to be fully accepted by local society, and eventually turned back against the military in the hope of persuading its leaders not to pursue policies that were seen as negative for local society. Thus the military brothel had come to be seen as an essential presence on Jinmen, necessary protection for local civilians from the predatory male soldiers. This perception was of course inextricably linked to the material benefits derived from the system, a connection that Jinmen shared with many other places where selling sexual services to soldiers was an important part of the local economy. But because in this case the actual prostitutes were not wives and daughters, fellow members of local society, but outsiders, the issue was disconnected from any other concerns about women's roles and statuses.

The changes to military prostitution were not the only way in which demilitarization affected gender on Jinmen. In calling for a public discussion about compensation for female militia (a subject discussed further in the next chapter), Weng Mingzhi noted that the National Day review participants had been "forced to neglect their family duties" in order to train for the review, where they "did a pretty dance for the high officials to watch."[33] This was perhaps the first time that the sexualized element of the female militia was ever explicitly addressed. What made it particularly interesting was Weng's suggestion that with the end of the female militia, women would be able to resume their appropriate role within the family without risk of interruption. Here was a clear recognition that it was the state of emergency that had drawn women out of the domestic sphere. Now that the emergency was over, they could return there. Demilitarization presented the possibility that with their role of self-sacrifice for the sake of the nation eliminated, women on Jinmen might face the resumption of a traditional patriarchy.

Smugglers, tourists, and Three Small Links

As we saw in chapter 6, for decades regulating communication across the waters that separated Jinmen from the mainland had been a major priority for the WZA. Small-scale smuggling had long been going on between fishing boats from the two sides. Li Yumin remembers meeting up at sea with mainland fishermen to drink beer and exchange news in the 1980s. After martial law was lifted, applications for fishing licenses rose as Jinmen residents looked for opportunities to profit from smuggling. The authorities fought a rearguard action, but halfheartedly, for the smuggling was impossible to stop and it relieved to some extent the economic hardship of residents. By the mid-1990s, a journalist for the *New York Times* estimated that 60 to 70 percent of all the produce consumed on the island was smuggled.[34] With smuggling an open secret, a new term entered the local vocabulary. Goods from the mainland were said to have "floated over" (*piao guolai*).

In 2000, responsibility for maintaining coastal security was transferred from the navy to the coast guard, and smuggling of mainland products moved from the waters off Jinmen to its beaches. Fishing boats from the Xiamen area began to cross over to Little Jinmen every day. Elderly villagers in some villages began wearing finely crafted wool Sun Yat-sen suits and traditional *qipao* gowns, made to measure by mainland tailors. Mainland fishermen equipped with cell phones could even transmit orders from the beach back to the mainland, to ensure prompt delivery. The next year, as cross-strait relations continued to deepen, the ROC government authorized direct transport links between Jinmen and Xiamen. This became known as the "Three Small Links" (*xiao santong*), in distinction to direct links between the mainland and Taiwan, which the ROC government continued to forbid. Daily ferry service was set up. The dense social and economic ties that had formerly linked Jinmen to the nearby mainland, but that had been cut off since 1949, began to revive. Local people reconnected with lost relatives. ROC soldiers who had settled on Jinmen went back to the mainland to take young wives from the poor fishing villages of the coast. Wealthy Jinmen residents began to invest on the mainland, and many people purchased property in Xiamen. A running joke on Jinmen today is that when older folk greet one another in the local dialect, they no longer ask "Have you eaten yet?" but "Have you been to Xiamen lately?"

Tourism and smuggling converged to provide a new source of income for residents. This change is apparent outside the temple of Wang Yulan. When tour buses first began to stop at the temple in the early 1990s, Qingqi villagers built rough stalls to sell local products such as peanuts, snacks, and cleavers. In the next few years, as tourist visits grew into the tens and then hundreds of thousands, the villagers pooled resources to construct a tin roof over their stalls. Their business also shifted. They now sell mostly products smuggled from the mainland: herbal medicines, specialty foods like mushrooms and dried shellfish, and manufactured items such as clothes and toys. Many of the stall-holders are local women who used to be involved in G. I. Joe business but have now reoriented themselves to tourist business. This shift from selling local goods to smuggled mainland goods is widespread on the island. So too is the shift in the location of their business, from locations near bases to locations near tourist attractions. Purchasing smuggled mainland products is now part of an authentic Jinmen tourist experience, even though many Taiwanese travel to the mainland themselves. One shopkeeper revealed to me that most of the mainland items in his Jincheng shop, such as teapots and porcelain figures, are acquired quite legally through a Hong Kong firm that tranships the goods from the mainland via Hong Kong and Taiwan. But it is crucial to his business that the customers believe that the items are smuggled directly across from the mainland.[35]

The temple of Wang Yulan is a useful site to explore other changes since the lifting of the state of emergency besides the rise of smuggling. Tourists now make up the vast majority of visitors to the temple. On any given day, as many as 1,000 tourists from Taiwan now visit the temple precincts, mostly on group tours. There are three attractions at the temple site: the temple itself, the open air market, and a branch of a Jinmen tourist chain store specializing in local products. When tourists step off their bus, they are shepherded by their guide into the shop (no money changes hands with the guide, but some sort of consideration presumably ensures both the prominence of this site on the tour and the highlighting of the shop during the site visit). After exiting the shop, they visit the open air market or the temple or both. While virtually every member of every tour group visits the market, from a typical bus-load of forty to fifty tourists about half usually enter the temple. The majority of these perform no religious ritual, but simply stand briefly before the images in the temple, then step outside to view the grave. In most groups, though, a handful of tourists perform a more elaborate ritual. They make a contribution to the donation box (there are actually two boxes; the temple-keeper collects the receipts of one to support himself), in exchange for which they take incense sticks and paper money from a side table. After offering the incense with the appropriate bows before each station, they may leave other offerings such as skin cream, and cast divination blocks (see chapter 11). Visitors often use a video camera to record their visit.

My interviews with the tourists were by necessity brief, and typically interrupted by the tour bus driver honking angrily and signaling his intention to leave the interviewee behind. They offer similar sorts of explanations for their behavior to what one would hear at a temple to a popular deity in Taiwan. The temple has been represented to them as part of an authentic experience of Jinmen, so worshiping is part of their pursuit of authenticity. They also worship the deity in the hope of obtaining benefits, both concrete, in the sense that the deity can provide protection and grant wishes, and psychological, in the sense that worshiping the deity can give a sense of comfort and a "renewal of energy" (*buchong nengliang*). With their offerings of cosmetics, the tourists have unselfconsciously introduced their own innovation into ritual performance. They do so based on their experiences in Taiwan, where shrines to the ghosts of unmarried women are common. Such ghosts are believed to appreciate offerings of cosmetics and fashionable clothing by analogy with the perceived desires of living unmarried women.[36] By offering cosmetics to Wang Yulan, the tourists are in effect resexualizing her, reinterpreting her in terms different from both the nationalist symbol of the military and the protective deity of the villagers.

Wang Yulan and the politics of identity

Since demilitarization, the internal politics of the cult of Wang Yulan has become the site of a debate about Jinmen's identity and its future. A division has arisen between those who hold different visions of that future. Recall that Hong Duoyu held that after her initial revelation, the deity had never again possessed a medium. The actual situation is more complex. Since the late 1990s, Chen Meixin, an elderly woman from Qingqi village who used to operate a stall in the temple market, has claimed to be possessed by the spirit of Wang Yulan on a number of occasions. Like many mediums in Jinmen, Chen was first possessed by the spirit of a dead soldier some thirty-five years ago. Through training by another medium, Chen developed her abilities to communicate with the spirits and to prepare illness-curing charms. Some years ago, Chen was unexpectedly possessed by Wang Yulan, who asked that a ritual of "burial transfer" (*zhuanzang*) be performed to comfort her. Not surprisingly on an island where fishing used to be an important livelihood, this is a common ritual performed when the spirit of a person who dies at sea continues to trouble the living, and involves a Daoist ritual and offerings of clothes and other things the dead might want. The timing of Wang Yulan's revelation probably had some connection to the spread of tourism, for it was the tourists who, bringing with them their experience from Taiwan, first made offerings of things considered as appropriate for a living woman. This renewed attention to her sexuality had the effect of highlighting the extent to which Wang remained a dead human, and had not completed the transition from ghost to god. Wang has since possessed Chen several times. In June 2002, Chen reported that Wang had expressed a wish to return to her home on the mainland. This is a practice that has become increasingly common among temples on Taiwan that claim to be offshoots of temples on the mainland. Taiwanese worshipers of Mazu, the goddess of seafarers, often make pilgrimages to Mazu's founding temple in Fujian. But Hong Duoyu, who sees Wang's divinity as arising from her resistance to Communism, refused to accept that Wang would have any interest in mainland China. So he now denies the legitimacy of Chen's possession, which is why he says that Wang has never possessed any medium since her initial revelation. Opinion in Qingqi is divided on the matter. Discussion about Wang's return is a proxy for discussion of whether Jinmen's future lies in closer ties to the mainland. As Katherine Verdery has written of post-socialist Eastern Europe, dead bodies can be one of the vehicles through which people "reconfigure their worlds of meaning in the wake of . . . profoundly disorientating changes."[37]

Hong Duoyu's disagreement with Chen Meixin reflects disagreements about Jinmen's relationship with the mainland. He and other temple leaders also have other strong opinions about Wang Yulan that bear on disagreements about Jinmen's relationship with Taiwan. Hong is scathing about most of the tourists who visit her temple. Some enter the temple only to gawk, others do not bother to enter at all. "Why would they worship here – they don't even respect their parents? . . . Of every 100 tourists from Taiwan, only two will worship. Most of them just bow. They don't even make offerings. The temple has become just a tourist attraction." The distinction between bowing and offering is of great concern to Hong because his livelihood depends on worshipers making donations in exchange for incense and paper money. But he sees tourist attitudes as indicative of a greater problem, the moral collapse of Taiwanese society. "The great culture of our Chinese people has been destroyed. Education in Taiwan has become hooligan education (*liumang jiaoyu*), not Confucian education. There are even cases of fratricide, of matricide, even of incest in Taiwan." He feels the Republic of China on Taiwan has abandoned its self-proclaimed role as the defender of traditional Chinese culture. This renunciation is linked, he feels, to the greed and materialism that now permeates Taiwanese culture. The clearest evidence of this greed is that Taiwanese businessmen "are going abroad, leaving the people impoverished." By this he means they are shifting investment to the People's Republic. The political leadership is also to blame. "Our leaders do nothing to help the situation."

The question of whether Wang Yulan wishes to return to the mainland, and Hong Duoyu's critique of Taiwanese society, are symptomatic of a fundamental crisis of identity currently besetting the people of Jinmen. This identity crisis is partially, in turn, one of the lingering consequences of the decades of militarization and geopoliticization. The state of emergency continues to cast a shadow on contemporary society and identity.

Already in the martial law period, activists on Taiwan had begun to articulate a distinctive Taiwanese identity as a rebuttal to the KMT and PRC claims that Taiwan is part of China and as part of their efforts to legitimize the idea of Taiwanese independence. This articulation of a new identity has since become more elaborate and taken root in society at large. The main historical elements in this construction are Taiwan's distinctive history of migration from the mainland beginning in the seventeenth century, the period of Japanese colonialism from 1895 to 1945, and then rapid economic and social development since 1949 (the history of Taiwan's aborigines is also increasingly celebrated in narratives of Taiwanese distinctiveness). This version of Taiwanese identity is very challenging for the people of Jinmen. They share little of this history in common with Taiwan. Jinmen's lineages are said to have moved to the island more than a thousand years ago; the Japanese occupation of eight years left few lingering consequences, and the rapid economic growth of Taiwan bypassed Jinmen because of militarization.

One response to this dilemma has been efforts to construct Jinmen as an intermediary or a bridge between the two societies, the mainland and Taiwan. As Chen Shuizai's successor as magistrate commented on the county's website:

From the perspective of the external environment, Jinmen's status is now in a state of uncertainty due to cross-strait instability. Politically, we should try to make the best of Jinmen's geographical vantage point to shape the island into a special experimental zone for cross-strait interaction, and mold it into a free, prosperous, functional cultural city by exploiting the resources on both sides of the strait. At the current stage, Jinmen must get rid of its past image as a bastion of anti-communism and national recovery, and move to reestablish its image as an open, prosperous city that serves as a linking bridge across the strait.[38]

This is a viewpoint that is often articulated by the local government; it is also what many Jinmen residents are doing in practice, by rejuvenating traditional ties with the mainland, investing there, and traveling frequently back and forth. As with so much of Jinmen's recent history, though, the question of whether this approach can become a sustainable vision for Jinmen's future depends on larger forces over which Jinmen residents and officials have little control. Moves to closer ties, such as direct transport links between Taiwan and the mainland, would make Jinmen largely irrelevant as a bridge between the two societies.

A small number of Jinmen residents have decided to embrace the new vision of Taiwan. They have thrown their support behind the DPP, which grew out of the Taiwan independence movement into the most important political party to have emerged since democratization. Political activism related to Jinmen issues took full advantage of the space created by dissidents on Taiwan, and there was a certain community of interest between the two groups in the late 1980s. Weng Mingzhi was widely criticized when he joined the DPP, and two essays he wrote in response to that criticism are instructive. In the first, "Why do I want to join the DPP," he explained that his general commitment was to a system in which multiple parties contended for power, thereby ensuring the greatest benefit went to the people and limiting corruption. His support for the DPP was simply support for democratic transition. Blaming all of Jinmen's problems on the "powerful party-state-army clique," he also argued that a small number of activists could not hope to effectively oppose the clique. They had to seek allies.[39] Few local people agreed with him, in part because of suspicion about the implications of the DPP policy of promoting Taiwan independence, and in part because the major mass organizations on Jinmen remained under the control of the KMT. The large numbers of civil servants and employees of state-owned enterprises were likewise disinclined to support an opposition party. The first organized DPP rally on Jinmen, in late November 1992, drew only about twenty participants.

Jinmen suspicion of the DPP grew the following year, when two party leaders visiting the US told reporters that the future of Jinmen was up to the people of Jinmen to decide democratically. While this was seemingly inoffensive, it followed logically from their position that Jinmen and Mazu are not part of Taiwan's territory. This sparked immediate outrage on Jinmen and among Jinmen expatriates. The DPP central office distanced the party from the comments, affirming that the DPP position was that the national territory of the Republic of China included Jinmen. The issue arose again in 1995, when the party chairman, Shi Mingde, called for the withdrawal of all troops from Jinmen. As he put it, "why should the sons of Taiwan run the risk of being held hostage on Jinmen?" Though the DPP tried to calm public opinion by presenting a white paper on economic development on Jinmen, Shi's remarks were widely interpreted as a call for the ROC to abandon Jinmen. Rumors circulated that the DPP had offered a secret deal to the Communists, to turn over the offshore islands in exchange for a cross-strait peace settlement.[40]

It was one thing to ignore the DPP when it was a force in the political wilderness; quite another when it became a ruling party. The election of the DPP's candidate, Chen Shuibian, to the office of ROC president in 2000 was a shocking development for Jinmen. Residents realized that they could no longer assume a KMT-led government would protect their interests. A county DPP branch was hurriedly organized, says one party member, "because we realized we had lost all ties to the central government . . . When I signed my party application, my eyes were all red, because I felt I was betraying myself. But joining the DPP gives us an opportunity to help our native place. All we need to do is increase the number of votes [for DPP candidates at various levels] and the center will start to pay attention to us."[41] There were now also potential personal and professional benefits to DPP support. Due to his years of anti-KMT activism, both within and without the DPP, Weng Mingzhi was appointed the secretary of the Fujian provincial government.

But the overall voting pattern on Jinmen remains strongly pro-KMT. In the current political environment of the ROC, this means the island votes for the pan-Blue coalition. As of 2007 this included the KMT and two splinter parties. Compared to its opponents, the pan-Blue coalition favors closer ties to the mainland even as it moves away from a position of support for eventual unification. The politics of the local people thus are consistent with their everyday behavior, bound increasingly to the mainland both through the revitalization of old ties that had been broken in 1949 and the creation of new ones. For like other divided Cold War societies, it was precisely as the PRC's role as mirror-image and mirror-opposite in the fashioning of Jinmen declined that in material terms the two sides of the Strait began to grow closer.

Conclusions

Virtually nothing about Jinmen's strategic position changed between the early 1980s and the late 1990s. But the period saw the reversal of the decades-long course of militarization and the demilitarization of local society. The causes of this shift were not military but political. They were linked to issues and agendas in Beijing, Washington, and especially Taibei. Thus demilitarization did not indicate the delinking of Jinmen from geopolitical concerns, but rather simply a new phase in its geopoliticization. This is not to say that Jinmen was a serious factor in geopolitical decision-making as it had been in the 1950s – clearly, it was not. But geopolitics continued to shape local society in direct and immediate ways. That this influence was direct and immediate is not to say that it was deliberate. The ways in which lives were changed on Jinmen, in the ways people made a living or organized their families, were generally unanticipated, products of the interaction between these larger geopolitical shifts and the agency of local individuals and groups. Militarization had been closely connected with the ways in which local authorities, civilian and military, had pursued and promoted modernity for local society. The legacies of militarization proved highly problematic for the achievement of certain outcomes associated with modernity, especially economic ones. When tourism replaced G. I. Joe business as the mainstay of the local economy, Jinmen exchanged one form of dependency for another, and economic modernization remains a major challenge for the long-term well-being of local society. The course of militarization and subsequent demilitarization also leaves their traces in contemporary politics and in the construction of local identity. As we shall see in the next chapter, it also has a profound impact on the way militarization is remembered by the people most affected by it, and on individual as well as collective subjectivity.

13   Memory and politics

The history of a place consists not only of the record of its past but also of how that past is remembered. Because people's memories of the past are shaped by their concerns in the present historians need to consider not one but two additional dimensions to history, the past as it is produced in memory and the past as it is deployed in politics. Previous chapters have concentrated on the first dimension; this chapter explores the second and third, and the connections between them. Beginning from the assumption that the sense of the past is a reality that can also fruitfully be analyzed in its own right, it revisits some of the historical phenomena discussed earlier and asks how they are remembered today.

There is much in the popular memory of Jinmen civilians that is at odds with the documentary record. For example, it is widely remembered that emigration from the island to Taiwan was forbidden. I have found no evidence of any official regulation prohibiting emigration to Taiwan, and the tens of thousands of emigrants also contradict this interpretation. Rather, as we have seen, movement to Taiwan was regulated, which is something rather different. There was a process. It involved finding a guarantor, filling out paperwork, and getting approvals. Crucially, there were procedures to ensure that moving to Taiwan was not a way to evade military obligations. Male residents of Jinmen were liable for militia service and male residents of Taiwan for temporary conscription, and one could in principle take advantage of the difference – for example by claiming to be a Jinmen resident while residing on Taiwan. There were certainly cases of individuals who were not allowed to move to Taiwan. But there was never a restriction against emigration *per se*. Many residents, however, remember things differently. They often say that they were forced to remain on Jinmen against their will and despite the danger. There is little interest in simply asserting that popular memories of restricted emigration are false. Rather, the interesting challenge is to explore how and why such memories have taken form in people's minds.

One central element in the collective memory of Jinmen residents is the question of the individual's relationship with the nation. As previous chapters have shown, militarization constructed the civilian on Jinmen as an archetype of the mobilized citizen. To ask how this is remembered is to turn to the issue of subjectivity. Homi Bhabha helpfully distinguishes between the pedagogical and performative aspects of national subjectivity, the former being a set of practices and discourses that call into being a subjective identification with the nation, the latter the expression of an agency that is not entirely derived from the discourses that produce it.[1] On Jinmen, the pedagogical production of national subjectivity was particularly deliberate and methodical, because the goal was not just to produce citizens but to produce citizens who could be a model for other citizens. But in the decade since the end of martial law and the War Zone Administration (WZA), the performative aspect has emerged as a central element in local politics. The case of Jinmen thus shows how the interplay between these two elements, the pedagogical and the performative, is highly specific to context.

Much recent literature on social or collective memory concentrates on the contrast between dominant or official memory and private or popular memory.[2] In official memory, the past is often used as a justification or legitimization of the present, while popular memory may be a way of criticizing or otherwise resisting contemporary arrangements. The situation on Jinmen fits this general pattern but with an interesting complication. Popular memory has in the past decade appropriated many elements of official memory for its own purposes. This appropriated official memory has now become an important tool in contemporary political struggles, not, as is often the case, with the state deploying official memory to oppose the claims of citizens, but with citizens using official memory to support their claims on the state. To put this in Bhabha's terms, people use the legacy of the pedagogical production of subjectivity in performing their politics today.

Another noteworthy aspect of memory on Jinmen is the level of convergence, at times even unanimity, in oral history. It is hard to recapture how people perceived their experiences at the time, but there are striking commonalities in how they remember those experiences today, or at least how they represent their memories to the oral history interviewer. Several common themes, many of them already discussed in previous chapters, recur throughout the oral history record, regardless of who provided the testimony and who collected it. The confiscation of doors in 1949, the unfairness of having to purchase one's own militia uniform or provide one's own meals during training, and the hardship of feeding a family during the 1958 bombing are topics raised by virtually every informant, regardless of age, gender, or class. These examples strongly support the insight of Maurice Halbwachs, the influential historian of memory, that while it is individuals who remember, it is social groups that determine what is remembered.[3] Some of these collective memories clearly have a strong symbolic dimension, and it may be that these impositions are the ones most often brought to light in oral history because other aspects of life under martial law – the arbitrary detentions and the threat of rape, for example – remain too painful or too risky to discuss with outsiders. But I will argue that at least part of the explanation for this unanimity has to do with contemporary political struggles, specifically for compensation or other forms of redress. Positions in these struggles are widely shared by civilian residents, so one would expect them to have common memories of the relevant issues.

To say that there are commonalities is not to suggest that there is a single memory of the past. On the contrary, the people of Jinmen have multiple ways of remembering the past. A single individual can simultaneously recall the past as a history of glorious service to the nation in the face of threats to its survival, and as a history of repression. These multiple versions of the past mirror the different ways in which Jinmen was represented in official discourse during the period of militarization for internal and external consumption. The propaganda was often mutually contradictory, just like the memories that are linked to it. For example, depending on the purpose to which the propaganda was to be put, Jinmen was constructed either as rich and prosperous or as poor and backward. An appeal to citizens on Taiwan from 1955, just after the first crisis, reports that "for many residents, their houses having been hit by the continuous shelling from the Communists, are now on the verge of destitution, with no reserves of food and no homes in which to live."[4] But a report on agricultural development from only a few years later claims that despite Communist efforts to starve the civilians and military and force them to withdraw, "efforts at economic construction on Jinmen have turned the poor soil into a fertile oasis, creating a prosperous society and a firm fortress of freedom."[5] The difference is not simply the passage of time, but the different political purposes to which representations of Jinmen were put. No one was subject to more of these representations than the people of Jinmen themselves, and the intensive and exaggerated application of propaganda affected their perception of the situation at the time as well as their subsequent memories.

While much of the propaganda they received focused on the enemy just across the strait, the PRC and life under Communism do not figure much in popular memory. This absence may be a lingering consequence of the general prohibition on contact, and the pressure put on civilians to hand over the propaganda material from the other side without even looking at it. So to know and remember anything of the other side is manifestly to have disobeyed orders. But oral history informants and essayists show little hesitation in discussing other sensitive aspects of life under martial law. The more important factor is probably that while the PRC may have been the collective enemy, daily interactions and daily battles that local people fought were with the ROC state and its army, and these are much more the stuff of personal and collective memory. Younger informants do remember the anti-Communist education they received in schools, but not necessarily for the reasons intended. "When I was in school in the 1970s, a few times each year mainland fishermen were brought to our class. We were grateful not to have been born on the other side – from a young age you'd have to go fishing . . . in the foggy season you might go to the wrong harbor and then you'd end up being paraded around as a model, and have to worry about ever getting home."[6] In other words, the lesson learned was that people on the mainland were subject to use in national political propaganda, which was of course precisely the experience of people on Jinmen.

While Communists and PRC residents themselves play little role in the memories of the people of Jinmen, the larger geopolitical interaction with the PRC does play a crucial role in framing those memories. "When the army retreated to Jinmen," "before the 1958 Crisis," "during the 1960 shelling," "when the PRC and the US normalized relations" – these are how residents structure their memory of the past. The rhythm of everyday life was shaped by geopolitical issues and events, so too was the rhythm of individual and collective memory. In the remainder of this chapter, I explore three different types of memory that coexist in contemporary Jinmen: a discourse of suffering, a discourse of agency, and a nostalgia discourse. I then offer explanations, two contemporary and one historical, for each of these three modes.

A discourse of suffering

Central to the memory of many residents of Jinmen is the suffering they endured during the martial law period. To subject these memories to analysis is in no way to pass judgement on their experiences, but rather to recognize that these memories themselves are part of the history of the period. Memories of suffering can be divided into two types, recollections of the trauma of war and combat, and recollections of the suffering caused by the actions of the state regime and its agents, such as the WZA and the militia command. The two types overlap in the often still-painful memories of the events around 1949. One elderly informant, her eyes full of tears, recalled for me how she and her parents had fled their home in Guningtou when the battle began. They stayed with relatives inland for some weeks.

When we came back, our house had been emptied. Everything had been stolen. When we came back, soldiers were guarding our house. They pointed bayonets at us, and demanded to know our business. They wouldn't let us in . . . We had two houses in those days; they were paid for by remittances from the Philippines . . . They destroyed our beautiful houses. I can't even talk about it anymore.[7]

Besides whole structures confiscated or destroyed, people have strong memories of the specific items of property taken, especially wooden doors. Other items that are remembered are precisely those that locate the speaker in his or her own history, a history of village and family. "When the soldiers tore down tombstones to use them for bunkers, it enraged the people. But what could we do?"[8] Even ancestral tablets were destroyed, probably for fuel. "Now we don't even know the names of some of those ancestors."[9]

Distinct from memories of official confiscation, ostensibly for the sake of defense construction, are memories of outright theft. "At the time, the National Army soldiers had three criteria for things they didn't take: anything they couldn't see, anything they couldn't move, and anything that was worthless." Some soldiers made token gestures to conceal their theft. "Whatever the G. I.s wanted they took; in the best case, they might just give you a few coins as a gesture." In the hard months after the Battle of Guningtou, theft by soldiers was as much a matter of desperation as the quest for plunder and booty. But this mattered little to the villagers whose houses were emptied and whose crops were pulled up long before they were ready for harvest. "They stole all our crops in the field. It was as if we had worked for nothing."[10] Said one farmer, "to put it nicely, we were serving the people; to put it in a way that is less pleasant to hear, it was just like we were slaves."[11]

Memories of the shelling of the island, both the more intense shelling of the crises and the alternate day shelling of the subsequent decades, are often formulaic and depersonalized. ROC propaganda efforts to link the shelling to the cruelty of the Communist enemy have had little impact on popular memory. Except for those militia members who were assigned above-ground duties such as portering ammunition and carrying messages, what comes to mind when most people are asked about these times is the initial panic, the cramped and dirty conditions in the shelter, and the struggle to feed themselves and their families. People speak at greater length today of their resentments against the state and its local agents. Indeed, it is these remarks that have animated much of the preceding text. "At that time, [militia] service was obligatory. We didn't have any rights; we didn't get any benefits. You even had to provide your own meals. If you were told to work, you had to work; if you were told to do something, you just had to do it. You couldn't hesitate or you'd be punished under military justice." People remember the difficult conditions under which they were forced to labor. "When we were working, our rice rations were brought in a manure bucket. When we ate we just had to hold our noses and swallow it down. Otherwise how would we have had the energy to work?" Harsh and arbitrary punishments are also an important part of local memory. Sun Bingshu remembers going to militia assembly with his belt unbuckled: "I was beaten on the spot, and then I was sent to . . . headquarters and locked up for three days." Even those who did not personally suffer such punishments recall them as part of everyday life. "In those days, if they wanted to make trouble for you, they'd just lock you up." "If you didn't show up [for militia assembly] within thirty minutes, you'd be locked up and labeled a Communist spy."[12]

The perceived danger of Communist subversion and the atmosphere of surveillance and fear that grew out of that perception is also an element in many people's memories. "The political training officer secretly kept an eye on our speech and conduct. There was no democracy at all. If you had any dissatisfaction or resentment toward your superior, you'd be accused as a spy or a traitor." "We were afraid; we didn't dare to speak out."[13] Besides the more serious cases discussed in chapter 3, the White Terror on Jinmen affected many others, sometimes with long-term consequences. Chen Ailing tells the story of a cousin who made an off-hand remark that was critical of the Nationalist Party (KMT) in the 1980s. He was jailed for three months while the matter was investigated, which meant that he missed the university entrance examinations. Many anecdotes relate how casual remarks or actions could bring one under suspicion.

Some of the memories of suffering only fully make sense with the passage of time. That is, the significance of these memories is only revealed when they are historicized. Militia members were required to store a supply of rice. Because these reserves in turn typically came from expired military reserves, by the time it reached the villagers the grain was often several years old. "The rice was always yellow with mold; the cadres told us this was because vitamins had been added to it." To prevent further spoilage, the villagers ate their oldest stores first, so newly bought rice typically was stored for several more months before being eaten. A 1996 medical study on Mazu found that while overall death rates were similar to those on Taiwan, the incidence of cancer was significantly higher. The report linked the cancer rate to the presence of aflatoxins in rice that had been stored for too long.[14] While no similar study has been done on Jinmen, many residents are convinced that they too have suffered long-term health problems as a result of the martial law period.

What links all of these memories together is the theme of suffering. These memories are about the civilians of Jinmen enduring a wide range of indignities, some at the hands of the Communist enemy, many more at the hands of the ROC state, the WZA administration, and the militia officers. This mode represents residents as passive victims with little capacity to influence their own fates. It suggests a recognition of geopoliticization, a sense that their suffering is tied to political conflicts that are not of their own making, but an entirely negative recognition.

A discourse of agency

Like people everywhere, Jinmen residents explain their history in terms that make sense within the community's own values and worldview. In this version of history, the People's Liberation Army (PLA)'s failures at the Battle of Guningtou were not the result of poor logistical support or inadequate provision for reinforcements, but the intervention of the gods who blew the PLA boats away from their intended landing site and then stranded them by the retreating tide, allowing the ROC soldiers to torch them.[15] In this version, the outbreak of plague in the early 1950s was the result not of their own backward hygiene, as the official representation has it, but because the troops ate the snakes that had previously kept the rat population down.

This type of popular or folk memory is not necessarily at odds with official representations. For example, older residents typically explain that so many local men joined the regular army in the 1960s and 1970s because of the close relations that developed between local children and the soldiers billeted in their homes. These memories echo the contemporary propaganda that celebrated the friendly relations between soldiers and civilians, in which "military and civilians are all one family" (*junmin yijia*). These accounts both minimize the tension and hostility that was part of the soldier–civilian relationship during this period and ignore the fact that one unanticipated consequence of the regime of militarization was to effectively eliminate most access to higher education and upward mobility. A military career was for many Jinmen youth the best route out of poverty.[16]

But in other areas folk memory diverges from the official story. For example, the ROC soldiers who died defending the island are officially memorialized as virtuous martyrs to be emulated. Their bodies are buried at the cemetery at the foot of Mount Taiwu, built by Hu Lian in late 1952. In front of the cemetery Hu built a "Shrine to Loyal Martyrs," and erected a statue of Sun Yat-sen. These sites were explicitly constructed as part of efforts to build Jinmen into a "spiritual fortress" to harden the resolve of the ROC citizenry.[17] They are sites for political education and nationalist ritual. Soldiers, civilians, and visitors are often taken to the shrine to bow and offer incense to the souls of the heroic dead. While the cemetery and shrine construct the spirits of the dead as heroes to be venerated and emulated, in popular culture they are hungry ghosts, potentially predatory and dangerous. This representation is expressed in the ghost stories that circulate on the island, in which the spirits of dead soldiers – tormented, mischievous, sometimes malicious – complicate the lives of local people. It is also expressed in a more material way in the dozens of small "Temples to the Generals." We have seen that these are a local variant of the shrines to hungry ghosts that were used in traditional society to deal with the threat of unknown spiritual forces. This representation of the souls of the dead is also reflected in popular understandings of the layout of the martyrs' cemetery. Among his many talents, Hu Lian is credited with being an outstanding geomancer. The bronze statue of Sun Yat-sen, people say, was placed by Hu Lian in front of the cemetery so that the father of the nation could keep an eye on the souls of the dead soldiers and prevent them from causing any trouble to the world of the living.[18]

Irony, humor, and sexual innuendo play an important role in this mode of memory. When old folks gather to talk about their experiences under martial law, a common theme is the mutual misunderstanding between soldiers and civilians in the early days, because the civilians at that time did not speak modern standard Chinese (Mandarin). One often hears the story, typically part of the standard account of the first commanding officer (CO)'s beneficence to the local people, of how Hu Lian ordered that military vehicles offer rides to civilians. "All you had to do was raise your hand and they'd stop. The old ladies didn't speak good Mandarin, so they'd ask, 'G. I. Joe, can I be your wife?' (*zuo ni de qizi*) instead of 'can I have a ride in your car?' (*zuo ni de chezi*)."[19] In this mode, soldiers' efforts to trick or mock the villagers invariably backfired, as in the well-known story of the old lady who asked a soldier to teach her how to say "thank you" in Mandarin. The soldier instructed her to say "*wangbadan*" ("bastard," literally "turtle egg"). She had her first chance to use the phrase at an official function, when she shouted it out to Hu Lian.[20]

The cunning of the local people often enabled them to get the better of the ROC government and its commanders. For example, after 1949 fishing was forbidden and most of the fishing fleet destroyed, ostensibly to yield materials for use in defensive fortifications (as noted in chapter 2, the real reason was probably to make it harder for ROC soldiers to defect back to the mainland). Eventually the prohibition was repealed. Elderly fishermen explain how this was accomplished: the closure of the coast "was really tough on us fishermen. One time, some fishermen went out secretly. Then they took their catch to the commanding officer. He was from the interior of the mainland. He'd never tasted anything like fresh fish. He thought it was really good. So he had to allow them to start fishing again."[21] To get around the restrictions on expenditures for religious activity, villagers learned to apply to sponsor an operatic performance not in the name of their village deity but as *laojun*, entertainment for the sake of nearby troops.[22]

Villagers also recall how adept they became at manipulating the language of mobilization and patriotism in order to use it against the regime of control and regulation. A man who was late for curfew was held up at a roadblock on the way home. He told the guards that he was late because he had been watching a film about the life of Sun Yat-sen. Naturally he could not have walked out on such a film in the middle, so the guards allowed him to pass. But often their little victories were simply the result of the fact that local people were much cleverer than the soldiers, who were easily taken advantage of. "When they were building bunkers, they'd demand we provide bricks. But sometimes it was really impossible to find enough bricks, so we'd take advantage of noontime when the soldiers were busy [with their lunch] and steal back some of the bricks to give to them [again]."[23] Other memories, such as the story of how a militia team found time while unloading ships in the 1958 Crisis to pilfer beer intended for the US Military Advisory and Assistance Group (MAAG), highlight the *sangfroid* of the people.[24] Such humorous accounts appear often in the essays on the supplements page of the *Jinmen Daily*. This genre of story in the Chinese press has long lent itself to short, funny anecdotes of this sort. But the same type of story also appears frequently in oral history, suggesting that it is not simply a product of the genre.

A popular memory that interprets events in terms that make sense to the popular worldview and popular values is a widespread, perhaps almost universal, phenomenon. What is distinctive about this mode of memory on Jinmen is the way it ascribes not just agency but geopolitical significance to the actions and behaviors of local people. In other words, in this mode of memory, not only does geopolitics affect their lives, but their lives affect geopolitics. Their courage in the face of Communist aggression is remembered as a crucial factor in the history of the unfinished Chinese civil war, the cross-strait relations, and indeed the larger global Cold War. The Battle of Guningtou and the Artillery Wars of 1954–5 and 1958 are recalled as great victories. This is how one former soldier from the mainland, who settled on Jinmen and married a local widow, remembers the 1958 Crisis:

Mao Zedong said that if they could capture Jinmen, then it would be impossible to defend Taiwan . . . On August 23rd they started firing. Our side was ready, we loaded our shells, but we didn't fire. We waited for orders. Their guns were weak; the shells fell in the sea. We weren't afraid . . . We drove away their planes. Their losses were much heavier than ours. They had many more casualties. We lost only one landing craft; they lost so many. After twenty days, they still hadn't won victory. So Mao Zedong was forced to leave office (*xiatai*). Liu Shaoqi took over from him. It was Liu who decided on the idea of shelling on alternate days . . . We were really tired [from the fighting]. If you fought in a battle for two, three, or five hours, you'd be exhausted. You're an American – you'd have to go see a therapist. But we fought for twenty days. We were so tired. But we defeated them.[25]

Mao Zedong did indeed step back from his day-to-day leadership position in the early 1960s. But most historians ascribe this decision to the disastrous consequences of the Great Leap Forward, not the heroism of the people of Jinmen. The idea that the alternate day shelling was the PRC response to an ROC victory in 1958 is common on the island, as is the sense that it was not just the regular army, but also the civilian population, who deserve the credit for the victory. "The Communists started to shell us every other day, because they knew they couldn't defeat us." The survival of Jinmen was a continued irritant for the enemy, "a mote in the eye of the Communists."[26]

In this mode of memory, the survival of Jinmen has been critical in ensuring the security of Taiwan. After all, had the Communist propaganda loudspeakers not blared their intention to "wash Taiwan in blood" during the 1950s? But the people of Jinmen had held them off, thwarting their evil intentions, and this in turn had allowed Taiwan to enjoy decades of extraordinary economic development in relative peace. "Without the Jinmen military miracle, there would have been no Taiwan economic miracle." As the local historian Dong Qunlian puts it, "It was only because the militia provided support to the army that victory was won in 1958. It was only because victory was won in 1958 that Taiwan and Penghu enjoyed several decades of peace, enabling economic development and prosperity and the democratization of society. All of these accomplishments in Taiwan are intimately connected to the victory in 1958." Former government officials go even further, crediting Jinmen with significance to the overall conduct of the Cold War by the US and its allies. "It's really a strategic question. It was part of the larger US strategy. The US needed Taiwan to defend the Pacific, to keep the Communists out of the Pacific. So Jinmen had to be held."[27] A critical part of this agency is that it be remembered as voluntary. As Chen Shuizai puts it, "People on Jinmen are more loyal to the nation than people in other places, because they were always under threat from the mainland. There were heavy losses in the first few decades. Gradually there developed a revenge psychology, a philosophy of life and death. If you don't shoulder your gun, you won't survive. You have no choice. So we did not need much propagandizing or [political] education; there was no thought control. Every person realized they must shoulder their weapon to survive."[28]

It is perhaps a universal element of local consciousness to identify what is special about one's native place. The people of Jinmen, though, remember their locality not only as a special place but also as an important place. While in the discourse of suffering the martial law period is remembered as a time of hardship and unfair treatment, of arbitrary exactions and punishments, in the discourse of agency the same period is remembered as a time of heroism, of patriotic contributions to the collective nation. Both discourses coexist in the memory of Jinmen people today.

Nostalgia

A third mode of memory that appears in oral history is nostalgia. Many people intersperse complaints about militia service with positive memories of life under martial law. It is remembered as a time when people were unselfish and mutually supportive. "In those days when there was a problem somewhere, everyone put out a little effort [and the problem was solved]. People helped one another." This memory of mutual aid and support extends to the relationship between soldiers and civilians as well. "We talked to the soldiers; we helped one another. When the harvest was ready, we'd ask them for help. We'd help them when they needed to dig trenches. We'd lend them our tools." There is also a sense that despite the ever-present military threat, life was secure and stable. "In those days there were no thieves. It was safe. There was no traffic. The people were united." Former cadres say part of the reason was the greater authority of the government. "It's not like today – you give one order and there are lots of different opinions, lots of different responses. In those days, there was one order and one response."[29]

When Jinmen residents reflect nostalgically on their experience, they often recognize the mirror-imaging of the policies they experienced and those used on the other side of the Taiwan Strait. "The thinking was just the same, only the terms were different. We would say [cadres needed to be] reformed; they would say they needed to be criticized. It's all mostly the same." Former magistrate Chen Shuizai has a similar understanding. "The militia had military *and* political functions. It was used to control the people of Jinmen. If war broke out, then the whole population of Jinmen would become like an army. It was very similar to the Communists. The issue was how to control people."[30] With these comments, Chen indicates that he is well aware that the policies of the WZA were not simply about enhancing military readiness, but also about creating and exercising power.

Interpreting the three discourses

The three discourses of memory are not completely discrete but occasionally intertwine. Thus, for example, when thinking back on the militia's contribution to local defense, Hong Futian becomes nostalgic about an earlier, simpler time. "The militia's determination to sacrifice themselves for the sake of protecting their home and nation never wavered. But with democratization on Taiwan, each person began to stress their own interest. This tendency led the members of the militia to ask themselves, 'Why is the nation's burden on the people of Jinmen so heavy? Are all the legal restrictions appropriate? What does the state do for us? Is our sacrifice on the front line worth it?' "[31] Agency and suffering are simultaneously invoked in Weng Shuishe's recollections of deployments during the 1958 Crisis, when militia members were ordered to stand guard at coastal checkpoints while regular forces withdrew to more secure locations. "Civilians were put on the front line, and soldiers on the second line. Fuckers! When the Communists started shelling, we weren't even able to fire right away; we had to wait for orders . . . If you deserted the ranks you'd be dealt with by wartime justice. At the time I was deputy squad leader; I complained to the officers. What was the result? I was locked up for two months."[32] But despite this overlap it is useful to keep the three types of memory analytically separate, because this makes it possible to identify the distinct underlying issues that structure these modes. Collective memory is underpinned by a complex relationship between past experience and contemporary concerns. We can identify a historical or contemporary political issue that helps explain or account for each of the three modes of memory.

In 1992, a few days after the lifting of martial law, Weng Mingzhi submitted a petition to the Jinmen county government. It included three demands for compensation: for property seized or damaged; for unpaid service and labor by the militia, and for injuries suffered at the hands of both the Communists and the ROC government.[33] Such demands may have first occurred to people on Jinmen when the government began to offer compensation and redress to Taiwanese residents who suffered under KMT rule, especially the victims of 2–28, the incident on February 28, 1947, when Taiwanese protests against the KMT had been suppressed with military force, leaving thousands dead and imprisoned. The episode and its subsequent cover-up had long been a source of resentment for Taiwanese natives, and the decision to investigate it was widely seen as an opportunity for reconciliation between disaffected Taiwanese and the KMT. One contributor to the Jinmen newspaper began his essay with the observation that when he watches television, he sees "everyone on Taiwan telling stories about 2–28, but no one wants to hear our stories of Jinmen. This column is not as good as television, but at least it gives us the chance to tell our stories."[34] Others wanted more than simply the chance to tell their stories:

I thought about back when I was young, I was wounded while helping the army carry ammunition. At the time, the county government just gave me NTD120 and a bag of rice. It was really pitiful. But we humble folk didn't dare make any demands. Later, on Taiwan, they started to give out compensation for various incidents, one after the other. So I started to bring up the events of the past at the village assembly. Every time there was an assembly, I'd call on the government to compensate those of us who were wounded in combat. But the officials would just write it down, write it down. They never followed up.[35]

Within a few years of Weng's petition, the ROC government announced that it would introduce compensation for various injustices of the previous decades, in order to close conclusively that chapter of local history. Though the government did not acknowledge the role of activism in shaping its decision, there was clearly a link, for compensation was offered in categories that corresponded to those demanded by Weng. Residents were allowed to make claims for land that had been seized and houses destroyed by the military. In all, more than 8,000 claims were made (Chen Shuizai suspects that at least some of these were false). Most were resolved in favor of the complainant; the military was required to come to an agreement with the owner to purchase, rent, or return the land. The land problem did not prove very difficult to resolve, since the process began precisely as the withdrawal of the troops was accelerating, so much of the land in question was no longer being used by the army. A second type of compensation was for death or injury of civilians in wartime. Compensation was only payable if the injury was suffered at the hands of the ROC's own troops; victims of PLA shelling in 1954–5 or 1958 were not eligible. Over 100 suits were filed on behalf of the dead and a larger number by the injured. The families of the dead received payments to a maximum of NTD1.5 million, and the injured smaller amounts depending on the seriousness of their injury. The third type of compensation was for militia service. In 1995 the county announced that militia veterans would be assigned a number of points depending on their length of service, dangers faced, and whether they had been decorated. The number of points determined the amount of compensation, with a maximum payment of NTD245,000. In all, there were over 40,000 recipients of compensation (this figure includes recipients from Mazu). Chen Shuizai estimates the total payment was in the order of NTD6 billion.[36]

Some calls for compensation for service remain outstanding. No compensation was paid to the tens of thousands of guerrillas, former members of the Anti-Communist National Salvation Army, who had served on Jinmen and the other offshore islands, apparently because the costs of paying them the equivalent of a military salary were prohibitive. For many others there is lingering dissatisfaction with the amount of compensation. Lin Yongju's father had been wounded carrying messages for the army during the 1958 shelling. He survived, and lived into the early 1990s. Lin Yongju sought compensation for the injury, but was told that since his father was already dead, there was no way to assess the seriousness of his injury, despite the various medical records he was able to present. He remains bitter. "You can see how unreasonable the law is. It can't really compensate for the sacrifices and the contributions of the militia at that time." Others complain that the compensation has not been distributed fairly. "Even public servants [who served in the militia] get compensation, but they didn't have to risk their lives."[37]

The criteria for allocating compensation and the discourse of suffering in popular memory are closely connected. Part of the reason that Jinmen people today deal with the past by reflecting on their suffering is because this is precisely how the ROC government deals with it. The categories into which they divide their suffering, and the types of suffering which do and do not feature prominently in their memories, match neatly the categories for which compensation is paid. By keeping memory of their suffering alive in the context of their campaign for compensation, residents of Jinmen reject an earlier political rhetoric that calls on citizens to make willing sacrifice for the sake of the nation. The calls for compensation for militia service cleverly exploit contradictions within official rhetoric. Militia service was represented as the fundamental obligation of citizenship on Jinmen just as military service in the regular army was the fundamental obligation of adult males on Taiwan. But conscripts from Taiwan were paid a salary; militia members were not. Those who now demanded compensation were turning the logic of Taiwan's neo-liberal political economy against the political rhetoric, demanding financial compensation for their labor and material losses. This mode of memory is thus a form of citizenship discourse applied toward the past but driven by contemporary concerns.

In the recollections of the people of Jinmen, the discourse of suffering co-exists with the discourse of agency that turns the island's civilians into heroes. One hears frequently about the great victories won in 1949, 1954–5, and 1958 by the residents with the help of the army. These memories may seem rather naive, but rather than disputing the triumphalist version of causation offered by Jinmen informants, it is more interesting to ask about the contemporary implications of these memories. We have seen above that the vision of heroism began to appear in government propaganda very early in the martial law period. Identifying when the vision of heroic agency took root in popular memory is not easy. It first enters the documentary record in forms other than government propaganda in the speeches and writings of political activists in the crucial 1987–92 period. But it probably was a powerful element in local identity long before it was turned into a political tool. A fully elaborated version appears in the manifesto of a 1993 demonstration in Taiwan:

Since the Battle of Guningtou and the August 23rd Artillery War up to the present day, the lives of many of our people have been sacrificed to the heartless artillery fire for the sake of the safety of the nation, and for the sake of protecting the stability and prosperity of Taiwan and Penghu. Many have also been conscripted into forced labor, into the militia, and to serve as porters for ammunition . . . [Referring to the recently issued six-year economic development plan for Taiwan,] What about Jinmen? It is still a "battlefield." It is still the "front line." It is still the same Jinmen, where the people are impoverished, where the damage has yet to be repaired . . . What about Jinmen? What about the people of Jinmen, who have sacrificed themselves in countless numbers for the sake of the nation?[38]

Similar perspectives are today very widespread. One former militia member, asked about his feelings toward the ROC government, answered, "I hate them. What makes me the most indignant is that during the 1958 Strait Crisis, the people gave so much for the government. The museum of military history doesn't have any memorial to us; we haven't received adequate compensation. It's only because of our sacrifices that Taiwan exists today."[39] The discourse of agency is one of the most frequently deployed tools in local efforts to improve central government funding for the local economy. In his speech on taking office as the first elected magistrate of Jinmen county in 1993, Chen Shuizai summarized the pressing tasks of his administration: "First, to speedily resolve and overcome the question of popular resentments that have accumulated over forty years; second, to accelerate investment and development in order to create the ideal Jinmen of the future."[40] The discourse of agency is thus inseparably linked to the discourse of suffering. Whether it comes in the form of political manifestos or personal reminiscences, this rhetoric links past and present. During the martial law period, the ROC state adopted a certain argument in order to justify its policies on Jinmen. Today, that same rhetoric is being appropriated by the people of Jinmen, who redeploy it to their own purposes. It is a variation on official memory, not popular counter-memory, that is being used subversively here. The appropriated official history of militarization has become central to activist rhetoric. It has also become an important element in local popular memory, precisely at a time when the contemporary reality that is served by memory is shifting so dramatically.

These contemporary shifts also help explain the nostalgia in popular memory today. This is not unique to Jinmen; an interest in the past is very common in societies undergoing abrupt and destabilizing changes. Nostalgia for the martial law period reflects in large part dissatisfaction with the contemporary state of local society and uncertainty over the future. The nostalgia of Jinmen residents for a simpler time in which they were celebrated as model citizens resembles in some ways that of other groups undergoing socio-economic displacement as well as cultural marginalization. Lisa Rofel shows that former industrial workers in state-owned enterprises in the PRC hold similar memories. Formerly celebrated as the heroes of the nation, they are now mostly cast aside both materially and ideologically.[41] For them, as for the people of Jinmen, the past now seems a more desirable place than the present.

The discourses of agency and nostalgia converge in reconstituting previous repression as self-sacrificing patriotism. The extent of this reconstitution is difficult to gauge, for locals had to some degree accepted state propaganda, making them heroes even before that propaganda began to disappear. But its influence on subjectivity has evidently grown since the dramatic shifts in contemporary politics. The overall process has been that the ROC made a variety of claims to justify its policies on Jinmen. These claims are now being redeployed by the people of Jinmen in their politics. Many of these claims are about the past, about Jinmen's links to the mainland and Taiwan before 1949, and about Jinmen's function, real and symbolic, as defender of Taiwan and the free world. These modes of memory are thus part of a debate over Jinmen identity today. This debate is waged publicly through political activism, and internally through the development of individual subjectivities that mix the three modes of memory.

Adding further complexity to the situation is that when these modes of memory are deployed openly for political reasons, they are shots fired at a moving target. The ROC state is not an eternal, unchanging, and unified entity. In the years since martial law it has itself undergone dramatic changes such as democratization and the emergence of multiple political parties. At times, the state or elements in it have begun to repudiate the claims of its predecessors. The growing sense of a distinctive Taiwanese identity, discussed in chapter 12, has been encouraged by the Democratic Progressive Party (DPP) but is now more than simply a political campaign. As the decades of efforts to recover the mainland and then to prevent any division between China and Taiwan seem to many increasingly like delays on the road to Taiwanese statehood, the heroism of Jinmen's civilians seems increasingly irrelevant to the people of Taiwan, and is thus less and less persuasive in efforts to secure investment or other favorable policies from the central government. To put this another way, the various discourses of memory discussed here are different ways in which the past is

deployed in contemporary campaigns about citizenship and democratization. On Jinmen, these campaigns are shaped by rhetorics of compensation, exchange, and fairness. They thus combine a geopolitical, Cold War
rhetoric and a liberal, market rhetoric. But the first of these is decreasingly
relevant to the ROC and therefore decreasingly effective as a political tool.
One may wonder if it may gradually decline in importance in local memory,
even before the heroes of the 1950s have passed from the scene.

Conclusions

A central element in Jinmen's history over the last five decades has been
its construction as a political symbol.[42] To better understand that history,
we must look not only at how that symbolism was generated, but also at
how it was interpreted by residents themselves. As we have seen, the ROC
regime and its agents were never completely successful in generating a
constant sense of impending threat from the mainland. Rather, in the lives
of Jinmen residents, the main challenge was to adapt to and strategize
within the constraints of the system imposed by the ROC itself. It is really
only since the military threat receded that the people of Jinmen began to
use the images created by the state, deploying them in their dialogues with
that state. This is yet another way in which the history of Jinmen shows
the embeddedness of global issues in local contexts. The discourses surrounding those global issues can themselves become political resources.
The deployment of these rhetorics by the local people and their activist
representatives has not been very successful – no one on Jinmen seems to
be satisfied with the way the government in Taibei has dealt with the outstanding issues. This is part of a general uncertainty about the future that
residents of the island must live with. One of the ways in which their
ambivalence about the present is represented is through nostalgia for the
past, when political instability and military threat paradoxically provided
economic and social stability. The full story of Jinmen under martial law
also involves analysis of these various modes of remembrance.

14   Conclusion: redoubled marginality

When soldiers were first billeted in civilian homes in 1949, their officers painted slogans on village walls to inculcate militaristic values in both the soldiers and the civilian population. Later, political instructors developed more permanent media, mounting concrete medallions on the walls of homes and temples. One could trace the chronology of militarization on Jinmen from these inscriptions on the island's built environment: "Exterminate the Traitors of Mao and Zhu" (1949); "Liberate our Compatriots on the Mainland" (1950s); "Soldiers and Civilians Unite" (1956); "Never Forget our Time in Ju" (1966); "Implement the Three Principles of the People and Recover the Mainland" (1984) [Fig. 14.1].[1] For this book I have relied instead on different kinds of historical sources, primarily the oral history of local people. For the people of Jinmen today, as for other people in other times and places, uncertainty about the future has generated great interest in the past. Their memories have created resources that allow us to move beyond the official record in exploring the interaction of communities with the great global forces of the last half-century.

The main goal of this book has been to show how social life on Jinmen was affected by the island's changing connection to regional and global conflicts, a phenomenon I have labeled geopoliticization. It is analytically crucial to reconstruct the geopolitical context behind War Zone Administration (WZA) policies in order to understand both the policies themselves and their social impacts. The interplay between geopoliticization and militarization has been the most important relationship in the history of the island since 1949. The path of the relationship has been complex. To summarize the arguments made in the first part of the book, early militarization was an *ad hoc* measure triggered by the unexpected outcome of the Battle of Guningtou and the need to secure that symbolic victory. As the situation stabilized, temporary arrangements were replaced by more formal ones. In 1953, civilian government was restored to the island in order to strengthen the claim that Jinmen was a bastion of freedom. The ROC–US relationship, in particular Chiang Kai-shek's efforts to secure US support for the defense of the islands, led to huge

Fig. 14.1 "Soldiers and Civilians Work Together; Fight Communism
and Oppose the Soviets" (photo by Jiang Bowei)

increases in the size of the garrison, which soon came to exceed the civilian population. Chiang deliberately invested Jinmen with much of his
total troop strength so that the fall of the island would be a dreadful blow
to morale and thus threaten the very survival of the ROC regime. This
was his way of ensuring that the defense of Jinmen remained a Cold War
and not simply a cross-strait issue. His decision prompted further
refining and institutionalization of militarization, with the county government firmly subordinated to the military through the increasingly
elaborate Experimental War Zone Administration regime. Thus already
by the mid-1950s the militarization of Jinmen had less and less to do with
military concerns narrowly defined and more to do with the larger political struggles of the Cold War. These changes had huge social consequences for the local people.

If the 1958 Crisis was indeed linked to Mao's wishes to intensify the
sense of threat to the PRC so as to mobilize and militarize the populace in
support of the Great Leap Forward, then one consequence was a parallel
response on the part of his enemy. For the ROC state in turn emphasized
the threat from *its* enemy, leading to new heights of mobilization and militarization on Jinmen. At this point domestic militarization on the mainland and on Jinmen moved virtually in lockstep, two gears linked by the
third gear of Maoist foreign policy.

Two years later the relationship reversed itself. The 1960 call to construct Jinmen as a Three People's Principles Model County was also a reaction to developments on the mainland. But whereas in the earlier phase changes on the mainland resulted in Jinmen and mainland society becoming more alike, the 1960 policies were intended to highlight the differences between the two societies. Recognizing that the economic crisis on the mainland represented a propaganda opportunity for the ROC, the focus of policy on Jinmen shifted to civilian social and economic development, or what I have called militarized development. These new policies did not signify an end to militarization, for they were ultimately driven by military and geopolitical considerations and led to new forms of authoritarian control and labor extraction. This was not the return of a repressed civilian politics, but rather a change in the trajectory of militarization.

In the late 1960s militarization entered another new phase on Jinmen with the combat village system, the content of which was actually inspired by a Communist insurgency in another context where Cold War and civil war intertwined, Vietnam. The Cultural Revolution on the mainland may have played a role in the initial stages of this phase, but unlike a decade earlier it was not primarily heightened militarization on the mainland that inspired a similar response on Jinmen. On the contrary, by the late 1960s the actual military threat to Jinmen was beginning to recede. The main inspiration for the combat village system over the next decade was rather the desire to highlight the threat posed by the PRC in the hope of bolstering international support for the ROC. This involved representing the cross-strait conflict in terms of a stark bipolar Cold War world that in fact no longer existed. This international propaganda strategy, however, proved ineffective, and Taiwan's diplomatic and international standing continued to deteriorate. The ROC state on Taiwan also faced growing internal challenges, and the militarization of Jinmen also came to be used as a tool to legitimize continued authoritarianism by drawing attention to the imminent danger of PRC attack. Jinmen now became even more militarized as mainland society grew less. The key variable influencing the degree of militarization was no longer on the mainland; now it was on Taiwan.

Militarization of Jinmen was thus always profoundly connected to larger geopolitical forces, but not in a consistent way. In the early phases, domestic policy considerations on the mainland shaped foreign policy decisions that in turn shaped militarization policies on Jinmen. In later phases, the relevant units of scale were both larger and smaller. They were global, the Sino–American relationship, and domestic, internal politics on Taiwan. Though the overall trend was to ever-greater levels of militarization, the relationship between militarization and military threat was basically reversed over the course of the period. This relationship, summarized in Table 14.1, was direct in the early phases and inverse in the later phases, as militarization was increasingly driven by political rather than military concerns.

While the specific trajectory of militarization on Jinmen was distinctive, it is also illustrative of a broader phenomenon. Everywhere the history of nations and local communities in the Cold War was a product of the interplay of global geopolitics with regional, national, and local issues. In *Seeing Like a State*, Scott argues that grandiose schemes of social transformation typically originate in a combination of four factors: the administrative ordering of state and society; a "high-modernist ideology" of faith in the possibility of state planning; an authoritarian state, and the weakness of civil society, and that the combination of these four elements often leads to disaster.[2] This study of Jinmen suggests that for the latter half of the twentieth century there could often be a fifth factor, the local articulation of the global conflict. State schemes were produced not only by domestic ambitions and interests but also geopolitical ones. The US–ROC relationship shaped the particular version of development that was promoted on Jinmen, but this relationship had only the most marginal connection to the interests of the people of the island. Nationalist Party (KMT) planning for Jinmen was only in part about "improving the human condition," to use Scott's phrase.[3] It was also about responding to changing enemy policies, highlighting difference from the enemy, and generating sympathy from the superpower ally. So even when state schemes did not lead to outright disaster, their success or failure could depend on the geopolitical interests that drove them as much as on the actual targets of social engineering. Sometimes schemes failed when the external context changed and the scheme could no longer serve the purposes for which it was intended. While the people of Jinmen certainly enjoy a higher standard of living today than they did in 1949, the skyscrapers of Xiamen call into question the ultimate success of militarized utopian modernism as a mode of demonstrating the superiority of the ROC system.

The complex inter-relationship between geopolitical developments and local militarization is only part of the story of Jinmen. Throughout the period, Jinmen remained in a state of emergency, and this in turn enabled the implementation of the ambitious, self-consciously modernizing agenda that I have called militarized utopian modernism. This agenda, shared in its broad outlines not only with the rest of the ROC but also with many other places in the world, was crucial to how the state and its agents staked out sovereignty over the personal and social lives, even the corporeal lives, of the civilian population. The content of this agenda was modulated by the specifics of the local context as well as the unconscious

Table 14.1 A chronology of militarization on Jinmen

Phase	Period	Significant changes	Geopolitical trigger
Ad hoc militarization	1949–1956	Extraction of civilian labor; breakdown of existing networks; regime of surveillance and indoctrination	Battle of Guningtou
War Zone Administration (WZA)	1956–1960 (WZA in place to 1992)	Expansion of garrison; formalization of existing regime; subordination of civilian to military administration; civilian logistical support	US–ROC Mutual Defense Treaty and Formosa Resolution
Three Principles of the People Model County	1960–1968	Development militarization: infrastructure and economic development	Great Leap Forward and consequences
Combat village/underground Jinmen	1968–1979 (phase 1)	Civilian militia as combat fighters; tunnel projects within villages; massive defense projects; renewed ideological education	US–PRC rapprochement (also Cultural Revolution; Vietnam War as model)
	1979–1992 (phase 2)		ROC domestic legitimacy crisis
Demilitarization	1992–	Restoration of civilian government and end of military rule; renewal of ties to Xiamen; economic crisis	Political reform on Taiwan; continued reform on mainland

assumptions of its authors. National and local officials brought their own understandings of the meaning of health, backwardness, and discipline to the construction of "modernity," focussing on certain issues to the neglect of others. Many of the crucial discourses of Chinese awakening or modernity as identified by Fitzgerald, Harrison, and others, such as questions of hygiene, mobilization, civic ritual, and education, were reshaped by militarization.[4] All of these discourses, for example, were instrumentalized on Jinmen. What had previously been ends of modernization now became means in the pursuit of national security, by ensuring military readiness, preventing enemy infiltration, and promoting domestic cohesion and international support. The thinking of local and national officials was also shaped by what they understood to be elements of Chinese tradition. Their notions of the centrality of the family, mutual responsibility, and appeals to individual ethics are quite different from modern self-discipline in the Foucauldian sense.[5] As the capillaries of militarization extended themselves into local society, the Cold War and geopolitics became immanent in diverse areas of daily life. Militarization changed the ideas and experience of gender, reworking but not eliminating inherited assumptions. New religious forms appeared and became subject to state regulation and manipulation, creating new sites of interaction between state and society. Global economic discourses were reworked to suit distinctive conditions, and local people responded to the incentives created by those conditions with their own decisions. The Cold War could affect the construction of even the most seemingly apolitical aspects of life.

In the Introduction I discussed three meanings of the term geopoliticization: as influence, as symbol, and as everyday life. The closing chapters on memory suggest a fourth meaning. In their oral history testimony and in their own writings, the people of Jinmen also show that geopoliticization became a part of their identity. Geopoliticization can describe a type of subjectivity in which one's life takes its meaning in part from the role of oneself and one's community in geopolitical affairs. This sense of geopoliticization invites comparison with recent discussions of globalization. When used in reference to subjectivity, globalization often means the way in which the meanings of people's lives are destabilized and even stripped of value by their participation in a global economy. Geopoliticization meant that events on the national and international stages constantly affected the lives of people on Jinmen. Though it is at times difficult not to see the people of Jinmen as pawns in the larger political processes, this is not how they themselves remember this period. At every significant juncture they have a counter-memory that puts them at the center of events, their wits and determination undermining those, both friend and enemy, who would take advantage of them. To call this counter-memory a form of resistance does not take us very far. Nor should their acquiescence in many aspects of the regime be taken as shifting responsibility for that regime onto the shoulders of local people. Rather, as Farquhar and Zhang have written, we must recognize that people may "obscurely" perceive the distribution of powers in a society, and respond in ways that are simultaneously political and nonconfrontational.[6] Within the militarization system, residents of Jinmen were not simply pawns, but exercised their own agency in various spheres.

Though the stakes were strongly weighted to one side, militarization like other state regimes was also a process of reception and negotiation. Building on Chi Chang-hui's insight that the people of Jinmen became a kind of "political capital" in the global Cold War, we might consider the varied political uses of the island to be a kind of deterritorialization, an effort to axiomatize Jinmen in order to secure maximum political value. People's negotiations with the bureaucratic regime were then efforts to reterritorialize local society, recoding it to recover and redeploy cultural and social forms.[7]

In the long term, constantly being reminded of their central importance in world politics has created a distinctive mode of memory among the people of Jinmen that accepts and celebrates this importance, a mode I have labeled the discourse of heroic agency. It coexists with a discourse of suffering that remembers the powerlessness and victimization of local people. Today, those same people use these two modes of memory to criticize the past *and* to criticize the present. Their memories shaped the course of the democratic transition on the island and continue to shape their lives today. This appropriation of state-sponsored rhetoric from the past and its deployment in political struggle in the present raises another way in which the Jinmen case can contribute to Scott's findings on schemes of state transformation. Given his larger argument, he focusses on the tragic disasters of well-intentioned schemes gone awry. But the Jinmen case reveals another set of unanticipated consequences that may also be part of a broader phenomenon. The use of memory in contemporary Jinmen society shows how participation in such schemes can become political resources that local agents use in their negotiations with the state. Claims of adherence to the policies of state transformative schemes can thus be deployed in political struggles by the very people who did not adhere to them, even long after the schemes themselves have been abandoned. The efficacy of these claims will be shaped not only by the behavior of local agents but also by how these schemes fit into the contemporary state's image of itself. The long-term legacies of militarized utopian modernism are thus manifold indeed.

Jinmen in the world

Most studies of militarization in history are shaped by a teleology leading to the outbreak of war. The purpose of the story is typically to explain how militarization, militarism, and war are connected. The central question is then to identify the causes of militarization, or alternatively to identify what it was in society that failed to prevent war.[8] But just as militarization has no necessary relation to military threat, it need have no connection to militarism, the reliance on military force in political and diplomatic affairs. On Jinmen, of course, militarization did not lead to war, and this makes it possible to examine the phenomenon of militarization from a different perspective, to ask not how it leads to war but how it shapes and distorts culture and society.

A senior local official who granted me several interviews was always very concerned that my research not present the people of Jinmen in a comical light. "Many things about Jinmen seem ridiculous today," he told me several times. "You mustn't laugh at Jinmen."[9] He usually made this remark just after an observation about how life on Jinmen in this period resembled the situation on the mainland. His worry was that such similarities lend themselves to caricature. Such statements are perhaps the local articulation of what Michael Herzfeld calls cultural intimacy – "the recognition of those aspects of a cultural identity that are considered a source of external embarrassment but that nevertheless provide insiders with their assurance of common sociality."[10] At the same time, the official was also articulating in his own way the issue of representativeness and particularism that all local historians must think about. The changes I have traced on Jinmen are the changes of the militarized states of the twentieth century in miniature and sometimes in exaggerated form. Militarization led to shifts of local geography: some places were depopulated, others expanded. It led to shifts in translocal geography: some old networks were destroyed and new ones created. These new networks were not equal ones; Jinmen's relationship with Taiwan, like that of many highly militarized communities, shares similarities with the relations of dependency characterizing colony and metropole. There were shifts in political economy, with the rise of a bureaucracy and a class of micro-entrepreneurs to serve the troops. Some groups in society benefited from these changes, others lost. But the status of every group came to be judged by its relationship to the military threat. Militarization does not explain every aspect of Jinmen's history in this period, but there were few aspects of life that were not touched in some way by militarization. This is not unique to Jinmen.

Because of the importance of global factors throughout the period, I have used the phrase Cold War to describe the overall context from the Battle of Guningtou all the way to demilitarization in the early 1990s. Certainly the ongoing struggle between the ROC and the PRC arising out of the Chinese revolution was central to Jinmen's history. But super-power, especially American, interests and interventions profoundly shaped the framework within which that struggle unfolded. Jinmen's distinctive status derived in the first place from the internationalization of the Chinese civil war in 1950. This initial geopoliticization continued to shape the broad context for the next forty years. In 1958 Mao's decision not to try to take Jinmen was determined by the specifics of the US–ROC alliance. So long as the US guaranteed the security of Taiwan, seizing Jinmen would have worked against the ultimate goal of reunification by encouraging the separation of Taiwan from the mainland. The alternate day bombing resulted from Mao's recognition of this reality. Even in the decades since 1958, ROC policies toward Jinmen continued to be shaped by the US relationship. American models of economic and political change continued to shape policy choices.[11] Even more important, the construction of Jinmen as a symbol of anti-Communist struggle was a policy aimed at least partially at the US. A second reason for the use of the term Cold War is that it encourages comparison. There are of course limits to the possibilities of comparison. There was much that was distinctive, even unique, to Jinmen. The cross-strait relationship was not simply the local version of the US–Soviet Union confrontation. On a deeper level, even as we pursue the project of a global comparative social and cultural history of the Cold War, we must acknowledge that there was not one but many Cold Wars. The differences are most obvious in those places where the Cold War did not remain cold. More broadly, there were profound differences between the Cold War in Europe and in its former colonies. A developing strand of scholarship on the period rightly points out that interpreting decolonization primarily in terms of Cold War conflict is a new incarnation of the Orientalist silencing of non-Western peoples that was brilliantly revealed by Said.[12] Unlike in Latin America, the geopoliticization of Jinmen was not primarily expressed as a conflict between the forces of entrenched privilege and of social revolution. Unlike much of Southeast Asia, the geopoliticization of Jinmen was little connected to the struggles of decolonization. On the other hand, insisting that the Taiwan Strait conflict was purely domestic is a long-standing, politically motivated tactic, a self-referential and perhaps also self-Orientalizing move that needlessly and unhelpfully isolates China and Taiwan from the global networks and processes in which both have long been embedded. By considering the history of Jinmen not simply in terms of episodic outbursts of military confrontation or the unfinished business of the Chinese civil war, we can more clearly see its history as more than a political or military or ideological standoff, as tied to widespread social processes that could be similar across different locales.

We might think first of all about Jinmen in relation to the Republic of China on Taiwan. Bruce Cumings has identified a distinctive regional pattern of state formation, of which Taiwan is an example, that he labels the Bureaucratic–Authoritarian–Industrializing Regime (BAIR). The BAIR is characterized by relative state autonomy, high degrees of central coordination and bureaucratic planning, high flexibility in moving in and out of industrial sectors, the exclusion of labor from politics, low state expenditures on social welfare, and authoritarian repression. Moving beyond the literature on the developmental state, Cumings shows that the formation of BAIR regimes must be seen not only in a national but also in a regional context, tied to US hegemony.[13] While Cumings concentrates on issues of political economy the study of Jinmen fleshes out some of the many social implications of the BAIR regime. Moreover while Cumings notes that the interaction of external hegemonic forces (the US) with domestic societies led to different political outcomes in different states, Jinmen's history shows that the constitution and consequences of a regime could vary considerably even within a single state. As Meredith Woo-Cumings has noted, the ROC state was able to harness the energies of its population in the service of its development plans in part by highlighting the security threat. Woo-Cumings has written that the "genius" of the ROC state, among others, "was in harnessing real fears of attack and instability toward a remarkable developmental energy."[14] On this argument, Jinmen's main significance, especially after its military importance lessened, was to focus the anxiety of the population on Taiwan so that it would be more malleable in the service of the developmental state. Much of what we have seen about Jinmen applies also to Taiwan as a whole. In both societies deliberate efforts were made to construct the civilian population as an anti-Communist polity, a process involving productive as well as repressive power. Other more mundane issues such as the settlement and treatment of old male soldiers were also common to both places. But over time, as political and social life grew more open on Taiwan, the two places diverged. Jinmen became truly a state of exception within the state of exception, a localized form of the extreme politics ostensibly necessitated by geopolitical confrontation. The ROC's construction of Jinmen was thus an attempt to concentrate or localize threat-driven militarization, the better to keep it in the public mind without allowing it to interfere with economic development. Jinmen also offered a localized site to which concentrated resources could be applied to the recycling or revival of the personal projects of authoritarian leaders, reversing the past failures of those projects.

Jinmen is also a useful case study to explore the question of the similarities and differences in the histories of the two regimes on either side of the Taiwan Strait. We have seen numerous examples of extraordinary similarities between policies adopted on Jinmen and in the PRC, from the household registration system, to the use of mass campaigns for the elimination of pests, to the modes of propaganda, and also in some of the outcomes of those policies. Similar obsessions, for example with promoting hygiene or controlling the flow of information to and fro across the border, exercised officials on both sides. The two regimes also shared common approaches to dealing with the problems they identified, often by launching campaigns of popular mobilization that combined material incentives with ideological exhortation. Both the PRC and Jinmen authorities also frequently identified problems, such as the persistence of practices that were seen as backwards and un-modern, that on closer analysis turn out to be creations of those same authorities. They created the very targets of their own interventions.

Some of the similarities seem to derive from a shared inheritance of Chinese political culture. Both regimes often blamed policy problems on the failings of the populace, and therefore saw moral education and transformation as critical to successful implementation. It is hard not to see echoes of the Confucian imperative to educate and transform (*jiaohua*) in many policies on Jinmen and on the mainland. Solutions to problems were often sought first in state intervention. This fundamental statism implies an approach to governing that Alexander Woodside traces back to early modern Chinese history, the tendency to convert political questions to technical issues, that is, to assuming that the resolution of a political issue lay in finding the appropriate policy solution.[15] By converting political problems into technical issues, both regimes frequently allowed administrative goals to become ends of policies rather than means. The common origins of the two parties as Soviet-influenced Leninist parties that saw themselves as a vanguard for mobilizing the population and transforming society also help explain the similarities.

But it is not just their shared past that explains the parallelism between the two regimes. In his study of kinship in East and West Berlin, John Borneman notes that the two societies cannot be understood in isolation but only in relation to one another.[16] Like the two Germanys, the ROC and the PRC did not only imagine the enemy as the opposite of self but also engaged in the active fashioning of self in contrast to the enemy. This process of "mirroring" could take two very different forms. Many of the changes discussed in this book have been the results of efforts to construct Jinmen as the "mirror opposite" of the mainland. The conscious, selective appropriation of what was perceived to be Chinese cultural tradition by ROC state authorities was one way in which the ROC sought to distinguish itself from the PRC. Difference was used as a tool of legitimacy. But there are also other examples of Jinmen being constructed as the "mirror-image" of the situation on the mainland. Sometimes this was deliberate. The parallels in modes of propaganda were a deliberate effort to ensure that the enemy could not seize any advantage. The combat village system was adopted from another Cold War enemy because it was seen as effective. There were other parallels, like the campaigns against pests, that were unwitting and ironic.

Without downplaying the horrific human consequences of the Maoist period, by drawing attention to the extraordinary similarities to policies and responses across the Strait, this parallelism has implications for our understanding of Chinese political culture since 1949. It shows that models of political behavior that focus on the overarching ideology to which the regime claimed allegiance, or the idiosyncrasies of individual leaders, or the bureaucratic politics within the regime are all inadequate to explain fully the trajectories followed by the two regimes. To these must be added the shared inheritance from the past, the common origins of the two regimes as Leninist modernizing revolutionary groups, with common visions of mobilization and modernization, and also the parallel processes of self-definition in a context of mutual antagonism. Militarization in a state of emergency yielded patterns of policymaking and implementation that shared many similarities on both sides of the Taiwan Strait.

Another useful comparison for Jinmen is with other highly militarized societies. The creation of huge military bases and of new frontiers in the global Cold War had similar consequences on communities around the world, from Fayetteville, North Carolina, outside Fort Bragg, to Subic Bay in the Philippines. Environmental damage and disruption to the local economy, the rise of the sex trade, the importance of the military as a career path – all of these are broadly similar across many locales. Militarization's impacts often appeared in unexpected places, for example the gendering of citizenship, an argument made by Seungsook Moon.[17] The similarities also extend to the political uses of these societies and to contemporary legacies. Okinawa, for example, like Jinmen, was used as a localized site for the concentration of militarization that could therefore be reduced in the larger society to which it belonged. The question of local identity and its relation to national identity was a central concern for the authorities in both places (though on Okinawa this question went back to the nineteenth century). Comparisons of the postmilitarization period seem even more apposite. Gavan McCormack's description of Okinawa's position today is similar to that of Jinmen, even to the point of mirroring the split between marginality and the naively optimistic hopefulness of local officials. Okinawa, like Jinmen, now faces "a choice between being incorporated in the nation-state-centered regional and global order as a hyper-peripheral, hyper-dependent backwater . . . or alternatively, becoming a base for the creation of the twenty-first century's new, decentralized, sustainable and naturally balanced order."[18]

Moving beyond immediate comparisons, I have tried to outline in the preceding chapters a politics of Cold War militarized modernity, to show in a localized context the way concerns and interests around the global Cold War, national conflict, and the quest for modernity have been understood and deployed, and how they are remembered in the present. This is not a politics of modernity in general, but a politics directly shaped by the geopolitical specificities of time and place, which is why I call it a politics of Cold War militarized modernity. At the core of this politics has been militarization, the penetration of military concerns into social life. The justification of militarization of society on the basis of a specific emergency, a perceived national security threat that was in turn linked to global geopolitical issues, was common throughout Asia in the second half of the twentieth century, especially in the three (six?) divided states of the region, but also under other authoritarian regimes. Militarization has been a factor in many other states of Asia in the twentieth century, and indeed has been central to the political economy of some. Militarization shaped the way modernization was understood and pursued throughout the region, which is why Jinmen should be seen as but one example of a broader phenomenon of the regional inflection of the Cold War and global modernity. In some states, it was an unfinished civil war that drove continuing militarization; in others superpower interventions. But regardless of their ideological orientation the consequences of this phenomenon of militarization were broadly comparable across states. They included the geopoliticization of society and the pursuit of certain approaches to modernization. Putative military threat gave great scope to state authorities to implement desired policies regardless of resource constraints or the need for popular support. Modernization policies such as economic development, education, and hygiene were transformed from ends of modernization, the desirable outcomes that modernization was to create, into means of pursuing geopolitical survival. (This is perhaps a postcolonial echo of a familiar issue of anti-colonial and anti-imperialist resistance in Asia, wherein these ultimate goals were also transformed into instrumental means of overthrowing the colonial power.) Under such conditions, civilian noncompliance or evasion was more than just resistance; it was collaboration with the enemy. These policies produced many unanticipated outcomes that linger to the present day. Among these legacies is the way participation in or compliance with state efforts has subsequently become a political resource for the people involved.

These complex and often unpredicted consequences of geopoliticized militarization were not limited to Asia. My discussion has rested on the premise that the level of militarization on Jinmen was out of all proportion to the specifics of the military threat. This was a widespread phenomenon in the post-Second World War world. Where the Cold War remained cold, the appropriate level of militarization, in the narrow and broad sense, was unquantifiable. Whereas specific responses to specific threats might also have required large armies, the task of demonstrating determination and reassuring allies was open-ended. Michael Sherry argues that part of the power of militarization in the US derived from the fact that it was never centrally directed or coordinated as it was in states like Nazi Germany. It was the tool rather than the goal of diverse interests. "Its force derived from the manner in which all sorts of conflicts become subsumed under or attached to dominant anxieties about national security." Though Jinmen lies somewhere in the middle of the continuum of militarization that Sherry implies, its outcomes could be just as quixotic and unpredictable. Around the world, the Cold War threat was internal as well as external, so it had profound impacts on issues of social control and surveillance. Militarization led to the politicization of many aspects of daily life. For militarization is a way of creating and exercising power as much as a national security strategy. Militarization drove social changes but also determined the forms they would take, forcing some changes and circumscribing others. As Elaine Tyler May has written of America, "The politics of the cold war and the ideology and public policies that it spawned were crucial in shaping postwar family life and gender roles." [19]

Above all, the study of the local history of the Cold War reveals the crucial importance of breaking down traditional boundaries between international relations history and the history of domestic processes. Theorists of international relations have long recognized the importance of domestic considerations in the making of foreign policy. But social historians must also recognize that international considerations can profoundly shape domestic policy decisions and therefore lived human experience. To fully understand the Cold War in its local instantiations requires shifting back and forth between multiple scales of analysis. A geopolitically informed social history is as crucial as a socially informed geopolitical history. Otherwise historical developments are allowed to generate their own meanings at a level of abstraction far removed from how they were actually experienced. The story of Jinmen is not only the story of diplomatic and military crisis, but also of new patterns of daily life. And a truly comprehensive cultural and social history of the Cold War must include not just life in the superpowers and those places in the Third World where the Cold War became hot. It must also consider those many other parts of the world where geopolitical confrontation and superpower intervention shaped communities and families and distorted society and culture.

The themes that animated the body of this study, geopoliticization, modernization, and militarization, remain useful ways to think about the profound changes on Jinmen since 1992. During the martial law period, as part of efforts to draw attention to the geopolitical significance of the island, the WZA sought to highlight Jinmen's location on a border. This was a military boundary and also an ideological border: the point where the forces of global Communism and the forces of freedom faced one another. While this border was often represented as being impermeable, in fact it not only could be permeated but had to be permeated in order for Jinmen to play its desired role. Thus the WZA efforts were to demarcate and strictly regulate the border. Even before the 1992 lifting of martial law, the border was increasingly becoming a borderland, a more fluid zone of interactions and flows of people, goods, capital, and ideas. This shift from border to borderland is a concrete expression of the shift from geopoliticization to globalization. Under geopoliticization, the inter-connectedness of different places is rooted in the power of nation-states and their agendas. Under globalization, that inter-connectedness is based, at least in principle, on neo-liberal economic relations. The nostalgia that is so widespread in Jinmen today is in part a response to the disruption caused by the displacement of geopoliticization by globalization. Authorities on Jinmen today hope that the new flows that have developed in the last decade will bring to Jinmen the prosperity that evaded it under martial law. They define modernization in rather different terms than their army predecessors, in terms of economic liberalism and the social welfare that they hope will follow from it. What were formerly the means of winning a propaganda war – educational facilities, health care, infrastructure – have now once again become the ends of the modernization project.

Jinmen ultimately escaped its cycle of militarization. But it still bears many scars of this encounter – scars on its landscape, on its people, and on its potential for the future. In the 1960s, the people of Jinmen could be confident that they were at the very center of world affairs. By the 1970s, this confidence was shaken by the increasing marginalization of the Republic of China on Taiwan. Then, as the people of Taiwan began to articulate an identity tied to history rather than politics alone, Jinmen became increasingly marginalized from Taiwan as well. Today Jinmen is doubly marginalized, both with Taiwan and from Taiwan. This sense of double marginalization, and the desire to fight it, has become part of the identity of the people of Jinmen. In today's globalized world, it is hard to imagine how Jinmen could possibly be any more peripheral than it is. Never again will Jinmen be the center of world attention as it was in 1958. It will be little consolation to its residents today, but perhaps it is as a lesson of the consequences of militarization and the implementation of the state of emergency that Jinmen's significance lies.

I opened this book by describing how metaphor was a dominant trope in representations of Jinmen. These arguments for Jinmen's importance to comparative history are, in a sense, indications that I too perceive the island as a metaphor for the experience of the Cold War. Perhaps the metaphor can be extended even further. To a degree that was quite unanticipated by the great nineteenth-century social theorists whose thinking so much still shapes our own, militarization and the violence of war characterized global society in the twentieth century.[20] If Jinmen saw militarization taken to extremes, it can therefore stimulate reflection on the more general condition. Jinmen's story shows that militarization may occur for reasons that have little to do with military threat or military ambition, and that militarization in different contexts may produce similar policies and social outcomes regardless of the ideology behind it. It shows how militarization and modernization can become intertwined and how together the two can produce a distinctive politics. In genuine or claimed democracies emergency is always the justification for militarization, and the aporia of emergency, its self-representation as necessity, and its ambiguous position between law and absence of law, is what enables militarization to extend itself into so many domains of life and then to normalize its extension. Emergency can be invoked to justify not only authoritarianism or repression but all manner of political, social, economic, and cultural policies. These developments are never inevitable responses to objective circumstances. They are always linked to and conditioned by politics, local and trans-local or even global. And they are always negotiated by the individuals and communities affected by them. Agamben has argued that since the beginning of modern democratic thought, governments have simultaneously claimed to be expanding the realm of freedom while actually undermining it through appeals to necessity and emergency.[21] On this interpretation, the state of exception or martial law can be considered a paradigmatic form of modern government. To the extent that militarization was a widespread phenomenon of the twentieth century and that the invocation of the state of emergency remains a concern today, the experience of Jinmen and its people may be emblematic and instructive rather than singular and irrelevant.

Appendix

Table A.1 Civilian population and garrison size (selected years)*

Year	Civilian population	Size of garrison	
		Troops	Units
1945	50,865		n.a.
1949			9 divisions
1954		42,000 (+ 6,000 guerrillas)	6 divisions
1956	45,347		
1958		95,000 (Wu Lengxi) 86,000 ("US Military Policy")	
1959	41,014	80,000–100,000 (?)	5 divisions
1961	47,528		
1966	56,842		
1970	61,008		
1975	59,668		
1980	51,883		
1985	48,846	60,000–80,000 (?)	4 divisions
1990	42,754		
1993	45,807	30,979	
1997	51,080	15,974	4 brigades
2000	53,832		
2004	64,456	10,709	

* The figures for the civilian population come from various statistical collections and are probably quite reliable (*JMXZ*, 355–62; *JMTJ*, no vol. number (1961); *JMTJ* LI (2004), 29). The figures for the size of the garrison are more tentative. For military secrecy reasons the ROC government did not release precise numbers before the 1990s. The figure for 1954 comes from a CIA report (Central Intelligence Agency: Office of Current Intelligence, "The Chinese Offshore Islands," 1954, DDRS, 3. The reliability of this figure is somewhat called into question by the estimate of the civilian population as 6,000, a number that is wrong by a factor of six or more, but this was not the priority of the authors). Mao Zedong, whose intelligence was presumably good, used the figure of 95,000 in a meeting at Beidaihe in mid-August 1958. (Wu Lengxi, "Wuzhang yu

Table A.1 note (cont.)

wenzhang: Paohong Jinmen neimu," 6). US government sources from September 1958 give the figure of 86,000. ("US Military Policy and Objectives in Formosan Area – Draft Script for McElroy–Sandys Talks, September 22–October 3 1958," DDRS, 5–6). An assessment that appears often in the scholarly literature is that in 1958 the garrisons of Jinmen and Mazu consisted of one-third of the ROC army. This can, I think, be traced back to remarks early in the crisis by Eisenhower that were probably based in turn on CIA estimates. Since the ROC army at the time numbered over 450,000, and the total armed forces approximately 600,000, this was clearly an overestimate, and caused some confusion at the time. A CIA Special National Intelligence Estimate that is cited in Halperin seems to have arrived at the one-third figure by comparing the combined total for the garrisons of Jinmen (86,000) and Mazu (23,000) against the estimated 320,000 combat-ready troops. Eisenhower may also have been referring to unit rather than troop numbers. Of twenty-one divisions of the ROC army, six were located on Jinmen and one on Mazu. Alternatively, he may have been deliberately manipulating the ambiguity for political purposes ("Transcript of the President's News Conference on Foreign and Domestic Matters," *New York Times*, August 28, 1958; Morton Halperin, *The 1958 Taiwan Straits Crisis: A Documented History*, 4–5.) The figures for the number of units and for troop numbers after 1993 come from "Jinfang bu zuzhi xitong dishan duizhao biao." This is a photocopied document which was provided to me by a source on Jinmen. There is no reason to doubt the authenticity of the document. Its cover is printed with the shield of the Jinmen Defense Headquarters (JDHQ), improper use of which would presumably be a serious offense. In the ROC army, a division is a unit that consists of between 10,000 and 20,000 troops. So the numbers for divisions accord well with rough figures given to the media and visitors that the total garrison was between 60,000 and 100,000. In 1983, one division was relocated to Taiwan, leaving behind four. The number of divisions remained constant at four over the next decade. In 1997 the four divisions were downgraded to brigades.

Notes

Abbreviations used in the Notes

DDRS	Declassified Documents Reference Service, US
FRUS	*Foreign Relations of the United States*
GFBA	Guofangbu (Ministry of Defense) archives, ROC
GSGA	Guoshiguan (Academia Historica) archives, ROC
JMBD	*Jinmen baodao* (*Jinmen Reports*)
JMJCJA	Jinmen jingchaju (police bureau) archives, ROC
JMMFFT	Dong Qunlian (ed.), *Jinmen jieyan shiqi de minfang zuxun yu dongyuan fangtan lu* (Taibei: Guoshiguan, 2003–)
JMMFTDJL	Xu Weimin *et al.* (eds.), "Jinmen minfang dui de tiandiao jilu," *Jinmen Daoshang Minfangdui shiji ji Guo-Gong zhanyi diaocha yanjiu qizhong baogao* (Jinmen: Jinmen guojia gongyuan, 2000)
JMRB	*Jinmen ribao* (*Jinmen Daily*)
JMTJ	*Jinmen tongji nianbiao* (*Jinmen Statistical Annual*)
JMXZ	*Jinmen xianzhi* (Jinmen: Jinmen xianzhengfu, 1992)
LYA	Lieyu (Little Jinmen) township archives, ROC
NARA	National Archives and Records Administration, US
SSJY	*Zhonghua Minguo shishi jiyao* (Taibei: Guoshiguan 1971–)

PREFACE

1 Dwight Eisenhower, *Waging Peace, 1955–1961: The White House Years*, 304.
2 US$ figures are from Samuel Ku, "The Political Economy of Regime transformation: Taiwan and Southeast Asia," 59–78; historical rates from investintaiwan.nat.gov.tw/en/env/stats/exchange_rates.html

1 INTRODUCTION: ORDINARY LIFE IN AN EXTRAORDINARY PLACE

1 This account is drawn from Dong Qunlian (ed.), *Jinmen jieyan shiqi de minfang zuxun yu dongyuan fangtan lu* (*JMMFFT*), I:313 ff and other oral history.

2 For example Morton Halperin, *The 1958 Taiwan Straits Crisis: A Documented History*; Thomas Stolper, *China, Taiwan, and the Offshore Islands*.

3 A comprehensive list of the literatures in each of these fields would be unwieldy. Representative works in each field include Robert Accinelli, *Crisis and Commitment: United States Policy toward Taiwan, 1950–1955*; Chen Jian, *Mao's China and the Cold War*; Gordon Chang, *Friends and Enemies: The United States, China, and the Soviet Union, 1948–1972*; Qiang Zhai, *The Dragon, the Lion and the Eagle: Chinese–British–American Relations, 1949–1958*; Thomas Christensen, *Useful Adversaries: Grand Strategy, Domestic Mobilization, and Sino-American Conflict, 1947–1958*, and Gordon Chang, "To the Nuclear Brink: Eisenhower, Dulles, and the Quemoy–Matsu Crisis."

4 I often use the term Cold War as shorthand for this system and the larger geopolitical conflicts in which Jinmen's history was embedded, including the global conflict between ideologies and political and economic systems, and the conflict between the PRC and the ROC on Taiwan. The reasons for this usage go beyond mere felicity. The term draws attention to the ways in which historical developments on Jinmen throughout this period were tied to larger political forces. Of course, this usage oversimplifies a more complex reality and becomes increasingly problematic after Sino–American rapprochement in the 1970s. This issue is discussed further in the Conclusion.

5 Militarization need not refer exclusively to states, but the exceptions are uncommon.

6 Cynthia Enloe, *Maneuvers: The International Politics of Militarizing Women's Lives*, 291. For a discussion see Catherine Lutz, "Militarization," 318–31. The broader meaning is captured rather well by the Chinese term *junshihua*, which in the twentieth century included the idea of transforming civilian values and behavior to bring them closer to those of the army.

7 Other US agencies were also involved more tangentially. For example, the US Escapee Program that funded aid to defectors from the Communist bloc was used to recruit guerrillas from Hong Kong and transfer them to Jinmen. "Report on the US Escapee Program for Refugees Seeking Political Asylum in the Free World," August 17, 1954, Declassified Documents Reference Service (DDRS).

8 The invasion was initially planned under Eisenhower but was approved by Kennedy. Arthur Schlesinger, *A Thousand Days: John F. Kennedy in the White House*, 225–56.

9 Rosendo Canto, *Between Champagne and Powder*, 30.

10 One might begin by exploring what Jinmen/Quemoy meant to the millions of ROC men who served there as adolescent conscripts; to the thousands of Chinese Youth Anti-Communist National Salvation League members who visited for paramilitary training; to the countless audiences in the PRC who heard the comedic dialogue (*xiangsheng*) "Bombard Jinmen on August 23rd"; to US television viewers of the 1965 episode of the program *I Spy* that

involved the heroes recovering stolen plans of the island's defenses, and to the residents of Quemoy Court, in a Colorado sub-division near Buckley Air Force Base.

11 Greg Grandin, *The Last Colonial Massacre: Latin America in the Cold War*, 17. Also see Susan Bucks-Morss, *Dreamworld and Catastrophe: The Passing of Mass Utopia in East and West.*

12 There is a huge literature on modernity and more recently on its unstable and multiple character. Two works that have been particularly influential in my understanding of modernity on Jinmen are Michel Foucault, "Governmentality," 87–104, and Seungsook Moon, *Militarized Modernity and Gendered Citizenship in South Korea.*

13 James Scott, *Seeing Like a State*, 1–4.

14 For the period from the 1950s to the 1980s I use the term state to refer to both the ROC state and the KMT since the roles and functions of the two were closely intertwined. Party-state would be a more accurate but more cumbersome term. As William Kirby argues, in principle "the government existed to execute the policies dictated by the party." "The Nationalist Regime and the Chinese Party-State, 1928–1958," 213. Hung-mao Tien shows how this principle was put in practice on the mainland through the construction of a parallel system of party and state organizations. *Government and Politics in Kuomintang China, 1927–1937*, chs. 1–2.

15 Odd Arne Westad, *The Global Cold War: Third World Interventions and the Making of our Times*, 404.

16 There is a growing literature on the continuities across the two regimes even after 1949. Some key works include Paul Cohen, "Reflections on a Watershed Date: The 1949 Divide in Chinese History"; Joseph Esherick, "Ten Theses on the Chinese Revolution"; Kirby, "Nationalist Regime."

17 John Borneman, *Belonging in the Two Berlins: Kin, State, Nation*, 17; Patrick Major and Rana Mitter, "East is East and West is West? Towards a Comparative Socio-Cultural History of the Cold War," 2.

18 Though it is not my main purpose, this book can also be situated in relation to two other bodies of literature, local studies from Taiwan and those from the PRC. As scholars of Taiwan have pointed out, many of the first group of works use Taiwanese communities to try to understand Chinese culture, thereby ignoring both history and Taiwanese distinctiveness. The works of the second group typically focus on the domestic transformation since 1949, to the neglect of the geopolitical context that shaped that transformation. This book thus bridges the two bodies of literature but more importantly situates local communities in the global as well as national context. Keelung Hong and Stephen Murray, *Looking through Taiwan: American Anthropologists' Collusion with Ethnic Domination*; two classic works of the second group are Edward Friedman, Paul Pickowicz, and Mark Selden, *Chinese Village, Socialist State*, and Anita Chan, Richard Madsen, and Jonathon Unger, *Chen Village under Mao and Deng.*

19 The "new Cold War history" is exemplified in the work of John Lewis Gaddis, *We Now Know: Rethinking Cold War History*; see Major and Mitter, "East is East." Key works on cultural history include Margot Henriksen, *Dr. Strangelove's America: Society and Culture in the Atomic Age*; Stephen Whitfield,

The Culture of the Cold War. For a discussion see Robert Griffith, "The Cultural Turn in Cold War Studies." Gaddis has more recently, in *The Cold War: A New History*, characterized the Cold War as a low-tension war punctuated by high brinkmanship, that involved primarily military and ideological confrontation. This formulation is largely applicable to Jinmen. But the overall privileging of the European theater of the conflict casts into historical oblivion the millions of victims of the Cold War in other parts of the world, and the clear demarcation of winners and losers, moreover, continues to sidestep the question of the conflict's complex impacts around the world.

20 Giorgio Agamben, *The State of Exception*, 7.

21 Interviews were conducted mostly in modern standard Chinese (Mandarin, or *guoyu*) which is widely spoken on Jinmen by all except elderly women. Informants frequently switched back and forth between *guoyu* and the local Minnan dialect; research assistants helped with interpreting dialect material on the spot. Interviews conducted in dialect were interpreted by research assistants, recorded and transcribed. Interviewees were disproportionately male and disproportionately over the age of sixty, that is, people who had lived through much of the martial law period. I did not attempt an analysis by cohort to explore how the period was experienced and remembered differently by people of different ages.

22 Where possible I have provided a reference to the published oral history so that interested readers can follow up with this rich source themselves.

23 Philomena Goodman, *Women, Sexuality, and War*, 5.

24 When I first began to use them, the files were stored in several dozen plastic garbage bags. In citing them, I provide where possible the name of the village, the details of the document and the date.

25 The wealth of source material and the intimate scale of Jinmen created an unanticipated ethical issue. Most of the published oral history from Jinmen provides names and personal details of interviewees. Because in my own interviews I ask informants to discuss personal and sensitive topics and sometimes even reveal illegal activities, I use pseudonyms to protect their anonymity. I was also required by the local government to use pseudonyms for people mentioned in archives. But some people appear in multiple sources. For example, some of my informants have also been interviewed by other historians who have published their oral histories using their real names. This raises ethical and methodological questions. For example, how should I deal with an informant who had given a published interview that was clearly sanitized, but had also given me an interview in which she revealed embarrassing personal information on condition of anonymity? What about a person who had written a signed newspaper essay and who also appeared in archival materials? I have settled on a compromise about which it is best to be explicit. For individuals whose oral histories have appeared in other books but whom I have not interviewed myself or read about in archives, I use real names as published (the information has already been publicly disclosed, and I am simply excerpting and translating it). For individuals named in the archives or interviewed by me whose real names have not been published elsewhere, I have removed the name or used a pseudonym. For individuals whom I have interviewed or read about in the archives *and* who have published oral histories, I have also used

pseudonyms and changed minor details to protect their identity. To make this effective, I have had to mis-label some excerpts from published interviews as if they were my own interviews (otherwise, it would be a simple matter to cross-reference the published interview and learn the true identity of the informant). I acknowledge that this is not a completely foolproof method of maintaining anonymity, but I think it is the best possible compromise. A final category is public figures, by which I mean people who have run for or held public office or who have published books under their own names. They are referred to by their real names. There are five such individuals mentioned in this book.

PART I GEOPOLITICIZATION ASCENDANT

2 THE BATTLE OF GUNINGTOU

1 The Jinmen gazetteer records that he was hit by bullets in the back of the head. *Jinmen xianzhi* (*JMXZ*), 417.

2 The seasick soldiers had taken too long to unload; none of them could swim so the boats had to be brought in to the shallows, and they had not expected to be under fire. When the tide began to ebb early in the morning, the lead boats were stranded on the beach, and the other boats were ensnared by anti-landing fortifications that had been laid on the tidal sands.

3 Liu Yazhou, "Wu Jinmen zhi zhan, wu jinri Taiwan."

4 These statistics, now widely accepted, are considerably lower than earlier figures produced in the ROC for propaganda purposes. For example, a 1969 work reports a total invasion force of over 20,000, with 7,000 captured and the remainder killed. Jinmen fangwei silingbu zhengzhi zuozhan bu (ed.), *Nian nian: Guningtou dajie nian zhou nian ji*, i.

5 Guoshiguan shiliao chu (ed.), *Jinmen Guningtou, Zhoushan, Dengbudao zhi zhanshi shiliao chuji*, 48–9; Zhang Huomu, *Jinmen gujin zhanshi*, 47.

6 An official combat history of the PLA blames the defeat primarily on inadequate logistical preparations and the fact that remaining military tasks were necessarily neglected when the army was suddenly faced with the task of administering the city of Xiamen after its fall. Mu Yang and Yao Jie, *Zhongguo renmin jiefangjun zhanshi*, III:340–1. A recent book singles out Guningtou as the PLA's only unsuccessful amphibious operation. Qi Dexue, *Zhongwai denglu zuozhan jingyan jiaoxun*, 30.

7 Henceforth, I use the term Jinmen to describe the two islands collectively and also for the larger of the two islands, and Little Jinmen to describe the smaller island.

8 The first reliable population figures are from the mid-eighteenth century, and give a total population of 60,623. *Maxiang tingzhi*, cited in *JMXZ*, 355.

9 The history of the period is explored in Li Shide, *Shiqi shiji de haishang Jinmen*.

10 *JMXZ*, 356.

11 Li Jinsheng, *Jiyan shanding tan Zhushan lishi*, 107–8.

12 Zhang Qicai, *JMMFFT*, I:214.

13 Li Qingquan, cited in Dong Qunlian, "Zhandi Jinmen shihua"; Li Tiansong, *JMMFFT*, II:62.

14 Li Jinchun, *JMMFFT*, II:19–20; Li Qingquan, cited in Dong, "Zhandi Jinmen."

15 A 1996 PRC document dealing with informal relations with Taiwan reportedly recorded 7,000 similar cases, but this number seems too high. Yang Shuqing, *Jinmen daoyu bianyuan*, 5. A 1955 US report mentioning "a good deal of civil traffic" between Jinmen and the mainland must be a misunderstanding, perhaps of ROC reports of infiltration missions by guerrillas or of traffic between Jinmen and Taiwan. A. J. Goodpaster, "Memorandum for the Record," DDRS.

16 Wu Wuquan, *JMMFFT*, II:86; Li Qingzheng, *JMMFFT*, I:16; Li Jinchun, *JMMFFT*, II:20; Wang Qinglin, *JMMFFT*, I:347.

17 Shanhua, "Xiangye beiwu"; Li Tiansong, *JMMFFT*, II: 62.

18 Wu Wuquan, cited in Dong, "Zhandi Jinmen"; Cai Xiujuan, cited in Xu Weimin *et al.*, "Jinmen minfang dui de tiandiao jilu," (*JMMFTDJL*) 215.

19 Shanhua, "Xiangye".

20 Wu Wuquan, *JMMFFT*, II:92.

21 Weng Xiongfei, "Fenghuo taonan ji"; Li Qingquan, *JMMFFT*, II:44.

22 PLA officer Liu Yazhou reports that local villagers told him decades later that many of the PLA wounded had been buried alive. "With their bare heads and eyes wide open, their moans were heard all over . . . One young kid, about sixteen or seventeen, was waving his hands as he was buried alive. It was a brutal and horrid sight" ("Jinmen zhi zhan"). I have not heard such reports in oral history.

23 Li Tiansong, *JMMFFT*, II:63; Wang Zhichang, cited in Dong, "Zhandi Jinmen"; Chen Zonglun, *JMMFFT*, III:53–4.

24 Dulles and Eisenhower's commitment was rather more hedged that Hu's interpretation of it. Christopher Tudda, " 'Reenacting the Story of Tantalus': Eisenhower, Dulles, and the Failed Rhetoric of Liberation," 3–35.

25 Hu Lian, *Jinmen yijiu*, 83.

26 Wu Quanjian, cited in Dong, "Zhandi Jinmen."

27 Besides Jinmen, the ROC also retained control of several other islands in late 1949. The most significant were the Mazu group just to the north of Jinmen; the Dachen group farther to the north, opposite Zhejiang province, and the island of Hainan far to the southwest. Hainan fell to the Communists in 1950, and the Dachen group was evacuated in 1955 after one of the smaller islands was taken in battle (see chapter 4).

3 POLITICS OF THE WAR ZONE, 1949–1960

1 Shanhua, "Xiangye."

2 Hu served two terms as commanding officer (CO) of the JDHQ, from December 1949 to April 1954 and July 1957 to November 1958.

3 There was therefore also a Zhejiang Provincial Government, with jurisdiction over the northern offshore islands until these were abandoned in the 1950s.

4 These visits are recounted in detail in the section on "Distinguished Visitors" in the county gazetteer. *JMXZ*, 1659–99. Articles about Jinmen that appeared in world media are translated in Jinmen fangwei silingbu, *Nian nian*, 43–76.

5 Chen Yangjin interview (all interviews conducted by the author, on Jinmen); Xu Rongxiang, *JMMFFT*, I:64–5.

6 Wu Zongqi, "Jinmen diqu shiyan zhandi zhengwu ji qi zhidu zhuanxing zhi yanjiu," 101.

7 Most of the guerrillas came from one of two places. Some were former inhabitants of other offshore islands. Many of these were modern-day privateers, former pirates and bandits who had been given authorization by the ROC government to continue their attacks under the flag of harassing Communist shipping and raiding the mainland. Others were refugees, many of them KMT soldiers and officers, who had escaped to Hong Kong. In the early 1950s, out of fear of Communist infiltration, the ROC imposed strict requirements on such refugees before they could be allowed to continue to Taiwan. Anyone who could not find a guarantor was forced to remain, mostly destitute, in Hong Kong. Hu Lian sent a team to Hong Kong to recruit these men to serve as officers in the guerrilla forces. In all, about 2,800 were recruited, with US financial assistance. Foreign Operations Administration, *Report to Operations Coordinating Board*, August 17, 1954, DDRS.

8 Their activities are described in Frank Holober, *Raiders of the China Coast: CIA Covert Operations during the Korean War*. Holober was a CIA employee who trained and at times accompanied the guerrillas on their raids of the mainland.

9 Zhang Qicai, *JMMFFT*, 1:215.

10 Originally named the Institute for Research into the Realization of the Revolution, in 1952 the institute was renamed and transferred to the Ministry of Defense's General Political Department, headed at the time by Chiang Ching-kuo. Guofangbu shizheng bianyi ju, *Guojun waidao diqu jieyan yu zhandi zhengwu jilu*, 6–7, 187.

11 The key legal document behind the WZA was the Experimental Regulations for the Jinmen and Mazu War Zone Administration, enacted by the Ministry of Defense in July 1956. The legal basis for these regulations was the constitutional provisions for martial law and the Temporary Provisions Effective During the Period of Communist Rebellion, a constitutional revision enacted by the National Assembly in 1948 that granted the President extraordinary powers to respond to the national emergency. Wu Zongqi, "Shiyan zhandi," 38.

12 Bruce Dickson, *Democratization in China and Taiwan: The Adaptability of Leninist Parties*.

13 *JMXZ*, 598; Yang Xiaoxian, *Jinmen jindaishi yanjiu*, 137. Wu Zongqi, "Shiyan zhandi." Though both the county government and WZA budgets were published, the finances of civilian government on Jinmen prior to 1992 are murky. The available statistics do not include transfers via the WZA from the Ministry of Defense and other central government agencies. Also, much capital construction was done by the army, and the statistics do not distinguish between purely military construction and construction such as schools and roads that also benefited the civilian population. Yang Dongwen and Lin Jinwei interviews; *Jinmen tongji nianbiao* (*JMTJ*) (various years); Guofangbu (Ministry of Defense) archives (GFBA), 00002716, "Jinmen fangwei siling bu 43 niandu shizheng jihua," 1955.

14 Fu Kuncheng and Li Jinzhen, *Jinmen zhandi zhengwu de fagui yu shixian*, 323.
15 The theoretical link to Sun Yat-sen's principle of military tutelage provided an explicit justification for the system from an unimpeachable source. It was not only objective necessity that justified the state of exception, but also the authority of the nation's founding father.
16 Lin Tiansheng, in Lin Mateng and Lu Yunzai, *Cong Dongkeng tanqi*, 134.
17 Wang Qingbiao, *JMMFTDJL*, 164.
18 Xue Chengzu interview.
19 Dong Zhenhan interview.
20 Zheng Shihua, *JMMFFT*, I:458.
21 Xue Chengzu interview; Yan Boyi, *JMMFFT*, III:271; Ni Jiujing, cited in Dong, "Zhandi Jinmen."
22 Wen Shizhong, *JMMFFT*, I:199–201.
23 Wu Guihai, *JMMFFT*, I:513.
24 Zheng Shihua, *JMMFFT*, I:460–1.
25 When a household obtained or lost one of these items, it was required to report the change to the village office, which kept its own register, the registry of floatable objects. Surviving registers from Little Jinmen village show that the system was implemented strictly. Lieyu (Little Jinmen) township archives (LYA), Xikou, "Xikou cun piaofu dengji liguan ce," October 1969 to July 1981.
26 Xue Liujin interview.
27 Chen Changqing interview.
28 The earliest surviving mutual responsibility agreement in the archives dates from 1967. It reads: "The members of the mutual responsibility group and their family members declare that if there are violations of the household registration administration or the regulations of Article 5 of the Measures for Mutual Responsibility and Punishment by Association for Inspecting and Eliminating [contact with] Communist agents, the members of the group will accept strict punishment by association." LYA, Xikou, "Huji," 1967, "Xikou/Huji/Gezhong huji dengji shenqing shu."
29 Yang Luyin, "Shequ zuzhi yu dongyuan zhi tantao – yi Guan'ao wei li," 226–7.
30 Xu Rongxiang recalls that in the early days of the pass system, violators could be locked up for as long as three months. Xu Rongxiang, *JMMFFT*, I:73.
31 Chi Chang-hui, "The Politics of Deification and Nationalist Ideology: A Case Study of Quemoy," 117.
32 Zhang Qicai, *JMMFFT*, I:218–19
33 Xu Minghong, *JMMFFT*, I:288–9.
34 Li Jinlian, *JMMFFT*, II:252; Hong Futian, *JMMFFT*, I:392.
35 Xue Chengzu interview; Dong Guangxin, *JMMFFT*, III:17; Xu Minghong, *JMMFFT*, I:288–9; Xue Qijin interview.
36 Xue Chengzu interview; Fu Wenmin, *JMMFFT*, I:364–5.
37 On the survival of traditional social forms on the mainland, see Sulamith Heins Potter and Jack Potter, *China's Peasants: The Anthropology of a Revolution*.
38 Chen Cangjiang (ed.), "Jinmen baise kongbu ge'an dang'an ziliao huibian."
39 Xu Mingliang, *JMMFFT*, II:131.

40 Zhang Zhangyuan, *JMMFTDJL*, 177; Han Zhenpin interview; Yang Luyin, "Guan'ao," 226.
41 Pan Shuqi interview. Li's case is also discussed in Chen Rongchang, *Wutu Wumin: Wudao Jinmen ren de zhenqing gushi*, 124–6 and Yang Shuqing, *Jinmen daoyu*, 159–62. Documents are in Chen Cangjiang, "Jinmen baise kongbu."
42 Chi Chang-hui, "Politics of Deification," 112; Jiang Bowei personal communication.
43 The main source for the story of Wang Fangming is Chen Rongchang, *Wutu*, 118–23. Wang's story was also discussed in interviews with Pan Shuqi.

4 THE 1954–5 ARTILLERY WAR

1 Zheng Qingli, *JMMFFT*, I:409–10.
2 *Foreign Relations of the United States* (hereafter *FRUS*), 1952–4, XIV:600.
3 Karl Rankin, *China Assignment*, 205.
4 The diplomatic negotiations also made clear that the US would not support ROC efforts to retake the mainland, a project that would now have to be deferred. Jinmen residents recall this transformation clearly. "At first, the slogan was 'Prepare in the first year, counter-attack in the second year, do battle in the third year, win victory in the fourth year.' Then the slogan changed to 'This will be the year of the counter-attack.' But the counter-attack never happened . . . So the slogan changed to 'Within a minimum of three years and a maximum of five, we will attack.'" Wang Wende interview. Another expression of the change was Hu Lian's decision to provide immediate compensation to people whose homes had been damaged or destroyed in 1949. Hu Lian, *Jinmen yijiu*, 44; Han Zhenpin interview.
5 Chang, "To the Brink," 106.
6 *JMXZ*, 1250. Christensen, *Useful Adversaries*, 194–5. Some recent work by scholars in the PRC seeks to salvage Mao's plan from this largely negative assessment, suggesting that in addition to testing US resolve, he also used the crisis to reaffirm the commitment to liberate Taiwan; to distract the ROC from the immediate target of the northern offshore islands, and to raise tension between Washington and Taibei. In all of these regards, the crisis had succeeded by the spring of 1955, so it made sense to ease the tension. Gong Li, "Tension across the Taiwan Strait in the 1950s: Chinese Strategy and Tactics." Chen Jian, *Mao's China*, 175–81, largely supports this analysis.
7 Li Jinsheng, *Jiyan shanding tan Zhushan lishi*, 117.
8 Li Yumin interview.
9 Dong Wunan, *JMMFTDJL*, 160.
10 Chen Zonglun, *JMMFFT*, III:67–8; Li Jinsheng, *Zhushan*, 119.
11 He recalls hiding under his bed, which may mean that he was from a nearby village rather than Guqu itself or that he has confused multiple incidents. Yuping, "Shensi Guqu danyaoku jingbao yu cunmin shangtong."
12 Huang Xi'an, cited in Dong, "Zhandi Jinmen."
13 Wu Guihai, *JMMFFT*, I:510.
14 Huang Xi'an, cited in Dong, "Zhandi Jinmen."
15 It is easily forgotten today, but at the time the US was concerned not only about aggression from the mainland but also that ROC activity in the strait

might provoke a PRC response and thereby draw the US into war. So the US, which had coordinated the guerrillas in the early 1950s, now called on Chiang to leash them in. Their units were eventually disbanded, and their members resettled on Taiwan or on Jinmen itself.

16 Hong Zhidi, in Lin and Lu, *Dongkeng*, 140.

17 Chen Jinzhen, *JMMFFT*, III:154; Fu Wenmin, *JMMFFT*, I:368; Li Qingquan, *JMMFFT*, II:55; Huang Pingsheng and Xu Rongxiang, cited in Dong, "Zhandi Jinmen."

18 *FRUS*, 1955–7, III:617.

5 MILITARIZATION AND THE JINMEN CIVILIAN SELF-DEFENSE FORCES, 1949–1960

1 There is some variation in the unit number depending on the age of the informant – elderly people use the term Unit 805; if the teller of the story is middle-aged, the unit is often Unit 108, or $108, presumably because of inflation. Several younger informants used the 805 figure, probably because they learned the story from their parents and grandparents. In most versions, the old man is anonymous, but in some he is identified by name. An example is Xu Pimou, *JMMFTDJL*, 154. Another version appears in Ouyang Yangming, *Huaiyi Jinmen*, 144–5.

2 Aaron Friedberg, *In the Shadow of the Garrison State: America's Anti-statism and its Cold War Grand Strategy*, 149.

3 Elizabeth Perry, *Patrolling the Revolution: Worker Militias, Citizenship, and the Modern Chinese State*, ch. 1.

4 Annual "combat summer camps," that brought Taiwanese youth of the Chinese Youth Anti-Communist National Salvation League to Jinmen were one important way this message was communicated.

5 Chen Yongcai, *JMMFFT*, I:432–3.

6 Du Tiansheng, in Lin and Lu, *Dongkeng*, 97.

7 Former magistrate Chen Shuizai was also given similar figures. Chen Shuizai interview.

8 Du Tiansheng, in Lin and Lu, *Dongkeng*, 97.

9 The most important regulations were the "Jinmen and Mazu counties civilian defense force organizational regulations," issued by the Ministry of Defense in late 1957, about a year after the creation of the War Zone Administration.

10 The regulations also specify the relationship between militia units and the nearby army units. Under peacetime conditions, the local commander exercised "supervision and support, through the local WZA Committee." In combat, the militia came under his direct command. Fu and Li, *Fagui yu shixian*, 285–7.

11 Xu Rongxiang, *JMMFFT*, I:59–60; Dong Qiming, *JMMFTDJL*, 149; Lin Jinshu, *JMMFTDJL*, 211.

12 Xu Qingqi, *JMMFTDJL*, 167.

13 A 1984 WZA document defines the purpose of a Thunder Exercise as: "to capture Communist infiltrators, or defectors who have disappeared without

a trace, and to confiscate prohibited items, in order to ensure the security of the defense zone." LYA, Xikou, "Fagui," "Leiting yanxi cunluo sousu jihua shishi guiding," December 1984.

14 Yang Luyin, "Guan'ao," 231.
15 Actual defections to the PRC grew quite rare, with the best known case in 1979, when a rising star in the ROC army, Captain Justin Lin Yifu, defected to the PRC from his post on Jinmen. Lin went on to earn a PhD in economics at the University of Chicago, and became Professor of Economics at Peking University. In 2008 he became chief economist of the World Bank.
16 LYA, Xikou, "Fagui," "Leiting yanxi"; Yang Luyin, "Guan'ao," 231.
17 Yang Shuqing, *Jinmen daoyu*, 203 ff.
18 Sun Bingshu, *JMMFTDJL*, 141–2; Xu Rongxiang, *JMMFFT*, I:78.
19 Xu Rongxiang, *JMMFFT*, I:62–3; Zheng Chengda, *JMMFTDJL*, 180; Dong, "Zhandi Jinmen."
20 Hong Futian, *JMMFFT*, I:396; Xie Gulong interview; Wu Sanjin interview.
21 Wen Shizhong, in Shi Maxiang, Zhuang Zhenzhong, and Chen Xiuzhu, (eds.), *Rongmin koushu lishi*, 83.
22 *Defense of Quemoy and the Free World*, 14.
23 Wang Farong, *JMMFTDJL*, 196.
24 Li, cited in Dong, "Zhandi Jinmen."
25 Dong Guangxin, cited in Dong, "Zhandi Jinmen."
26 Dong, "Zhandi Jinmen."
27 This was one of many examples of Hu using a historical analogy to legitimize policies on Jinmen. He compared the building of the wall to the famous story of Tao Kan, a fourth-century general, who kept in fighting trim while in exile by carrying bricks. "Tao Kan," said Hu, "carried bricks. We carry stones. The times are different; but the significance is the same." Dong, "Zhandi Jinmen." Only a few years later, Communist leaders would also be photographed helping with public works projects in the run-up to the communization movement.
28 Wu Fuma, cited in Dong, "Zhandi Jinmen".
29 Li Jinliang interview; Xu Minghong, *JMMFFT*, I:285.
30 Fu and Li, *Fagui yu shiyan*, 293–4.
31 Sun Bingshu, *JMMFTDJL*, 141; Xu Pimou, *JMMFTDJL*, 154; Lin Huocai, *JMMFTDJL*, 145.
32 Xu Naiyu, *JMMFTDJL*, 165; Zheng Chengda, *JMMFTDJL*, 181; Wang Zhenchun, *JMMFTDJL*, 191–2. The believability of the story is supported by the fact that on September 25, 1958, Chiang Kai-shek himself ordered an airdrop of moon-cakes and cigarettes to the soldiers on the Jinmen front-line, to help them celebrate the upcoming Mid-Autumn Festival. "Jiang zongtong guanhuai qianxian jiangshi," *Zhongyang ribao*, September 27, 1958, reprinted in *Zhonghua Minguo shishi jiyao* (*SSJY*), July–September 1958, 989.
33 Wang Farong, *JMMFTDJL*, 196.
34 Chen Jinbu, *JMMFTDJL*, 143–4; Ou Ganmu, *JMMFTDJL*, 161.
35 Xu Pimou, *JMMFTDJL*, 153; Zhuang Huokan, *JMMFTDJL*, 186.

6 THE 1958 ARTILLERY WAR

1 Ke Huizhu, in Lin and Lu, *Dongkeng*, 190–1.

2 Hong Futian, *JMMFFT*, I:391.

3 This analysis is largely borrowed from Christensen, though his categorization differs slightly. For examples of the literature on each explanation, see *Useful Adversaries*, 201–4. Interestingly, Western analysts at the time thought the US intervention in Iraq and Lebanon was an important factor; recently released Chinese materials confirm this. Wu Lengxi, "Wuzhang yu wenzhang." But Christensen shows that this argument would make more sense had the attack on Jinmen been launched a month earlier; by late August, the tension in the Middle East was already declining. *Useful Adversaries*, 237–40.

4 Christensen, *Useful Adversaries*, 217; Chen Jian, *Mao's China*, 179–80; Xu Yan, *Jinmen zhi zhan, 1949–1959*, 189.

5 Mao Zedong, *Mao Zedong waijiao wenxuan*, 344. Roderick MacFarquhar in a personal communication suggests that these remarks were Mao's retrospective attempts to justify having brought China to the brink of war without achieving the desired pedagogical effects on the Soviet Union or the US. A recent translation concludes the sentence with the phrase "and can therefore promote the Great Leap Forward in economic construction," but I do not find this explicit link in the original text. Li Xiaobing, Chen Jian, and David Wilson, trans., "Mao Zedong's Handling of the Taiwan Strait Crisis of 1958: Chinese Recollections and Documents," 216.

6 Perry, *Patrolling the Revolution*, 185–8.

7 Chen Zonglun, *JMMFFT*, III:75; Mao Zedong, *Xuexi wenxuan*, 297–8.

8 Mao Zedong, *Jianguo yilai Mao Zedong wengao*, VII:348.

9 Chen Zonglun, *JMMFFT*, III:76. According to a mainland popular history, the local PLA commander interrogated three captured ROC soldiers in great detail in the days preceding the battle, and this is why the first sortie was so accurate. Shen Weiping, *823 paoji Jinmen*, 132.

10 The lower figure for military casualties was reported in the media at the time and used recently by a Jinmen county official; the higher figure is used by a PRC scholar. "Quemoy Casualties at 229," *New York Times*, August 24, 1958; Yang Xiaoxian, *Jinmen jindaishi*, 115; Xu Yan, *Jinmen zhi zhan*, 222. Civilian casualty figures also vary depending on the source, see *JMXZ*, 252–3.

11 Lao Fandian, "Paoda Meiren shan"; Wang Qitao, cited in Dong, "Zhandi Jinmen."

12 Hong Fujian, *JMMFFT*, I:389–90.

13 Pan Shuba interview. The common elements of people's personal stories from this period are widely shared, both in the sense that many people had roughly similar experiences, and in the sense that these experiences are talked about frequently in everyday social life even today. So the earliest memories of many Jinmen people who were small children at the time are tied up with the bombing, though it sometimes seems that these memories are collective ones that they have internalized as their own. Hong Chunqing, a local schoolteacher, wrote one of the first essays of personal experience to appear in the early 1990s. Her language suggests a certain awareness of the complex relationship between personal and group memory. "I was a child of two on the

battlefield. I personally underwent this baptism by fire. But I have no memory whatsoever of the heat of battle. What I can remember, with reluctance, is hearing the distant sound of shelling, and my mother carrying me, carrying me for a long time down a narrow path, and then being crowded in with the other people in the shelter." Hong Chunqing, "Zhandi 35."

14 Ke Huizhu, in Lin and Lu, *Dongkeng*, 190–1; Dong, "Zhandi Jinmen." In one of the more extraordinary parallels between life on Jinmen and life on the mainland, this was also a time when peasants on the mainland recall eating meat. The circumstances were very different. During the early days of the Great Leap Forward, peasants often slaughtered and consumed their livestock to avoid having to turn them over to communal ownership.

15 Some of these rumors persist in the ghost stories that circulate on Jinmen up to the present, such as the tale of an abandoned tunnel complex at Xintou, haunted by the souls of the soldiers who were killed there by shellfire in 1958. Wang Kui, *Jinmen junqu naogui dang'an*; Hong Tianyuan, in Lin and Lu, *Dongkeng*, 200.

16 Weng Shuishe, *JMMFTDJL*, 147; Yang Luyin, "Guan'ao," 219; Li Yanjie, *JMMFFT*, II:13.

17 Yang Shiying, *JMMFFT*, I:236.

18 Chen Jian, *Mao's China*, 197–8; Mao Zedong, *Wengao*, VII:424–5.

19 Xu Yan, *Jinmen zhi zhan*, 198; Christensen, *Useful Adversaries*, 196.

20 As he told the State Council, "Now the US is committed to a system of overall responsibility over here . . . They've fallen into our noose. The US's neck is in China's steel noose . . . One day we will give them a kick, and they won't be able to get away, because they are stuck in our noose." Mao Zedong, *Waijiao wenxuan*, 341.

21 Xu Jiazhuang, *JMMFFT*, II:280–1.

22 Yang Shuqing, *Jinmen daoyu*, 295. Using classified American military sources, Halperin calculated that a total of 2,455 tons of supplies was offloaded at the beach between September 7, with the arrival of the first US-escorted convoy, and the cease-fire of October 6. There is no way to disaggregate the weight offloaded by militia as opposed to regulars. In addition, 2,132.5 tons of supplies were dropped by air in the same period. Halperin, *1958 Crisis*, 298 ff, 305. Portering of air-dropped materiel is mentioned in the oral history, but only rarely. I do not know whether this is because militia did less of this work, presumably because it was less dangerous and so regulars were used, or because, being less dangerous, it figures less in people's memory.

23 Chen Jian, *Mao's China*, 199; Gong Li, "Tension," 164.

24 Mao Zedong, *Waijiao wenxuan*, 344.

25 "Quemoy Unbowed Despite Shelling," *New York Times*, September 27, 1958; "Children Live in Caves," *New York Times*, October 1, 1958.

26 Lin Meilan interview.

27 Huang Xi'an, *JMMFFT*, I:269; Dong Wenju, *JMMFFT*, III:28.

28 Xue Liujin interview.

29 Dong Wenju, *JMMFFT*, III:28–9; Xue Chongwu, "823 dashuqian," in *Jinmen Xueshi zupu*.

30 In the late 1960s, the earliest time for which there are statistics, excess of births over deaths on Jinmen averaged 1,650 per year. Assuming this figure

was relatively stable, perhaps half the increase was due to natural increase. Most of the remainder would be returned evacuees. *JMTJ* (1961), 13 for population figures; *JMXZ*, 370 for birth and death figures.

31 Chen Changqing interview.

32 Chen Zonglun, *JMMFFT*, III:86.

33 Gong Li, "Tension," 170.

34 According to Wu Lengxi, the chief editor of the *People's Daily* and one of Mao's political secretaries, at a Politburo Standing Committee meeting on October 21, Mao proposed the alternate day idea: "From a military standpoint, this might seem like a joke. Never in the history of warfare has there been such a thing. But this is political warfare, and political battles are fought this way." Wu Lengxi, *Yi Mao Zhuxi: Wo qinsheng jingli de ruogan zhongda lishi shijian pianduan*, 89.

35 Can Wenfan interview.

36 Chen Shunde, "Laojun dianying qiule wo yiming."

37 *JMXZ*, 252.

PART II MILITARIZATION AND GEOPOLITICIZATION CHANGE COURSE

1 Vladislav Zubok and Constantine Pleshakov, *Inside the Kremlin's Cold War*, 210.

2 Thomas Gold, *State and Society in the Taiwan Miracle*, 4–5.

3 For Taiwan see papers of Wellington Koo, cited in Steve Tsang, "Chiang Kaishek and the Kuomintang's Policy to Reconquer the Chinese Mainland, 1949–1958," 57–8; for the US, see Robert Accinelli, "A Thorn in the Side of Peace," 112–13; for the PRC see the comments by Mao in chapter 6.

7 THE 1960S: CREATING A MODEL COUNTY OF THE THREE PRINCIPLES OF THE PEOPLE

1 Weng Mingzhi interview. Weng's account is confirmed by village archives on the 1977 campaign, which set a quota of 200,000 sparrow claws, roughly one per civilian per month, for the four months of the campaign. LYA, Xikou, "Jianshe zajian," 1977, Lieyu township office to Xikou village office re "Hufa ge xiangzhen buniao wang," June 25, 1977; LYA, Xikou, "Busha maque fangfa," March 30, 1979.

2 The Three Principles of the People – nationalism, democracy, and people's livelihood – was the ideological formulation developed by Sun Yat-sen to which both the ROC and the PRC nominally pledged allegiance. Chiang's speech is excerpted at Guofangbu, *Jieyan*, I:191.

3 "Ruhe jianshe Jinmen wei sanmin zhuyi moufan xian," 1963, in *JMXZ*, 559–60.

4 The massive starvation caused by the program would only come to light later.

5 Even as the campaign sought to distinguish Jinmen from the mainland, much of the rhetoric associated with it seemed to resonate with the slogans on the mainland. The people of Jinmen were called on to "overcome the barriers of

their environment, use their spirit to overcome material deficiencies, use their labor to overcome shortages of funds, embrace an attitude of service, and help the masses lead the masses." "Ruhe jianshe Jinmen wei sanmin zhuyi moufan xian," 1963, in *JMXZ*, 559–60. There is no causal link with Jinmen, but within a few years, the "bureaucratic restoration" in the PRC meant a demilitarization of the mainland as well.

6 *JMXZ*, 558.

7 Prasenjit Duara reminds us that there is nothing natural about such efforts. Even "within" nations, efforts to transform the identities of the citizenry are closely akin to "cultural imperialism." Failure to acknowledge this is to naturalize and normalize the nation-state. Prasenjit Duara, *Sovereignty and Authenticity: Manchukuo and the East Asian Modern*, 18–19.

8 Michel Foucault, *History of Sexuality*, 140.

9 Mark Berger, *The Battle for Asia: From Decolonization to Globalization*; Westad, *The Global Cold War*.

10 Arif Dirlik, "The Ideological Foundations of the New Life Movement: A Study in Counterrevolution," 945–80.

11 Fu and Li, *Fagui yu shiyan*, 347 ff.

12 Ruth Rogaski, *Hygienic Modernity: Meanings of Health and Disease in Treaty-Port China*.

13 *JMXZ*, 403.

14 *Ibid.*, 113.

15 Hu Lian, *Jinmen yijiu*, 16.

16 Guoshiguan (Academia Historica) archives (hereafter GSGA), 081–1083–14, "43 nian fangzhi Jinmen shuyi gongzuo baogaoshu," May 1955.

17 GSGA, 081–1083–2, "Fangzhi Jinmen shuyi gongzuo zong baogao shu," May 24, 1950; Qiu Kongrong, "Jinmen shuyi fangzhi qianjian," *Zhengqi bao* c. 1952 (inserted in GSGA 081–1083).

18 GSGA, 081–1083–3, Taiwan Province Hygiene Office to Ministry of Internal Affairs, April 18, 1951.

19 GSGA, 081–1084–2, Liu Yung-mao, "A Rapid Sanitary Survey of Kinmen Military Area, Feb 8–9, 1952"; GFBA, 00050794, "Junmin linshi lianhe fangyi weiyuan hui di'er ci huiyi jilu," May 11, 1951.

20 GSGA, 081–1083–14, "43 nian fangzhi shuyi"; *JMTJ*, XXXII (1985), provides annual tallies for rat tails submitted. The highest number is 226,000, submitted in 1973.

21 GSGA, 081–1083–9, "Fujian sheng Jinmen xian fangzhi shuyi jihua shu," April 1951.

22 Xu Jiazhuang, *JMMFFT*, II:278; also LYA, Shanglin, "Jinmen Lieyuxiang zhongyao zhengling xuandao gangyao," 1964.

23 Li Zenghua, *JMMFFT*, I:524; also Wu Mafu, *JMMFFT*, I:493–4.

24 LYA, Shanglin, "Dushu miecang," August 13, 1982; LYA, Shanglin, "Miecang yundong jihua," June 16, 1977; Chen Huajin interview.

25 Li Zenghua, *JMMFFT*, I:526.

26 Li Jinliang interview. The secondary market is confirmed (though the article itself is intended to be humorous) in Wu Huasheng, "Jinmen de shan laoshu mei weiba." Also see Xu Yucun, "Guojia liliang, renkou liudong yu jingji bianqian – yi Jinmen Guan'ao weili," 70.

27 Li Zenghua, *JMMFFT*, I:525.
28 Wu Huasheng, "Jinmen de laoshu mei weiba."
29 LYA, Xikou, "Jinmen diqu mieshu jihua jiantao xietiao hui huiyi jilu," August 11, 1978.
30 LYA, Xikou, "Minjiao gu weisheng," June 30 to September 1, 1975.
31 This is the impression given in the archives, which reports payments for "supplementary submissions." LYA, Shanglin, Lieyu township office to Shanglin village office, June 22, 1977.
32 LYA, Xikou, "Jinmen diqu mieshu jihua jiantao xietiao hui huiyi jilu," August 11, 1978.
33 Xu Yucun, "Guojia liliang," 70.
34 Zhang Yufa *et al.* (eds.), *Liu Anqi xiansheng fangwenlu*, 169.
35 LYA, Shangqi, county government to Shangqi village office, June 6, 1973.
36 Pan Shuqi interview; Chen Yangjin interview.
37 Dong Zhenhan and Wang Xiaodong interview.
38 *JMXZ*, 1261.
39 *Ibid.*, 659. Of 3,199 in the overall statistics, only 554 are listed as having been sent on to Taiwan. While the number resettled on Jinmen is not given, it cannot have been very large. *JMXZ*, 1261; *JMTJ*, XXXII (1985), 523.
40 Chen Shuizai interview; *JMXZ*, 1263.
41 According to Yang Shuqing, a 1996 report by the Jinmen native place association on the mainland describes 7,000 similar cases, but this figure is not credible. See chapter 2, note 15. Not all of these cases date from the fall of Xiamen in 1949. In 1965, massive anti-Chinese demonstrations broke out in Indonesia, connected to a purported Communist coup. As ethnic Chinese became targets of mob violence, the PRC dispatched ships to repatriate Overseas Chinese. Some of them were natives of Jinmen, who apparently believed that they would be allowed to return home. Instead, they were resettled on farms in the vicinity of Xiamen, and were prevented from completing the last few miles of their journey home for decades. *Jinmen daoyu*, 32.
42 There were other dangers besides the weather: "Once we were fishing for a long time, then collecting our nets – while we waited for the nets to fill, we'd fish using rods – the soldiers didn't always pay attention. They'd sometimes fire around the ship. We'd get soaked [from the spray of shells hitting the water]. When we got back we'd complain. They'd just say 'Oh, it wasn't us; there must be some troops that have just arrived [on Jinmen]. The old mainlanders [i.e. the old soldiers who had come over from the mainland in 1949] had the best aim. One guy got hit with a bullet in the stomach back in the 60s." Li Diaoyu interview.
43 DeWitt Copp and Marshall Peck, *The Odd Day*, 11.
44 *Jinmen diqu yumin shouce*. Some of the most tragic stories of the martial law period are those of Jinmen fishermen who provided support to CIA-sponsored ROC guerrilla actions on the mainland, and who were captured or killed there. Yang Shuqing, *Jinmen daoyu*, 43 ff.
45 In a novel about 1958 by the Taiwanese writer and former soldier Zhu Xining, a group of soldiers on Jinmen are kept awake by the constant loudspeaker broadcasts from the mainland. The broadcasts include an entreaty by the aged mother of the CO of the JDHQ, begging her son to come home. *Ba er san zhu*, I:95–8. Zhu's novel is in some ways a complement to this book, for it

presents a fictionalized soldier's perspective on many of the issues discussed here from the civilian perspective.

46 Wang Aimei interview.

47 *JMXZ*, 1258–9; propaganda materials displayed at the August 23rd Museum, Jinmen.

48 Li Diaoyu interview.

49 LYA, Shanglin, "Jian'ao feiwei xuanchuan pin," c. 1984.

50 LYA, Shangqi, "Jingwei zonghe," county government to Shangqi village office, May 2, 1977.

51 LYA, Shangqi, "Jinmen xian zhengfu ling" re "Wei lingchuan chajin sicang feiwei xuanchuanpin you," October 19, 1964.

52 LYA, Shanglin, "Jian'ao feiwei xuanchuan pin," c. 1984; Wu Dawei interview. Reports on regular security inspections of schools and government offices frequently mention the discovery of Communist propaganda leaflets in their criticisms of the unit in question. For example, the report of October 1974 in LYA, Shanglin, "Baomi jiancha," 1974–1985.

53 Li Jinliang interview.

54 Sang Pinzai, *An yu an*, 102; Zhu Xining, *Ba er san zhu*, I:107; Li Jinliang interview.

55 My analysis here follows Bonnie Honig, *Democracy and the Foreigner*.

8 THE 1970S: COMBAT VILLAGES AND UNDERGROUND JINMEN

1 *JMXZ*, 276.

2 *Ibid.*, 125.

3 Local authorities were ordered to apprehend the "criminal plotters" who had started these rumors "in order to harm military morale," but the rumors themselves could not simply be dismissed. LYA, Shanglin, "Minfangdui," 1968, Jinmen militia command Lieyu brigade HQ to Shanglin squadron, February 9, 1968.

4 LYA, Shanglin, "Minfangdui," 1968, county government to "squadron" (*zhongdui*), February 9, 1968.

5 Yang Shiying, *JMMFFT*, I:248. The rationale is provided in "Combat Handbook for Combat Villages," issued by the WZA Committee on September 1, 1968, a few days after the official establishment of the program. *Zhandou cun zhandou shouce*, 1.

6 *Ziwei zhandou shouce*, 11–13.

7 *Weiji zhi shezhi yu paichu shouce*, 2–31.

8 *Zhandou cun zhandou shouce*, 1.

9 Lin Jinwei interview.

10 *Zhandou cun zhandou shouce*, 2.

11 Yang Shiying, *JMMFFT*, I:249–51.

12 Jiang Bowei, "Zongzu yimin juluo kongjian bianqian de shehui lishi fenxi," 172.

13 Cai Fulin, cited in Dong, "Zhandi Jinmen"; Yang Xiaoxian, *Jinmen jindaishi*, 144.

14 Systems of mutual responsibility continued to be used to enforce compliance. Any militia member applying for an exit permit to travel to Taiwan needed to

have a guarantor. If the traveler did not return on schedule, or immediately if an emergency was declared, the guarantor was punished by forced labor. *Jinma diqu yinan yizhong guominbing houbei junren chujing guanzhi guiding.* According to one resident, for a while married women also needed their husband's permission to apply for an exit permit. Zhenhan, "Dakai tiantang de yaoshi," *JMRB*, April 19, 2004.

15 Weng Xiongfei, "Zhuiyi guonian Tai-Jin jiaotong," *JMRB*, January 22, 2004. The converse was also true. Said a graduate of a teachers' college in 1970 who was assigned to a Jinmen primary school over the summer break: "It wasn't easy doing all the paperwork for the entry permit. At that time, the paperwork for going to the frontline on Jinmen was the same as that for going to a foreign country." You Jianpeng, "Nanwang Jinmen suiyue."

16 LYA, Huangpu, "Jinmen zhandi zhengwu weiyuan hui – Jinmenxian san-minzhuyi shiyan xian 6 nian jianshe jihua dagang," July 1, 1976.

17 Stanley Larson and James Collins, *Allied Participation in Vietnam*, 115.

18 Guojia anquan huiyi zhandi zhengwu weiyuan hui, *Yuenan xinshengyi zhi yanjiu.* The ROC publications refer to the program by the term *Ap Tan Sinh* (corresponding to the Chinese *xinshengyi*).

19 On *Ap Tan Sinh* and *Ap Doi Moi*, see John Donnell, "Pacification Reassessed," 567–76.

20 Cai Fulin, cited in Dong, "Zhandi Jinmen."

21 As an incoming head of the militia recalls being told by his army superior, the militia must learn "the methods used by the Vietnamese in the Vietnam War." Qu Zhiping, *JMMFFT*, I:88.

22 Zhang Qicai, *JMMFFT*, I:220. The combat village system, abstracted from Vietnam and transported to Jinmen, is perhaps an example of what Bruno Latour calls "immutable mobiles." *Science in Action: How to Follow Scientists and Engineers through Society*, 227.

23 A potential alternative explanation is that beefing up local self-defense capabilities on Jinmen would enable the ROC to redeploy forces elsewhere. But the evidence does not support this interpretation. Though exact numbers of troops remain secret, from July 1961 to October 1982 the overall size of the main force on Jinmen stayed roughly constant at five combat divisions and ancillary units. The major change was the 1976 withdrawal of the small US MAAG unit.

24 LYA, Shanglin, "Qingzhu liushiliu nian shuangri Guoqing jie Jincheng diqu xuangua biaoyu fenpei biao," October 1977.

25 GFBA, 00035750, "Jinmen zhandou ying." Another part of this propaganda campaign involved the celebration of earlier phases in Jinmen's militarization. In the mid-1980s, a state-owned movie company released the film *The Jinmen Bombs (Ba-er-san paozhan)*. While the main story line deals with a group of soldiers in 1958, local residents figure in some subplots. Granny Wang, for example, is irritated by the soldiers' interference in village life in the summer of 1958. But when the bombing begins, she asks an officer to take her savings to the commanding officer, to help pay for rifles and shells. As Granny Wang is being evacuated, her daughter informs her that she is staying behind, having volunteered for the Army Women's Corps. How these and other messages were received by the people of Taiwan must be the subject of another book.

26 Cai Fulin, *JMMFFT*, I:539–40.

27 *JMXZ*, 106; Hu Lian, *Jinmen yijiu*, 90–1. Chiang's detractors have argued that he had actually muddled two very different historical tales thus demonstrating that despite his pretensions to be the guardian of Chinese culture, he was a vulgar man of no erudition. Li Ao, *Choulou de Zhongguoren yanjiu*, 5–8.

28 Hu Lian, *Jinmen yijiu*, 89; Jiang Bowei, *Jinmen Juguang lou*.

29 Zhongguo qingnian fangong jiuguo tuan zongtuan bu, *Luqi piaoyang sanshi nian*, 389–90.

30 The movement called on the whole of the ROC to emulate three aspects of the ancient king's travails in Ju: the commitment to erase shame and recover the nation; the ability to defeat greater numbers; and the willingness to endure great hardship. Zhongguo qingnian fangong jiuguo tuan zongtuan bu, *Bentuan zhongyao wenxuan*, I:309–10.

31 *JMXZ*, 853.

32 Allen Chun, "From Nationalism to Nationalizing: Cultural Imagination and State Formation in Postwar Taiwan," 128.

33 LYA, Shangqi, "Guoshe jiao," 1971, "Jinmen xian tuixing Zhonghua wenhua fuxing yundong zai tuijin jihua gangyao fenggong jindu biao," August 20, 1971.

34 *JMXZ*, 1606.

35 LYA, Shanglin, "Anquan yewu," 1965, township head to Shanglin village office re "54 nian wuyuefen cunmin dahui richengbiao ji xuandao gangyao," May 17, 1965.

36 LYA, Shangqi, "Jingwei zonghe," 1978, county government to village offices, May 29, 1978.

37 LYA, Shanglin, commanding officer and member of WZA Committee to village offices re "Jinmen xian minzhong ziweidui 70 niandu xuesheng shuqi xunlian shishi guiding," August 1, 1979.

38 LYA, Shangqi, "Juguang ri," 1978, "Jinmenxian 66 (*sic*) nian 12 yuefen 'Juguang ri' jiaoyu jiaocai ziliao," January 5, 1978.

39 LYA, Xikou, "Zajian," 1979, county government to village offices. Compare Jeremi Suri's discussion of how investment in education in West Berlin served to showcase the superiority of the non-Communist approach but at the same time nurtured political opposition. Modifying Daniel Bell's famous phrase, Suri calls this revolt of the privileged "a cultural contradiction of the Cold War." "The Cultural Contradictions of Cold War Education: The Case of West Berlin," 2.

40 *Jinmen zhanshi xinzhan gaojian*, 24.

PART III LIFE IN COLD WAR-TIME

1 Lutz, "Militarization," 321.

9 COMBAT ECONOMY

1 Wu Dawei interview. Collecting shell fragments is part of the childhood memories of many people who grew up on Jinmen in this period. Itinerant peddlers on Jinmen became scrap dealers, trading shell fragments for spun sugar candy. Yang Shuqing, *Fanshu wang*, 33.

2 Communist propaganda materials were another favorite souvenir, but of course this was illegal. LYA, Shanglin, "Anquan," 1984, "Jian'ao feiwei xuanchuan pin."
3 Wu Dawei interview.
4 A summary of the literature on the developmental state is found in Meredith Woo-Cumings, "Introduction: Chalmers Johnson and the Politics of Nationalism and Development."
5 Hong Xiangming, *Xuedao: baqian zhuangshi zhansi Jinmen jishi*, 69.
6 Michael Coe, personal communication. In a subtle indication of Southeast Asian influence on local culture, the local term for the daily market was *Basha*, a transliteration of the word bazaar.
7 Lin Manqing interview.
8 Hu Lian, *Jinmen yijiu*, 21 ff.
9 *Jinmen tudi gaige*, 2.
10 The JCRR was founded in 1948 to administer US economic aid to the Republic of China. The JCRR moved with the ROC government to Taiwan, which became the focus of its activities. Until 1965, the JCRR was financed by the US government, and its total disbursements were almost US$400 million in 1979 dollars. As part of the China Aid Act, the ROC government was required to contribute annually an amount equal to the aid delivered into a special fund. When US funding was cut off in 1965, the JCRR continued to operate using this fund. After the breaking of diplomatic relations with the US, the JCRR was renamed the Council for Agricultural Planning and Development. Its activities should be seen in the context of the larger global discourse on development economics in this period; indeed, its key figure, Dr. James Yen, would go on to establish rural reconstruction agencies in the Philippines, Colombia, Guatemala, India, and Thailand. Joseph Yager, *Transforming Agriculture in Taiwan: The Experience of the Joint Commission on Rural Reconstruction*.
11 *Jinmen tudi gaige*, 27. The reason the figure for owner–cultivators was not 100 percent is that households of Overseas Chinese or with members in the military were exempt from the obligation to sell all their excess land. The comparable figures for Taiwan are 61 percent before land reform and 85 percent after. Lin Si-dang and Lin Li, *Land Reform on Kinmen*, 40.
12 Dai Zhongyu, "Preface," in *Jinmen tudi gaige*.
13 *Jinmen tudi gaige*, 33.
14 Hui-sun Tang, *Land Reform in Free China*.
15 Land reform statistics may unintentionally provide some sense of the scope of seized land. Thirty percent of all surveyed land was listed as public land. This was land for which no owner could be established. In an interview, former WZA official Lin Jinwei explained that many residents assumed the land survey was an excuse to impose new taxes, so they denied ownership of their land. In theory all of this land should have been redistributed. But only about one-third of it was. No mention is made of the disposition of the remainder, about 20 percent of all land on Jinmen. Presumably this land, together with other land that was never surveyed, came under the control of the military. Lin and Lin, *Land Reform*, 16, 23, 53–4.
16 Chen Shuizai interview.
17 Dickson, *Democratization in China and Taiwan*, 45.
18 Zhang Mingzhai, *JMMFFT*, I:168.

19 Wu Santeng interview.
20 Shen Zonghan, *Taiwan nongye zhi fazhan*.
21 Fu and Li, *Fagui yu shiyan*, 469–73.
22 *JMXZ*, 373 ff.
23 Chen Shuizai interview. The symbolic value of residents of the front line islands devoting themselves to national defense meant that soldiers from Jinmen were often selected for special, highly visible, duties on Taiwan. More than a hundred members of Chiang Kai-shek's personal bodyguard were Jinmen natives. Lin Zhong, "Jinmen 108 tiao haohan zuoguo suiyue," *JMBD*, inaugural issue (*chuangkan hao*), August 6, 1990.
24 Hu Lian, *Jinmen yijiu*, 17.
25 See chapter 3, note 13. *JMTJ*, XXXII (1985), 314, 327. These statistics also include profits from other state-owned enterprises. The most important of these was the ceramics factory that was essentially a part of the liquor business since its main product was liquor bottles. The other enterprises were minor.
26 Wen Shizhong, the political instructor in Zhushan, remembers that militia members were given a quota of five trees per year. Other militia members recall the number being much higher. Li Qingzheng, *JMMFFT*, I:35; Wen Shizhong, *JMMFFT*, I:201; Chen Yongcai, *JMMFFT*, I:433.
27 *JMXZ*, 1008.
28 *The Invincible Island: Ten Years of Reconstruction on Kinmen*, 10.
29 *Ibid.*, 57.
30 "Tight Little Island – Off China," *New York Times*, August 19, 1956.
31 Copp and Peck, *The Odd Day*, 5.
32 See Susan Reid, "Cold War in the Kitchen: Gender and Consumption in the Khrushchev Thaw," 211–52.
33 *JMTJ*, LI (2004), 29.
34 Fu Zizhen, cited in Li Jinsheng, *Fenghuo honglou moufanjie*, 196.
35 Chen Yongguo, *JMMFFT*, III:159; Hong Hongcheng, *JMMFFT*, III:136.
36 Wang Yingchuan, *JMMFFT*, II:211.
37 *JMXZ*, 946.
38 Hu Lian, *Jinmen yijiu*, 34.
39 *JMTJ* (1961), 13–14.
40 Fen Jinsan interview.
41 *JMXZ*, 946.
42 Baitouweng, "Xiayanxia de jianwen yishi."
43 Yang Yonghe, *JMMFFT*, II:170.
44 Zhai Fen interview.
45 Xiao Shengyi interview.
46 *Ibid.*
47 Zhang Mingchun, "You Jinmen junren xiaofei xingge kan Guan'ao shangdian de fazhan guocheng," 189–91.
48 Zhang Mingchun, "Junren xiaofei," 190–1; Zhai Fen interview.
49 Xue Qijin interview; Chen Changqing interview.
50 One of Zhang Mingchun's informants tried to save money by looking after the pool hall himself rather than hiring an attendant. But he had no trade because the soldiers would not come to his shop, so the business soon folded. Zhang Mingchun, "Junren xiaofei," 196.

51 *JMTJ*, XXXII (1985), 116–17 for numbers of public servants, 483 for household size; LI (2004), 29 for population statistics.
52 Zhang Mingchun, "Junren xiaofei," 202.
53 See Ping-Chun Hsiung, *Living Rooms as Factories: Class, Gender, and the Satellite Factory System in Taiwan.*
54 Zhai Fen interview.
55 Xue Liujin interview.
56 Chen Xiangxin, "Biying weilin, suijun er ju de tongnian."
57 Xingshibao, "Jinmen neng xiang junguan shuo zaijian?"
58 These villages were Yangzhai, Xiazhuang, Dingbao, Xiaojing, and Donglin. Construction statistics for market development tell the story. Yangzhai market was rebuilt in 1966 with 59 shops; Xiaojing market was built in 1968 with 42 shops; Donglin market was built in 1964 with 145 shops. *JMXZ*, 252–3.
59 Weng Tianzhen, *JMMFFT*, II:231.
60 Gao Kangwen interview.
61 Xiao Shengyi interview.
62 LYA, Shanglin, "Zonghe," 1970, Jinmen county police bureau to village offices re "Yanjin guanbing xiang minjian shangdian sheqian," June 21, 1970; LYA, Shangqi, "Zonghe," 1980, Lieyu township office to village offices re "Jiansong fangqu dui minjian ge shangdian banli qiejie shu moshi," June 23, 1980.
63 LYA, Shanglin, township head to Shanglin village office re "Yanjin fei junren chuanzhc junfu junmao," May 14, 1965; Zhenhan, "Datou de chuanqi"; LYA, Shanglin, county government to village offices re "Yanjin zhuanmai junyong youliao," October 1, 1964, 1–398; LYA, Shanglin, "Cunmin dahui," 1965, "Cunmin dahui tuizun yaodian," April 13, 1965.
64 Wang Kui, *Naogui dang'an*, 106–22.
65 Zhai Fen interview.
66 Jin Mengren, "Jieyanxia Qiangsheng dazuo"; Hong Dahai, "Lieyu junmin jinru lengzhan shiqi"; Lin Genben, "Jinmen baiwan jichengche". Reportedly the WZA used the threat of embargoes against G. I. Joe business to ensure that Jinmen residents cast votes in local elections (where the sole candidate was WZA-nominated and supported), thus explaining the extraordinarily high rates of voter turnout. Luo Deshui, "Liang'an guanxi fazhan yu Jinmen dingwei bianqian zhi yanjiu," 168; "Wugu renku shenmi kongbu," *Shidai zhoukan*, February 1988, reprinted in Liu Jiaguo, *Wo de jiaxiang shi zhandi: Jin-Ma wenti mianmianguan*, 17.
67 LYA, Shangqi, "Cunmin dahui," 1979, "Lieyu xiang 67 nian (*sic*) di'er ci cunmin dahui jianyi shixiang fenban biao."
68 Xiao Shengyi interview.
69 This process might usefully be compared to Kate Xiao Zhou's account of rural economic growth in the PRC as a spontaneous, unorganized, leaderless, nonideological, apolitical movement (SULNAM). *How the Farmers Changed China: Power of the People.*
70 Berger, *Battle for Asia*, 1–2.
71 Zhonghua Minguo Taiwan diqu guomin suode, 2001, 115; http://www.stat.gov.tw/public/data/dgbas03/bs4/94yb/index1/index1-2.xls (accessed November 22, 2007).
72 Catherine Lutz, *Homefront: A Military City and the American Twentieth Century.*

10 WOMEN'S LIVES: MILITARY BROTHELS, PARADES, AND EMBLEMS OF MOBILIZED MODERNITY

1 Lü Jiang, "*Liangge baba*," in *Lü Jiang ji*, 121–147. There are hints in the story that the woman is a member of a Taiwanese aboriginal tribe. The politics of gender and of the relationship between respectable women and prostitutes are typically threaded through with ideas about ethnicity and sub-ethnicity. How distinctions between non-Han aboriginal people, Han Chinese from Taiwan, and Han Chinese from the mainland played out in the history of the sex trade on Jinmen is an unexplored but potentially very important part of the story.

2 This approach borrows from Jon Solomon's argument that Taiwan under martial law rested on a sexual division of labor in which men were mobilized for war and women were reduced to "social immobility through categories of either-prostitute-or-mother." "Taiwan Incorporated: A Survey of Biopolitics in the Sovereign Police's Pacific Theater of Operations," 237.

3 Enloe, *Maneuvers*, xii.

4 Partha Chatterjee, *The Nation and Its Fragments*; Duara, *Sovereignty and Authenticity*.

5 It was not only the presence of male soldiers that destabilized gender but also the mere existence of female soldiers. For their perspective see *Nü qingnian dadui fangwen jilu*.

6 Lin Manqing interview; Lin Meilan interview; Wang Zhupan, *JMMFFT*, II:182.

7 Chen Changqing interview.

8 Wu Wuquan, *JMMFFT*, II:96; Zhang Qicai, *JMMFFT*, I:214–15. No one knows the source of Hu Lian's inspiration in setting up the system. He does not raise the subject in his memoirs. Possible explanations include that he was influenced by the comfort stations established by the Japanese army during the second world war; that the solution was suggested by the US Military Assistance and Advisory Group (MAAG), or that he was emulating a model established on Penghu by officers there to deal with rape of civilians. Xie Huihuang, "Jun leyuan de chuangyi ren."

9 GFBA, 00002716, "Jinmen fangwei siling bu 43 niandu shizheng jihua," 1955; Chen Changqing, *Zouguo fenghuo suiyue de Jinmen teyue chashi*, 16.

10 Gu Yan, "Junzhong leyuan tanmi," 16–17; Chen Changqing, *Jinmen teyue chashi*, 36 ff. Informants, both WZA officials and men who worked in the brothels, are very insistent that prostitutes came to Jinmen voluntarily. Whether this is accurate or not, this insistence is likely another example of how memory of the past can be shaped by contemporary concerns. As we shall see in chapter 12, in the late 1980s opposition politicians in Taiwan began to criticize the KMT government for operating military brothels. They drew parallels with the comfort women, sex slaves of the Japanese army in the Second World War whose international campaign for redress was growing at the time. So when informants stress that the recruitment of 831 prostitutes was voluntary, what they are really doing is denying the validity of this comparison.

11 Chen Ailing interview.

12 Compare, for example, the description of American Town in Katharine Moon, *Sex Among Allies: Military Prostitution in US–Korean Relations*, ch. 1.

13 Chen Changqing interview.
14 Li Ao, *Zhongguo xing yanjiu*, 229; Sang Pinzai, *An yu An*, 100; Jinmen jingchaju (police bureau) archives (hereafter JMJCJA), Item 75 caigan 1191, November 2, 1986; Chen Changqing interview.
15 Chen Changqing interview; JMJCJA, no item number, "Guofangbu Jinmen teyue chashi guanli yuanze."
16 Li Ao, *Zhongguo xing yanjiu*, 268; Chen Changqing, *Zouguo fenghuo suiyue*, 46.
17 Li Ao, *Zhongguo xing yanjiu*, 287 n13.
18 Chen Changqing interview.
19 Chen Changqing, *Zouguo fenghuo suiyue*, 49–50.
20 This transition is captured in a scene in Hou Xiaoxian's 1986 film *Dust in the Wind* (*Lianlian fengchen*). In the barracks recreation center, two older soldiers talk about their favorite 831 prostitutes, referring to the women by their number. The protagonist, a young conscript from rural south Taiwan, does not participate in their banter, pining for his girlfriend from the village.
21 Zheng Mingxin interview.
22 Chen Changqing interview; Chen Ailing interview.
23 Many informants report a black market in 831 tickets.
24 LYA, Shanglin, "Cunmin dahui," 1965, "Cunmin dahui tuizun yaodian," April 13, 1965; LYA, Shangqi, "Anquan yewu," 1980, county government instruction re "Minzhong bude yu fangqu teyue chashi shiyingsheng sheji dubo . . .," March 21, 1980; Chen Changqing interview. An exception to the rule against civilians using the military brothels was made in the 1980s for cadres and teachers from Taiwan. As the civil service on Jinmen expanded, the civilian authorities must have decided that, like soldiers, male civil servants also needed sexual outlets in order that social harmony be preserved. So a "social section" was opened for unmarried cadres and teachers. But specific shifts were set aside so that the cadres and soldiers did not overlap.
25 Li Ao, *Zhongguo xing yanjiu*, 252 ff.
26 Foucault, *History of Sexuality*, 140.
27 Li Ao, *Zhongguo xing yanjiu*, 265.
28 *Ibid.*, 278. Another brothel couplet was more graphic: "The hero wields his gun to wipe out the bandits; the maiden opens her gate to receive the fruits of victory." Chen Changqing, *Zuoguo fenghuo suiyue*, 40.
29 JMJCJA, Item 75 caigan 1191, November 2, 1986.
30 See Yuki Tanaka, *Japan's Comfort Women: Sexual Slavery and Prostitution during World War II and the US Occupation*, ch. 6; Enloe, *Maneuvers*.
31 Chen Changqing interview.
32 Lin Jinwei interview; personal communication from Cynthia Enloe.
33 Chen Zonglun, *JMMFFT*, III: 61; Lin Jiongfu interview.
34 Weng Xiongfei, "Guzao de san-ba xinniang."
35 Zhai Fen interview.
36 Kuishan, "Zhuan yun ei xiao dai jinzai."
37 Chen Huajin interview; Lin Jiongfu interview; Leshan, "Yinshui si yuantou – Junmin qingshen pian."
38 Zheng Mingxin interview.
39 The stereotype appears in many Taiwanese movies, for example *Jinmen nübing* (1983); *Ba-er-san paozhan* (1986).

40 There were also horror stories of soldiers who had lured local women to Taiwan with the promise of marriage, and then forced them into prostitution. Less horrifying, but still a cause of disappointment, were soldiers who exaggerated their wealth in order to trick local women into agreeing to a marriage. "One of them promised that he was really rich. Then his wife came back from Taiwan for a visit, and she said that her life there was even poorer than on Jinmen." Chen Huajin interview.

41 Chen Huajin interview. Postings to internet discussion groups for former ROC soldiers indicate that soldiers believed this rumor to be true. For example, www.rocmp.org/archiver/tid-9025.html (accessed February 20, 2006).

42 LYA, Xikou, "Huji zonghe," 1978, County government to village offices re "Zhumin X, yin fufu bulu," February 19, 1978.

43 *The Defense of Quemoy and the Free World*, 16.

44 *JMTJ*, LI (2004), 46–7. People on Jinmen calculate their age in *sui*, which typically overstates their actual age by one year. The total population also includes a small number of divorced and widowed.

45 Chen Zonglun, *JMMFFT*, III:62.

46 There is no reference to brideprice in any of Yang Tianhou and Lin Likuan, *Jinmen hunyin lisu*; Xie Yuping, "Jinmen chuantong shengyu lisu zhi tantao"; Xu Minhua, "Ming–Qing shiqi Jinmen chuantong funü jiating shenghuo yanjiu". A late nineteenth-century gazetteer comments that the costs of marriage, formerly modest, have recently increased, but it is unclear if this refers to brideprice or, more likely, dowry. Lin Kunhuang and Lin Zhuoren, *Jinmen zhi*, 350; Weng Xiongfei, "San-ba xinniang."

47 The village cadres who were required to fill out the forms, unlike their superiors, were perfectly aware of what caused the rise in brideprice: "Because so many young women of the region are taken away by soldiers there is a supply shortfall." LYA, Shanglin, "Fengsu diaocha biao"; Chen Zonglun, *JMMFFT*, III:63. Jinmen was not strictly speaking a colony, but it experienced many of the processes that we would typically associate with colonialism: the total reorganization of space, both public and private, extraction of resources including labor, and new modes of surveillance, classification, and control. On the similarities between colonial and modernizing projects, see Timothy Mitchell, *Colonising Egypt*, ix, and Bruce Cumings, *Parallax Visions: Making Sense of American–East Asian Relations at the End of the Century*, 72–3.

48 *JMXZ*, 422.

49 Susan Glosser, *Chinese Visions of Family and State, 1915–1953*, 128 ff.

50 LYA, Shanglin, "Jinmen diqu di shiwu jie jituan jiehun shishi yaodian," December 30, 1977; Glosser, *Chinese Visions*, 129.

51 LYA, Shanglin, Lieyu township to Shanglin village office re "Jiansong benxiang xianyi dinghun duixiang guli canjia di shiqi jie jituan jiehun," December 5, 1979.

52 "Xinwen xianfu juban jituan jiehun," *JMRB*, December 4, 1965.

53 LYA, Shanglin, "Jinmen diqu di shiwu jie jituan jiehun shishi yaodian," December 30, 1977.

54 Wang Wensan interview.

55 *JMXZ*, 629.

56 Michel Foucault's model of the family moving from a model for governance to the object of governance seems to apply here. "Governmentality," 87–104.

57 LYA, Shanglin, "Funü jie biaoyu," 1976.
58 Reid, "Cold War in the Kitchen," 252.
59 *JMXZ*, 683.
60 Kenneth Rose, *One Nation Underground: The Fallout Shelter in American Culture.*
61 Wu Mafu, *JMMFFT*, I:493; Li Gangshi, "Nü ziweidui yiwang"; Xu Shupei, *JMMFTDJL*, 152.
62 Chen Zonglun, *JMMFFT*, III:73; Chen Zengjian, *JMMFFT*, II:263.
63 Elaine Tyler May, *Homeward Bound: American Families in the Cold War Era*; Michael Sherry, *In the Shadow of War: The United States since the 1930s*, 150–1.
64 Ming Qiushui (ed.), *Jinmen (Jiang zongtong yu Jinmen)*, 56. The distinctive female uniform was not unique to the Jinmen militia. The "Women's Youth Brigade," an auxiliary modeled on the US Women's Army Auxiliary Corps (WAAC), wore similar uniforms. *Nü qingnian*, 21.
65 Ilene Feinman, *Citizenship Rites: Feminist Soldiers and Feminist Antimilitarists.*
66 Duara, *Sovereignty and Authenticity*, 139; Chatterjee, *The Nation and its Fragments*, ch. 6.
67 The mobilization of women on the mainland is mentioned in many accounts of women in the PRC, though the link to militarization is not always made.
68 Ou Ganmu, *JMMFTDJL*, 161.
69 Lin Caikuan, in Lin and Lu, *Dongkeng*, 104.
70 *Ibid.*
71 Vivienne Shue explores a comparable example from the PRC, linking the rapid spread of collectivization to the fact that the complex problems of semi-socialist agriculture overwhelmed the capacities of rural cadres. *Peasant China in Transition: The Dynamics of Development Toward Socialism, 1949–1956*, ch. 7.
72 *Zhandou cun zhandou*, 63–4.
73 Lin Caikuan, in Lin and Lu, *Dongkeng*, 104.
74 LYA, Shanglin, "Chuji minjiaoban guowen buxi jiaocai, xia," 1966.
75 Lin Caikuan, in Lin and Lu, *Dongkeng*, 104.
76 Li Gangshi, "Nü ziweidui yiwang."
77 Tan Shuling interview.
78 Du Tiansheng, in Lin and Lu, *Dongkeng*, 98.
79 Lin Meilan interview.
80 Xu Shupei, *JMMFTDJL*, 152.
81 "Zhandou de duo mianshou Li Mengqi"; "Panshan cun funü duizhang Weng Shuhui de caiyi chaoren."
82 Wang Tingqing, *JMMFFT*, I:127.
83 Xu Minghong, cited in Dong, "Zhandi Jinmen."
84 Lin Jindou, *JMMFTDJL*, 157.
85 Chen Xiuzhu, *JMMFTDJL*, 231.
86 Lin Jindou, *JMMFTDJL*, 157.
87 The famous photo can be seen at www.princeton.edu/~nanking/html/image_1.html (accessed September 20, 2007).
88 Duara, *Sovereignty and Authenticity*, 133.
89 Enloe, *Maneuvers*, 123.
90 Gail Hershatter, *Dangerous Pleasures: Prostitution and Modernity in Twentieth-Century Shanghai*, 305.

11 GHOSTS AND GODS OF THE COLD WAR

1 Wang Kui, *Naogui dang'an* is one collection of such stories. One now also finds Jinmen ghost stories on the blogs of former conscripts stationed there. For example, bbs.yuhome.net/thread-316579-1-8.html (accessed March 27, 2007).

2 Chi Chang-hui, "Politics of Deification," ch. 5.

3 *Ibid.*, 155.

4 Li Diaoyu interview.

5 See chapter 2.

6 LYA, Shanglin, "Shejiao huodong," "Jinmen diqu qingzhu Guningtou zhanyi shengli sa zhounian shishi yaodian," 1979.

7 Prasenjit Duara, *Rescuing History from the Nation: Questioning Narratives of Modern China*, ch. 3; Rebecca Nedostup, "Religion, Superstition, and Governing Society in Republican China."

8 Lin Manqing interview.

9 LYA, Shanglin, "Minjian baibai," 1977, county government to Shanglin village office re "Jumin X weigui chufa," September 8, 1977.

10 Tian Shuzhang, "Zhenlie ciji"; Yang Tianhou and Lin Likuan, *Jinmen simiao yinglian beiwen*, 197.

11 Tian Shuzhang, "Zhenlie ciji"; Yang and Lin, *Jinmen simiao*, 197.

12 Mark Elvin "Female Virtue and the State in China," 111–52.

13 Chun, "Nationalism to Nationalizing," 128.

14 Chiang Kai-shek, "Two Supplementary Chapters to Lectures on the Principle of People's Livelihood," 311.

15 Dao Lieyu interview.

16 Lie Zhangguan interview.

17 Jun Siling interview. This response corresponds closely to what Robert Weller identifies as the "elite style of interpretation" in Chinese popular religion. *Unities and Diversities in Chinese Religion*, 125.

18 "Lienü miao zhi."

19 Chen Lili interview; Hong Duoyu interview.

20 "Lienü miao zhi."

21 Chi Chang-hui perceptively notes that this is clearly a projection of Hong and other villagers' vulnerability to the arbitrary treatment and accusations of spying by the ROC military and to "the nightmare of living under authoritarian rule." "Politics of Deification," 204–5.

22 Steven Sangren, "Female Gender in Chinese Religious Symbols: Kuan Yin, Ma Tsu, and the 'Eternal Mother,' " 4–25.

23 For example, Kristofer Schipper, *The Taoist Body*.

24 Dao Lieyu interview.

25 The discussion in this section owes much to Prof. Stephen Teiser's comments on an earlier version of this chapter. Prof. Teiser is also responsible for the dreadful pun in the section title.

26 William Christian, "Religious Apparitions and the Cold War in Southern Europe," 239–66.

27 Weller, *Unities and Diversities*, 158–60.

28 Robert Hymes, *Way and Byway: Taoism, Local Religion and Models of Divinity in Sung and Modern China*.

29 Heonik Kwon, *After the Massacre: Commemoration and Consolation in Ha My and My Lai*; Shaun Malarney, *Culture, Ritual and Revolution in Vietnam*.

PART IV DEMILITARIZATION AND POSTMILITARIZATION

1   The unanswered question of the extent to which these changes in Taiwan were only made possible by the dramatic change in direction of the PRC after the death of Mao Zedong complicates this issue, but does not make the domestic changes any less important. I also ignore the question of whether the PRC's subsequent missile build-up reduced Jinmen's strategic importance even as the threat to Taiwan intensified. As previous chapters have shown, military threat alone does not explain militarization.

12 DEMILITARIZATION AND POSTMILITARIZATION

1   LYA, Xikou, "Anquan fanghu," 1978, county government to village offices re "Wei yin ying Zhong-Mei duanjiao zhi jushi bianhua," December 29, 1978; LYA, Shangqi, "Shehui jiaoyu," 1979–80, "Zhong-Mei gongtong fangyu tiaoyue feizhi hou guonei xuanchuan gongzuo de zuofa," December 17, 1979.
2   news.xinhuanet.com/ziliao/2003-01/24/content_705059.htm (accessed March 7, 2007).
3   Chen Jinhua interview.
4   Yang Shuqing, *Jinmen shehui diaocha*, 109.
5   Yang Xiaoxian, *Jinmen jindaishi*, 195.
6   Yang Shuqing, *Jinmen daoyu*, 328–9.
7   See chapter 2.
8   The comparison appeared frequently in Taiwan newspapers in the late 1980s. Examples are reprinted in Liu Jiaguo, *Wo de jiaxiang*, 22, 28, 54. Other documents from the Jinmen democracy movement are collected in Yang Shuqing, *Jinmen daoyu* and *Jinmen shehui diaocha*, and Weng Mingzhi, *Wuchao pengzhang*.
9   Chen Shuizai interview.
10 Unfortunately for scholars, when no agency could be found that would house the militia archives, the soon to be jobless cadres simply began to burn the archives that remained. Xu Minghong, *JMMFFT*, I:309.
11 De-mining by private companies continues at time of writing. Chen Shuizai considers one of the main accomplishments of his term to be the clearing of mines from most of the economically important parts of the island. NTD400 million was allocated by the ROC government to clear minefields in areas that were needed for further economic development during 2006–8. Chen Shuizai interview; "Landmine Monitor report 2005 – Taiwan," at www.icbl.org (accessed March 19, 2007).
12 Guofangbu shizheng bianyi ju, "Jieyan," 94 ff.
13 Yang Shuqing, *Jinmen shehui diaocha*, 33.
14 Gao Kangwen interview.
15 "Jinfang bu zuzhi xitong dishan duizhao biao." See Appendix.
16 *JMTJ*, LI (2004), 293. Other sources give a slightly higher figure of US$5,228 for 1991. Chen Shuizai, *Jinmen jieyan qianhou*, 65.

17 Xiao Shengyi interview.

18 Tan Keqi interview.

19 Huang Shiming, "1980 niandai hou Jinmen yu Nantou shehui li de fuxian: Taiwan fazhan jingyan zhong liangge difang shehui de fenxi," 94 ff.

20 Some of the pros and cons are discussed in Chen Ziqiang, "Wei guanguang, xian kaiguang."

21 On which see Robert Weller, *Discovering Nature: Globalization and Environmental Culture in Taiwan and China*.

22 Yang Shuqing, *Jinmen shehui diaocha*, 382–3.

23 Jiang Bowei, *Jinmen zhanshi jilu ji diaocha yanjiu*, II: 76.

24 Catherine Bell, *Ritual: Perspectives and Dimensions*, 242.

25 John Shepherd, "Commodification, Culture and Tourism," 192.

26 Jin Yilei, "Jinmen kaifang guangguang de shehui bianqian yanjiu," 63–77.

27 Hong Duoyu interview.

28 The company book-keeper says their business is worth about NTD18 million. Wu Kuaiji interview.

29 Weng Tianzhen, *JMMFFT*, II:231; Xiao Shengyi interview.

30 JMJCJA, Item 75 caigan 1191, November 2, 1986.

31 *Ibid.*

32 Chen Changqing interview; JMJCJA, "Letter from three retired soldiers," no item number; Yan Chen and Dong Huifang, "831 chetuihou 9 yue 7 ri Jinmen fasheng shouzong junren qiangbao minfu an."

33 Weng Mingzhi, *Wuchao pengzhang*, 34–5.

34 Li Yumin interview; "For Taiwan's Frontier Islands, the War is Over," *New York Times*, October 4, 1995.

35 Tan Keqi interview.

36 Lin Fushi, *Guhun yu guixiong de shijie: Bei Taiwan de ligui xinyang*; Huang Pingying, "Taiwan minjian xinyang 'guhun' de fengsi – yige Taiwan shehuishi de kaocha."

37 Katherine Verdery's discussion of why dead bodies work this way in postsocialist societies also makes for interesting comparisons with Jinmen. Among other factors she cites "political issues specific to a given polity . . . property restitution, political pluralization, religious renewal, and national conflicts tied to building nation-states." *The Political Lives of Dead Bodies: Reburial and Postsocialist Change*, 50, 52–3.

38 www.kinmen.gov.tw/English/eng_main2.htm (accessed November 24, 2002).

39 Weng Mingzhi, *Wuchao pengzhang*, 25–6.

40 This is chronicled in Yang Shuqing, *Jinmen shehui diaocha*, 11 ff.

41 Wu Zengyun interview.

13 MEMORY AND POLITICS

1 Homi Bhabha, "DissemiNation: Time, Narrative, and the Margins of the Modern Nation," 297. Ann Anagnost points out that Bhabha's distinction restates Foucault's dual notion of the subject, as subject to rule and agent of one's own identity. "Constructing the Civilized Community," 347.

2 Michael Kammen, *Mystic Chords of Memory: The Transformation of Tradition in American Culture*; John Bodnar, *Remaking America: Public Memory, Commemoration, and Patriotism in the Twentieth Century*.

3 Maurice Halbwachs, *On Collective Memory*.

4 Hu Tieji, *Cong baowei Jinma dao fangong dalu*, 213.

5 Shen Zonghan, *Taiwan nongye*, 237.

6 Yang Wenwei, "Laiqu chi biandang."

7 Li Shanwen interview.

8 Luo Jianfa, in Shi Maxiang *et al.* (eds.), *Rongmin koushu lishi*, 35.

9 Lin Manqing interview.

10 Wu Huating, in Shi Maxiang *et al.* (eds.), *Rongmin koushu lishi*, 28; Ou Ganmu, *JMMFTDJL*, 162; Lin Manqing interview.

11 Chen Zonglun, *JMMFFT*, III:86.

12 Hong Futian, *JMMFFT*, I:384; Lin Huocai, *JMMFTDJL*, 146; Sun Bingshu, *JMMFTDJL*, 141; Xiao Shengyi interview; Lin Huocai, *JMMFTDJL*, 145.

13 Lin Jinshu, *JMMFTDJL*, 212; Xue Zuyao interview.

14 Chen Ailing interview; Yang Shuqing, *Jinmen shehui diaocha*, 142.

15 Li Tiansong, *JMMFFT*, II:61.

16 Chen Shuizai interview.

17 Hu Lian, *Jinmen yijiu*, 83.

18 Pan Shuqi interview.

19 Li Yumin interview.

20 Pan Shuqi interview. A variation on this story is in the memoirs of Jinmen resident Ouyang Yangming, *Huaiyi Jinmen*, 262.

21 Li Diaoyu interview.

22 Lin Manqing interview.

23 Yingxi, "Dangnian yemu dichuishi"; Zheng Chengda, *JMMFTDJL*, 180.

24 Chen Zonglun, *JMMFFT*, III:82–3.

25 Lin Jiongfu interview.

26 Pan Shuqi interview; Yang Shiying, "Kegu mingxin de 825."

27 Hong Futian, *JMMFFT*, I:385; Yang Shiying, *JMMFFT*, I:232; Dong Qunlian, "Zhandi Jinmen"; Chen Yangjin interview; Zhang Zhichu interview.

28 Chen Shuizai interview.

29 Lin Huocai, *JMMFTDJL*, 146; Chen Dading interview; Pan Shuqi interview.

30 Li Jinliang interview; Chen Shuizai interview.

31 Hong Futian, *JMMFFT*, I:396–7.

32 Weng Shuishe, *JMMFTDJL*, 147.

33 Weng Mingzhi, "San da yaoqiu, wu da xiwang," in Weng Mingzhi, *Wuchao pengzhang*, 53.

34 Weng Xiongfei, "805 budui de gushi."

35 Wu Wuquan, *JMMFFT*, II:96.

36 Chen Shuizai interview.

37 Lin Yongju, in Lin and Lu, *Dongkeng*, 179; Ou Ganmu, *JMMFTDJL*, 162.

38 Yang Shuqing, *Jinmen shehui diaocha*, 99–100.

39 Weng Shuishe, *JMMFTDJL*, 148.

40 Chen Shuizai, *Jinmen jieyan*, 97.

41 Lisa Rofel, "Liberation Nostalgia and a Yearning for Modernity."

42 A thorough analysis would also include consideration of official representations of Jinmen's past, such as those conveyed by memorials and museums,
both during the WZA period and after. Jiang Bowei has done just such an
analysis in his "Shei de zhanzheng lishi?"

14 CONCLUSION: REDOUBLED MARGINALITY

1 Photographs of these and other slogans are collected in Lin Baobei,
Qiangshang fenghuo.
2 Scott, *Seeing Like a State*, 4–5.
3 It is a commonplace observation that the formation of the nation-state followed distinctive paths when it took place under the threat of imperialism.
Distinctive state formation under the threat of emergency is perhaps a
modern avatar of this phenomenon.
4 John Fitzgerald, *Awakening China: Politics, Culture and Class in the Nationalist
Revolution*; Henrietta Harrison, *The Making of the Republican Citizen: Political
Ceremonies and Symbols in China, 1911–1929*.
5 In other words, the regime of militarization sought to invoke ancient forms of
productive or generative power to support its disciplinary apparatus.
6 Judith Farquhar and Qicheng Zhang, "Biopolitical Beijing: Pleasure,
Sovereignty, and Self-Cultivation in China's Capital," 310.
7 Chi Chang-hui, " Politics of Deification," 73. The notions of deterritorialization and reterritorialization are taken from Gilles Deleuze and Félix
Guattari, though this argument stretches their usage considerably;
Anti-Oedipus, 34–5.
8 A classic example is Richard Smethurst, *A Social Basis for Japanese Militarism:
The Army and the Rural Community*. More infrequently, the question is turned
around and becomes the issue of what in society succeeds in preventing war,
as for example in Friedberg, *Garrison State*.
9 Li Jinliang interview.
10 Michael Herzfeld, *Cultural Intimacy: Social Poetics in the Nation-State*, 3.
11 Westad, *The Global Cold War*, 30 ff.
12 Jeremi Suri, "The Cold War, Decolonization, and Global Social Awakenings:
Historical Intersections," 354; Matthew Connelly, "Taking Off the Cold
War Lens: Visions of North-South Conflict during the Algerian War of
Independence," 739–69; Edward Said, *Orientalism*.
13 Bruce Cumings, "The Origins and Development of the Northeast Asian
Political Economy: Industrial Sectors, Product Cycles, and Political
Consequences," 1–40. On the developmental state in Taiwan, see Gold, *State
and Society in the Taiwan Miracle*.
14 Meredith Woo-Cumings, "National Security and the Rise of the
Developmental State in South Korea and Taiwan," 336.
15 Alexander Woodside, *Lost Modernities: China, Vietnam, Korea, and the Hazards
of World History*, chs. 3–4.
16 Borneman, *Belonging*, 17.
17 See, for example, Lutz, *Homefront*; Cynthia Enloe, *Bananas, Beaches and Bases:
Making Feminist Sense of International Politics*, ch. 3; Moon, *Militarized
Modernity*, ch. 5–6.

18 Gavan McCormack, "Okinawan Dilemmas: Coral Islands or Concrete Islands?," 278.
19 Sherry, *Shadow of War*, 177; May, *Homeward Bound*, 208.
20 One could, I think, read Zygmunt Bauman's interpretation of the Holocaust as less a survival of pre-modern barbarity than as located in the very character of modernity as an extraordinary exploration of this point. *Modernity and the Holocaust*.
21 Agamben, *Exception*, 11–22.

Bibliography

ARCHIVES

Guofangbu (Ministry of Defense) archives, Taibei, ROC (GFBA)
Guoshiguan (Academia Historica) archives, Taibei, ROC (GSGA)
Jinmen jingchaju (Jinmen police bureau) archives, Jinmen, ROC (JMJCJA)
Lieyu (Little Jinmen) township archives, Jinmen, ROC (LYA)
National Archives and Records Administration, US (NARA)

OTHER SOURCES

Accinelli, Robert. *Crisis and Commitment: United States Policy toward Taiwan, 1950–1955* (Chapel Hill, NC: University of North Carolina Press, 1996).
   " 'A Thorn in the Side of Peace': The Eisenhower Administration and the 1958 Offshore Islands Crisis," in Robert Ross and Jiang Changbin (eds.), *Re-examining the Cold War: US–China Diplomacy, 1954–1973* (Cambridge: Harvard University Asia Center, 2001).
Agamben, Giorgio. *The State of Exception.* Trans. Kevin Attell (Chicago: University of Chicago Press, 2005).
Anagnost, Ann. "Constructing the Civilized Community," in Theodore Huters, Bin Wong, and Pauline Yu (eds.), *Culture & State in Chinese History: Conventions, Accommodations, and Critiques* (Stanford: Stanford University Press, 1997).
Baitouweng. "Xiayanxia de jianwen yishi," *JMRB*, October 7, 2003.
Bauman, Zygmunt. *Modernity and the Holocaust* (Ithaca, NY: Cornell University Press, 1989).
Bell, Catherine. *Ritual: Perspectives and Dimensions* (Oxford: Oxford University Press, 1997).
Berger, Mark. *The Battle for Asia: From Decolonization to Globalization* (London: RoutledgeCurzon, 2004).
Bhabha, Homi. "DissemiNation: Time, Narrative, and the Margins of the Modern Nation," in Homi Bhabha (ed.), *Nation and Narration* (London: Routledge, 1990).
Bodnar, John. *Remaking America: Public Memory, Commemoration, and Patriotism in the Twentieth Century* (Princeton: Princeton University Press, 1992).
Borneman, John. *Belonging in the Two Berlins: Kin, State, Nation* (Cambridge: Cambridge University Press, 1992).

Bucks-Morss, Susan. *Dreamworld and Catastrophe: The Passing of Mass Utopia in East and West* (Cambridge: MIT Press, 2000).

Cai Zuqiu. "Fenghuo lijian ji," *JMRB*, March 1, 2003.

Canto, Rosendo. *Between Champagne and Powder* (Taibei: Free China Review, 1959).

Central Intelligence Agency, Office of Current Intelligence. *The Chinese Offshore Islands*, September 8, 1954, DDRS.

Chan, Anita, Richard Madsen, and Jonathan Unger. *Chen Village under Mao and Deng*, second edition (Berkeley: University of California Press, 1992).

Chang, Gordon. *Friends and Enemies: The United States, China, and the Soviet Union, 1948–1972* (Stanford: Stanford University Press, 1990).

"To the Nuclear Brink: Eisenhower, Dulles, and the Quemoy–Matsu Crisis," *International Security* 12:4 (Spring 1988), 96–123.

Chatterjee, Partha. *The Nation and Its Fragments: Colonial and Postcolonial Histories* (Princeton: Princeton University Press, 1993).

Chen Cangjiang (ed.). "Jinmen baise kongbu ge'an dang'an ziliao huibian," unpublished (2007).

Chen Changqing. *Jinmen teyue chashi* (Jinmen: Jinmen xian wenhuaju, 2006). *Zuoguo fenghuo suiyue de Jinmen teyue chashi* (Taibei: Dazhan, 2005).

Chen Jian. *Mao's China and the Cold War* (Chapel Hill, NC: University of North Carolina Press, 2001).

Chen Rongchang. *Wutu Wumin: Wudao Jinmen ren de zhenqing gushi* (Jinmen: Jinmen wenhua zhongxin, 2002).

Chen Shuizai. *Jinmen jieyan qianhou* (Taibei: Daotian, 2001).

Chen Shunde. "Laojun dianying qiule wo yiming," *JMRB*, May 1, 2003.

Chen Xiangxin. "Biying weilin, suijun er ju de tongnian," *JMRB*, October 4, 2003.

Chen Yongfa. *Liang'an fentu: Lengzhan chuqi de zhengjing fazhan* (Taibei: Zhongyang yanjiu yuan, 2006).

Chen Ziqiang. "Wei guanguang, xian kaiguang," *JMBD*, no. 18, June 26, 1992.

Chi Chang-hui. "Militarization on Quemoy and the Making of Nationalist Hegemony, 1949–1992," in Wang Qiugui (ed.), *Jinmen lishi, wenhua yu shengtai guoji xueshu yantaohui lunwenji* (Taibei: Shih Ho-cheng Cultural Foundation, 2004), 523–44.

"The Politics of Deification and Nationalist Ideology: A Case Study of Quemoy." PhD dissertation, Boston University (2000).

Chiang Kai-shek. "Two Supplementary Chapters to Lectures on the Principle of People's Livelihood," in *San Min Chu I: The Three Principles of the People, with Two Supplementary Chapters by Chiang Kai-shek*. Trans. Frank Price (Taibei: China Publishing Company, no date).

Christensen, Thomas. *Useful Adversaries: Grand Strategy, Domestic Mobilization, and Sino-American Conflict, 1947–1958* (Princeton: Princeton University Press, 1996).

Christian, William. "Religious Apparitions and the Cold War in Southern Europe," in Eric Wolf (ed.), *Religion, Power and Protest in Local Communities: The Northern Shore of the Mediterranean* (Berlin: Mouton, 1984), 239–66.

Chun, Allen. "From Nationalism to Nationalizing: Cultural Imagination and State Formation in Postwar Taiwan," in Jonathan Unger (ed.), *Chinese Nationalism* (Armonk, NY: M. E. Sharpe, 1996), 126–47.

Cohen, Paul. "Reflections on a Watershed Date: The 1949 Divide in Chinese History," in Jeffrey Wasserstrom (ed.), *Twentieth-century China: New Approaches* (London and New York: Routledge, 2003), 29–36.

Connelly, Matthew. "Taking Off the Cold War Lens: Visions of North-South Conflict during the Algerian War of Independence," *American Historical Review* 105:3 (2000), 739–69.

Copp, DeWitt, and Marshall Peck. *The Odd Day* (New York: Morrow, 1962).

Cumings, Bruce. "The Origins and Development of the Northeast Asian Political Economy: Industrial Sectors, Product Cycles, and Political Consequences," *International Organization* 38 (1984), 1–40.

Parallax Visions: Making Sense of American–East Asian Relations at the End of the Century (Durham, NC: Duke University Press, 1999).

The Defense of Quemoy and the Free World (Taibei: Asian People's Anti-Communist League, 1959).

Deleuze, Gilles, and Félix Guattari. *Anti-Oedipus.* Trans. Robert Hurley, Mark Seem, and Helen Lane (New York: Viking, 1977).

Dickson, Bruce. *Democratization in China and Taiwan: The Adaptability of Leninist Parties* (Oxford: Clarendon Press, 1997).

Dirlik, Arif. "The Ideological Foundations of the New Life Movement: A Study in Counterrevolution," *Journal of Asian Studies* 34:4 (1975), 945–80.

Dong Qunlian (ed.). *Jinmen jieyan shiqi de minfang zuxun yu dongyuan fangtan lu* (Taibei: Guoshiguan, 2003–4) (*JMMFFT*).

"Zhandi Jinmen shihua," *JMRB*, 38 parts, July 15 to October 24, 2003.

Donnell, John. "Pacification Reassessed," *Asian Survey* 7:8 (1967), 567–76.

Duara, Prasenjit. *Culture Power, and the State: Rural North China, 1900–1942* (Stanford: Stanford University Press, 1988).

Rescuing History from the Nation: Questioning Narratives of Modern China (Chicago: University of Chicago Press, 1995).

Sovereignty and Authenticity: Manchukuo and the East Asian Modern (Lanham, MD: Rowman and Littlefield, 2003).

Eisenhower, Dwight. *Waging Peace, 1955–1961: The White House Years* (Garden City, NY: Doubleday, 1963).

Elvin, Mark. "Female Virtue and the State in China," *Past and Present* 104 (1984), 111–52.

Enloe, Cynthia. *Bananas, Beaches and Bases: Making Feminist Sense of International Politics* (Berkeley: University of California Press, 1990).

Maneuvers: The International Politics of Militarizing Women's Lives (Berkeley: University of California Press, 2000).

Esherick, Joseph. "Ten Theses on the Chinese Revolution," *Modern China* 21:1 (1995), 45–76.

Farquhar, Judith, and Qicheng Zhang. "Biopolitical Beijing: Pleasure, Sovereignty, and Self-Cultivation in China's Capital," *Cultural Anthropology* 20:3 (2005), 303–27.

Feinman, Ilene. *Citizenship Rites: Feminist Soldiers and Feminist Antimilitarists* (New York: New York University Press, 2000).

Fitzgerald, John. *Awakening China: Politics, Culture and Class in the Nationalist Revolution* (Stanford: Stanford University Press, 1996).

Fitzpatrick, Sheila. *Everyday Stalinism: Ordinary Life in Extraordinary Times: Soviet Russia in the 1930s* (Oxford: Oxford University Press, 1999).

Foreign Operations Administration, Office for Refugees, Migration and Voluntary Assistance, United States Escapee Program, "Report to Operations Coordinating Board," August 17, 1954, DDRS.

Foucault, Michel. "Governmentality," in Graham Burchell, Colin Gordon, and Peter Miller (eds.), *The Foucault Effect: Studies in Governmentality* (London: Wheatsheaf, 1991), 87–104.

History of Sexuality. Trans. Robert Hurley (New York: Vintage, 1988).

Friedberg, Aaron. *In the Shadow of the Garrison State: America's Anti-statism and its Cold War Grand Strategy* (Princeton: Princeton University Press, 2000).

Friedman, Edward, Paul Pickowicz, and Mark Selden. *Chinese Village, Socialist State* (New Haven: Yale University Press, 1991).

Fu Kuncheng and Li Jinzhen. *Jinmen zhandi zhengwu de fagui yu shixian* (Jinmen: Jinmen xianzhengfu, 2004).

Gaddis, John Lewis. *The Cold War: A New History* (New York: Penguin, 2005).

We Now Know: Rethinking Cold War History (Oxford: Clarendon, 1997).

Garver, John. *The Sino–American Alliance: Nationalist China and American Cold War Strategy in Asia* (Armonk, NY: M. E. Sharpe, 1997).

Glosser, Susan. *Chinese Visions of Family and State, 1915–1953* (Berkeley: University of California Press, 2003).

Gold, Thomas. *State and Society in the Taiwan Miracle* (Armonk, NY: M. E. Sharpe, 1986).

Gong Li. "Tension across the Taiwan Strait in the 1950s: Chinese Strategy and Tactics," in Robert Ross and Jiang Changbin (eds.), *Re-examining the Cold War: US–China Diplomacy, 1954–1973* (Cambridge: Harvard University Asia Center, 2001).

Goodman, Philomena. *Women, Sexuality, and War* (New York: Palgrave, 2002).

Goodpaster, A. J. "Memorandum for the Record," March 18, 1955, DDRS.

Grandin, Greg. *The Last Colonial Massacre: Latin America in the Cold War* (Chicago: University of Chicago Press, 2004).

Griffith, Robert. "The Cultural Turn in Cold War Studies," *Reviews in American History* 29 (2001), 150–7.

Gu Yan. "Junzhong leyuan tanmi," *Xinwen tiandi* 16:38 (September 17, 1960), 16–17.

Guofangbu and Jinmen xianzhengfu (eds.). *Jinmen tongji nianbiao* (Jinmen, 1961–2006) (*JMTJ*).

Guofangbu shizheng bianyi ju. *Guojun waidao diqu jieyan yu zhandi zhengwu jilu* (Taibei: Guofangbu, 1996).

Guofangbu zong zhengzhi zuozhan bu. *Zhengzhi zuozhan gongzuo shouce* (1977).

Guojia anquan huiyi zhandi zhengwu weiyuan hui. *Yuenan Xinshengyi zhi yanjiu* (Taibei. 1968).

Guoshiguan shiliao chu (ed.). *Jinmen Guningtou, Zhoushan, Dengbudao zhi zhanshi shiliao chuji* (Taibei: Guoshiguan, 1979).

Jinmen Guningtou, Zhoushan, Dengbudao zhi zhanshi shiliao chuji (Taibei: Guoshiguan, 1982).

Halbwachs, Maurice. *On Collective Memory.* Trans. Lewis Coser (Chicago: University of Chicago Press, 1992).

Halperin, Morton. *The 1958 Taiwan Straits Crisis: A Documented History* (Santa Monica, CA: RAND, 1966).

Harrison, Henrietta. *The Making of the Republican Citizen: Political Ceremonies and Symbols in China, 1911–1929* (Oxford: Oxford University Press, 2000).

Henriksen, Margot. *Dr. Strangelove's America: Society and Culture in the Atomic Age* (Berkeley: University of California Press, 1997).

Hershatter, Gail. *Dangerous Pleasures: Prostitution and Modernity in Twentieth-Century Shanghai* (Berkeley: University of California Press, 1997).

Herzfeld, Michael. *Cultural Intimacy: Social Poetics in the Nation-State,* second edition (London: Routledge, 2005).

Holober, Frank. *Raiders of the China Coast: CIA Covert Operations during the Korean War* (Annapolis, MD: Naval Institute Press, 1999).

Hong Chunqing. "Zhandi 35," *JMBD*, no. 22, July 6, 1993.

Hong Dahai. "Lieyu junmin jinru lengzhan shiqi," *JMBD*, no. 33, May 1993.

Hong, Keelung and Stephen Murray. *Looking through Taiwan: American Anthropologists' Collusion with Ethnic Domination* (Lincoln, NE: University of Nebraska Press, 2005).

Hong Xiangming. *Xuedao: Baqian zhuangshi zhansi Jinmen jishi* (Guangzhou: Huacheng, 1995).

Honig, Bonnie. *Democracy and the Foreigner* (Princeton: Princeton University Press, 2001).

Hsiung, Ping-Chun. *Living Rooms as Factories: Class, Gender, and the Satellite Factory System in Taiwan* (Philadelphia: Temple University Press, 1996).

Hu Lian. *Jinmen yijiu* (Taibei: Liming wenhua, 1976).

Hu Tieji. *Cong baowei Jinma dao fangong dalu* (Taibei, 1955).

Huang Pingying. "Taiwan minjian xinyang 'guhun' de fengsi – yige Taiwan shehuishi de kaocha." MA thesis, National Central University (2000).

Huang Shiming. "1980 niandai hou Jinmen yu Nantou shehui li de fuxian: Taiwan fazhan jingyan zhong liangge difang shehui de fenxi." PhD dissertation, National Taiwan University (1995).

Huang Yongtuan. "Yongyuan jiyi," *JMRB*, August 24, 2003.

Hymes, Robert. *Way and Byway: Taoism, Local Religion and Models of Divinity in Sung and Modern China* (Berkeley: University of California Press, 2002).

The Invincible Island: Ten Years of Reconstruction on Kinmen (Taibei: Joint Commission on Rural Reconstruction, 1963).

Jiang Bowei. *Jinmen Juguang lou* (Jinmen: Jinmen xianzhengfu, 2002).

Jinmen zhanshi jilu ji diaocha yanjiu II (Jinmen, 2005).

"Shei de zhanzheng lishi? Jinmen zhanshiguan de guozu lishi vs. minjian shehui de jiti jiyi," *Minsu quyi* 156 (2007), 85–155.

"Zongzu yimin juluo kongjian bianqian de shehui lishi fenxi." MA thesis, National Taiwan University (1994).

Jin Mengren. "Jieyanxia qiangsheng dazuo," *JMBD*, no. 11, July 6, 1991.

Jin Yilei. "Jinmen kaifang guanguang de shehui bianqian yanjiu." MA thesis, Zhongxing University (1994).

"Jinfang bu zuzhi xitong dishan duizhao biao," photocopy.

Jinma diqu yinan yizhong guominbing houbei junren chujing guanzhi guiding (1975).

Jinmen Daoshang Minfangdui shiji ji Guo-Gong zhanyi diaocha yanjiu (Jinmen: Guojia gongyuan, 2001).

Jinmen fangwei silingbu zhengzhi zuozhan bu (ed.). *Nian nian: Guningtou dajie nian zhou nian ji* (Jinmen: Jinmen fangwei silingbu zhengzhi zuozhan bu, 1969).

Jinmen tudi gaige (Jinmen: Fujian sheng zhengfu, 1955).

Jinmen xianzhi (1922).

Jinmen xianzhi (Jinmen: Jinmen xianzhengfu, 1992) (*JMXZ*).

Jinmen Xueshi zupu (Jinmen: Zhushan wenxian hui, 1991).

Jinmen zhanshi xinzhan gaojian (Jinmen: Jinmen fangwei silingbu, 1968).

Jinmen zhengwu weiyuan hui (ed.). *Zhonghua minguo Jinmen xian xianmin suode baogao* (Jinmen, 1976).

Jinmen ziwei budui xinzhang hanhua gaojian (Jinmen: Jinmen xian ziwei zongdui, 1975).

Kammen, Michael. *Mystic Chords of Memory: The Transformation of Tradition in American Culture* (New York: Knopf, 1991).

Kirby, William. "Engineering China: Birth of the Developmental State, 1928–1937," in Yeh Wen-hsin (ed.), *Becoming Chinese: Passages to Modernity and Beyond* (Berkeley: University of California Press, 2000), 137–60.

"The Nationalist Regime and the Chinese Party-State, 1928–1958," in Merle Goldman and Andrew Gordon (eds.), *Historical Perspectives on Contemporary East Asia* (Cambridge: Harvard University Press, 2000), 211–37.

Kirk, Donald. "Still Waiting for War," *New York Times*, November 28, 1976.

Ku, Samuel. "The Political Economy of Regime Transformation: Taiwan and Southeast Asia." *World Affairs* 165:2 (2002), 59–78.

Kuishan. "Jinggui jinglushui," *JMRB*, July 7, 2003.

"Zhuan yun ei xiao dai jinzai," *JMRB*, March 9, 2004.

Kwon, Heonik. *After the Massacre: Commemoration and Consolation in Ha My and My Lai* (Berkeley: University of California Press, 2006).

Lao Fandian. "Paoda Meiren shan," *JMRB*, May 20, 2003.

Larson, Stanley, and James Collins. *Allied Participation in Vietnam* (Washington, DC: Dept. of the Army, 1975).

Latour, Bruno. *Science in Action: How to Follow Scientists and Engineers through Society* (Milton Keynes: Open University Press, 1987).

Leshan. "Yinshui si yuantou – Junmin qingshen pian," *JMRB*, May 29, 2003.

Li Ao. *Choulou de Zhongguoren yanjiu* (Taibei: Li Ao, 1989).

Zhongguo xing yanjiu (Taibei: Li Ao, 1995).

Li Gangshi. "Nü ziweidui yiwang," *JMRB*, July 26–7, 2003.

Li Jinsheng. *Fenghuo honglou moufanjie* (Jinmen: Jinmen xianzhengfu, 1999).

Jinmen shuitou (Jinmen: Jinmen xianzhengfu, 2000).

Jiyan shanding tan Zhushan lishi (Jinmen: Jinmen xianzhengfu, 1998).

Li Shide. *Shiqi shiji de haishang Jinmen* (Jinmen: Jinmen xian wenhua ju, 2004).

Li Xiaobing, Chen Jian, and David Wilson (trans.). "Mao Zedong's Handling of the Taiwan Strait Crisis of 1958: Chinese Recollections and Documents," *Cold War International History Project Bulletin*, nos. 6/7 (1995), 207–25.

"Lienü miao zhi." Inscription at temple of Wang Yulan, Little Jinmen (1995).

Lin Baobei. *Qiangshang fenghuo* (Taibei: Fuyang, 2000).

Lin Fushi. *Guhun yu guixiong de shijie: Bei Taiwan de ligui xinyang* (Taibei: Daoxiang, 1995).

Lin Genben. "Jinmen baiwan jichengche," *JMBD*, no. 2, October 6, 1990.

Lin Kunhuang and Lin Zhuoren. *Jinmen zhi* (1882) (reprint Taibei: Zhonghua congshu, 1955).

Lin Mateng and Lu Yunzai. *Cong Dongkeng tanqi* (Jinmen: Jinmen Lieyu xianggongsuo, 2003).

Lin Si-dang and Lin Li. *Land Reform on Kinmen* (Taibei: Joint Commission on Rural Reconstruction, 1958).

Lin Zhong. "Jinmen 108 tiao haohan zuoguo suiyue," *JMBD*, inaugural issue (*chuangkan hao*), August 6, 1990.

Liu Jiaguo. *Wo de jiaxiang shi zhandi: Jin-Ma wenti mianmianguan* (Taibei: no publisher, 1988).

Liu Yazhou. "Wu Jinmen zhi zhan, wu jinri Taiwan," *Shang bao*, May 23, 2004.

Lü Jiang. *Lü Jiang ji* (Taibei: Qianwei, 1992).

Luo Deshui. "Liang'an guanxi fazhan yu Jinmen dingwei bianqian zhi yanjiu." MA dissertation, Tamkang (Danjiang) University (1999).

Lutz, Catherine. *Homefront: A Military City and the American Twentieth Century* (Boston: Beacon Press, 2001).

"Militarization," in David Nugent and Joan Vincent (eds.), *A Companion to the Anthropology of Politics* (New York: Blackwell, 2004), 318–31.

Major, Patrick, and Rana Mitter. "East is East and West is West? Towards a Comparative Socio-Cultural History of the Cold War," *Cold War History* 4:1 (2003), 1–22.

Malarney, Shaun. *Culture, Ritual and Revolution in Vietnam* (Honolulu: University of Hawai'i Press, 2002).

Mao Zedong. *Jianguo yilai Mao Zedong wengao* (Beijing: Zhongyang wenxian, 1992).

Mao Zedong waijiao wenxuan (Beijing: Zhongyang wenxian, 1994).

Xuexi wenxuan (1964).

May, Elaine Tyler. *Homeward Bound: American Families in the Cold War Era* (New York: Basic Books, 1988).

McCormack, Gavan. "Okinawan Dilemmas: Coral Islands or Concrete Islands?" in Chalmers Johnson (ed.), *Okinawa: Cold War Island* (Cardiff, CA: Japan Policy Research Institute, 1999), 261–82.

Ming Qiushui (ed.). *Jinmen (Jiang zongtong yu Jinmen)* (Jinmen: Jinmen zhandi weiyuanhui, 1971).

Mitchell, Timothy. *Colonising Egypt* (Cambridge: Cambridge University Press, 1988).

Moon, Katharine. *Sex Among Allies: Military Prostitution in US–Korean Relations* (New York: Columbia University Press, 1997).

Moon, Seungsook. *Militarized Modernity and Gendered Citizenship in South Korea* (Durham, NC: Duke University Press, 2005).

Mu Yang and Yao Jie. *Zhongguo renmin jiefangjun zhanshi* (Beijing: Junshi kexue, 1987).

Nedostup, Rebecca. "Religion, Superstition, and Governing Society in Republican China." PhD dissertation, Columbia University (2001).

Nü qingnian dadui fangwen jilu (Taibei: Zhongyang yanjiu yuan, 1995).

Ouyang Yangming. *Huaiyi Jinmen* (Taibei: Wenshizhe, 2006).

"Panshan cun funü duizhang Weng Shuhui de caiyi chaoren," *Jinri Jinmen*, no. 15, May 1, 1974, 29.

Perry, Elizabeth. *Patrolling the Revolution: Worker Militias, Citizenship, and the Modern Chinese State* (Lanham, MD: Rowman and Littlefield, 2005).

Potter, Sulamith Heins and Jack Potter. *China's Peasants: The Anthropology of a Revolution* (Cambridge: Cambridge University Press, 1990).

Qi Changhui. See Chi Chang-hui.

Qi Dexue. *Zhongwai denglu zuozhan jingyan jiaoxun* (Beijing: Junshi kexue, 2006).

Rankin, Karl. *China Assignment* (Seattle: University of Washington Press, 1964).

Reid, Susan. "Cold War in the Kitchen: Gender and Consumption in the Khrushchev Thaw," *Slavic Review* 61:2 (2002), 211–52.

Rofel, Lisa. "Liberation Nostalgia and a Yearning for Modernity," in Christina Gilmartin *et al.* (ed.), *Engendering China: Women, Culture and the State* (Cambridge: Harvard University Press, 1994).

Rogaski, Ruth. *Hygienic Modernity: Meanings of Health and Disease in Treaty-Port China* (Berkeley: University of California Press, 2004).

"Nature, Annihilation, and Modernity: China's Korean War Germ-Warfare Experience Reconsidered," *Journal of Asian Studies* 61:2 (2002), 381–415.

Rose, Kenneth. *One Nation Underground: The Fallout Shelter in American Culture* (New York: New York University Press, 2001).

Roy, Denny. *Taiwan: A Political History* (Ithaca, NY: Cornell University Press, 2003).

Rubinstein, Murray (ed.). *The Other Taiwan: 1945 to the Present* (Armonk, NY: M. E. Sharpe, 1996).

(ed.). *Taiwan: A New History*, second edition . (Armonk, NY: M. E. Sharpe, 2007).

Rushkoff, Bennett. "Eisenhower, Dulles and the Quemoy-Matsu Crisis, 1954–55," *Political Science Quarterly* 96:3 (1981), 465–80.

Said, Edward. *Orientalism* (New York: Pantheon, 1978).

Sang Pinzai. *An yu an* (Taibei: Erya, 2001).

Sangren, Steven. "Female Gender in Chinese Religious Symbols: Kuan Yin, Ma Tsu, and the 'Eternal Mother,' " *Signs* 9:1 (1983), 4–25.

Sanmin zhuyi dingneng zhansheng gongchanzhuyi jianyi wenda (Zhengzhi jiaoyu fuzhu jiaocai 2) (Jinmen: Jinmen xian minzhong ziwei zongdui, 1976).

Schipper, Kristofer. *The Taoist Body* (Berkeley: University of California Press, 1993).

Schlesinger, Arthur. *A Thousand Days: John F. Kennedy in the White House* (Boston: Houghton Mifflin, 1965).

Scott, James. *Seeing Like a State* (New Haven: Yale University Press, 1998).

Shanhua. "Xiangye beiwu," *JMRB*, October 23, 2002.

Shen Weiping. *823 Paoji Jinmen* (Beijing: Huayi, 1998).

Shen Zonghan. *Taiwan nongye zhi fazhan* (Taibei: Shangwu, 1963).

Shepherd, John. "Commodification, Culture and Tourism," *Tourist Studies* 2:2 (2002), 183–201.

Sherry, Michael. *In the Shadow of War: The United States since the 1930s* (New Haven: Yale University Press, 1995).

Shi Maxiang, Zhuang Zhenzhong, and Chen Xiuzhu (eds.). *Rongmin koushu lishi* (Jinmen: Jinmen guojia gongyuan, 2003).

Shue, Vivienne. *Peasant China in Transition: The Dynamics of Development Toward Socialism, 1949–1956* (Berkeley: University of California Press, 1980).

Smethurst, Richard. *A Social Basis for Japanese Militarism: The Army and the Rural Community* (Berkeley: University of California Press, 1974).

Solomon, Jon. "Taiwan Incorporated: A Survey of Biopolitics in the Sovereign Police's Pacific Theater of Operations," in Thomas LaMarre and Kang Nae-hui (eds.), *Impacts of Modernities* (Hong Kong: Hong Kong University Press, 2004), 229–54.

Stolper, Thomas. *China, Taiwan, and the Offshore Islands* (Armonk, NY: M. E. Sharpe, 1986).

Suri, Jeremi. "The Cold War, Decolonization, and Global Social Awakenings: Historical Intersections," *Cold War History* 6:3 (2006), 353–63.

"The Cultural Contradictions of Cold War Education: The Case of West Berlin," *Cold War History* 6:3 (2006), 1–20.

Szonyi, Michael. *Practicing Kinship: Lineage and Descent in Late Imperial China* (Stanford: Stanford University Press, 2002).

"The Virgin and the Chinese State: The Cult of Wang Yulan and the Politics of Local Identity on Jinmen (Quemoy)," *Journal of Ritual Studies* 19:2 (2005), 87–98.

Tanaka, Yuki. *Japan's Comfort Women: Sexual slavery and prostitution during World War II and the US occupation* (New York: Routledge, 2002).

Tang, Hui-sun. *Land Reform in Free China* (Taibei: Joint Commission on Rural Reconstruction, 1954).

Tian Shuzhang. "Zhenlie ciji," inscription at temple of Wang Yulan, Little Jinmen (1956).

Tien, Hung-mao. *Government and Politics in Kuomintang China, 1927–1937* (Stanford: Stanford University Press, 1972).

Tsang, Steve. "Chiang Kai-shek and the Kuomintang's Policy to Reconquer the Chinese Mainland, 1949–1958," in Steve Tsang (ed.), *In the Shadow of China: Political Developments in Taiwan since 1949* (Honolulu, HI: University of Hawai'i Press, 1993), 48–72.

Tubilewicz, Czeslaw. "Taiwan and the Soviet Union During the Cold War: Enemies or Ambiguous Friends?" *Cold War History* 5:1 (2005), 75–86.

Tucker, Nancy Bernkopf. *Taiwan, Hong Kong and the United States, 1945–1992* (New York: Twayne, 1994).

Tudda, Christopher. " 'Reenacting the Story of Tantalus': Eisenhower, Dulles, and the Failed Rhetoric of Liberation," *Journal of Cold War Studies* 7:4 (2005), 3–35.

"US Military Policy and Objectives in Formosan Area – Draft Script for McElroy–Sandys Talks, September 22–October 3, 1958," DDRS.

Verdery, Katherine. *The Political Lives of Dead Bodies: Reburial and Postsocialist Change* (New York: Columbia University Press, 1999).

Wang Kui. *Jinmen junqu naogui dang'an* (Taibei: Heyang, 1995).

Weiji zhi shezhi yu paichu shouce (Jinmen: Jinmen fangwei silingbu, 1971).

Weller, Robert. *Alternate Civilities: Democracy and Culture in China and Taiwan* (Boulder, CO: Westview, 1999).

Discovering Nature: Globalization and Environmental Culture in Taiwan and China (Cambridge: Cambridge University Press, 2006).

Unities and Diversities in Chinese Religion (London: Macmillan, 1987).

Weng Mingzhi. *Wuchao pengzhang* (Jincheng: Weng Mingzhi fuwu chu, 1994).

Weng Xiongfei. "805 budui de gushi," *JMRB*, October 19, 2003.
"Fenghuo taonan ji," *JMRB*, April 4, 2004.
"Guzao de san-ba xinniang," *JMRB*, March 5, 2004.
"Huasheng yuan de huanghun," *JMRB*, August 16, 2003.
"Zhuiyi guonian Tai-Jin jiaotong," *JMRB*, January 22, 2004.
Westad, Odd Arne. *The Global Cold War: Third World Interventions and the Making of our Times* (Cambridge: Cambridge University Press, 2005).
Whitfield, Stephen. *The Culture of the Cold War*, second edition (Baltimore, MD: Johns Hopkins University Press, 1996).
Woo-Cumings, Meredith Jung-En. "Introduction: Chalmers Johnson and the Politics of Nationalism and Development," in Meredith Woo-Cumings (ed.), *The Developmental State* (Ithaca, NY: Cornell University Press, 1999), 1–31.
"National Security and the Rise of the Developmental State in South Korea and Taiwan," in Henry Rowen (ed.), *Behind East Asian Growth: The Political and Social Foundations of Prosperity* (London: Routledge, 1998), 319–37.
Woodside, Alexander. *Lost Modernities: China, Vietnam, Korea, and the Hazards of World History* (Cambridge: Harvard University Press, 2006).
Wu Huasheng. "Jinmen de shan laoshu mei weiba," *JMBD*, no. 15, November 6, 1991.
Wu Lengxi. "Wuzhang yu wenzhang: Paohong Jinmen neimu," *Zhuanji wenxue* (1994), 5–11.
Yi Mao Zhuxi: wo qinsheng jingli de ruogan zhongda lishi shijian pianduan (Beijing: Xinhua, 1995).
Wu Zongqi. "Jinmen diqu shiyan zhandi zhengwu ji qi zhidu zhuanxing zhi yanjiu," PhD dissertation, Wenhua daxue (2004).
"Wugu renku, shenmi kongbu," *Shidai zhoukan*, February 1988, reprinted in Liu Jiaguo, *Wo de jiaxiang shi zhandi: Jin-Ma wenti mianmianguan* (Tabei: no publisher, 1988), 14–19.
Xianying (Shining), Zhushan village magazine, 1920–49.
Xie Huihuang. "Jun leyuan de chuangyi ren," *JMRB*, May 24, 2005.
Xie Yuping. "Jinmen chuantong shengyu lisu zhi tantao." MA thesis, Mingchuan University (2005).
Xingshibao. "Jinmen neng xiang junguan shuo zaijian?" *JMBD*, no. 1, September 6, 1990.
Xu Minhua. "Ming–Qing shiqi Jinmen chuantong funü jiating shenghuo yanjiu." MA thesis, Mingchuan University (2002).
Xu Ruzhong (ed.). *Xin Jinmen zhi* (Jinmen: Jinmen xianzhengfu, 1959).
Xu Weimin *et al.* (eds.). "Jinmen minfangdui de tiandiao jilu," in *Jinmen Daoshang Minfangdui shiji ji Guo-Gong zhanyi diaocha yanjiu qizhong baogao* (Jinmen: Jinmen guojia gongyuan, 2000) (*JMMFTDJL*).
Xu Yan. *Jinmen zhi zhan, 1949–1959*. Reprinted in *Taihai dazhan, I: Zhonggong guandian* (Taibei: Fengyun shidai, 1992).
Xu Yucun. "Guan'ao de shengji huodong yu shengtai huanjing xitong de guanxi," in Yu Guanghong and Wei Jiezi (eds.), *Jinmen shuqi renleixue tianye gongzuo jiaoshi lunwenji* (Taibei: Zhongyang yanjiuyuan, 1994), 65–81.
"Guojia liliang, renkou liudong yu jingji bianqian – yi Jinmen Guan'ao weili." MA thesis, National Taiwan University (1996).

Xu Zhijie. "Jinmen Zhushan Xuexing xueyuan juluo kongjian bianqian de yanjiu." MA thesis, Gaoxiong Normal University (2003).

Yager, Joseph. *Transforming Agriculture in Taiwan: The Experience of the Joint Commission on Rural Reconstruction* (Ithaca, NY: Cornell University Press, 1988).

Yan Chen and Dong Huifang. "831 chetuihou 9 yue 7 ri Jinmen fasheng shouzong junren qiangbao minfu an," *JMBD*, no. 26, October 6, 1992.

Yang Luyin. "Shequ zuzhi yu dongyuan zhi tantao – yi Guan'ao wei li," in Yu Guanghong and Wei Jiezi (eds.), *Jinmen shuqi renleixue tianye gongzuo jiaoshi lunwenji* (Taibei: Zhongyang yanjiuyuan, 1994).

Yang Shiying. "Kegu mingxin de 825," *JMRB*, July 3, 2003.

Yang Shuqing. *Fanshu wang* (Taibei: Lianjing, 2003).

Jinmen daoyu bianyuan (Taibei: Daotian, 2001).

Jinmen shehui diaocha (Taibei: Daotian, 1998).

Yang Tianhou and Lin Likuan. *Jinmen hunyin lisu* (Jinmen: Jinmen shiji weihu hui, 1996).

Jinmen simiao yinglian beiwen (Taibei: Daotian, 1998).

Yang Wenwei. "Laiqu chi biandang," *JMRB*, October 12, 2003.

Yang Xiaoxian. *Jinmen jindaishi yanjiu* (Jinmen: Jinmen xianzhengfu, 2005).

Yingxi. "Dangnian yemu dichuishi," *JMRB*, August 3, 2003.

You Jianpeng. "Nanwang Jinmen suiyue," *JMRB*, February 18, 2004.

Yuping. "Shensi Guqu danyaoku jingbao yu cunmin shangtong," *JMRB*, October 5, 2003.

Zhai, Qiang. *The Dragon, the Lion and the Eagle: Chinese–British–American Relations, 1949–1958* (Kent, OH: Kent State University Press, 1994).

Zhandou cun zhandou shouce (Jinmen: Jinmen zhandi zhengwu weiyuanhui, 1968).

"Zhandou de duo mianshou Li Mengqi," *Jinri Jinmen*, no. 15, May 1, 1974, 26.

Zhang Huomu. *Jinmen gujin zhanshi* (Taibei: Daotian, 1996).

Zhang Jiajie. "From Battlefield to Tourist Destination: Production and Consumption of the Battlefield Tourism Landscape in Kinmen, Taiwan." BA thesis, Department of Geography, National University of Singapore (2007).

Zhang Mingchun. "You Jinmen junren xiaofei xingge kan Guan'ao shangdian de fazhan guocheng," in Yu Guanghong and Wei Jiezi (eds.). *Jinmen shuqi renleixue tianye gongzuo jiaoshi lunwenji* (Taibei: Zhongyang yanjiuyuan, 1994).

Zhang Yufa, Chen Cungong, and Huang Mingming (eds.). *Liu Anqi xiansheng fangwen jilu* (Nangang: Zhongyang yanjiuyuan, 1991).

Zhenhan. "Dakai tiantang de yaoshi," *JMRB*, April 19, 2004.

"Datou de chuanqi," *JMRB*, February 14, 2005.

Zhongguo qingnian fangong jiuguo tuan zongtuan bu. *Bentuan zhongyao wenxuan* (Taibei: Zhongguo qingnian fangong jiuguo tuan zongtuan bu, 1966).

Luqi piaoyang sanshi nian (Taibei: Zhongguo qingnian fangong jiuguo tuan zongtuan bu, 1982).

Zhou, Kate Xiao. *How the Farmers Changed China: Power of the People* (Boulder, CO: Westview, 1996).

Zhu Xining. *Ba er san zhu* (Taibei: Sansan, 1979).

Ziwei zhandou shouce (Jinmen: Jinmen zhandi zhengwu weiyuan hui, 1976).

Zubok, Vladislav, and Constantine Pleshakov. *Inside the Kremlin's Cold War* (Cambridge: Harvard University Press, 1996).

Index